W9-BZI-907

ALL FALL DOWN

GARY SICK

All Fall Down

AMERICA'S
TRAGIC ENCOUNTER
WITH IRAN

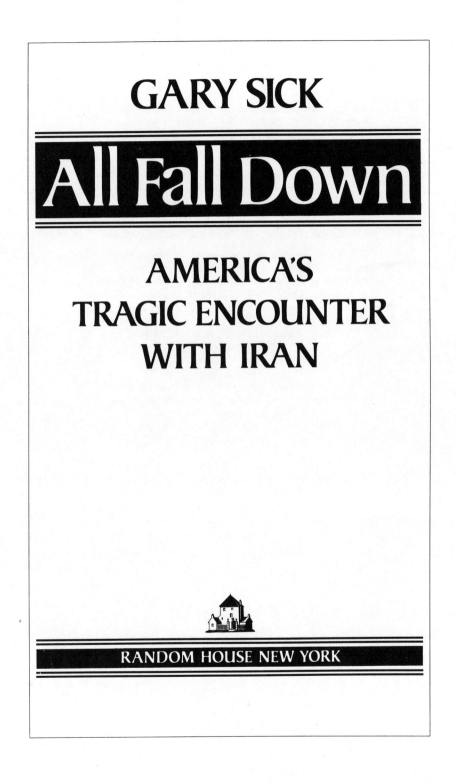

RANDOM HOUSE NEW YORK

Grateful acknowledgment is made to the following for permission to reprint previously published material:

Westview Press: Excerpt reprinted from *International Mediation in Theory and Practice,* Saadia Touval and I. William Zartman, eds. (Boulder, Colo.:Westview Press, 1985).

Yale University Press and the Council on Foreign Relations: Material excerpted from "Military Options and Constraints" by Gary Sick, and published in *American Hostages in Iran: Conduct of a Crisis,* a Council on Foreign Relations Book, by Warren Christopher, et al. (New Haven: Yale University Press, 1985).

Library of Congress Cataloging in Publication Data
Sick, Gary Gordon, 1935–
All fall down.
Includes index.
1. Iran Hostage Crisis, 1979–1981. 2. United States—
Foreign relations—Iran. 3. Iran—Foreign relations—
United States. I. Title.
E183.8.I55S53 1985   955'.054   84-45772
ISBN 0-394-54488-9

Manufactured in the United States of America
Typography and binding design by J. K. Lambert
24689753
First Edition

To Karlan
for everything

PREFACE

This book is the chronicle of a political and strategic disaster. The uprising of the Iranian people under the leadership of Ayatollah Ruhollah Khomeini, the collapse and exile and death of Mohammad Reza Shah Pahlavi, the establishment of an Islamic government in Tehran and the political and ideological transformation of Iran—symbolized most painfully for Americans by the attack on the U.S. embassy in Tehran and the holding of U.S. citizens hostage for 444 days—represented nothing less than a political earthquake in one of the most sensitive regions of the world.

Genuine revolutions are rare. The mobilization of an entire populace to demand, at risk of personal violence, the radical transformation of their own society is historically uncommon, particularly in large nations of great strategic importance. However, when such an upheaval does occur, it alters the landscape of an age and generates political aftershocks that continue to reverberate long after the initial dust has settled. Arguably, the Iranian revolution was such an event.

Ideologies and political movements that arrive in a burst of fireworks, proclaiming their intention to reform the world, all too often seem to deteriorate into sad caricatures of the regimes they replaced. As Charles Issawi once remarked, "Revolutions revolve, 360 degrees." Indeed, six years after millions of Iranians united with Khomeini to overthrow the shah, the people of Iran groan under a reign of repression whose abuses surpass the excesses attributed to the shah even by his enemies.

Still, it would be an error to imagine that a genuine revolution is merely the same wolf in a different skin. It is not. True revolutions dig at the marrow of society, altering fundamentally the chemistry of the body politic. Whatever the excesses of the revolutionary authorities in Tehran, and whatever judgment history may reserve for this unique social experiment, it seems indisputable that Iran has been permanently, irrevocably changed. Curiously enough, so has the United States of America, though in very different ways. Not since the fall of Saigon had a series of foreign policy events so shaken the United States. The events of those few years not only undermined the strategic position and international credibility of the United States but also contributed to a profound change in U.S. domestic political alignments and attitudes.

Yet when President Jimmy Carter arrived in the White House in January

1977 with an extensive agenda of foreign policy objectives, Iran was not in-cluded on the list and was not expected to be a problem. Iran appeared to be stable, the shah seemed to be firmly in control, and the policy differences between Iran and the United States were regarded as relatively minor and manageable. In the end, however, it was Iran that dominated the critical last years of Jimmy Carter's presidency and contributed substantially to his elec-toral defeat. This book will trace the process as events in Iran elbowed their way into the U.S. national consciousness and eventually imposed their own peculiar logic and rhythms on a superpower halfway around the globe.

I participated in those events, and in some respects I am a product of them. During the years of the Carter presidency I was the principal White House aide for Iran on the National Security Council staff, serving as a point of contact between the White House and various agencies of the government. I was both adviser and amanuensis, analyzing policy and preparing the offi-cial records of government meetings throughout the Iranian revolution and the hostage crisis. My position ensured me an unsurpassed vantage point from which to observe every element of the policy process, from the per-sonalities and politics of the White House to the internal policy disputes within the State Department.

This book draws on my own personal experiences, the working files that I maintained at the NSC, the internal government records of the period, and additional files and materials that were made available to me by my colleagues in the NSC and other agencies of the government. I have also benefited from the many firsthand accounts by other participants, including memoirs by President Carter, Cyrus Vance, Zbigniew Brzezinski, George Ball, Hamilton Jordan and William Sullivan, among others.

I had four reasons for writing this book. First, I wanted to produce a complete and accurate account of an extraordinary period in the history of U.S. foreign policy. I also hoped to preserve a sense of the human dimension of high policy from the perspective of one who was both observer and partici-pant. Further, I thought it was important to go beyond a purely descriptive account to ask why events unfolded as they did and whether there are more general lessons to be derived from the experience. Finally, I hoped to present this rich array of original material in a narrative style that would be accessible and appealing to the interested non-specialist.

As suggested by the title, this story has no heroes. No one had it right, and the system itself inhibited the flow of accurate information and hampered judgment. Moreover, these shortcomings were not limited to the United States. Other major countries with substantial interests in Iran—Great Britain, France and Israel—performed no better. The evidence suggests that we are poorly equipped to deal with revolutionary societies, and when religion is added to revolution, we are paralyzed.

America's encounter with the Iranian revolution continues to be the subject of a flood of articles and memoirs, in part because it evokes memories of a moment of national passion and frustration, but also because it raises profound questions about how a large and powerful state can or should conduct its relations with smaller nations in the throes of revolutionary change. It is a fascinating case study in international politics. It is also a rousing good story. I hope this book will do justice to both.

G. S.

ACKNOWLEDGMENTS

Any book of this size, covering more than four intense years of political history, necessarily owes more debts of gratitude than can be acknowledged in a few paragraphs. However, I have benefited so greatly from the help of friends, associates and colleagues that an expression of gratitude is called for —even if it must be brief and incomplete.

First, I must recognize my friends and colleagues on the National Security Council staff and in other agencies of the government who worked, wrote, sweat and shared together the experiences of a prolonged crisis. Some of their names appear in the text and notes of the book, and they will not be repeated here. Many others, however, should not be forgotten.

I am particularly grateful to William Quandt. We shared the same suite of offices in the Old Executive Office Building throughout the period of the Iranian revolution and the fall of the shah, and he was unfailingly generous with his time, his knowledge of the Middle East and his friendship at some crucial and lonely moments. Robert Hunter shared the same offices during the hostage crisis, and he also became a close friend whose political acumen and policy judgment I valued. Other key associates whose support and assistance were invaluable at various stages of the crisis and after include Janice Schechter, Jennie M. D'Amico, George Van Eron and Julianne McLeod.

Richard V. Allen graciously invited me to remain at the NSC after the change of administrations to complete the initial research on this book. Brenda Reger, director of information policy and security review, coordinated the review of the manuscript with all the appropriate government agencies. Her professionalism, sensitivity and dedication in overseeing this complex process were everything an author could hope for.

While on the NSC staff, I was also an officer on active duty with the U.S. Navy. The Navy introduced me to the Middle East and to international politics, sponsored my graduate education and provided generous support during eight years in Washington policy jobs. During those years, I especially valued the counsel and assistance of Admiral Bobby R. Inman.

When I left the government in 1981, the Manhattan transfer was made possible by the support and encouragement of J. C. Hurewitz—a great scholar and dear friend who was at that time the director of the Middle East Institute

at the School of International Affairs at Columbia University. He offered me
a position, supplied me with a marvelous office looking out over the rooftops
of Manhattan, made available to me the resources of a great academic institution, provided an expert review of the final draft of the manuscript and otherwise sustained me and my family with his wisdom and personal assistance. He
and his wife, Miriam, contributed freely of their experience at every stage of
the research and writing.

After one year in New York, I joined the Ford Foundation. Franklin
Thomas, the president of the Foundation, Vice President Susan Berresford,
Enid Schoettle, and many other colleagues and associates were unfailingly
helpful and considerate as I pursued a double life of institutional responsibility
for programs on U.S. foreign policy during the day, and research and writing
at night and on weekends. They gave me time off when I badly needed it and
provided both material and moral support in abundance.

Many scholars and foreign policy experts gave generously of their time in
reviewing the manuscript at various stages and offering comments and suggestions. These include Robert Jervis, Nikki Keddie, Warren Christopher, David
Newsom, Ervand Abrahamian, Harold Saunders and Richard Bulliet. In addition, I was fortunate to have the benefit of interviews with many individuals
with special knowledge and experience of Iran and U.S. Iranian policy, including James Schlesinger, Assad Homayoun, Richard Helms, John Pustay and
Mohammed Yeganeh. Some prefer anonymity. Many others who provided
interesting nuggets—or merely a patient ear—are too numerous to list.

In the Notes section in the back of the book I have provided citations in
those cases where I relied on published work by others. There is one important
exception, however, that deserves mention. The Congressional Research Service, under the direction of Clyde R. Mark, produced *The Iran Hostage Crisis:
A Chronology of Daily Developments,* which was published by the U.S. Government Printing Office in March 1981 as a report for the Committee on Foreign
Affairs of the U.S. House of Representatives. I relied constantly on this exceptional collection of public information for my research on the hostage crisis.

As a new author, I could have asked nothing better than to work with the
expert staff of Random House and editor Peter Osnos, whose own depth of
knowledge about Washington and international politics sharpened the focus
of the book in several key areas. Leona Schecter, a talented literary agent,
provided shrewd advice and assistance throughout.

Needless to say, although the institutions and individuals named above have
all helped to improve this book, I have not heeded them in each and every case
and none of them should be held responsible for any failures and shortcomings.
Those are my responsibility alone.

Some portions of this book have appeared in different form in two earlier
volumes. A paper on "The Release of the American Hostages in Iran" was
included in I. W. Zartman and Saadia Touval, eds., *International Mediation
in Theory and Practice,* Westview Press, 1985. A paper on "Military Options
and Constraints" was prepared for a study group jointly sponsored by the

Council on Foreign Relations and the Bar Association of the City of New York and published in Warren Christopher, et al., *American Hostages in Iran: The Conduct of a Crisis,* Yale University Press, 1985. I am grateful to the editors and publishers of these volumes for their permission to use some of the same material in this book.

This book is dedicated to my wife, without exaggeration. My parents, Lois and Ralph Sick, have followed all of this from a safe distance in Russell, Kansas, with the proper mixture of interest and skepticism. My son, Jeffrey, and my daughter, Gyneth, spent their high school and early college years first with the seemingly endless crisis, then with the seemingly endless writing. I have no idea what effect it may have had on them, but it is my impression that both of them found it almost as interesting and exciting as I did—at least when they took time from their own busy lives to think about it. Together, this smart and loving group made even the worst of times the best of times. I am very lucky.

CONTENTS

Preface   vii

I   America and the Shah   3

II   Early Signs and Signals   22

III   The Revolution Begins   43

IV   Communications Fail   65

V   Thinking the Unthinkable   81

VI   The End of a Bad Year   102

VII   Last Gasps   130

VIII   The Politics of Revolution   157

IX   Hostages   175

X   The Embassy Is Taken   195

XI   The Diplomatic Offensive   217

XII   A Long Shot That Just Missed   250

XIII   The Military Option   280

XIV   The First Year Ends   303

XV   Endgame   319

XVI   Personal Notes: Inauguration Day, 1981   339

Notes   343

Index   361

ALL FALL DOWN

AMERICA
AND THE SHAH

E arly on Thursday morning, November 2, 1978, the White House received two messages from U.S. Ambassador William H. Sullivan in Tehran. The first was a straightforward account of his most recent meeting with the shah. This message, though highly classified, was intended to satisfy the curiosity of the foreign policy establishment and to divert attention from the shorter message that followed. The second message was a bombshell, and its distribution was limited to the inner circle of foreign policy decision makers at the Department of State and the White House.

Sullivan, who had by this time been in Iran for nearly eighteen months, had a flair for the dramatic. He took pride in his terse reporting, and his cables were peppered with irreverent observations and sardonic asides. There could have been no doubt in his mind that this particular telegram would be read by every senior official in the national security hierarchy, including the president.

In good journalistic style, he put the entire message in the opening line. During his meeting with the shah on Wednesday evening, he said, he had detected the first signs that the shah might be considering abdication.

Sullivan was one of the most senior officers on active duty with the U.S. Foreign Service. He was canny and sophisticated in the ways of Washington, having had more than his share of experience with policy crises in Vietnam, Laos and elsewhere. He was well aware that the Carter administration was distracted with a crushing array of foreign policy concerns. These ranged from the final negotiations on a strategic arms limitations treaty with Moscow to the intricacies of negotiating a peace treaty between Egypt and Israel, in addition to the complex and difficult negotiations on normalization of relations with the People's Republic of China. It was not a good moment to relay bad tidings.

Officials in Washington were, of course, aware that the shah was in serious trouble. Evidence of swelling insurrection had been accumulating for months. However, at the beginning of November, Washington continued to believe that the shah was merely experiencing a crisis of confidence.

Ambassador Sullivan had contributed to that attitude. He had routinely reported on the outbursts of opposition activity in Iran, but he had suggested at each stage that the shah was very much in command and entirely capable of coping with the crisis. Only the week before, when the Department of State had solicited his views about a possible overture to the Ayatollah Ruhollah Khomeini in Paris, he had dismissed the idea out of hand with characteristic brio. "Our destiny," he had declared, "is to work with the shah." Now, only a few days later, he was about to reverse himself and set off a policy firestorm in Washington.

Mohammad Reza Shah Pahlavi had commented to Sullivan the night before that he would rather leave the country than submit to a referendum on the monarchy (as certain opposition politicians were suggesting). Fixing on this statement, Sullivan inferred that the shah was contemplating abdication. His cable to Washington predicted that the shah would seek his advice within forty-eight hours, and he asked urgently for guidance from Washington about how he should respond.

A corner had deftly been turned. With this message, the focus of Washington's attention suddenly shifted from the question of how to buck up the shah to the (previously inadmissible) consideration of whether he would survive at all. Officials were under notice that they had a first-rate crisis on their hands, with just forty-eight hours to decide how to jump. Moreover, the ambassador's previous comments were instantly rendered inoperative as thoughts turned to new initiatives to respond to new realities. By seizing on the shah's remark, Sullivan transformed the nature of the Iranian debate without so much as suggesting that he had changed his mind and even without venturing his own opinion on the subject. A prettier example of nimble ambassadorial footwork —what a Washington colleague once characterized as "an imperceptible 180-degree turn"—would be difficult to imagine.

The crisis in Iran had begun long before, but for harried decision makers in Washington the real policy crisis began that Thursday morning with Ambassador Sullivan's skillful reversal of field. There had been no absence of reports, memos and even periodic spurts of activity in Washington relating to Iran over the preceding months, but the sustained, high-level policy attention characteristic of a genuine crisis had been curiously absent. To understand that inattention, it is necessary to appreciate the unique relationship that had developed over the years between Washington and the shah of Iran.

The American Experience with Iran

Despite a century of sustained contact, Iran remained *terra incognita* for almost all Americans. Public education, religious association, historical accident and even popular literature combine to establish some rudimentary level of information about certain exotic and ancient cultures in the U.S. consciousness. Egypt, China, Japan and India probably evoke at least some stereotypical and cliché-ridden images in the minds of most Americans. In the case of Iran —a nation with two and a half millennia of proud history and culture— mention of the name typically drew a blank, at least prior to the crises that are the subject of this account.

Reference to Persia (as Westerners had called Iran until the mid-1930s, when the shah's father insisted on use of the traditional name) might evoke an image of carpets or perhaps a romantic verse from the *Rubáiyát*. Historically minded athletes might even recall that the legendary run from Marathon to Athens delivered the news of a Persian defeat at the hands of the Greeks. However, it is not an exaggeration to say that America approached Iran from a position of almost unrelieved ignorance.

American diplomats, soldiers and political leaders experienced their first sustained encounter with Iran during and after World War II. In 1941, British and Soviet forces invaded Iran in a move to forestall the growth of German influence, to secure the oil fields of Iran and to acquire a route for the transport of supplies to the Soviet Union. The British and Soviets deposed Reza Shah and installed his twenty-two-year-old son, Mohammad Reza Pahlavi, on the Peacock Throne. Two years later, when Roosevelt met with Churchill and Stalin in Tehran, the United States took the lead in promoting a formal declaration of support by all three major powers for Iran's independence and territorial integrity once the war was over.

The purpose of such a declaration, though not spelled out, was quite plain —to prevent the Red Army from transforming its military occupation of Iran into permanent political hegemony. From the earliest stages of its entry into northern Iran, the USSR had systematically set about creating a pliable client state on its southern border. When the war ended, the British and Americans withdrew their military forces from southern Iran within the six-month period provided by treaty. The Soviets, however, let the deadline pass while stepping up a blatant campaign of manipulation and intimidation aimed at establishing a puppet regime.

Strong U.S. support for Iran in the United Nations and elsewhere was a critical factor in persuading the Soviets to withdraw their troops in mid-1946 and to refrain from direct intervention when the Communist regime in Azerbaijan was subsequently overthrown by the Tehran government. This direct clash of wills can legitimately be regarded as one of the opening salvos of the Cold War.

The twenty-seven-year-old shah was profoundly affected by this crisis, as he was by a crisis of comparable proportions six years later. In April of 1951 the Majles (Iranian parliament) voted to nationalize the concessions and installations in Iran of the Anglo-Iranian Oil Company (AIOC), which had dominated the development and sale of Iranian oil since 1909, the year after oil was first discovered in Iran by an Australian, William D'Arcy. The British government had acquired a controlling interest in the company in 1914, which had assured British influence in economic and political affairs in Iran for more than forty years. The young shah, faced with a genuine nationalist revolt against foreign intervention, responded by appointing Mohammad Mossadegh as prime minister.

Negotiations with the British soon broke down, and the British initiated a very effective world-wide boycott of Iranian oil. The United States attempted to mediate the dispute, but efforts collapsed. Although Iran was experiencing economic disruption because of the boycott, Mossadegh's uncompromising campaign against a foreign power was immensely popular in Iran, and the prime minister's National Front won handily in the January 1952 elections. In the meantime, Mossadegh was arrogating more and more power to himself, at the expense of the shah. When he demanded control of the armed forces in July 1952, the shah dismissed him, only to be confronted with massive popular riots. Mossadegh was reinstated and, several months later, felt secure enough to dismiss the Majles altogether.

The outgoing Truman administration was deeply concerned that the failure to resolve the dispute with the British would force Iran to move closer to Moscow. Those fears were given substance by anti-American riots in Tehran. Washington made a last concerted effort to devise an acceptable compromise in late 1952, but AIOC and the British government rejected it. At the same time, Mossadegh's internal support was eroding. He had never had the support of the army in his efforts to undermine the power of the shah, but now the clergy and significant elements of the commercial and financial community of the bazaar deserted him. In contrast, the Communist Tudeh Party, which had originally opposed him, now swung its support to Mossadegh. By January 1953, when the shah threatened to leave the country in protest, the reports of his intentions were greeted by an outburst of demonstrations in favor of the young king and against Mossadegh.

In Washington the newly installed Eisenhower administration thus inherited a stubborn stalemate that had resisted all efforts at mediation and was leading to progressive economic deterioration in Iran. Mossadegh's internal support was waning, and he was becoming increasingly dependent on the Tudeh Party, leading to fears in Washington that the USSR was laying the groundwork for a pro-Communist coup. Simultaneously, popular support for the shah was growing. Under these circumstances the Eisenhower government approved U.S. participation in a plan to oust Mossadegh in favor of the shah. This plan, originally proposed by the British and code-named Ajax, was coordinated by Kermit Roosevelt of the CIA, who described his activities in a slim volume written a quarter century after the event.[1]

Reading that account in the light of the events of 1978 and 1979 is bemusing. A small group of Westerners with no special knowledge of Iran, disposing of relatively small sums of money and some basic communications, were able to coordinate and orchestrate the dismissal of an ambitious prime minister by the ruling monarch and make it stick by a rousing show of public enthusiasm and support. Without dismissing the importance of the U.S. role, it seems likely that when the shah told Kim Roosevelt, "I owe my throne to God, my people, my army—and to you!" he had the order roughly correct.[2] Roosevelt himself was quite explicit that without the "heartfelt strength" of popular support for the shah, the plan would never have succeeded.[3]

Regardless, the belief that the United States had single-handedly imposed a harsh tyrant on a reluctant populace became one of the central myths of the relationship, particularly as viewed from Iran. The United States government has a short memory. The rapid rotation of new faces in and out of Washington ensures that anything that happened more than a quarter century before—even an event of singular importance—assumes the pale and distant appearance of ancient history. In Washington, by 1978 the events of 1953 had all the relevance of a pressed flower. Recollections of a frightened and irresolute young shah had been replaced by the realities of dealing with a testy and imperious monarch. In Iran, however, the memory (or mythology) of 1953 was as fresh as if it had happened only the week before, and the popular image of the shah as a pliant creature of the United States was a vivid political reality.

Whatever interpretation one chooses to place on the objectives and consequences of Operation Ajax, it abruptly and permanently ended America's political innocence with respect to Iran. Until 1953 the United States had played an essentially benevolent role in the great-power politics of Iran, restraining both British and Soviet appetites during WWII, firmly opposing Soviet encroachments immediately following the war, and playing the honest broker between Iran and the AIOC five years later. But the direct intervention in 1953 cast the United States in the role so common in Iranian history of the cynical external power prepared to manipulate Iranian political circumstances for its own benefit. Whether or not such a description is a fair characterization of U.S. policy, it is unfortunately true that after 1953 the United States would never again be able to enjoy the presumption of benign objectives and enlightened self-interest when engaging itself in the affairs of Iran.

Dealing with the Shah

It is of more than academic interest that in the same fateful year of 1953, the new vice president of the United States, Richard M. Nixon, arrived in Tehran in the course of a good-will and fact-finding tour. Vice President Nixon was instantly taken with the ambitious young monarch and found that they shared a common viewpoint on regional security matters. Nixon found the shah prepared to cooperate with the United States in opposing Soviet ambitions in the Persian Gulf, and he was intrigued at the prospect of a close strategic relationship between the two countries.

There is no evidence that this enthusiastic interpretation by his vice president had any significant effect on President Eisenhower. In fact, Eisenhower later demonstrated a healthy skepticism about the shah's gloomy assessment of the security threats facing Iran and rather brusquely rejected as excessive the shah's importunate requests for advanced military technology. However, the Nixon-shah relationship endured and eventually resurfaced nearly twenty years later, when it would recast the relationship between the United States and Iran.

The shah referred to the events of August 1953 as "the national uprising," and he deliberately designated that date as the beginning of the remarkable spurt of Iranian economic growth that he hoped and expected would epitomize his reign.[4] Indeed, the two decades that followed the defeat of Mossadegh were a period of extraordinary prosperity in Iran.

During the first ten years of this period the United States, under Presidents Eisenhower and Kennedy, pursued an intricate and sometimes ambiguous policy toward Iran. The United States was generally sympathetic to Iran's interest in developing an effective defense. Military assistance in the amount of $829 million was provided between 1950 and 1963, and $1.3 billion worth of new weapons systems was made available. Nonetheless, the levels of financing and technology constantly fell short of the shah's requests.

The United States government repeatedly found itself in the uncomfortable position of having to insist that Iran's most pressing problems were internal and that the shah should not permit his preoccupation with military development to interfere with the process of nation-building. But the shah was impatient with such advice, and he persevered from year to year and from one U.S. president to the next.

The pattern of this dialogue was established early in the Eisenhower administration and continued off and on throughout the decade. The shah wrote regularly to President Eisenhower, describing the threats to Iran's security from every side and requesting in urgent tones the most advanced military equipment. Eisenhower questioned the shah's analyses and toned down the requests in replies that were blunt and authoritative. Coming from the general who had directed the Allied offensive in Europe, these messages left small opportunity for a royal rejoinder. However, some of Eisenhower's successors, perhaps less confident of their own military judgment, were more reluctant to challenge the shah's strategic assessments and the lengthy "shopping lists" of high-technology weaponry that inevitably accompanied them.

The two great crises of the shah's life to that time—the trauma of foreign military occupation during and after WWII and the near-loss of political control to Mossadegh in the early 1950s—had taught the shah two lessons that shaped his attitudes and behavior in the decades to follow. The first was the vital importance of a strong, well-equipped Iranian military force to deter foreign intervention. The other was the political danger of permitting an independent or charismatic rival close to the seat of real power.

The shah's concern with issues of military security provided the dominant leitmotif of the U.S.-Iranian relationship almost from the beginning. His preoccupation with military affairs was, in fact, a family tradition. His father, Reza Khan, had been the commander of the Persian Cossack Division and led his forces in a successful nationalist takeover of the government in 1921 that ended the previous Qajar dynasty. Using his military position as a springboard to power, Reza Khan first became prime minister and then, in 1925, had himself crowned as Reza Shah Pahlavi. A physically powerful man, Reza Shah dominated his son's early years and personally managed his military education.

Although Reza Shah's son lacked the intimidating physique and presence of his father, he understood very well the importance of the military in bringing the Pahlavi family to power and keeping it there. As early as 1943 the young shah described himself as "burning" to discuss Iran's "need for planes and tanks."[5] That burning interest never subsided; in fact it ripened almost to the point of obsession by the mid-1970s.

The shah's instinct for accumulating all real power in his own hands and operating through compliant ministers and political representatives was evident from at least 1953. General Fazlollah Zahedi, a retired officer whose support within the military had provided the critical alternative to Mossadegh, was appointed as the first prime minister after the "countercoup" of 1953. Zahedi (his son later became the Iranian ambassador to the United States and played an important role during the revolution) was genuinely popular. His nationalist views (he had earlier been a key organizer for the National Front) and his contacts in the army gave him the potential of becoming a strongman in Iranian politics. The shah dismissed him after twenty months.

During the Kennedy administration, key officials in both the White House and the State Department concluded that the shah was wrong to emphasize military expansion at the expense of political liberalization. As time went on, opinion in Washington increasingly gravitated toward Dr. Ali Amini as someone who might be able to introduce and carry out a program of political and economic reform in Iran.

Ali Amini belonged to one of the great landholding families in the country. He had been a cabinet minister under Mossadegh and again under General Zahedi. He had spent three years as the Iranian ambassador in Washington, where he impressed observers as an intelligent, moderate, reform-minded political figure. President Kennedy and some of his advisers made no secret of their belief that Amini would be the ideal individual to carry out a meaningful and badly needed reform program.

The shah, feeling himself under pressure "too strong . . . to resist"[6] appointed Dr. Amini prime minister in May 1961. However, as is often the case, Washington's blessing proved to be a curse in disguise. The Tehran rumor mill permanently tagged Amini as "Washington's man," while the shah recognized in Amini a potentially serious rival for real power and reacted accordingly. The combination was deadly, and it was compounded by Washington's unwillingness or inability to provide the kind of prompt, tangible support that might have improved Amini's chances of pushing through a controversial program of political and economic reform.

After only fifteen months the shah dismissed Amini and introduced his own program of land reform and modernization, which he called the White Revolution (to distinguish it from the Marxist, or Red variety). Never again would he permit a potential rival so close to the seat of power. Amini, as we shall see later, would reappear as a key adviser to the shah as the revolution came to a climax in late 1978.

Rehearsing Revolution: The Riots of 1963

The third great crisis that influenced not only the shah's behavior but also the fundamental course of events leading to the revolution of 1978 was his confrontation with the clergy in 1963. In many respects, the 1963 incident was a rehearsal for the revolutionary uprising a decade and a half later. Public opposition to the shah's economic and political program was directed—in 1963 as in 1978—by a fiery *mujtahid* (religious authority) named Ruhollah Khomeini, who was then sixty years old.[7]

Khomeini had written in opposition to the shah's father in the early 1940s but had remained essentially silent during the politically turbulent 1950s. In 1963 he returned to the political scene with blistering denunciations of the corruption, constitutional violations and "Westoxication"—the indiscriminate imitation of things Western—of the shah's regime.[8]

Khomeini was briefly under arrest in March, after the religious school where he taught was attacked by paratroops, but he immediately returned to his inflammatory attacks on the regime. Again he was arrested, on June 4, the anniversary of the martyrdom of Husaýn, who is revered as the first imam of the Shi'i faith. This ignited three days of violent protests throughout Iran that the shah's forces harshly suppressed, killing hundreds of dissidents, including religious students in the holy city of Qom.

After more than two months in prison, Khomeini was released and again resumed his political protests. When he called for a boycott of the parliamentary elections of October 1963, Khomeini was arrested a third time and remained in prison for nearly eight months.

When he emerged from prison he soon launched back into opposition activity, this time against a proposed "status of forces" agreement between the Iranian government and the United States. Such agreements routinely include a provision that exempts U.S. military personnel from jurisdiction of national courts, in effect granting them the same immunity accorded to diplomats. Although the United States had similar agreements with most of its closest allies (e.g., Germany, Japan and Great Britain), the provision smacked of the kind of extraterritorial privileges that were viewed in Iran as distastefully reminiscent of the colonial past.

As a direct result of this fourth clash with the government, Khomeini was exiled to Turkey in October 1964. From there he traveled on to Iraq. He did not set foot in Iran again for more than fourteen years. It is disappointing that this violent episode, which had so many parallels with the 1978 revolution, went almost entirely unreported in the United States.[9]

During this period the U.S. government and media devoted their attention almost exclusively to the shah's six-point program of land reform, female suffrage, forest conservation, denationalization of state-owned industries, profit sharing for industrial workers and rural literacy. These objectives corresponded perfectly with the philosophy of economic and cultural development then in vogue in U.S. academic circles, and the shah's harsh tactics were accepted as an unpleasant but necessary effort to break the hold of reactionary elements standing in the way of social progress.

That was very much the way the shah perceived it as well. However, that judgment failed to recognize the depth of resistance within Iranian society to the wholesale imposition of Western values. His subjects were, for the most part, impoverished, illiterate and traditional in their attitudes toward religion and society. So long as Iran was prospering, the veneer of success would conceal the underlying discontent; but if the economy should falter, the frustrations would re-emerge with a vengeance. That critical point was not well understood by the shah or even by the most sophisticated Western observers.

On the contrary, the shah preferred to insist—then and later—that it was all a plot. The 1963 riots were inspired, he said, "by an obscure individual who claimed to be a religious leader, Ruhollah Khomeini." It was certain, the shah added, that Khomeini "had secret dealings with foreign agents," and he even owed his title of *ayatollah* to "radio stations run by atheist émigrés belonging to the Tudeh Party."[10]

Confronting the Mullahs

The failure in both Washington and Tehran to understand the underlying significance of the 1963 events proved to be a costly error. When the rebellion began to grow in 1978, scarcely any American was familiar with the name of Khomeini or what he stood for. Thus, the seemingly pathological hatred that Khomeini displayed toward the United States during the hostage crisis was incomprehensible to all those Americans who did not know that his arrest, imprisonment and fourteen years of exile were the direct result of his opposition to "Westoxication" and, in particular, the granting of special rights and privileges to Americans in Iran.

The 1963 experience did, however, confirm a lesson that the shah had learned from his father—that the power of the clerics (the mullahs) could be successfully confronted only with force and repression. Both father and son shared a bottomless scorn for the traditionalist clerics, whom they saw as obscurantist relics of a benighted past—black reactionaries who stood in the path of modernization and progress—to be dealt with by impatient injunction backed by coercion. It must be added that there were many in Iran, especially in the professional and modernizing middle classes, who agreed with these attitudes, if not always the methods.

After the riots of 1963 had been crushed, and especially after the ringleader, Khomeini, was packed off to exile, most observers inside and outside Iran could be excused for believing that the shah had definitively broken the power of the clergy as a political force. And so it appeared for almost a decade and a half. But the shah and other observers had ignored the warning of an old Iranian proverb: "Do not step on a Persian carpet or a mullah, for it increases its value."[11]

The riots and demonstrations of 1963 marked the end of open resistance to the shah's White Revolution. The country plunged into a frenzy of construction and modernization fueled by dramatic increases in oil production and oil revenues, which climbed from $555 million in 1963 to $5 billion in 1973. Iran made striking improvements in virtually every field of human and industrial development during the late 1960s and early 1970s, though the benefits were not equally distributed.

The shah, apparently satisfied with the results of his personal revolution, chose in October 1971 to commemorate 2,500 years of Iranian history with one of the most lavish displays of wealth, power and pageantry in history. At the spectacular ruins of the palace of Cyrus the Great near Persepolis, he constructed an elegant tent city and for several days entertained heads of state and influential political figures from nations around the world. Maxim's of Paris catered the event, boasting that it could satisfy the whim of the most discriminating royal palate, relying on a special airlift of ingredients from any part of the globe.[12]

Hours of parades, by soldiers in uniforms of the past, celebrated the centuries of Iran's military triumphs. Standing at the tomb of Cyrus, the ancient warrior who created the Persian Empire, the shah addressed his predecessor in confident tones. "Rest in peace," he cried out, "the Iranian flag is flying today as triumphantly" as ever in the past.

The extravagance of this spectacle exaggerated the contrast between the almost limitless wealth of the court and the abject poverty of much of the country. Some of those who later became active in the revolution identified this occasion as the key turning point in their decision to oppose the shah and to dedicate themselves to revolutionary activities. However, even the most fervent among them had to admit that at the time, in the days of pomp and splendor at Persepolis, with all its symbolism of the wealth and power available to the shah, their cause appeared to be beyond hope.

Nixon, Kissinger and the Shah

By 1972 the shah was at the peak of his personal power, and Iran appeared to be making an altogether remarkable transition into the ranks of the developed states. In the United States, Richard Nixon had become president, and by early 1972 he had achieved several triumphs of his own. In February of that year, President Nixon visited the Forbidden City in Peking, meeting with Mao Zedong and, in a single dramatic stroke, effectively rearranging all the pieces on the diplomatic board. In May, responding to Vietnamese intransigence in secret negotiations, he ordered the mining of North Vietnamese ports, thereby risking the breakdown of the SALT negotiations and the forthcoming summit meeting with the Soviets. The Soviets, however, studiously looked the other way and received Nixon in the Kremlin scarcely two weeks after the bombing. Not only was he the first U.S. president to visit the two great Asian capitals (and that within the breath-taking space of ninety days), but President Nixon came away from Moscow with a strategic arms limitations treaty and an agreement on "Basic Principles of Relations" between the two superpowers. All of the pieces seemed to be coming together.

Nixon flew directly from Moscow to Tehran, where he was greeted by the shah. Curiously, this heady moment can be viewed in retrospect as the high-water mark in the careers of both leaders. Each had overcome seemingly impossible odds and had triumphed absolutely. Nixon would go on to a smashing electoral victory that November, and the shah had new triumphs ahead of him; but it was already true (if unknowable) that the greatest achievements of both leaders were behind them and that the seeds of tragedy were quietly beginning to germinate beneath the surface of events.

Less than three weeks after the Nixon-shah meeting, a bizarre band of burglars was apprehended during an attempted break-in at the Democratic National Committee in the Watergate apartments in Washington, D.C., thereby setting in motion a train of events that would lead to Nixon's resignation in 1974. In the same year that Nixon was undergoing the agonies of the Watergate scandal, the shah was secretly informed by two French physicians that he was suffering from a form of cancer that had resulted in the deaths of other members of his family in the past. Nixon, although disgraced, would survive. The shah would not.

In Iran, President Nixon and his national security adviser, Henry Kissinger, had spent two and a half hours in formal meetings with the shah on May 30 and 31, 1972. The outcome was a bargain that radically restructured the U.S.-Iranian relationship. The United States agreed, among other things, to increase substantially the number of U.S. uniformed advisers and technicians living and working in Iran, and guaranteed the shah access to some of the most sophisticated non-nuclear technology in the U.S. military arsenal. The shah, in turn, agreed to accept a principal role in protecting Western interests in the Persian Gulf region.

For the shah, this was a personal triumph beyond his wildest expectations. For years he had dealt with successive U.S. presidents but had always been kept on a short leash. President Eisenhower had dismissed his strategic analyses with unceremonious bluntness; President Kennedy had pressed him for social reforms and President Johnson had only grudgingly yielded to his requests for modern fighter aircraft after the traumatic events of the Arab-Israeli War of 1967. Now, at last, he was recognized as a world-class strategic thinker by no less an authority than Henry Kissinger,[13] and the U.S. arsenal of high military technology was thrown open to him just at the moment when surging oil revenues gave him the means to indulge his taste in weaponry.

To President Nixon and his adviser, the security arrangement with the shah was an integral element of the new geopolitical structure that had been assembled at the Peking and Moscow summits. With the United States bogged down in Vietnam, with U.S. domestic opinion firmly opposed to any new military ventures abroad, with the withdrawal of the British from their strategic role east of Suez, and with the oil of the Persian Gulf beginning to be recognized as a key factor in Western security, there was an inescapable logic in asking a strong regional power to accept a security role that the United States was simply incapable of undertaking at the time.

All of this was expressed with startling candor and simplicity at the end of their meeting. Richard Nixon looked across the table to the shah and said simply, "Protect me."[14]

The shah accepted this new relationship with alacrity. The only significant opposition came from the Washington bureaucracy. No one in the official Washington community disputed the importance of a pro-Western, anti-Soviet Iran, and no one was prepared to question the wisdom of maintaining a close security relationship with the shah. Significantly, however, it was the Department of Defense that objected vigorously to the notion of selling the shah everything he wanted.

For years officials in the Defense Department had been required to produce studies and analyses of Iran's security situation; and year after year, through one administration after another, the result was the same. Pentagon studies routinely concluded that the military threats to Iran's northern and western borders could best be addressed by the steady, systematic development and training of its military forces, rather than the rapid introduction of massive quantities of complex high-technology equipment.

In the view of most military planners, the question was not whether the United States should provide military assistance to Iran. That was universally regarded as consistent with U.S. security interests. Rather, the question was whether the United States should suspend its own best professional judgment in deference to the shah's voracious appetite for large quantities of the latest military technology.

Kissinger attempted to cut the argument short. In July 1972 he issued a memorandum reiterating the president's decision to provide a wide range of the most modern weaponry and technical assistance to the shah. Iran would be encouraged to purchase U.S. equipment—as opposed to that of other nations—and technical information on such equipment would be provided to Iran on request. In the president's name, Kissinger formally served notice to the bureaucracy that, henceforth, decisions on purchases of U.S. military equipment would be left primarily to the government of Iran.

A year later, in a memorandum to President Nixon, Kissinger summarized the policy in his own words. After the May 1972 meeting with the shah, he noted, "we adopted a policy which provides, in effect, that we will accede to any of the Shah's requests for arms purchases from us (other than some sophisticated advanced technology armaments and with the very important exception, of course, of any nuclear weapons capability . . .)."

There continued to be resistance to this unprecedented edict from scattered elements within the Department of Defense, but they were reduced to fighting rear-guard actions as the arms sale rush swung into high gear. The combination of vast quantities of money, a seemingly unquenchable Iranian appetite for hardware, and formal encouragement by the president of the United States created what can only be described as a stampede. In the first four years after the Nixon-Kissinger visit, the shah ordered more than $9 billion worth of the most sophisticated weaponry in the U.S. inventory, and the arms sale program quickly became a scandal.

Two successive secretaries of defense felt constrained to send personal representatives to Tehran to keep up with the action and try to impose some degree of order. Shortly after James Schlesinger became secretary of defense in 1973, he became concerned that the boom in arms sales would lead U.S. industry and the armed forces to push sophisticated equipment on recipients who were not prepared to absorb them. As the cabinet officer responsible for implementing U.S. security policy, Schlesinger was concerned that this dumping of high-technology military equipment would create problems of assimilation and would eventually erode confidence in the U.S. Department of Defense as a reliable partner and source of military assistance.

In late 1973, Schlesinger had the first of several meetings with the shah. In the course of those meetings he attempted firmly but politely to persuade the shah that his most pressing military problem was not a shortage of sophisticated equipment but rather a shortage of trained manpower capable of absorbing, maintaining and effectively using the vast arsenal that was being acquired. Schlesinger argued strongly for more selectivity in weapons purchases and better management of Iran's limited human resources. In these discussions Schlesinger felt free to raise questions with the shah about his program and to offer his own advice. However, in accordance with the explicit policy of President Nixon and Henry Kissinger, if the shah insisted on proceeding with a specific purchase, the secretary of defense was to defer to the shah's wishes and approve the sale.

As a result of these talks, the shah requested U.S. technical advice and assistance on a more regular basis. In response, Schlesinger sent a retired Army colonel, Richard Hallock, to Iran as his unofficial representative. Hallock was at the time a private consultant under contract to the Advanced Research Projects Agency (ARPA) of the Department of Defense. Hallock seemed to be a natural choice. He was a former colleague of Schlesinger's at the Rand Corporation and had worked with Schlesinger in the Budget Bureau. He had conducted a useful cost-effectiveness study for the Turkish military, and he was highly regarded as an analyst of military procurement and management. With Schlesinger's approval, he was to operate as an independent set of eyes and ears in Tehran.

Schlesinger continued to be uneasy about the situation he had inherited. In early 1974 he asked senior members of his staff to prepare a candid evaluation of the security relationship with Iran. That report confirmed that the White House directive of July 1972 was universally interpreted as a presidential order to the Defense Department to sell Iran whatever military equipment it desired, short of nuclear weapons.

Schlesinger was unwilling to accept that as the final word, and he appointed a personal representative to conduct a detailed review of the U.S.-Iranian military supply relationship within the Department of Defense. Schlesinger chose for this task a senior Defense Department civilian, Glenn Blitgen, from the staff of the Near East section of International Security Affairs (ISA). Secretary Schlesinger may have been aware that ISA was virtually the only place in the government that consistently resisted the avalanche of military sales to Iran.

By choosing Blitgen—a seasoned professional with a reputation for loyalty and discretion—and giving him a mandate to conduct a full-scale investigation in the secretary's name, Schlesinger accomplished several objectives. First, he could be certain that Blitgen would overlook nothing; he was a thirty-year veteran of the Pentagon who could not easily be misled or diverted. Second, he could have high confidence that the report would not leak before he was ready to make use of it. Finally, Schlesinger could be confident that Blitgen's systematic progress through the intricacies of the Pentagon bureaucracy would ensure that everyone associated with arms sales to Iran would soon be aware that the secretary of defense was personally concerned about the situation.

However, there was one area that remained off-limits—the activities of Richard Hallock. Hallock had been well received by Ambassador Richard Helms in Tehran, and his acceptance by the Iranians went beyond Schlesinger's expectations. Hallock established an office immediately adjacent to the Iranian vice minister of war, Air Force General Hassan Toufanian, who was the shah's principal aide for military procurement, and inserted himself directly into the Iranian chain of command for procurement decisions.

A Senate study of the U.S.-Iranian military relationship in 1976 concluded that Hallock's role was "(1) to provide the shah and General Toufanian with independent analyses on weapons procurement and (2) to keep Schlesinger informed of the shah's views and/or problem areas as they developed."[15] This description helps to explain the extreme delicacy and sensitivity of Hallock's mission. On the one hand, he was to assist the shah in sorting out the multitude of weapons sales proposals by U.S. companies, thus potentially giving him power to influence literally billions of dollars' worth of contracts. At the same time, he was to report directly to the U.S. secretary of defense and the ambassador about the shah's concerns and problems with the arms sales program. To add a further element of complexity to the picture, Hallock, who had his own consulting practice, was independently on retainer to the government of Iran throughout this entire period. So Hallock was at any moment balancing three sets of interests—Iran's, America's and his own. Not surprisingly, as time went on, questions began to be raised about the propriety of Hallock's actions.

This unorthodox arrangement was only a further embellishment on the Byzantine tangle of political and commercial interests that flourished in the hothouse climate of the arms bazaar in Tehran. Orthodox or unorthodox, Schlesinger's methods of introducing a cautionary note into the system began to have an effect, particularly after President Nixon resigned in August 1974.

Prior to the Nixon resignation, any attempt to place constraints on the U.S.-Iranian relationship was doomed to failure, since it was assured of opposition from both the president and Henry Kissinger, who had, since August 1973, added the job of secretary of state to his function as national security affairs adviser. It was only after the Nixon resignation that Schlesinger asked Blitgen to conduct his inquiry. The Iranian arms sales issue thereafter became intertwined with the running power struggle between Schlesinger at Defense and Kissinger at State, which dominated the Washington political landscape during 1975.

By September 1975, Schlesinger had placed the defense advisory role in Tehran on a more orthodox basis by replacing Hallock with a Defense Department professional, Eric Von Marbod. Then, with Blitgen's report in hand, Schlesinger drafted a six-page memorandum to President Gerald R. Ford expressing his "doubt whether our policy of supporting an apparently open-ended Iranian military buildup will continue to serve our long-term interests." He called for an interagency review of the Iranian situation.

However, Kissinger was not without resources. He still controlled the National Security Council staff, which managed the paper flow on foreign affairs issues to the president. Thus it was not surprising that the White House responded to Schlesinger's request with a deliberateness that could only be described as glacial. By November 1975 no answer had been received from the White House, and Schlesinger was replaced at Defense by Donald Rumsfeld.

Not until the spring of 1976 did the Department of Defense receive a response to the Schlesinger proposal. The response, in the form of a directive to conduct an interagency study, was not limited to Iran. In fact, Iran was scarcely mentioned. Instead, the directive called for a comprehensive review of all aspects of U.S. security policy in the Persian Gulf region. It proposed a detailed assessment of the evolution of U.S. policy in the past, a review of U.S. goals and objectives in the region generally, and the development of policy options over the next decade. The study was to be completed in thirty days.

The subject was so broad, the terms of reference so vague, and the divisions within the government so deep that such a study was doomed even before it began. The more cynical members of the bureaucracy, who by this time had several years of experience with the Kissingerian style of bureaucratic management, quickly concluded that this was nothing but a paper operation, intended to distract and divide the forces of opposition within the government rather than to inform and shape policy.

There was considerable evidence later that this view was far from unjustified. When the original deadline passed, there was no objection from the White House, and the months of interagency wrangling that followed apparently attracted no particular attention or evinced any special concern at the NSC. On the contrary, even when a study of sorts was finally assembled and sent to the White House, it languished in the in-boxes of General Brent Scowcroft, Kissinger's former deputy who became national security affairs adviser in the cabinet reshuffle of November 1975, and his deputy, William Hyland, also a close associate of Kissinger's. Despite some considerable exertions from the working level of the NSC staff, the study remained in bureaucratic limbo through the 1976 elections and the transition period that followed. In the end, the report was bequeathed to the Carter administration, to be incorporated in its major review of arms transfer policy conducted in the spring of 1977.

The Legacy of the Past

That is a brief review of the tangled history of U.S.-Iranian relations that the Carter administration inherited on January 20, 1977. Five years after Richard Nixon and Henry Kissinger visited the shah in Tehran, a new set of realities had been created in U.S.-Iranian relations, and those new realities were deeply embedded in U.S. policy. More than $10 billion worth of military equipment had been sold during those five years, and the pipeline was jammed with programs that would extend over decades to come. American strategy in the oil-rich Persian Gulf was heavily reliant on Iranian support. Richard Nixon's decision to rely exclusively on the shah for the protection of U.S. interests in the Persian Gulf had been so thoroughly institutionalized in U.S. policy and practice that the United States now lay strategically naked beneath the thin blanket of Iranian security.

The remarkable exchange between the shah and the president of the United States in May 1972 had laid the basis for an almost unique degree of mutual dependence. The shah relied absolutely on access to U.S. technology and expert assistance to transform his ambitious military and economic visions into reality. The United States, in turn, was dependent on the shah to protect U.S. interests in a region that was becoming increasingly important to the very survival of the Western industrial system.

Once committed, it was not easy to escape the inexorable logic of the situation. Each side was operating without a safety net. Even the prospect of failure was not to be admitted: it was too painful to contemplate.

This was the new reality, and it was understood even by those who had lingering doubts about the wisdom of making such a gamble. The die was cast, and the senior Washington bureaucracy—which has a short institutional memory at best—had fully engaged its massive capabilities in the effort to justify and explain the policy course irrevocably defined by its political leaders.

In later years Kissinger attempted to minimize the importance of the White House commitment. In his book *White House Years,* he dismissed criticisms of the "open-ended" commitment to the shah as "hyperbole" in view of the "readiness and skill with which our bureaucracy is capable of emasculating directives it is reluctant to implement."[16]

Quite apart from the dubious implication that one could or should safely rely on the bureaucracy to resist deliberate excesses by political leaders, this curious statement stands on its head what was presumably the original motive in issuing an iron-clad presidential directive, i.e., to ensure that the bureaucracy had no latitude to reinterpret what was clearly a controversial policy decision.

There was no precedent in U.S. history for an order directly from the president to the national security bureaucracy instructing it to rely on the judgment of a foreign leader in making decisions on arms transfers. It will not do to argue seven years later that the directive had no effect. It did. The president's order was unequivocal and comprehensive. It afforded not the smallest loophole for those who questioned the wisdom of a blank check to the shah. There were indeed rear-guard actions within the bureaucracy to attempt to moderate the effects of the decision, but they were largely futile. The order was implemented, with a vengeance.

Three years later, in the second volume of his memoirs, Kissinger took a different tack. This time he asserted "I had forgotten it,"[17] suggesting that the policy directive had been swept from memory by the events of Watergate and the advent of a new administration. It is apparent that, in retrospect, Kissinger would prefer that it be forgotten, but he need go no further than his own files to discover that the facts were quite different. As indicated above, the directive remained the object of hotly contested debate at the highest levels of the government through the very last days of the Ford administration, with Kissinger consistently supporting it against opposition within the government.

The Tail Wags the Dog

In the 1950s and 1960s, there were many in the U.S. government who had vivid memories of the shah as a beleaguered young monarch, uncertain of his throne and indecisive in the face of stormy political events over which he had only limited control. By 1976 those observers had disappeared into retirement or into jobs in other areas. The U.S. government bureaucracy was populated from top to bottom with individuals whose experience with Iran and its monarch reflected the new reality of the 1970s: a ruler who knew his own mind and did not take kindly to gratuitous advice from anyone (including the U.S. ambassador), firmly in command of a prosperous, modernizing nation whose most serious problem seemed to be the impulse to try to do too much too soon.

The days when Washington called the tune in relations with Iran, if remembered at all, were remembered with irony as Washington scrambled to accommodate the latest requests of the shah, frequently amplified by not too subtle prodding from the White House and State Department. Although many in the government retained strong personal doubts about the frantic pace of forced-draft industrialization and military expansion that the shah was imposing on his largely illiterate and traditional population, questions centered not on the shah's objectives of modernization and regional power but on the wisdom of attempting to do so much in so short a time with such limited resources.

Even these qualms tended to be submerged by the Washington cycle of the self-fulfilling prophecy. Attacks and criticisms from the press and the Congress about particular programs or policy decisions require public responses and congressional testimony. Although the criticisms register in the system, the system is energized to find arguments and justifications supporting the administration's position. Officials who speak to the media, the public and the Congress on these issues repeatedly expound the administration "line," which typically attempts to put the most favorable interpretation on a set of potentially embarrassing or controversial facts. Being human, those who constantly defend a position with arguments, facts and statistics eventually come to believe what they are saying.

In the case of Iran this was particularly seductive, since the administration had based its entire strategic concept for the Persian Gulf region on the strength and stability of the shah, and the White House was irrevocably wedded to that approach. In some respects, the strategic gamble that Nixon and Kissinger took in placing U.S. interests in a vital area of the world almost entirely in the hands of the shah was the equivalent of the gamble that the shah himself was taking in his attempt to fling his nation bodily into the world of industrialization and high technology.

This situation was described with exceptional honesty and candor in a report by the inspector general of the U.S. Foreign Service in the summer of 1976, just before Jimmy Carter was elected president. After four months of interviews and policy examinations in Washington and Iran, the report concluded that "The Government of Iran exerts the determining influence" in the relationship with the United States. Iran, the inspectors noted, contributed far more in financial terms than did the United States, and "He who pays the piper calls the tune." The United States, they noted, "should stand ready to assist the GOI [Government of Iran] to get the best U.S. goods and services at full cost . . . [and] the best is, usually, expensive."

Eighteen months before the revolution began, the inspectors were able to conclude that "There is no effective internal challenge to [the shah's] leadership." The major problem they saw was that many Americans deplored the authoritarian nature of his rule and were concerned that the unrestrained arms transfer policy would "lead to a conflagration rather than stability in the area."

Despite Kissinger's claim that his directive on arms sales had been forgotten, the inspectors were very much aware of it. They quoted it in full as an unequivocal statement of U.S. policy. Moreover, they noted that major decisions relating to Iran were taken by the most senior levels of the Department of State and the White House, while the assistant secretary, the ambassador and the State Department desk officer for Iran were "usually informed" of decisions in time to avoid "excessive confusion or false-stepping."

In short, the Nixon-Kissinger policy of placing U.S. security interests in the Persian Gulf almost exclusively in the hands of the shah had been fully absorbed by the bureaucracy and the U.S. power structure. By the time President Carter arrived in the White House, U.S. security policy in that important region of the world was in many respects hostage to the social and economic experiment that the shah was conducting in Iran. Whether one liked it or not, Iran was the regional tail wagging the superpower dog.

II

EARLY SIGNS AND SIGNALS

T he election of Jimmy Carter as president of the United States in November 1976 came as a blow to the shah of Iran. The shah's ambassador in London wrote in his diary on August 8 that the shah "fears that Jimmy Carter may have 'Kennedy-type pretensions' and would much prefer to see Ford re-elected."[1]

Carter had adopted as two of his principal campaign themes the issues of human rights and reduction of U.S. arms sales, each of which could be regarded as critical of existing U.S. relations with Iran. Moreover, the shah, in his many years of dealing with U.S. presidents, had always had more success with Republicans than with Democrats, so the shift in parties would have been unwelcome in any event.

In this case, however, the shah had reason to view the change of administrations with special poignancy. The personal and official ties that Richard Nixon and Henry Kissinger had woven between the United States and the shah were unique. Those close associations had been jarred by the events of Watergate but nevertheless remained intact during the presidency of Gerald R. Ford. So it must have come as a disagreeable shock to realize not only that the new U.S. president was a total stranger and a Democrat but, worse, that he had been elected on a platform that appeared to be hostile to many of the shah's policies.

It was quite apparent in Washington that the shah was apprehensive about the new Carter administration. It was also evident that the United States had no visible strategic alternative to a close relationship with Iran. Policy bridges had been burned years before. Consequently, the Carter administration devoted considerable efforts during its first year to reassure the shah that there was no intent to alter the basic nature of the relationship. The shah, for his part, realized that cooperation with the United States was critical to the success of his military and economic programs, and he moved quickly to establish the basis for a healthy relationship with the new president.

The use of torture and political persecution in Iran had become common-place during the 1970s. The feared and hated secret police known as SAVAK (the Farsi-language acronym for National Security and Information Organiza-tion) was given wide latitude to identify and intimidate political enemies of the shah. SAVAK also conducted essentially unlimited warfare against a collec-tion of urban guerrilla organizations committed to violent opposition to the shah's regime.

One close observer estimated that at least 341 guerrillas—most of whom were disaffected young intellectuals—were killed over an eight-year period.[2] The guerrillas, in turn, conducted hit-and-run operations against police sta-tions, border posts and other institutional targets, in addition to sporadic assassinations—including seven Americans. This largely covert struggle coin-cided with a period in Iran's relationship with the United States when the shah had reason to believe that a crackdown on opposition elements would be welcome in Washington and that his methods would be regarded with a considerable measure of tolerance.

Nevertheless, the assassinations of U.S. civilians and officials in Iran, to-gether with the persistently critical reporting of organizations such as Amnesty International and the International Commission of Jurists drew public atten-tion in the United States to the repressive side of the shah's government. The shah was very sensitive to the growing tide of uncomplimentary reporting in the U.S. media and its broader implications both for the presidential election and for Iran's overall relations with its most important foreign ally. That may help explain why the shah, during the period immediately prior to the U.S. elections and in the first year of the Carter administration, moved vigorously and publicly to decrease the use of torture, to reduce the number of political prisoners and to introduce some basic reforms into the judicial system.

The U.S. election, however, provides only part of the explanation for this change. The shah's decision to introduce limited reforms must also be seen as part of a larger plan intended to preserve the half century of Pahlavi rule into the future. The shah's son, Reza, was sixteen. He would be twenty—the age of majority in Iran—in 1980, and the shah was clearly grooming him to assume at least limited power. The fact that the shah knew he had cancer may have lent additional impetus to this program. Several individuals in the shah's entourage have recalled in conversation that they anticipated a mammoth national celebration on the shah's sixtieth birthday in October 1979 to proclaim the completion of his White Revolution. They understood that by that date all major projects under their supervision were to have been completed.

The shah himself was quite explicit in his own writings about his intentions to lay the foundations for political institutions that would survive him and that would facilitate a smooth transfer of power to his son at some point in the future. He was much less clear—in his writings and perhaps in his own mind —about the nature of the institutions he hoped to build. He experimented with a variety of political forms and political-party arrangements. In each case, however, he ringed these parties with so many restrictions on their freedom of action and packed them so tightly with his own men that they failed to gain credibility as independent institutions.

The shah appeared to have a genuine, if somewhat idealized, regard for democratic forms, perhaps as a result of his Swiss education. However, the inherently untidy operation of a free political marketplace was incompatible with his instinct for manipulation and control. As a consequence, his efforts at institution-building were tentative, carefully hedged and ultimately unconvincing. His attempted introduction of reforms in 1976 and 1977—the latest in a series of experiments with political forms—was unfortunately fated to be no exception to the rule.

Still, the election of Jimmy Carter provided an auspicious context for whatever liberalization measures the shah was prepared to undertake. Both in public and in private, the shah insisted that his order to terminate the use of torture in Iranian prisons, as well as the introduction of legal reforms and the general easing of restrictions on public expression, were unrelated to events in the United States. However, these steps were viewed in Washington as timely and welcome gestures of good faith. To a considerable degree, these well-publicized reform measures provided the essential rationale for the Carter administration's decision, in effect, to continue without change most of the policies of the previous five years.

Arms Sales: The AWACS Controversy

Despite the crushing array of special studies and policy analyses that were undertaken in the first hectic months of the Carter presidency, none was specifically concerned with Iran or U.S. policy toward the Persian Gulf. Iran was not considered to be a problem. On the contrary, the concept of relying on regional powers (or "regional influentials" in the terminology of Zbigniew Brzezinski) in the pursuit of policy objectives and interests was embraced as a cardinal tenet of Carter's foreign policy.

There was, nevertheless, a serious interest in bringing the arms sales program with Iran under effective control. That process was well under way when Carter arrived in the White House, due to the prior efforts of Defense Secretary Schlesinger and the Defense Department representative in Tehran, Eric Von Marbod. There was also a determination to use America's moral influence in the promotion of human rights. But the shah's timely efforts to introduce certain key reforms suggested that a strident and confrontational campaign on this issue would probably be unnecessary or even counterproductive in the case of Iran.

The overriding consideration for U.S. Iranian policy, however, was to ensure that the cooperative relationship that had been developed over nearly four decades would be preserved and that Iran would remain a strong, reliable and friendly ally in the vital region of the Persian Gulf. The importance of the security relationship was paramount—even if that relationship should require some accommodation in the areas of human rights or arms limitations.

The first high-level personal contact between the Carter administration and the Iranian regime occurred in May 1977, when Secretary of State Cyrus Vance visited Tehran for a meeting of the Central Treaty Organization (CENTO)— a mutual-security treaty comprising Iran, Turkey, Pakistan and the United Kingdom, with the United States participating in the work of some committees. During this visit, one of those mysterious "senior officials" who always seem to travel with secretaries of state let it be known to the press that the United States viewed the trends in Iranian civil liberties as favorable and that any sanctions against the shah were out of the question.[3] Vance also informed the shah that the United States would honor all existing arms sales contracts, and was prepared to offer to Iran the sale of airborne warning and control system (AWACS) aircraft.[4]

By all accounts, the shah was reassured by this conversation. In fact— contrary to later speculation—the shah gave no evidence of being at all intimidated or psychologically shaken by the policies of the new administration. When Secretary Vance informed him that the United States was prepared to proceed with the sale of 160 F-16 fighter aircraft—a difficult concession for President Carter—the shah responded with a quick word of thanks and then coolly put in an order for 140 more.

During that same month, the newly nominated ambassador to Tehran, William H. Sullivan, met with President Carter before proceeding to his new post. Sullivan specifically requested, and received, guidance on several sensitive issues between the United States and Iran. On the issue of arms sales, the president confirmed that he was prepared to make available to the shah all equipment already on order and that he intended to approve the sale of AWACS. He also said that he had no objection to selling nuclear power plants to Iran, provided that Iran agreed to appropriate safeguards, particularly on the disposition of spent fuel. Carter confirmed the continued importance to the United States of access to intelligence on the USSR acquired in Iran, and he reiterated his view of the importance of a secure and stable Iran for U.S. strategic interests in the Persian Gulf. These essential elements of U.S. policy were relayed to the shah by Sullivan when he arrived in Iran in June.[5]

The guidance that Sullivan received on the question of arms sales (and that Vance had earlier communicated to the shah) was soon translated into practice. In early July the Congress was officially informed of the president's intention to sell seven AWACS aircraft to Iran. The shah had originally requested ten such aircraft, and the case had aroused passionate debate within the administration.

President Carter had decided (in Presidential Directive 13 of May 13, 1977) that all arms sales cases would henceforth be reviewed personally by the president. That decision ensured that policy control of arms transfers would remain in the White House, and it deliberately placed the burden of proof on those within the bureaucracy who favored any particular arms sale. However, it also elevated the political risk of each case by ensuring that the president would be unable to dissociate himself from an unpopular or controversial decision.

The first case to be presented to President Carter after he signed PD-13 was the proposed sale of AWACS to Iran. The issue was presented to him in a brief, tightly drafted memorandum. The memo noted that the mobile AWACS, for all its expense and technological complexity, was cheaper and required fewer trained men than the alternative air defense system, which would have involved the construction of multiple radar sites on mountaintops throughout the north and west of Iran, including all the attendant construction of access roads, living accommodations, and the like.

The memorandum to President Carter described the opposition of some elements of the government to the sale. Curiously, the leading opponents of the sale were in the Department of State, despite the fact that Secretary of State Vance had personally delivered word to the shah the previous month that the AWACS sale would be approved. Evidently Vance had failed to inform his closest aides of the decision and his own participation in it. The memo also reminded the president that approval of the request, whatever the merits, would be seen by many as a contradiction of his own policy and would inevitably set off a bruising fight with the Congress.

Typically, this memorandum remained in the Oval Office for less than twenty-four hours. Years later it became almost a cliché to describe President Carter as "indecisive," but his working habits were the opposite. He absorbed large quantities of material quickly and made decisions without long, agonizing delays.

In this case, accepting the validity of Iran's need for an effective air defense system, Carter approved the sale of AWACS as the lesser of two unpleasant choices. However, he scratched out "ten" and inked in "seven" in his precise hand. The signal to be conveyed to Tehran seemed unmistakable. First, there should be no doubt that the United States would continue to sustain a security relationship with Iran, even when that entailed some political sacrifice. Second, however, it was equally clear that the days of blank checks were over: the United States would exercise its own independent judgment in reviewing Iran's requests, even if that meant occasional disagreements with the shah.

Although the original "signal" from President Carter to the shah seemed clear enough, it undoubtedly became muddied during the subsequent three months of intense public debate. The Congress, largely in response to the uncontrolled arms sales policy to Iran adopted by the Nixon administration, had written into law a provision under which it could veto any arms sales proposal by a vote of disapproval in *both* the House and the Senate. Although the intent of this legislation was admirable, in practice it usually left the administration with the worst of all possible worlds. The Congress was reluctant to reverse the administration on an important foreign policy issue, yet it was unwilling to be perceived as a rubber stamp for controversial decisions. The result was often an acrimonious and highly public political contest that the administration won only after the recipient nation was thoroughly embarrassed, thereby forfeiting most if not all the foreign policy benefits the administration may have hoped to achieve by approving the sale in the first place.

That is what happened with the AWACS proposal. The House Foreign Affairs Committee, by a close vote, rejected the sale. President Carter was forced to withdraw the proposal temporarily, while conducting negotiations with key members of Congress and with the government of Iran for written assurances about the precise nature of the equipment to be provided and the security measures to be adopted for protection of the sensitive electronic instrumentation. The shah found this process so humiliating that he considered withdrawing his request entirely.

After weeks of difficult talks, a set of assurances was produced that allayed some congressional fears. The proposed AWACS sale was reintroduced in September. The following month, after intense lobbying by representatives of the executive branch—including the president—the House Foreign Affairs Committee reversed its previous position by a voice vote, rendering a Senate vote unnecessary, and the sale was permitted to proceed.

Significantly, President Carter also approved $1.1 billion worth of additional military sales to Iran, including training and spare parts. Much of this latter amount was the "tail end" expense required to sustain programs already in place. President Carter's personal approval of this sizable package—at the very moment when the controversial AWACS package was still before the Congress —again conveyed an unmistakable, public message that he intended no dramatic shift away from the security relationship with Iran.

The unequivocal nature of this signal was diluted, in Iran, by the intense criticism leveled at Iran and the shah in the course of the congressional debate over AWACS. The State Department inspector general, in the 1976 assessment of U.S.-Iranian relations mentioned in the previous chapter, had observed that "many Americans—officials, congressmen and public opinion leaders—deplore the Shah's authoritarian regime and his policies, in particular the relatively low regard for human rights . . . and the Shah's role in keeping oil prices high. The idea of a 'special' relationship with Iran based on U.S. military support is also distasteful or repugnant to many." All of those concerns were given public expression during the AWACS debate in 1977.

Moreover, the unfortunate timing of this proposal—immediately after the announcement of a new policy of restraint on the sale of arms—and the administration's failure to reconcile the contradictions between the two, was an unfortunate early example of clumsy handling of the inevitable conflicts between competing policy objectives. This insensitivity to public perceptions and the lack of skill in communicating complex policy goals were to bedevil the Carter administration throughout its four years and to earn it a reputation for inconsistency and indecisiveness.

"Tears in the Morning and Tears at Night"

Nevertheless, by the time the shah arrived in Washington in November 1977, for his first meeting with President Carter, the basic course of U.S. policy on the difficult issues of arms sales and human rights was well established. The tone of policy in Washington had changed sharply from the days of Richard Nixon and Henry Kissinger, but the emphasis was definitely on gentle persuasion, not heavy pressure or fundamental shifts of alliances. If that was not evident to the shah prior to his arrival, there could have been little doubt in his mind after the nearly five hours of face-to-face meetings with President Carter on November 15 and 16.

The circumstances of the shah's arrival could scarcely have been less auspicious. In the week before his arrival, demonstrators from among the more than 60,000 Iranian students in U.S. schools poured into the capital. Wearing masks to prevent identification by SAVAK, they gathered each day in Lafayette Park across from the White House to shout anti-shah slogans. In response, the Iranian embassy helped organize counterdemonstrations by pro-shah students and military cadets, who were transported to Washington for the occasion. Both sides used bull horns to outshout each other, and the noise level around the White House was so excruciating and incessant that some employees became physically ill.

During the welcoming ceremony at the White House, the war of words between the opposing camps escalated to physical combat with staves and clubs. Police were forced to use tear gas to quell a battle on the nearby Ellipse, and whiffs of acrid gas wafted over the crowd assembled on the White House lawn. President Carter completed his remarks and the shah plowed through his formal statement despite the wave of coughing and choking, but it was scarcely a good omen. Newspaper photographs the following day showed President Carter wiping tears from his eyes as he listened to the shah.

That night, opening his toast at the state dinner, President Carter deadpanned: "There is one thing I can say about the shah—he knows how to draw a crowd." Everyone laughed and the tension was broken. Then, speaking extemporaneously, the president went on to deliver a brief but heartfelt statement about the importance of Iran to the United States and the need to preserve the relationship. By the end of the toast, I was surprised to see that the shah had tears in his eyes. At a luncheon the following day, very few understood the shah's reference to the emotional events of the day before as "Tears in the morning and tears at night."

A different facet of the shah's personality emerged later, during the White House entertainment. Mrs. Carter knew that the shah and his wife enjoyed jazz, so she had invited Sarah Vaughan and Dizzy Gillespie to give a brief but spectacular performance. Earl "Fatha" Hines had also been invited to the dinner as a guest, and the president coaxed him to the stage for a spirited jam session encore, in which Hines's piano dueled with Gillespie's horn. After Gillespie had conceded, and as the applause was swelling, the president and

Mrs. Carter went up to the stage to shake hands and congratulate the performers. The shah, however, sat stiffly in place. Empress Farah, in her brocade and emeralds, leaned over to urge him to go to the stage, to no avail. Finally she grasped his arm and virtually propelled him toward the stage, where he shook hands all around, in evident discomfort.

The incident provided an amusing insight into the personal relationship between the emperor and his consort. It also revealed something about the shah. He was basically a shy man. No politician in the Western sense, he lacked the common touch. Although impressive in the orchestrated ritual of statecraft, when confronted with the unexpected and the need for improvisation, he froze.

"An Island of Stability"

Scarcely six weeks later, President Carter and the shah met again, this time in Tehran on New Year's Eve and New Year's Day. Tehran served as a convenient intermediate stop between Warsaw, Poland, and New Delhi, India, in the course of a whirlwind presidential visit to three continents. It also provided an opportunity to pursue several substantive items of business that had been initiated in Washington.

During the ride in from the airport, between miles of soldiers standing almost shoulder to shoulder, Carter and the shah reached a verbal understanding concerning the nuclear non-proliferation agreement that was to accompany the sale of U.S. nuclear power plants to Iran.[6] The two heads of state also discussed President Carter's request for a consolidated list of Iran's anticipated military needs over the next five years. Carter hoped that the development of such a list would enable both countries to address the strategic underpinnings of Iran's security planning while introducing a measure of order and predictability into the arms sales relationship. Both of these initiatives were thwarted and lost in the violence of 1978.

Finally, the visit provided an opportunity for discussion on the Arab-Israeli question. The shah had a very real stake in the search for a comprehensive Middle East peace, and he was kept fully briefed on the status of discussions. Iran's willingness to provide oil to Israel had been a key element in achieving the Sinai disengagement of 1975, which Secretary Kissinger had negotiated. The Carter administration was attempting to launch a new peace effort following President Anwar Sadat's historic visit to Jersualem in November 1977 (less than a week after the shah's visit to Washington), and it was believed the shah might again play an important subsidiary role.

The schedule of events in Tehran was extraordinarily hectic. The presidential party spent less than twenty-four hours on the ground, during which there was a ninety-minute meeting with the shah, a state dinner, a New Year's Eve party, a morning meeting with King Hussein of Jordan (who had prevailed on his friend the shah for an invitation to meet with the president in Tehran), a second brief meeting with the shah, plus the usual elaborate arrival and departure ceremonies. The most notable event of the visit, however, was the state dinner.

President Carter used the occasion as an opportunity to reassure the shah once again that the relationship would remain sound. Many of those present at the dinner were genuinely touched by the president's graceful reference to human rights in his formal toast, citing the lines of the great Persian poet Saadi:

> Human beings are like parts of a body,
> created from the same essence,
>
> When one part is hurt and in pain, others
> cannot remain in peace and be quiet.
>
> If the misery of others leaves you indifferent
> and with no feelings of sorrow, then you
> can not be called a human being.

However, the line that is best remembered from that toast, and one that the president later had reason to regret, was his opening reference to Iran as "an island of stability in a turbulent corner of the world."[7] President Carter's remarks were consciously intended to flatter and reassure the shah, but the words he used also unconsciously reflected the prevailing image of Iran as it had come to be accepted by successive administrations in Washington over the previous decade.

The shah, after all, had been on the throne for thirty-seven years. He had lately resolved a historic border dispute with Iraq without resorting to arms. He had played a responsible and constructive role in regional affairs. He had maintained an intimate security relationship with the United States and the West while preserving beneficial relations with the Soviet colossus on his northern border. In short, discounting the hyperbole common to such occasions, the offending phrase was not inaccurate as a description of Iran's recent history as perceived by official Washington. It was, however, disastrously wrong as a prediction. Less than a month after these words were spoken, serious riots broke out in the religious city of Qom. Within a year, the shah was preparing to leave Iran for exile.

President Carter was not oblivious to Iran's internal unrest. The demonstrations that had recently occurred at Tehran University and the clashes between Iranian human rights activists and Tehran authorities were reviewed in the briefing materials prepared for his visit. One paper, prepared by the National Security Council staff, commented that "the shah undoubtedly sees this as a potential threat to his rule."

In late November 1977, after the shah's tumultuous visit to Washington and before President Carter's visit to Tehran, I had prepared an internal memorandum on these demonstrations and the systematic intimidation by the authorities that followed. Several U.S. experts on Iran, I noted, had recently told us that in their estimate, opposition to the shah's regime was deeper than one would suspect.[8] I wondered if perhaps the shah was truly running scared.

Nevertheless, these comments in no sense suggested that the shah was in serious danger of being overthrown. On the contrary, the briefing materials reflected the unspoken but unanimous view of virtually all observers at the time that the shah was Iran and Iran was the shah. President Carter did not invent that view. Neither did he question it. His willingness—and the willingness of those around him—to accept it at face value was to leave him singularly unprepared as the façade of Iranian "stability" crumbled with astonishing speed over the following twelve months.

On New Year's Day 1978 there was no reason to believe that the relationship with the United States and Iran was anything but secure. The shah himself, writing from exile two years later, recalled that "My talks with President Carter had gone well. Iran's relationship with the U.S. had been so deep and friendly during the last three administrations . . . that it seemed only natural that our friendship would continue. . . . Carter appeared to be a smart man. My favorable impression of the new U.S. President deepened when he visited Tehran. . . ."[9]

Similarly, Ambassador Sullivan later recalled the shah's sense of elation following Carter's visit to Tehran.[10] The defeats, the bewilderment and the shah's bitterness with Washington were all to come later and for a very different set of reasons.

The Failure of Communication

Many of the problems could be traced to fundamental differences of perception. Simply put, the world as seen from Tehran is not the world as seen from Washington. The university demonstrations and human rights clashes in Tehran during late 1977 provide an interesting case in point. I had the opportunity, four years after the event, to discuss these events with a man who had helped organize them. In 1977 he was in the forefront of the opposition to the shah; by the time I met him he had fled into exile to organize opposition to the Khomeini regime, as had many of his colleagues who were concerned with civil liberties.

He informed me that the timing of the November demonstrations, which occurred immediately after the shah's reception in Washington, was no coincidence. When the dissidents learned of the tear-gas incident on the White House lawn, they reasoned that such an event could have occurred only at the president's behest. Thus they quickly concluded that Carter had abandoned the shah and launched a series of protest demonstrations and meetings. Washington, of course, which had done everything in its power to avoid clashes during the shah's visit, could not have conceived of such an interpretation, and the relationship between the two events was totally overlooked.

This misunderstanding, though minor, was symptomatic of the perceptual gulf that separated the two societies and that bedeviled relations throughout the entire crisis. That problem was aggravated by the weaknesses of U.S. official reporting on Iran during much of the first year of the crisis.

For at least a decade the United States had viewed its relations with Iran almost exclusively as relations with the person of the shah. There probably was never a formal order to avoid contacts with Iranian opposition groups, but there was a clear awareness that the shah was annoyed and suspicious about such contacts and they gradually dried up. The State Department report of August 1976 put it succinctly: "The Embassy . . . has difficulty in developing information about dissidence . . . because of Iranian sensitivities and the Government of Iran's disapproval of foreign contacts with these groups." Thus, primary attention was devoted to contacts with officials in and around the court, rather than invite the shah's wrath. That decision was made easier by the fact that the disparate array of opposition groups had been operating to no apparent effect since the 1950s and were perceived in Washington and Tehran as largely irrelevant.

So deeply ingrained was the conviction that the shah was master in his own house and that the opposition constituted little more than a nuisance that even a year later, when the revolution was raging almost out of control, issues relating to internal dissension in Iran continued to receive little attention. For each major area of the world, Washington maintains one or more lists of problems that should be monitored by the various government agencies. In late 1978 the question of "domestic instability" in Iran was assigned a priority of three (on a scale of six) on one such list and, on another, a priority of three on a descending scale of one to three. As a consequence of these deeply institutionalized patterns of behavior, Washington received little reliable information about the activities or intentions of opposition groups during the early stages of the revolution.

A second factor that greatly complicated effective communications between Washington and Iran was the different voices each side chose to trust. The Carter administration paid careful attention to the shah's views as relayed to Ambassador Sullivan in official meetings, which became increasingly frequent as the crisis wore on. Washington also tended to discount to a considerable degree the more sensational reports coming through the press, particularly when those contradicted what was being reported officially from the embassy in Tehran. The shah, however, while meticulously cognizant of official U.S. expressions delivered in formal public statements or private assurances from Ambassador Sullivan, combed the Western media for evidence that the United States and its allies were weakening in their resolve and support for his efforts. Needless to say, he found no shortage of material to feed his concern.

In retrospect, both approaches were wrong. The Carter administration would have been well advised to have listened more carefully to some of the responsible voices in the press and elsewhere that often proved to be more farsighted and realistic than the embassy's reporting. Conversely, the shah would have been much wiser to have paid more attention to the explicit policy statements coming to him directly from Washington, and less to the distant rumblings of bureaucratic skirmishes.

The third and most important factor in the communications short circuit between Iran and Washington was the Iranian penchant for conspiracy theories. In my experience, Iranians assume that a simple, forthright explanation of events is merely camouflage concealing the devious intricacies of "reality." To this is added the conviction that any significant political, economic or social upheaval in Iran must be traceable to the manipulation of external powers. And finally, events are perceived as neither random nor aimless; rather, they must be understood as purposeful and integral to some grand scheme or strategy, however difficult it may be to fathom.

In a nation that has been invaded repeatedly, whose national life has often been manipulated by foreign powers for their own benefit, and whose national existence has all too often depended on international circumstances beyond Iran's control, the three characteristics outlined above may be entirely comprehensible and even practical. They are, however, far from the American experience, and they could hardly have been more foreign to the pragmatic engineer from a small Southern town who inhabited the White House at that critical moment.

President Carter was an activist president with a deep commitment to specific goals. But he was remarkably free of ideological preconceptions in his approach to a problem. His commitment to the promotion of human rights and the reduction of world-wide arms sales was beyond question; yet he was prepared to give the shah the benefit of the doubt in his efforts to introduce reforms, and he was prepared to engage the prestige of his office in a difficult legislative fight for an arms sale to Iran that he believed was consonant with U.S. security interests, to the discomfiture of many of his more ideological subordinates. Faced with a difficult problem, he dealt with it on its own merits, disassembled it into its component parts the better to understand and solve it. It would never have occurred to him to start his analysis by asking himself whether the problem was merely evidence of a sinister scheme.

The shah, however, approached the world quite differently. Former Vice President Nelson Rockefeller paid a private visit to the shah in May 1978, after several rounds of religious riots in Iran and following the coup in Afghanistan that placed a Communist faction in control of the government. Discussing these issues, the shah later wrote that he asked Rockefeller "pointblank" whether this meant that "the Americans and the Russians have divided the world between them?"[11]

This was not an idle question in a moment of depression. Rather, it was the beginning of a refrain that every American concerned about Iran was to hear dozens and dozens of times in multiple versions throughout the revolution. It expressed the underlying conviction that the revolution and regional events were part of a gigantic plot, that each new development was planned and carried out according to a sinister master plan in which Iran and the shah's regime were the unwitting victims.

Thus, long after Khomeini returned to Iran and U.S.–Iranian relations lay in ruins, it was common to meet sophisticated, well-educated Iranians whose inevitable question would be, "Why did the United States want to bring Khomeini to power?" The logic behind this question was inexorable. All the power was in the hands of the shah, who relied on the United States. Yet Khomeini had succeeded in overthrowing the shah. The only explanation was that America had withdrawn its support for the shah and had transferred it to Khomeini, otherwise it could not have happened.

American officials, who were baffled and frustrated about the breakdown in Iranian society, found these elaborate rationalizations so patently absurd that they tended to dismiss them out of hand. Yet some version of this story was accepted by virtually every Iranian, from the shah down to the unemployed construction worker swelling the ranks of the anti-shah demonstrations.

The effect all too often was of two cultures talking past each other. U.S. policy makers, operating on the assumption that Iran was a modernizing society under firm central leadership, were slow to recognize the magnitude of popular dissatisfaction and its deep historical roots. The Iranian leaders, in turn, predisposed to interpret political developments as evidence of external intervention, failed to comprehend the nature of the forces progressively tearing the country apart, and they instinctively took refuge in the wholly unrealistic expectation that they could or would be saved by some superpower *deus ex machina.*

Both, of course, were quite wrong. It is not clear that a more astute evaluation on either side would have materially affected the course of the revolution, which was proceeding according to its own rhythm and purpose; but there is no doubt that the perceptual chasm between Washington and Tehran at times lent an almost surrealistic air to communications between the two capitals.

"Doing the 40-40"

It is now commonly accepted that the revolution began in earnest during January 1978, in the religious city of Qom. The government-controlled press on January 7 published an article ridiculing Ayatollah Khomeini. This event came two months after the mysterious death of Khomeini's son, which many Iranians attributed to SAVAK. It coincided with the religious fervor associated with the end of the holy month of Moharram. It also happened to be one week after President Carter's whirlwind visit to Tehran.

Two days after the article appeared, a religious demonstration and march was organized in Qom. The police opened fire, killing a number of students and prompting the leading religious figure in Qom, Ayatollah Shariatmadari, to denounce the shah's government as anti-Islamic. The revolution had begun.[12]

In Shi'i Islam, a religious ceremony is traditionally held forty days after a death. The shootings in Qom set off a series of demonstrations at forty-day intervals throughout much of 1978, eventually culminating in the shah's departure. One high-level official in Khomeini's Islamic Republic who had participated in this cycle of demonstrations later referred to it as "doing the 40-40." He described the process as follows: "Clashes between the security forces and the people often led to deaths, which we commemorated on the fortieth day. New marches were often the outcome of the fortieth-day ceremony. From one 40 to the next, we had marches and demonstrations. We used to oppose the government, trying to put the regime's back up and weaken and eventually eliminate it."[13] Although the cyclical occurrence of anti-regime demonstrations soon became familiar to all observers of events in Iran, the initial outburst in Qom was overlooked entirely in embassy and other official government reporting until much later.

The fortieth day after the Qom shootings was February 18. On that occasion violence broke out in Tabriz, the capital of the northwest province of Azerbaijan. Several days later, I summarized the situation in a memorandum to Brzezinski:

Reports are beginning to come in about truly massive riots in Tabriz last week. Although the government is making reference to Communist support and outside involvement, it appears that these were the work of what may be the true threat to the shah's regime—the reactionary Muslim right wing which finds his modernization program too liberal and moving too fast away from the traditional values of Iranian society. This is a serious problem and one that is extremely difficult to control. The word is spread from the pulpits, and the religious hierarchy provides a backbone which is formidable indeed.

The U.S. consul in Tabriz reported that the bulk of the rioters were young men, mostly unemployed, and that the targets of the violence had been symbols of secular society such as movies and social clubs. He commented prophetically that religious and social forces had been unleashed that would not easily be contained.[14] The shah reacted to the Tabriz riots by replacing the governor general of the province and disciplining SAVAK and police officials. Nevertheless, forty days later there were again demonstrations and violence in cities throughout Iran.

Just prior to this new outburst on March 30, Secretary of State Cyrus Vance visited Iran for a CENTO foreign ministers meeting. He took advantage of this opportunity to brief the shah on developments in the Arab-Israeli situation following Prime Minister Menachem Begin's visit to Washington on March 21 and 22. During these discussions, neither the shah nor Secretary Vance raised the subject of Iran's internal difficulties.

On March 28 a decision was taken to approve an Iranian order for tear gas. Approval had been held up due to objections by Assistant Secretary of State for Human Rights and Humanitarian Affairs Patricia Derian. The Human Rights Bureau in this instance was doing precisely what it had been created to do: reviewing policy from the perspective of promoting human rights. But its recommendation in this case to deny a routine sale of tear gas was opposed by every other policy department in the government. David Aaron, who was Brzezinski's deputy at the NSC, called Derian and argued that it would be foolish to deny to the shah a non-lethal crowd-control measure that we had ourselves used at the time of the demonstrations during the shah's visit. The sale proceeded as scheduled.[15]

By April 1978 the embassy in Tehran was reporting on efforts by the Iranian authorities to break up opposition activities. The homes of certain opposition leaders were bombed and some individuals were beaten up by vigilante groups whose connection with SAVAK was never acknowledged but universally assumed. In a memorandum, I commented that the shah would have been more comfortable in a showdown with the left rather than the right, but that he seemed to be launching a general wave of repression in response to the three successive outbursts of opposition at forty-day intervals. "What is less clear," I commented, "is the degree of actual threat to the present regime by what appears to be a very widespread conservative groundswell of opposition. Most observers believe the danger is still latent, but cracks in the façade of Iranian social stability are becoming difficult to ignore."

During the same month, a pro-Communist faction overthrew the government of Mohammed Daoud in Afghanistan in a sudden and unexpected coup d'état. This was a profoundly unsettling event for the shah, who began to worry out loud whether there was an international conspiracy operating against him: the conspiracy of "the red and the black," or Marxism and the clergy. An Iranian embassy official relayed the shah's concerns to me, and I reported this to Brzezinski. I wondered how much time we had before the Soviet influence in Afghanistan's internal affairs would become irreversible. Noting that Iran and other regional states would probably be prepared to cooperate with us, I commented that quick participation with them as an indication of U.S. willingness to expend some political capital on this issue would be infinitely reassuring. "Afghanistan as Finland is probably inevitable," I believed, "but an Afghan Hungary is a positive danger to the long-term stability of the entire region." Brzezinski indicated his agreement, and this memo, recommending an active U.S. political response to the coup, was rewritten and sent to the president.

Early in May the shah wrote a long letter to President Carter about the situation in Afghanistan. He said that he had known all along that events in Afghanistan would finally take such a turn, but these had occurred earlier than he had expected. He indicated that he would have to step up his defense efforts and would rely on the United States to supply some of these needs, although he was not specific. He also noted that the oil companies had recently cut back sharply in their lifting of Iranian oil, and he expressed concern about his ability to pay for these expanded plans without increased levels of oil purchases.

Two weeks later Ambassador Sullivan reported from Tehran that a large body of Iranian public opinion appeared to have been surprised, disappointed and perhaps even a little frightened by what they perceived as indecisiveness, nervousness and imprecision in the way the shah conducted a public interview with domestic media representatives. During the interview he avoided answering questions and did not seem to be able to make up his mind between either a hard line or a soft and conciliatory line in response to recent internal events. The embassy attributed this indecisiveness to the unfamiliarity of the liberalization course on which the shah had embarked. They commented that the shah, over time, had come to consult fewer and fewer people. From this latest episode, the embassy noted, one could "draw the conclusion that the shah was losing his touch." In response to this troubling assessment, I asked the intelligence agencies to take a fresh look at the entire situation in the form of a new National Intelligence Estimate on Iran.[16]

My concern was also based on a series of personal contacts with diplomats in the Israeli and French embassies in Washington. In each case these careful professionals delivered what I interpreted to be personal assessments of the growing concern within their two governments about the deterioration of political stability in Iran.

Nearly two years later I learned that the senior Israeli representative in Tehran, Uri Lubrani, who functioned as Israel's ambassador in all but title, had written a gloomy prognosis in early June 1978, expressing the view that the shah might not survive for more than two or three years. Subsequently there were claims that Lubrani's report was passed to Washington, where it was dismissed.[17] I have been unable to verify this assertion. It was certainly never reported to the White House. Lubrani later stated publicly that he discussed his concerns with Ambassador Sullivan, but Lubrani's analysis was not mentioned in embassy reports or during Sullivan's consultations in Washington during the summer of 1978.[18]

The failure to heed the Lubrani report was symptomatic of a fundamental dilemma that goes beyond the routine collection and analysis of information. In the aftermath of virtually any sudden policy shock, it is possible to sift back through the record and find evidence that the event was clearly signaled in advance and should have come as no surprise. However, for each item of "significant" evidence as perceived in hindsight, there were hundreds, perhaps thousands, of items that were contradictory, ambivalent or merely competing for policy attention. The problem is always to sort the wheat from the chaff.

The more intractable problem arises from the underlying assumptions that are woven into the very structure of the policy itself and that prevent policy makers from asking the right questions. Few U.S. policy makers would deliberately have chosen the high-risk social and economic strategy that the shah was pursuing in his effort to modernize his country. However, in the early 1970s a conscious decision had been taken that the U.S. government would not "second-guess" the shah. His efforts to transform his nation into a regional power were consistent with U.S. policy interests, and the vast oil wealth pouring into his treasury liberated him from the usual array of persuasive leverage that a superpower might exercise in its relations with a "client" state.

For better or worse, the United States gambled that the shah's perilous experiment would succeed and boldly associated itself with the process. For most of a decade the gamble seemed to be paying off, and U.S. security strategy in the Persian Gulf rested on the assumption that Iran would remain stable, strong and aligned with the West.

When things began to go sour for the shah in the late 1970s, the United States became the victim of its own policies. U.S. reliance on the shah had removed the incentives to maintain independent sources of information and analysis, whether in Tehran or Washington. Rebuilding such a structure is a slow, costly and politically difficult task; but without it, it is hard to judge between competing and contradictory voices.

Moreover, elements of the U.S. bureaucracy had themselves developed a vested interest in relations with the shah's regime, and they were not inclined to seek out problems or promote solutions that risked interfering with the pursuit of important but essentially parochial objectives. In each of these areas, whether it was commodity imports, educational exchange, defense procurement, petroleum production or international banking and finance, the overwhelming daily reality was that of business as usual, and neither Iranians nor Americans wished to see that disturbed.

Finally, and most critically, U.S. policy had so thoroughly burned its bridges during the preceding decade that there was no place to turn. Like the gambler who faces financial destruction, there was a powerful incentive to risk another turn of the wheel rather than admit that the game was over.

From Chessboard to Hurricane

Governments are not well equipped to deal with decisions of catastrophic proportions. The classic model of foreign policy decision making is the chessboard, but the Iranian crisis was not in any sense comparable to a chess game. A chess game involves two opponents competing over a well-defined territory according to agreed rules, with the ability to observe each move as it takes place. The process is incremental, goal-oriented, competitive and fundamentally rational, although the greatest players display creativity and boldness as well. Governments are organized to deal with chesslike questions. They examine the position of the players, consider the relevant factors and evaluate available options.

There is another kind of decision making that is more of a hurricane model. The person whose home is threatened by a hurricane must decide whether to bring in the lawn furniture, seal the windows and ride it out or, alternatively, to get out of the way before the neighborhood gets torn apart. The potential victim of a hurricane tries to make a rational calculation, just as the chess player does, but his decision ultimately turns on a single judgment: will the force of the hurricane destroy the house or not? By definition, the answer to that question cannot be known with certainty. A hurricane is not a calculated act, and its internal logic can produce some whimsical twists and turns. Careful observation and a knowledge of historical patterns are helpful but seldom conclusive.

The Iranian revolution was not a force of nature. It was "man-made" in the sense that it was the tumultuous outcome of decades of accumulated human acts, encouraged and exploited by various men for their own political objectives. Unlike a hurricane, the revolution was susceptible to some measure of human manipulation and crude adjustment. Still, in its inchoate appeal to social destruction and its incalculable effects, the revolution was no nicely plotted move on the international chessboard. On the contrary, it was the fury of the player who smashes his fist into the board and showers the pieces about the room in an emotional demand for a fresh board, new players and a radically restructured rule book.

Foreign policy establishments, like officials at a chess match, are ill equipped to deal with an outburst of this nature. As bureaucracies, they are designed to function within a defined framework of rules and generally accepted patterns of behavior. The tacit but all-pervasive assumption of all governments is that tomorrow will, by and large, be very much like yesterday. Incremental changes in the environment are anticipated and sometimes encouraged. Elaborate study is devoted to the perceived moves of other players and the possible consequences of various strategies available to their own governments. Radical transformations such as wars, revolutions and assassinations are acknowledged as possible outcomes, and in circumstances where the stakes are relatively low, such events are factored in as an element of the process. However, when the stakes are extremely high and such an outcome would be catastrophic, analysis tends to focus on preventive measures and damage limitation. The system searches for points of leverage and control rather than contemplate massive destruction.

Such a system is eminently rational. More than 99 percent of all events in international politics can be adequately explained and dealt with by a foreign policy structure based on the triple assumptions of rational action, incremental change and partial control. It is therefore ironic and tragic that these excellent rules should prove to be illusory and dangerously fallacious when confronted with those rare but crucially important challenges to the very existence of the system itself.

History is littered with painful examples. The European powers in 1914 ensnarled themselves in the long, bloody conflict of World War I by the meticulous observance of policies originally designed to protect themselves from such an eventuality. The near-disastrous failures of the United States to anticipate a Japanese attack at Pearl Harbor in 1941 and of Israel to foresee an Egyptian attack across the Suez Canal thirty-two years later were due more to a failure of bureaucratic imagination than to any absence of warning. The wrenching trauma of America's intervention in Vietnam is a classic instance of persistent bureaucratic pursuit of a policy chimera, first mistaking a regional civil war for an international conspiracy and then employing finely tuned gradualist tactics against an adversary whose goals were absolute. Military organizations, themselves enormous bureaucracies, are peculiarly susceptible to such failures of judgment, retaining weapons systems such as battleships, or doctrines such as mass infantry assault, in which they have invested heavily, long beyond the moment when the weapons or tactics have been rendered ineffective by developments outside the control of those making decisions.

The failure of a policy maker to deal promptly and effectively with prospective radical change may of course be due to ignorance, ideological myopia or simple negligence. However, when confronted with evidence that the very foundations of a thoroughly institutionalized policy may be faulty, the reluctance of the policy maker to respond is more likely to be due to his awareness of the cost—and possible futility—of action rather than inattentiveness.

In the case of Iran, the policy maker had to ask not only whether the shah's regime was in trouble, which was obvious, but what remedies were available to protect U.S. interests. If one believed that the monarchy or even the existing political elite would survive the challenge in some form, then there was very little required of the United States beyond marginal adjustments to what might be expected to remain a basically friendly Iranian leadership. If, however, one concluded that the monarchy and its surrounding elite were about to be replaced by a new set of individuals and institutions hostile to the United States and the West, then a very different set of policy problems arose.

In fact, the implications of such a revolutionary transformation extended far beyond the borders of Iran and the bilateral U.S.-Iranian relationship. American security strategy for the Persian Gulf, the Indian Ocean and ultimately all of Southwest Asia had, over a period of more than a decade, come to be based squarely on the premise that Iran was and would continue to be a strong, stable regional power whose interests coincided with those of the United States. Over time, this judgment had been translated into specific decisions concerning U.S. military deployments in Asia and the Mediterranean. It affected decisions on military procurements and long-term planning for force structure and readiness. It was intimately associated with strategy on nuclear arms limitations negotiations with the Soviet Union. It was a small but important link in the complex effort to forge a peaceful settlement of the Arab-Israeli dispute, since Israel relied heavily on assured supplies of Iranian oil and on Iran's potential diversion of growing Iraqi military power away from the immediate arena of confrontation. It also had significant domestic implications in the United States in the form of vast commercial and financial undertakings, not to mention Iran's ancillary role in the development and procurement of advanced weapons systems for U.S. forces. Iran was the second largest oil exporter in the world, and any disruption of its exports of five million barrels per day would inevitably play havoc with international energy markets.

Over a period of many years, virtually every element of the U.S. government that had any influence on the making of foreign policy had acquired a vested interest in the status quo. These were the same entities that were responsible for monitoring developments in Iran—for judging the force of the approaching hurricane. Inevitably, caution prevailed. The official or the organization that concluded that the shah's regime was, in the words of Sartre's anti-hero in *Les Mains Sales,* *"non-recouperable,"* had to be prepared to answer the unavoidable next question: How can U.S. policy interests be preserved if the shah falls? There were, in fact, no satisfactory answers to that question, as events would demonstrate. Nothing less than a full-scale reconstruction of U.S. global policies and assets would suffice.

Reluctance to "Make the Call"

It is doubtful that any official ever put this question to himself in those terms, but there is no doubt that the immense responsibility of proclaiming a generation of U.S. policy bankrupt weighed heavily in the minds of those observing the ominous unfolding of events in Iran. First and foremost among these was the U.S. ambassador in Tehran. It was William Sullivan who was closest to the action in Tehran, and it was to him in the first instance that Washington looked for judgments about the meaning of those events. If in fact a hurricane was brewing that was likely to demolish the elaborate policy structure erected over more than a decade, he was in the best position to sound an early warning. Yet he did not. He reported fully and accurately on events as they occurred, but he stopped short of drawing any conclusions or expressing any personal judgments that the shah's regime might collapse.

This same reticence was repeated by the intelligence community, the Pentagon, the State Department and the White House. Everyone was aware of the virus in the Iranian body politic, but no one was prepared to pronounce it terminal. Moreover, with the possible exception of Ambassador Lubrani's report to Tel Aviv, this same caution was apparently displayed by other Western governments with extensive interests in Iran. I am aware of no large-scale contingency planning or major policy reorientation by any Western government—including the government of Israel—prior to the final hectic months of 1978.[19]

The proximate causes for this institutional myopia are twofold: first, the outcome was never as inevitable as it appears in hindsight; and second, premature precautionary moves might in fact have hastened the collapse. The shah, after all, had thirty-seven years' experience on the throne and had survived crises which, by appearances, were no less severe than the riots of 1978. He commanded vast wealth, a superbly equipped military force of some 400,000 men, and a security force whose sinister reputation was legendary. He had powerful friends in nearly every major capital of the world and a compliant legislature. Arrayed against this impressive phalanx of traditional power was an aged cleric who had fulminated against the shah from exile for fourteen years to no avail and a congeries of aging Mossadeghists, village ecclesiastics and disgruntled job seekers.

Given this uneven distribution of apparent power, it is perhaps not surprising that most outside observers would conclude that a resolution of Iran's troubles was within the shah's capacity through a combination of needed reforms and firm leadership. Moreover, since the problem was widely perceived to be the shah's own uncertainty and lack of decisiveness, any overt steps to prepare for a political collapse would only encourage the opposition and contribute to his failure of nerve. In short, the most logical policy seemed to be to provide reassurances to the shah to assist him out of his funk while waiting for events to sort themselves out in Iran.

This was, in fact, the practical response of most Western governments to the growing policy dilemma of Iran, and the superficially unassailable logic sketched above was replicated in countless policy papers and diplomatic conversations. Nevertheless, for an explanation of the nervous passivity of the United States and other Western states, one must look beyond the superficial rationale to an appreciation of the paralysis of bureaucratic structures in high-risk situations. If the events of early 1978 in Iran had taken place in a nation where U.S. and Western interests were marginal, there would have been little reluctance to speculate about a range of possible outcomes, including revolutionary overthrow of the existing power structure. In the normal course of events, there would have been papers discussing available options in the event the government fell, together with systematic consideration of precautionary adjustments in policy.

There was almost a total absence of such studies and speculative analyses in the case of Iran. No one in the bureaucracy, from the ambassador to the Washington analyst, wished to be the first to "make the call" that the shah was on his way out. As a consequence, each individual and each organizational element procrastinated, waiting for incontrovertible evidence before pronouncing such a fateful judgment.

That evidence came very late in the day and was doubly shocking when it arrived, since the system had done nothing to prepare for what was by then a virtual certainty. The president, who had relied on the system, was astonished and furious that he had been so poorly served. And that reaction was fully justified. However, what came to be known as the "intelligence failure" was not so much a failure of sources or observation or data as a structural inadequacy of the system itself to make the conceptual leap from chessboard to hurricane.

III

THE REVOLUTION BEGINS

On June 1, 1978, I reviewed the Iranian situation for the president. Three major eruptions had occurred since January, I noted in my report, and the end was not in sight. The religious leaders had had a taste of blood and seemed to like it. The shah's policies seemed incapable of controlling the mobs, and other sectors of the society were watching and wondering if this was a rising tide or merely an isolated explosion of social tension. The international community wondered too.

I suggested two opposing theories: either the religious leaders, who had previously been defeated by the shah, represented an interest group whose demands could be diffused by some accommodation to their special concerns, or, alternatively, the religious leadership had uncovered a deep layer of hostility to the abuses of modernization. The first theory assumed that the shah might have to make some compromises but that he was not in real trouble. The second theory, however, held that the powerful social forces at work represented a political threat that could topple or cripple the regime. The shah, in my view, preferred theory one; the opposition, two. I felt there was a considerable measure of wishful thinking on the part of both.

The fact is, I said, that no one knows. But after three major incidents of massive civil violence, no one was willing to dismiss it as a passing phenomenon, and concern about long-term Iranian stability was becoming a routine topic of discussion for the first time in many years. I noted that a new National Intelligence Estimate on Iran had been directed.

At about the same time, the United States received a new request from the shah for weapons and communications systems to outfit eight to twelve frigates that he intended to purchase in Europe. The shah also requested approval to purchase 31 F-4E aircraft with wiring built in to permit the subsequent installation of sophisticated radiation suppression equipment, plus one thousand Shrike anti-radiation missiles. These aircraft and missiles together would provide Iran a capability to neutralize air defense missile sites. The package also included requests for 84 8-inch and 214 155-mm. self-propelled howitzers and 100 associated M-548 cargo carriers. Although these requests had been under consideration between the Iranian military and the U.S. Military Advisory Group in Tehran for some time, the request was probably deliberately timed to arrive in Washington shortly after the shah's letter to the president on Afghanistan, which had foreshadowed additional arms purchases.

President Carter replied to the shah's letter on June 2, 1978, acknowledging the seriousness of events in Afghanistan and outlining his own views on the security situation in the region. The letter did not refer to Iran's internal problems and it made no commitment on the arms sales package that had just arrived and was under review by the Department of Defense and the State Department.

The proposed weapons package generated fierce controversy within the administration, and the debate that ensued in the following weeks largely diverted attention away from Iran's internal turmoil to the familiar issue of the U.S.-Iranian arms sales relationship. Several elements of the shah's request were potentially in conflict with President Carter's publicly announced policy on arms transfers. That policy stipulated that sales of a subsystem—e.g., the weapons and communications packages the shah was seeking for the frigates he intended to purchase in Europe—could be approved only if the United States was prepared in principle to sell the entire system, ships and all, and to permit U.S. firms to bid on the sale. Yet the entire system was too expensive to be accommodated within the overall dollar limit that the president had established to force a slowdown in the rate of U.S. arms sales.

The shah well understood this "Catch-22" in the new U.S. policy, which is why he had gone to European shipbuilders rather than to U.S. suppliers; but he understandably wished to maintain uniformity of guns and missiles among these new ships and the earlier U.S.-supplied equipment in his fleet. The question was whether the United States would be willing to accommodate this divergence between the strict interpretation of a new policy and the continuation of an established arms supply relationship.

More serious was the question of the wiring of the F-4 aircraft. The F-4G aircraft, equipped with radiation-suppression "black boxes," was considered too sensitive for export. The shah was not requesting the "black boxes," but he wanted the wiring built into the aircraft so the "black boxes" could be plugged in later, if and when restrictions were removed. Everyone was well aware that approval of the wiring was tantamount to approval of eventual sale of the F-4G. A further complication was added, since the F-4 production line was about to close down and the expense of installing the wiring was significantly less during initial production than it would be at some later date.

President Carter had made it clear to the shah that he was prepared to continue a generous arms supply relationship with Iran, though the "blank check" policy of the past would no longer apply. The president was also personally and politically committed to a reduction in the level of U.S. arms sales. The shah's arms request in the spring of 1978 highlighted some of the inherent contradictions between these two objectives and was widely regarded within the administration as a test case.

Throughout the month of June 1978, these issues were debated in a series of adversarial meetings and policy papers, some of which recalled the controversies of medieval scholastics in their fervor and parsing of differing texts. The issue was finally joined in a Policy Review Committee (PRC) meeting at the White House on July 5, chaired by Secretary of State Vance.

It was agreed in that meeting that the United States would sell Iran the artillery and cargo carriers. The United States would also approve the sale of weapons systems for the frigates to be built in Europe. American companies would be permitted to bid on the entire package, but the shah was to be reminded of the ceiling provisions of U.S. policy that would raise complications if the ship hulls were purchased from U.S. suppliers. The sale of F-4 aircraft with 1,000 Shrike missiles *and* with wiring was also approved. All of these decisions were subject to presidential review and were to be delivered to the shah by Undersecretary of State David Newsom during a previously scheduled visit to Tehran four days later.

It appeared that the proponents of a generous arms sales policy toward Iran had won on every count. However, flushed with victory, they made a serious tactical blunder. Senior officials at the Department of State, arguing that installation of wiring on the F-4 was, for all practical purposes, approval of the eventual release of the "black boxes" of the F-4G, went back to Vance with a proposal to make it official by formally approving the sale of the F-4G immediately. As a consequence, Vance had second thoughts and reversed himself about the original decision. By Saturday morning, July 8, with David Newsom already in the air on his way to Tehran, Brzezinski sent a memorandum to the president asking for his approval of all the recommendations of the PRC *except* the wiring for the F-4 aircraft.

The president, who had not been a party to these backstage maneuvers, approved the request with the laconic comment that the PRC seemed much too inclined to approve every arms request that came its way. The news was flashed to Tehran, and Newsom was given the unenviable task of informing the shah that a key element of his package was not approved.

Although the interagency decision-making process had been less than tidy, the final decision on this case was entirely compatible with Carter's fundamental objectives. It demonstrated a willingness to apply a liberal interpretation of his arms-transfer policy to accommodate Iranian defense requirements. The shah got most of what he wanted, including the modern artillery and armored transport that was of particular significance due to the increased threat from Afghanistan. However, the United States was not prepared to release the highly sophisticated technology associated with the F-4G and was unwilling to risk U.S. national security interests in deference to the shah's judgment.

The shah was visibly displeased with the decision, and the U.S. embassy strongly urged reconsideration. The issue was raised once more with the president in early August, but he refused to alter his decision. Iran eventually withdrew its request for the 31 aircraft.

Ambassador Sullivan's Holiday

During this period, and for the remainder of the summer, Ambassador Sullivan was on extended home leave. He made two brief visits to Washington, during which he argued forcefully in favor of the proposed arms package. Although he was not present at the PRC meeting of July 5, his views weighed heavily in the arms sales decision.

I took advantage of his presence during one of these visits to invite him for lunch at the White House mess, followed by a meeting with Brzezinski for a review of events in Iran. In these meetings Sullivan focused almost exclusively on the immediate bilateral problems of arms sales and other issues. He was decidedly upbeat about the shah's ability to deal with the internal disturbances and studiously avoided any hint of alarm. He was very well informed and seemed so confident of his optimistic prognosis about Iran that Brzezinski, no doubt recalling the very gloomy reports he had been receiving from me, gave me a quizzical glance. Sullivan was so optimistic and so certain of his assessment that I suffered a few pangs of regret for the shrill tone that had crept into my own reporting.

For some weeks, events in Tehran seemed to confirm Sullivan's judgment. The combination of a crackdown on the dissidents and the granting of some limited reforms, including the replacement of the chief of SAVAK, seemed to have had the desired calming effect. The fourth forty-day commemoration of the January Qom riots passed almost without incident. The shah seemed to believe that he had events under control, and all reports indicated that he exuded a new sense of confidence. In June a U.S. businessman who was intimately familiar with Iranian politics met with the shah and all of his top ministers. The visitor later told me that the shah seemed healthy and demonstrated his usual vigorous interest in political developments. His ministers reflected the same calm assurance. "These were not nervous men," he declared.

In late July and early August there was a spate of rumors that the shah had been shot in an assassination attempt. The U.S. embassy flatly discounted these reports and attributed the rumors to the fact that the shah had been away from Tehran for a vacation on the Caspian Sea. Some visitors had noted that he seemed a bit wan and pale after a reported bout with the flu or a cold, but there was no indication of anything seriously wrong with his health.[1]

The lull, however, was both deceptive and short-lived. In retrospect, it is evident that the peaceful nature of popular demonstrations in June was probably due to the intercession of Ayatollah Shariatmadari, the most respected Islamic figure living in Iran and a man who was often at odds with Khomeini's more extreme and highly politicized positions. In an effort to halt the cycle of killings, he called for the people to stay home in passive protests rather than take to the streets.[2] However, by the end of July, clashes resumed between religious demonstrators and police, resulting in more shootings and more deaths.

The Moslem fasting month of Ramadan, always the occasion of high religious fervor, began on August 5.[3] That date coincided with Constitution Day, and the shah used the occasion to make a major address to the nation, combining promises of political liberalization (free elections in 1979, greater press freedom, opening the political system to opposition elements) with warnings that he would deal firmly with those who stimulated violence.

The address seemed to have little effect. Major demonstrations again broke out throughout the country, and by August 11 Isfahan was placed under a dusk-to-dawn curfew after two days of intense riots. The same pattern was repeated in a number of other cities shortly thereafter. And finally, whatever residual effect the shah's speech may have had was swept from popular memory by one of the great tragedies of the revolutionary period.

On August 19 the Rex Cinema in the city of Abadan was set ablaze during a well-attended showing of an Iranian film. Some exit doors were locked, and 477 people died. The regime claimed that this was the work of Islamic fundamentalists, who had attacked cinemas throughout the country as symbols of Western values. The opposition, noting that the Rex was not frequented by Westerners and that the fire department had been suspiciously slow in responding to the alarm, accused the regime and SAVAK of setting the fire to generate opposition to the fundamentalist cause.

The truth of the matter may never be known, but the anti-regime interpretation was widely accepted. The effect was comparable to throwing fuel on a smoldering fire. Largely as a result of this incident, at the end of August the shah replaced the government with a new "reform" cabinet under Prime Minister Ja'far Sharif-Emami.

Sharif-Emami had been prime minister briefly in the early 1960s. It was he who was replaced by Dr. Ali Amini at the urging of the Kennedy administration in 1961. By 1978 he was viewed as a pale and ineffectual figure of the past. Although the new prime minister promised freedom of political participation to opposition parties, abandoned the hated imperial calendar (which calculated years from the time of Cyrus the Great) in favor of the Islamic calendar (which began with Mohammad's flight from Mecca in 622 A.D.), closed gambling casinos and some other egregious symbols of Westernization, and undertook a number of other steps intended to appeal to the religious community, his program failed to gain widespread support or credibility. The new prime minister himself was viewed as a loyal courtier and was generally believed to have shared in the corrupt practices of the past. Instead of silencing the opposition voices, these political maneuvers were regarded by the shah's enemies as a cynical appeasement effort and by his supporters as an admission of weakness and vulnerability.

All of this occurred while Ambassador Sullivan was completing his vacation of nearly three months. He returned to Tehran in late August, received briefings from his staff and met with the shah. In his summary report to Washington he stressed his conviction that the shah had made a fundamental political decision to transform his regime into a "genuine democracy," since the country had become too volatile to be governed through the present processes of "benevolent authoritarianism." However, in the ambassador's view, the Iranian public had not yet grasped the import of the shah's decision and seemed to regard the shah's announced intentions as being less than genuine. At the same time, he noted, Iranian military leaders were expressing doubts about the wisdom of the shah's chosen course, fearing that he was not acting with sufficient firmness. Caught between these two extremes, and anxious above all to preserve the monarchy, the shah was "remote, nervous and suspicious." Among other things, the shah suspected that the CIA was conspiring against him.[4]

Sullivan proposed that in order to help the shah through this difficult period, the United States offer a little private encouragement. To that end he included in his lengthy cable a draft text of a letter from President Carter to the shah. This proposed letter became the subject of considerable discussion in Washington during the week that followed.

The letter was so filled with flattering references to the shah that it might have been written by one of the shah's courtiers rather than the U.S. ambassador. Some of us considered its tone embarrassingly obsequious and insisted that it be tempered. The Department of State, displaying admirable institutional loyalty to one of its representatives in the field, manfully resisted wholesale changes to the ambassador's text. As a result, a tug of war developed over words and phrases that will be distressingly familiar to anyone who has ever worked in a government bureaucracy, where the expenditure of time and energy frequently seems to be directly proportional to the triviality of the subject matter at issue.

The course of this petty skirmish is of no consequence. The cable that launched it, however, was symptomatic of the state of U.S.-Iranian relations and deserves at least passing attention. Ambassador Sullivan's analysis, and even his deferential choice of language, were firmly in the tradition of a long succession of U.S. ambassadors to Iran. The shah tended to be regarded as a uniquely wise and farsighted ruler whose vision of a strong, prosperous and modernizing Iran was far ahead of his advisers and his people. That view had become firmly established in the U.S. government in the mid-1960s after the shah introduced his White Revolution of social reforms. It had become official U.S. dogma after 1972 when the president and his national security adviser formally relinquished control of U.S. arms sales decisions to the shah. Although circumstances had changed substantially during the first half of 1978, this image of a modernizing ruler leading his fractious and often reluctant nation into the twentieth century continued to dominate U.S. thinking in Tehran and Washington.

These attitudes were powerfully reinforced by the realities of political life in Iran, where, by the mid-1970s, virtually every government action, no matter how minor, involved the shah's personal knowledge and often his express permission. The elaborate court structure with which he surrounded himself was intended to impart a sense of mystery and majesty to the imperial presence. Although U.S. officials and others were prone to joke about these trappings after the shah had fallen, they evidently had their desired effect on Americans as well as the shah's subjects.

A colleague of mine who was subjected to a heavy dose of U.S. embassy reporting in the mid-1970s—long before Ambassador Sullivan arrived—remarked that he was startled by the almost reverential tone that crept into reports *from one American to other Americans* when referring to "His Imperial Majesty." Ambassador Sullivan was far less susceptible to this syndrome than many of his predecessors. However, his draft letter reflected the unquestioned reality of imperial discourse in the year 1978, however absurd it might sound coming from Jimmy Carter.

On September 6, while Sullivan's cable was under review, Washington received Iran's five-year plan for military purchases from the United States, which President Carter had requested during his meetings with the shah. The list was simply staggering. Major items included 70 F-14 fighters, 12 Boeing 707 tanker aircraft, 140 F-16 fighters, 7 P-3C maritime patrol aircraft, and 16 other systems, totaling at least $12 billion over the next four fiscal years. It was obvious that the events of the first eight months of 1978 had in no way persuaded the shah to scale back his long-term military objectives. Nor was there any evidence that Carter's arms sales policy had inhibited him in the slightest.

Also, on the morning of September 8, the Department of State released a cable authorizing the sale of tear-gas canisters, small-arms ammunition and a variety of other riot-control equipment, such as helmets and shields. This marked the latest phase in the running debate between the Human Rights Bureau and other offices within the State Department about whether the United States should provide riot-control equipment to the shah's forces. In this case, as in most others, it was decided to provide the equipment, after intense review and discussion.

A new thread of the story also emerged at this point. On September 5 I was informed by the Iranian embassy in Washington that Ambassador Ardeshir Zahedi had departed for Iran. I later learned that Zahedi's presence in Tehran had been requested by Empress Farah, who was concerned about the drift of events and asked Zahedi to return and "raise the morale of the shah and the middle class." Zahedi was more than happy to comply. According to his closest associates, Zahedi's compelling ambition was to become prime minister, and the erosion of authority in Tehran provided him an unparalleled opportunity. Among other things, Court Minister Amir Abbas Hoveyda had just resigned, leaving a vacancy at the very top of the government hierarchy. Before leaving on this mission, Zahedi sent word to Brzezinski and met privately with Henry Kissinger.

The embassy asked me to inform Brzezinski of Zahedi's unexpected departure and to assure him that Ambassador Zahedi would see him immediately upon his return. This was my first indication of a personal relationship between Brzezinski and Zahedi. That relationship would assume much greater importance as the revolution progressed.

Finally, in the week after the Sullivan cable, I conducted my own survey of the Iranian political situation, discussing the developments with a number of specialists within and outside the government. On September 7, I summarized the results in a memo for the president. The reactions to the situation in Iran, I reported, were universally pessimistic. The deep sense of dissatisfaction revealed by the continuing demonstrations and riots suggested that Iran could be ripe for full-scale revolution.

There was simply no experience in Iran, I observed, with democratic politics. So when the shah decided to move toward liberalization, he simply removed the repressive mechanisms and then seemed content to sit back to see what would happen. The religious leaders tasted a bit of freedom and decided to see how far they could push it. As the mobs got worse, the shah began tossing out a series of concessions piecemeal, without attempting to deal with the opposition as a responsible group of leaders. They in turn interpreted the concessions as a sign of weakness and decided to redouble their efforts and their demands. Finally the shah was forced to impose martial law. As a first tentative step in the direction of more liberal policies, I noted, this episode had to be counted a total disaster.

That gloomy judgment was tragically borne out sooner than anyone would have anticipated. The Sullivan letter, the arms request, and all previous political analyses were swept aside by a momentous new event.

The Jaleh Square Massacre

The opposition had begun a direct challenge to the new government of Sharif-Emami on September 4 and 5 with two very large demonstrations in Tehran celebrating the end of Ramadan. The government refused permission for these marches but did not interfere. Emboldened by their success, the more radical opposition leaders pressed for outright confrontation with the government and called a general strike. The government responded by imposing martial law. The new rules were announced in the evening of September 7 and did not receive much publicity until early the following morning.

By that time, up to 20,000 people were already beginning to congregate in Jaleh Square for a religious rally. Troops at the site ordered the crowds to disperse. When they refused to obey, the soldiers opened fire on the crowd.

Government reports later claimed that the fire was returned from some individuals in the crowd. In any event, the gunfire by the troops went on and on, and scattered firefights continued throughout Tehran for the remainder of the day.

Estimates of casualties varied enormously. The opposition claimed 1,000 deaths or more. The government estimated 122 killed and 2,000 to 3,000 wounded. Doctors who tended the casualties estimated some 300 to 400 dead and ten times that many wounded.[5]

All previous clashes between the government and the opposition paled into insignificance in comparison with this traumatic and bloody event. Its significance was recognized at the time, but in retrospect it can be identified as the turning point from sporadic acts of popular rebellion to genuine revolution.

Calls from Camp David

On September 5, President Sadat of Egypt and Prime Minister Begin of Israel had arrived in the United States to join President Carter at Camp David for nearly two weeks of intensive negotiations that resulted in the Camp David Accords. At the end of their second day of meetings, late on Friday, September 8, the three heads of state were informed of the tragic events in Tehran's Jaleh Square. The following day President Sadat placed a telephone call from Camp David through the Iranian embassy in Washington to the shah, to offer his personal assurances of continued support. A U.S. message was also sent to Tehran notifying Ambassador Sullivan that President Carter would place a call to the shah early on Sunday morning Washington time.

At about eight o'clock on Sunday morning, President Carter spoke to the shah for about five minutes. Carter told the shah that he was calling to express his friendship and his concern about events. He wished the shah the best in resolving these problems and in his efforts to introduce reform. Most of the conversation, however, was a virtual monologue by the shah. Speaking in a flat, almost mechanical voice, the shah described the events as part of a well-planned, diabolical plot by those who were taking advantage of his liberalization program. He felt that the whole question of Iranian liberty and independence was at stake.

The shah reiterated his determination to restore law and order and to proceed with his liberalization program. "There is no other way," he said. "The country must be prepared for democracy." He urged the president to "come forward as strongly as possible," otherwise his enemies would take advantage of it. Carter agreed, noting that his only purpose in making such a statement was to strengthen the shah's position in maintaining order and pursuing the principles of freedom.

A few hours later the White House released a statement noting the telephone conversation and reaffirming the close and friendly relationship between Iran and the United States. It indicated the president's regret over the loss of life and his desire that the violence would soon be ended. The statement expressed Carter's hope that the movement toward political liberalization in Iran would continue.

This was not the first occasion when a U.S. president had found himself in a quandary about how to respond to an outbreak of domestic violence in Iran. In June 1963, following the introduction of the sweeping modernization program that the shah called his White Revolution, massive demonstrations broke out throughout Iran, led by Khomeini and the clergy. The shah's troops on that occasion also responded with force. Khomeini was arrested, theological schools were invaded by the military, and thousands of demonstrators were shot. On that occasion, John F. Kennedy was confronted with the same dilemma that President Carter encountered fifteen years later: how to reaffirm the importance of the U.S.–Iranian relationship without directly associating the United States with the shooting of demonstrators in the streets of Iranian cities.

The results in each case were remarkably similar. President Kennedy wrote to the shah in July 1963 that he shared "the regret you must feel over the loss of life connected with the recent unfortunate attempts to block your reform programs." President Kennedy expressed his confidence that "such manifestations will gradually disappear as your people realize the importance of the measures you are taking to extend social justice and equal opportunity for all Iranians." In the same letter, Kennedy rejected the shah's most recent request to increase his military purchases.

The carefully chosen words in President Kennedy's private letter, as in President Carter's public statement many years later, could not hope to overcome the popular view in Iran that the shah was "Washington's man," that he was carrying out orders from the White House, and that the United States bore direct responsibility for the civilian deaths. Khomeini's deep hatred of the United States was permanently fixed by the events of 1963, and the bitter fruit of that personal obsession was to appear in all its fury in the revolution of 1978–1979.

There is a bizarre footnote to the story of the telephone conversation that deserves mention. The shah, in his memoirs written in exile, recounted these events as follows: "Sadat called me late on the night of September 9 and we talked for a few minutes. As always, Sadat offered his encouragement and his help. I have no way of knowing what he said to President Carter later that night. But I do know that reports widely circulated in the West about a Carter telephone call to me later that night are false. President Carter has never called me—except once at Lackland Air Force Base in December 1979."[6]

The telephone conversation between Carter and the shah occurred on September 10, not on the ninth, but it *did take place.* The shah would have had no reason to conceal the fact later, so it must be assumed that he truly had no memory of it. One can only speculate on the reasons for this lapse. Several observers who met with the shah after the Jaleh Square incident described him as a shattered man who looked to be on the brink of a nervous collapse. The evidence is overwhelming that throughout the summer of 1978, the shah believed that the demonstrations were the work of a small group (in which he often included the CIA), but that he, the shah, retained the support and affection of the Iranian people. He thought he was very much in command of events. At some point he must have come to the realization that the optimistic reports relayed to him by his loyal courtiers bore little if any relation to reality.

There must have been a moment when he, in effect, lifted the corner of the royal carpet and peered directly at what was stirring beneath. That sudden flash of recognition would have been a severe psychological shock to any man in his position; but to the shah, whose entire program was a race against time and who was deeply aware of his own mortality, it must have been devastating.

There is good reason to believe that the Jaleh Square incident was that moment. During his brief conversation with Carter, the shah sounded stunned and spoke almost by rote, as if going through the motions. His later inability even to recall the conversation suggests a man in shock—or someone under heavy medication.

This analysis, however, has the benefit of hindsight. At the time, the evidence of the shah's psychological state was ambiguous at best. Within ten days of the telephone conversation, a cable from Ambassador Sullivan reported two recent visitors to the shah as finding him "looking the picture of health, confident, almost feisty. While he exhibited emotion from time to time, this was frustration rather than depression or distraction."

This was a pattern that would be repeated on several other occasions during those last fateful months. Washington would receive a disturbing report suggesting that the shah was profoundly depressed and seemingly incapable of acting, only to be reassured several days later by an upbeat prognosis from the embassy. Presumably this seesaw reflected the ups and downs of the shah's personal moods, but it had the inevitable effect of forestalling the critical judgment that the shah was incapable of managing events in Iran. Throughout this period, Ambassador Sullivan contented himself with brief, one-line descriptions of the shah's appearance during his increasingly frequent audiences, while carefully avoiding in his reporting any basic judgments or generalizations about the shah's mental or physical capacity to deal with events.

Even in retrospect, it is difficult to reconcile the many contrary impressions. For example, British Ambassador Sir Anthony Parsons recalls the same period as follows: "On September 16th I had my first private audience with the Shah after my return to Tehran. [Parsons had also been away for more than three months over the summer.] I was horrified by the change in his appearance and manner. He looked shrunken; his face was yellow and he moved slowly. He seemed exhausted and drained of spirit." Parsons notes that when he saw the shah a few days later, "He looked fitter and was more alert."[7] Washington did not have the benefit of Parsons' reporting at the time, but the contrast with Sullivan's description above could hardly be more complete.

Ambassador Zahedi had also not been reassured by his brief visit with the shah during this critical moment. He returned to Washington on September 10, and according to an official of the Iranian embassy in Washington, the following day he arranged two long telephone conversations with Tehran. The first was a conference call involving Zahedi, the shah and Barbara Walters of ABC News, which was intended to convey to the U.S. media the impression that the shah was firmly in command. The second call was a lengthy effort by Zahedi to impress on the shah the importance of demonstrating that he was in charge and functioning well. That the shah tolerated a lecture from a man who was not a member of his inner circle underlines the dramatic change that had taken place in a very few days.

First Contacts with the Khomeini Camp

Several days after the Jaleh Square incident I was contacted by Richard Cottam, an academic specialist on Iran at the University of Pittsburgh, asking if I would be interested in meeting with a Dr. Yazdi from Houston, who claimed to be the representative of Khomeini in the United States. Dr. Ibrahim Yazdi was an Iranian resident of the United States who had been conducting medical research in Houston for a number of years. He was also a key figure in organizing and directing the anti-shah activities of Iranian students and citizens in the United States, and he later emerged as a key aide and associate of the ayatollah during his residence in Paris. This was the first time I heard his name.

Professor Cottam maintained close contact with Iranian opposition figures, and he argued that Khomeini's positions—apart from his absolute opposition to the shah—were relatively moderate and deserved a hearing. I got the clear impression that Yazdi was unenthusiastic about any direct contact with the U.S. government but that Cottam had persuaded him to consent to a meeting if it could be done discreetly.

I was intensely aware of the dangers of misunderstanding and possible propaganda abuse of meetings between opposition figures in *any* government and anyone closely associated with the National Security Council and the White House. This was particularly true in the case of Iran. Nevertheless, I believed that it was important to get a better understanding of the motives and objectives of the Iranian opposition forces. Therefore I called Harold Saunders, the assistant secretary of state for Near East and South Asian affairs, to discuss the possibility of a meeting between Yazdi and a lower-level State Department officer. Saunders agreed with me that such a meeting would be of potential value to gain a better insight into the workings of the Khomeini forces and that any adverse political effects could be minimized. So I suggested to Cottam that he get in touch with the Department of State to arrange a meeting. He and Yazdi were not enthusiastic about the idea but finally agreed to pursue that channel.

However, when the senior people at the Department of State learned of the plan, they vetoed any meeting at any level. This caution was no doubt an accurate reflection of attitudes in the White House as well, where every effort was being exerted to avoid the appearance of consorting with the opposition, thereby feeding the shah's fears of a U.S. conspiracy against him. As a consequence, when Cottam got in touch with the State Department, he was informed that no one was available for a meeting and that Yazdi should write a letter if he had anything to offer. Understandably, both Yazdi and Cottam felt insulted and concluded that their doubts about the U.S. government's attitude toward the opposition had been amply confirmed. Soon thereafter, Yazdi departed to join Khomeini in Iraq.

In the months to come, there was no shortage of opportunities to hear Yazdi's views—publicly, privately and in direct meetings with U.S. officials. In each case his objective was the same: to promulgate Khomeini's basic line in words tailored to appeal to a Western audience. Yazdi and a number of other Western-educated revolutionaries, such as Sadegh Ghotbzadeh and Abolhassan Bani-Sadr, served as "interpreters" of Khomeini's position, smoothing the rough edges of his rhetoric and packaging his ideas in terms that would be more intelligible and more attractive to Western ears. A key theme in these presentations was the expectation that these relatively moderate, devout and even technocratic men around Khomeini were the natural inheritors of the revolution. America had nothing to fear, it was suggested, from the humane, reformist government they hoped to introduce in place of the shah's repressive regime. Presumably that is the message that Yazdi intended to deliver in September 1978 and that he wanted the U.S. government to hear.

Even at the time, I was among those who were skeptical of the soft sell we were beginning to hear. In my report of the initial Yazdi contact I had commented to Brzezinski that it was apparent from my conversation with Cottam why communication between the shah and his opponents was difficult. This expert on Iranian politics, with long-standing ties to the liberal Iranian opposition, saw Khomeini and his followers as "centrist" in orientation and believed that the successor government to the shah would be composed of liberal, secular leaders backed by the religious leadership. I disagreed with this view, feeling that "the chaos surrounding the ouster of the shah would soon leave the more moderate secular leaders in the dust." "The moderates," I noted, "seem unaware that they would probably be swallowed up in the power struggles following the shah's departure, even if they should be the ones who engineered it."

Months later, these conflicting interpretations would harden into a major debate within the U.S. government. But in mid-September I argued that our skepticism about the moderates' prospects should not prevent us from acquainting ourselves more thoroughly with their views. I continue to believe that was correct.

The Shah Wavers

The extent of the shock delivered by the Jaleh Square incident became evident as the shah, for the first time in living memory, undertook an agonizing reappraisal of his ambitious military expansion program. By the end of September, clear signals were being received by our embassy in Tehran that major cutbacks were being planned in military purchases. General Toufanian, who supervised and managed the shah's immense military procurement program, told Ambassador Sullivan that the shah's favorite words to him in recent weeks had been "economize, reduce and stretch out."

The shah reportedly diverted more than $200 million from the defense budget to pay for damages to private and public property resulting from the months of riots and to compensate the families of those killed in the riots and the Rex Cinema fire. Symbolically, this was a momentous shift in priorities. In the popular mind, the huge military expenditures by the shah's regime were regarded as a payoff to Western military and industrial interests at the expense of the Iranian people. The truth was more complicated, since the shah's strategy was to undertake massive expenditures in virtually every sector of the economy simultaneously.

Nevertheless, even a small shift from the military budget to domestic welfare represented a major transformation in the shah's thinking. Such a move would have been virtually unthinkable before Jaleh Square. In response, the U.S. government quietly let it be known to Iranian officials that it would assist Iran in any way it could to revise existing contracts and would not press them to undertake additional military obligations during this difficult period. A high-level meeting to review Iran's five-year military expansion program was postponed pending clarification of the situation in Tehran.

On October 10, Ambassador Sullivan had what he described as a "long, somber audience" with the shah. The shah was "drawn looking and tense, but the conversation was animated." Sullivan described his purpose in this conversation to "try to snap the shah out of the current funk and to focus his attention on problems requiring his leadership," specifically, the reordering of budget priorities and preparations for the elections announced for the following June.

Perhaps understandably, the shah preferred to talk about more immediate problems. He was toying with the notion of inviting Khomeini to return to Iran. Sullivan responded that he thought the shah would be out of his mind to issue an unconditional invitation. The shah reviewed his latest efforts to pull together a coalition of elder statesmen, accompanied by a long lament about the Persian inclination to bicker rather than work as a team. For the first time, the shah referred to problems in the military, revealing the concern of his generals that the current disorders might spread to the troops. They were pressing him to clamp down sharply on all disorder, and the shah commented ruefully that they seemed to think he had gone soft when he held them back.

At approximately the same time, we received the first confirmed instance of military sabotage when a helicopter mysteriously exploded at an air base in

Isfahan. The shah ordered a 20 percent salary increase and bonuses for the military and cut back further on all nonessential training and military construction projects.

Khomeini Flees to Paris

The shah's suggestion to Sullivan that he was considering inviting Khomeini back to Iran was poignant evidence of a further dilemma bedeviling his government at the time. By September it had become unmistakably clear that Khomeini, from his residence in exile in nearby Iraq, was not only inspiring opposition to the shah's regime but was in fact orchestrating the rebellion. The steady stream of Iranian pilgrims to the holy city of Najaf came back armed with cassettes of the ayatollah's latest sermons attacking the shah, along with new instructions and marching orders that were quickly translated into action through the network of mosques.

The shah's government found this intolerable and prevailed on the Iraqis to clamp down. The secular Iraqi leaders probably required little persuasion, since they had to fear the effects of a militant uprising of their own Shi'i inhabitants, who comprised more than half of the Iraqi population. On September 23, Iraqi forces surrounded the ayatollah's house, severely limiting access to him.

During the first week of October, Khomeini yielded to the pressure and attempted to leave Iraq. At first he attempted to go to Kuwait. I learned of this when I received an urgent telephone call from Richard Cottam, who informed me that Khomeini and his party had cleared the border post in Iraq but were refused entrance into Kuwait. Iraq then refused to permit them to cross back, and the entire party was trapped in the no man's land between the two border posts. Cottam asked that the U.S. government intervene to resolve the impasse. I said there was nothing we could do.

Eventually Khomeini and his party were permitted to return to Baghdad, where they took a plane to Paris on October 6. The French government permitted them to enter, reportedly after consulting with Iran. French officials subsequently insisted that Iranian officials seemed entirely unperturbed by the ayatollah's arrival in Paris and made no effort to intervene. In fact, the Iranians seemed to have calculated that the ayatollah's great distance from Iran, without access to the steady flow of religious pilgrims, would make it much more difficult for him to influence events. That proved to be a colossal—and ultimately fatal—error.

The Iranian authorities overlooked the marvels of the direct-dial telephone system that the shah had installed in Tehran with U.S. assistance. Khomeini was as close to his lieutenants in Iran as he was to his telephone in the small suburb of Nauphle-le-Château near Paris. More important, the Iranian authorities probably never imagined that a dour medievalist, speaking only Farsi and Arabic, with no experience of the world outside the seminary and the esoteric politics of Shi'ism, would become the instant darling of the Western media. The shah's undisguised disdain for Khomeini as a benighted reactionary consistently led him to underestimate the ayatollah's political talents, his charisma and his instinctive understanding of publicity and propaganda. The shah was only the first of a long sequence of political enemies to fall into that trap.

The immediate effect of Khomeini's flight to Paris was a new outburst of demonstrations in Iran. As October wore on and the forty-day mourning date of the Jaleh Square deaths approached, conditions deteriorated throughout the country. New demonstrations occurred almost daily, with reports of new civilian deaths, and strikes began to hurt key industries, notably the vital oil industry, where production dropped to about one-tenth its normal level. There was also an increase in anti-American incidents, although mostly of a minor and apparently spontaneous nature.

Ambassador Sullivan again met with the shah on October 24, accompanying Deputy Secretary of Defense Charles Duncan. The shah scarcely participated in the discussion with Duncan, then cut the audience short and asked Sullivan to remain behind. To Sullivan's surprise, he and the shah were joined by the British ambassador, Sir Anthony Parsons, for a review of the situation.

Summarizing the progressive breakdown in public order, the shah said he was reviewing his options. One was to install a military government, which the shah said he personally felt was a non-starter since the military could not even begin to run the oil industry. Another option would be to try a coalition government, although he acknowledged that he had no confidence such a measure would succeed. He asked for the views of the two ambassadors.

Sullivan reported that he and Parsons argued that the situation was not quite as dark as the shah depicted it. Although there were disruptions, life was going on more or less normally in most of the country. They agreed that the problems in the oil fields were serious but not necessarily fatal, and they opposed both of the shah's options. They felt that a military government would worsen the situation and possibly lead to an explosion, and they believed the dismissal of the present government would only be destabilizing. Instead, they suggested bringing some opposition politicians into the present government.

The shah, who was "sober but not depressed," thanked them and indicated he would talk to them again in several days. Sullivan commented to Washington that he thought the Iranian military, who would like to take over in their own way, were deliberately feeding the shah the darkest possible views of the present situation.

Whatever their motives, Iranian military and security officials could scarcely have exaggerated the critical nature of the crisis facing the shah in late October. At the very time Ambassadors Sullivan and Parsons were conferring with the shah, the Department of State was putting the finishing touches on a comprehensive analysis of the situation for the president. This lengthy memorandum provided a grim summary of recent events, concluding that the shah's fortunes were at an extremely low ebb. It detailed the many direct expressions of U.S. support that had been delivered to the shah in recent months[8] but failed to find any evidence that the many visitors and high-level statements had had any visible effect on circumstances in Iran. Looking at possible courses of future action, the paper noted that the shah had an urgent need to establish an effective government within a few weeks. Otherwise, it was believed, the military would almost certainly intervene.

The paper, which was cabled to Tehran for Ambassador Sullivan's comments, rejected a military government on the grounds that such harsh repression would only inspire an equally harsh reaction from the mobs and that the military could not solve the problems facing the country, nor provide the required leadership. It proposed three basic thrusts for U.S. policy: first, firm support for the shah as the key element capable of leading Iran through the transition to a more broadly based and stable government; second, increasingly strong support for the shah's liberalization efforts, including a more active advisory role with the shah and offers of assistance to the Iranian government, especially in the economic field; and third, steadfast opposition to a military regime.

As an immediate initiative, it proposed that Ambassador Sullivan provide advice to the shah with "greater specificity" than in the past, though it did not indicate what the nature of that advice should be. It left open for possible future consideration the possibility of initiating contacts with Khomeini and the opposition forces as well as the possibility of sending a special envoy to the shah as a dramatic expression of U.S. support.

The paper explicitly recognized the limited ability of the United States to influence the course of events in Iran and conceded that the shah's fortunes might well continue to erode despite our best efforts—or perhaps even as a result of our actions. It expressed concern about the safety of the 41,000 Americans resident in Iran but felt that the situation did not yet require emergency measures.

Sullivan responded with a lengthy reply on October 27. He agreed with the State Department paper that a military intervention would be "a delayed disaster," but he felt that "deterioration between now and next June," when elections were scheduled, "would make such military intervention inevitable."

Sullivan described the efforts in which he was engaged to encourage the Iranian government to begin a political process that would bring moderate political leadership into the system through the preparations for the June elections. He rejected the idea of additional high-level statements of support or special emissaries on the grounds that this was the time for truly quiet diplomacy. He rejected the proposal (advanced by Deputy Secretary of Defense Duncan after his visit to Tehran) that the United States provide training and assistance to the Iranian military for purposes of crowd control. He did not, he said, "want to give the Iranian military the idea that we wanted to help them have the capability of maintaining themselves in power bloodlessly if they took over [sic]." Moreover, he felt the British were already providing about all the riot control matériel and training that the Iranians were prepared to absorb.

Finally, Ambassador Sullivan strongly opposed any overture to Khomeini, since he thought Khomeini would wish to lead the country toward radicalism. Khomeini, he said, "should be firmly quarantined. Our destiny is to work with the shah."

To any seasoned observer, Sullivan's message was clear. He had his own game plan, which he was actively pursuing; in the meantime, he could kindly do without interference and kibitzing from Washington. The State Department seemed inclined to accept this rebuke and quietly shelved its policy paper. As a consequence, neither the State Department paper nor the ambassador's response was ever passed to the White House, and President Carter never saw it.

In retrospect, it is unfortunate that this paper never became the subject of a policy discussion in Washington. It laid out the arguments against a military government in Iran, but those arguments were not universally accepted throughout the Washington policy-making community, as we shall see. In fact, as the State Department began to lobby more openly against the idea of a military government, Zbigniew Brzezinski was beginning to seek allies on the opposite side. Lines were beginning to be drawn for a major policy debate, but the potential adversaries were not confronting one another.

Strange as it may seem, by the end of October 1978, after some ten months of civil disturbances in Iran, there had still not been a single high-level policy meeting in Washington on this subject. The reason for this lapse was obvious. The intense diplomatic negotiations between Egypt and Israel that began at Camp David in September 1978 and continued through the signing of a peace treaty in March 1979—precisely the time span of the climax of the Iranian revolution—occupied the full attention of U.S. policy makers and officials concerned with the Middle East.

The State Department paper was intended to focus attention on Iran and to stimulate a policy debate that might clear the air. Instead, each side in this emerging battle continued to muster its arguments and allies almost in clandestine fashion, waiting for events to force the issue.

A Quiet Birthday Party

October 26 was the shah's fifty-ninth birthday. Normally, this date was the occasion for public celebrations in Iran and receptions at Iranian missions abroad. In 1978 the festivities were canceled. In Washington, Ambassador Zahedi decided to mark the occasion with a small dinner party at his residence in honor of the visiting crown prince, the shah's eighteen-year-old son who was undergoing flight training at a U.S. air base in Texas. Zbigniew Brzezinski was the most senior U.S. official present, but both the Department of State and the Pentagon were represented as well, together with a few non-government Washington personalities.

A number of us attempted to draw the crown prince into a discussion about the state of affairs in Iran, but the young man was much more interested in talking enthusiastically about his experiences in flight training. He was lively and charming, without a trace of pompousness or self-consciousness. My wife and Mrs. Brzezinski, who sat on either side of the young man at dinner, considered him to be an altogether normal teen-ager, with a range of interests and enthusiasms quite typical for his age.

I was reminded of my first encounter with Crown Prince Reza at the famous New Year's Eve party in Tehran only ten months earlier, when the shah repeatedly attempted to persuade him and his sister to turn down the volume of rock music they were playing. It may be of some comfort to nonroyal parents of teen-agers that the shah failed utterly.

At dinner, Ambassador Zahedi offered a brief toast to the United States and the U.S.-Iranian relationship. Brzezinski replied with an eloquent and obviously heartfelt statement that stressed the importance America ascribed to its relationship with Iran. His explicit words of support for Iran during its time of troubles were accompanied by very pointed assurances that the United States would back the shah in whatever decisions he took to resolve the present crisis. After dinner, as the guests lingered over coffee in the drawing room, Brzezinski and Zahedi withdrew to an adjoining room for a prolonged tête-à-tête. It was quite apparent that the relationship between these two men was rapidly becoming an important new dimension in the dialogue between Washington and Tehran.

That dinner party also came to have particular significance to me for quite a different reason. I happened to be seated beside columnist Carl Rowan, who had just returned from Iran, where he had televised an interview with the shah and a number of other Iranian personalities. We talked at length about his impressions, which were very pessimistic. As a result of this conversation I made a special effort to watch Rowan's TV report a few nights later. Even on camera, in a formal interview, the shah was listless and seemed unable to handle even relatively simple questions. There were long, embarrassing pauses between question and answer, and the shah seemed unable even to formulate a coherent opinion.

In late 1977 I had spent more than eight hours in various high-level meetings between President Carter and the shah, and I had had a number of other opportunities to observe him in a variety of settings, formal and informal. The image on the TV screen bore almost no resemblance to the man I had seen less than a year earlier. I had read the occasional reports about his indecisiveness and periodic lapses, particularly during private meetings, but this performance was of an entirely different magnitude. The interview was at a time and place of his own choosing, in a format similar to hundreds of other interviews he had given. A statesman of his lengthy experience should have been capable of fielding the kinds of questions he was being asked almost as a matter of routine. As any listener to the Washington talk shows is aware, it is not necessary to have an effective policy in order to produce a glib answer. On this purely technical level, the shah's performance was surprising; as a measure of his ability to lead, it was profoundly disturbing. Clearly, something was wrong.

On Crown Prince Reza's birthday, October 31, President Carter received him in the Oval Office. The brief photo session was intended to underline the president's support for Iran, and Carter made the following statement: "Our friendship and alliance with Iran is one of the important bases on which our entire foreign policy depends. We wish the shah our best and hope the present disturbances can soon be resolved. We are thankful for his move toward democracy, and we know that it is opposed by some who do not like democratic principles. But his progressive administration is very valuable, I think, to the entire Western world."

The Shah Surveys His Options

On the same day, Ambassador Sullivan met again with the shah and found him "somber but controlled and occasionally displaying a rather macabre touch of humor." The shah felt that the current government of Prime Minister Sharif-Emami had proved itself unable to seize the initiative. It was unable to get the universities open or the oil strike settled. In the meantime, Iran was melting away daily and time was running out. He saw only two alternatives available to him: a military government or a coalition government. The military government, he believed, would at best be a quick fix and in the long run no solution at all. He was therefore thinking in terms of a coalition, formed around a distinguished "neutral" figure who would be acceptable to all "constitutional" factions. He mentioned two venerable members of the National Front, both in their seventies, as potential candidates.

It is doubtful that this plan ever had any realistic chance. It was a classic example of the shah's repeated attempts to manipulate himself out of danger without making any substantive concessions in actual power terms. The concept of splitting the National Front—a revived grouping of nationalist and secular political figures who had played a central role in support of Mossadegh in the early 1950s—away from the religious leadership by bringing them into the government was a perfectly reasonable scheme. However, it was coming very late in the day, and the choice of septuagenarians for the prime minister's position suggested that the shah was more interested in preserving his own absolute dominance of the political system than he was in making the opposition an offer it could not refuse. The shah implied as much to Sullivan when he joked that one possible candidate to form a new government was so deaf that he might not be able to hear the offer.

The shah's proposal might have been attractive if it had been offered earlier, but by the end of October the shah had much less bargaining leverage. He would have had to concede some measure of independent political power to the secular forces to tempt them away from the Khomeini camp, which by that time had acquired enormous momentum. It was a case of too little too late.

The entire scheme collapsed within twenty-four hours. Karim Sanjabi[9] and several other National Front leaders had gone to Paris during the last week of October to attempt to strike a deal with Khomeini that would have preserved the monarchy in return for institution of a reform government. The point of reference for these political leaders, as well as many other secular political figures, was the constitution of 1906, which provided for Islamic review of Iranian legislation but which also contained the framework for Western-style parliamentary democracy, with guarantees of political and civil rights.

The shah and his father had systematically introduced changes in constitutional form and practice that placed all real power in the hands of the monarch. Although most of the secular leadership would almost certainly have been satisfied to return to the original constitution, with its constraints on monarchical power, that was not what the ayatollah had in mind.

Khomeini, in Paris, was totally unyielding. He insisted that the shah had to go, and the National Front leaders, who had political respectability but lacked both an effective popular organization and the kind of "troops" that Khomeini could put into the streets, reluctantly succumbed. By the time the shah's limited offer was conveyed to them, the National Front had already accepted Khomeini's terms, and the basis for any cooperation with the shah had vanished.

This fact was made known to Sullivan and British Ambassador Parsons during a meeting on November 1. The shah said that the National Front would not consider any cooperation unless the question of the monarchy was submitted to a national referendum. The shah said he would never accept such terms. After some discussion, during which the shah again referred to the pressures building on him to install a military government, the three concluded that the present government under Prime Minister Sharif-Emami was insufficient and that a further attempt should be made to form a coalition government, possibly using the threat of a military government as leverage. If that failed, the shah would try to form a neutral government for the sole purpose of holding elections.

This conversation was reported in full in the normal State Department channels. In a separate, more restrictive channel, Sullivan sent an additional commentary on the meeting that set off nearly four months of intensive activity in Washington. In his meeting of November 1, Sullivan said he had detected the first signs that the shah might be thinking of abdication when he said he would "rather leave the country than submit" to a referendum on the monarchy.

Sullivan believed that the dilemma facing the shah was much more severe than the choice between a coalition government or a neutral caretaker government. On the contrary, Sullivan believed that if the shah remained, he could only attempt to govern through the military. If he should leave, the military could be expected to take over in a coup without the shah. Of these two, Sullivan definitely preferred the former, believing that military government without the shah would be "repressive, brutal and totally unimaginative," abandoning any plans for liberalization and democracy.

Sullivan anticipated that within the following forty-eight hours the shah would conclude that his political efforts had failed and would seek U.S. advice whether to abdicate or to impose military government under his continuing rule. Sullivan was convinced that the shah would stay only if he could be sure of continuing support from the United States. He requested urgent guidance from Washington.

In some ten months of developing crisis, this was the first occasion when Ambassador Sullivan had asked Washington for guidance. Washington, in turn, convened the first high-level policy meeting to deal specifically with the Iranian crisis.

IV

COMMUNICATIONS FAIL

The crisis in Iran could scarcely have come at a worse moment for the Carter administration. President Carter had arrived in Washington in January 1977 with an extraordinarily ambitious agenda of foreign policy objectives. For nearly two years, each of these major initiatives was pressed forward relentlessly by Carter until, in the fall of 1978, each had generated independent momentum, demanding increasing amounts of time and personal attention at the highest level.

With the Camp David negotiations, SALT II and normalization of relations with China all coming to a climax at approximately the same moment, the national security policy apparatus of the United States government was stretched to the limit. As an activist and an extraordinarily energetic president, Carter had in effect generated a series of "crises" that were breaking just as the danger point arrived in Iran.

This coincidence in timing helps account for the curious absence of sustained attention that Iran received at the highest levels from August through October, when the crisis was brewing. That tendency was reinforced by a number of other factors. Ambassador Sullivan's very optimistic reports in June that the shah was firmly in command and quite capable of dealing with the problem had fed a sense of complacency, and the ambassador's prolonged absence throughout the summer had meant there was no high-level contact with the shah for nearly three months. The embassy in Tehran had continued to report dutifully on events as they occurred, but their reporting failed to provide the kind of political analysis that would help to put events in perspective. There was no sense of alarm.

Even after Sullivan returned to Tehran, and as the situation deteriorated dangerously, the ambassador's reports studiously avoided setting off alarm bells in Washington. Sullivan was an old pro and a veteran of many crises. He knew from experience that once the system was jolted into a crisis mode, the center of the action would shift away from the embassy to Washington, where his control would be limited. Until November, none of his reports requested policy guidance from Washington, and he made it unmistakably clear that he did not welcome "outside" advice.[1]

The Politics of Paralysis

At least equally important for the relative lack of attention paid to Iran during this critical period was the underlying realization that there were no attractive options available to Washington. Civil rebellion poses painful dilemmas not only for the nation involved but also for other states that have a stake in the outcome. Outside powers must ask themselves two fundamental questions: Will the existing leadership survive the challenge?, and if the answer is no, To what extent can or should an external power be prepared to intervene actively to promote an outcome favorable to its own interests? The Carter administration was exceptionally ill equipped to answer either of these momentous questions with respect to Iran.

The United States, over a period of nearly a decade, had permitted its own contacts in Iranian society to be concentrated almost exclusively on the court, the Western-educated elite and official relations with military and security institutions. Very few experienced officers in the embassy could speak the local language, and there was virtually no contact with the merchants of the bazaar, let alone the clergy. As a consequence, decision makers had almost no reliable, independent sources of information upon which to base a judgment about the shah's prospects.

The issue of intervention was even more difficult. Memories of Vietnam were painfully fresh, and neither Carter nor most of his key advisers were philosophically prepared to entertain the idea of massive U.S. intervention in an internal rebellion in a Third World country. Many individuals in the State Department, and to a lesser extent in the White House, were openly hostile to the shah, to his use of SAVAK and to his record of human rights abuses. Although these views in their most extreme form were not major determinants of U.S. foreign policy, the president's own deep convictions about human rights and the abuses of political power effectively established outer limits to the range of realistic policy options. Any suggestion that the United States should or could provide active support for bloody suppression of the opposition, for example, was just not credible—politically or morally.

These circumstances produced two results. First, since the normal channels of information were grossly deficient, those who were deeply concerned about the course of events tended to seek out their own sources. Brzezinski's reliance on Ambassador Zahedi was one such case that received a great deal of attention, but the fact is that virtually every individual and every office that was affected by events in Iran developed a network of private sources that it was reluctant to share with others, thereby breeding distrust and suspicion.

Second, since there were very few realistic policy options available, and since any substantial change in policy involved actions that were certain to be politically distasteful or worse, people were inclined to keep their thoughts to themselves. The combined effect was to stifle communication, to breed suspicion and to encourage procrastination in the hope that the situation would resolve itself somehow.

This unhealthy state of affairs was not limited to the United States. From my contacts with officials in the British, French and Israeli governments during the crisis and later, it was evident that they were also seized with a kind of policy paralysis. Everyone was aware of the dangers of the situation; in some diplomatic circles, there was talk of little else. But talk is cheap. None of these governments undertook any substantial adjustments in their policies toward Iran or launched any new initiatives until it was far too late.

The November 2 SCC Meeting

Ambassador Sullivan's alarming message was received on Thursday morning, November 2. At six o'clock that evening the Special Coordination Committee (SCC) of the National Security Council convened in the Situation Room of the White House for the first formal, high-level review of U.S. Iranian policy since the beginning of the crisis. Brzezinski chaired, as he did for all meetings of the SCC. Other participants were Deputy Secretary of State Warren Christopher; Secretary of Defense Harold Brown; General David Jones, chairman of the Joint Chiefs of Staff; Admiral Stansfield Turner, director of central intelligence; Brzezinski's deputy, David Aaron; and myself as note taker. Secretary of State Vance was not present.

Brzezinski opened the meeting by reading from Sullivan's urgent request for instructions. Brzezinski said he had discussed the matter with the president, with Secretary of State Vance and with Ambassador Zahedi. He had also spoken with Ambassador Sullivan in Tehran, who was engaged in a series of private meetings with leaders of the National Front. Zahedi, he said, had commented that Sullivan was being perceived in Tehran as somewhat ambiguous in his support of the shah. Brzezinski added that he had his own personal doubts about the nature of advice that the shah was receiving from British Ambassador Parsons, who was now accompanying Sullivan in his almost daily meetings with the shah. (Parsons had been outspoken in his opposition to military rule and in favor of a coalition government that would bring opposition figures into the cabinet.)

Brzezinski had also talked to a senior French official who felt the shah was suffering from a "crisis of will" and that he needed to regain his determination and authority. Finally, to complete his survey, Brzezinski reported that he had received a telephone call from former Vice President Nelson Rockefeller, who felt that the United States was doing nothing and wondered where the government stood on this issue—an attitude that, in Brzezinski's view, probably reflected a considerable body of U.S. public opinion.

Brzezinski had prepared a draft message for Sullivan to deliver to the shah that consisted of three basic elements. First, it expressed U.S. support for the shah "without reservation." Second, it noted the need for "decisive action" to restore order and the shah's authority and indicated that the United States would support the shah's decision fully, whether he chose a coalition or a military government. Third, once order and authority had been restored, it was hoped the shah would resume prudent efforts to promote liberalization and eradicate corruption.

Warren Christopher, speaking for the State Department, questioned the ability of a military government to resolve fundamental problems, and he stoutly supported Ambassador Sullivan against Zahedi's comments. Admiral Turner also felt that a military government would cause great problems. Secretary Brown contented himself with the remark that a military government with the shah was obviously better than one without the shah, and that comment was added to the message.

After some additional discussion, Brzezinski left the room to talk by telephone to the president, who approved the general thrust of the message. The president also asked Brzezinski to telephone the shah the following day.

That night, the message was transmitted to Tehran with only minor changes. It was sent as a personal message from Brzezinski to Sullivan, but in view of the policy dispute that was beginning to emerge in Washington, it was considered necessary to add a line assuring Sullivan that it had the express concurrence of Secretary Vance. That point was underscored the following day when Vance, at a press conference, made a strongly worded statement of support for the shah's effort to restore order before moving on to elections and other liberalization plans.

The White House vs. the State Department

Policy feuds are nothing new to Washington. They are the inevitable human side effects of the clash of powerfully held policy views. After the fact, they are often relished as part of Washington folklore, and some, as in the case of the bitter rivalry between Alexander Hamilton and Aaron Burr, attain legendary status. However, in my limited experience, they seldom result in good policy. That was certainly the case in Washington during the Iranian revolution. The erosion of mutual confidence hampered effective policy formulation and implementation at virtually every level.

As the point of contact between the White House and the various policy agencies, I was painfully aware of this phenomenon on a daily basis. However, it assumed its most extreme form in my dealings with Henry Precht, the country director for Iranian affairs in the Department of State.

Henry and I had first met in Egypt in the mid-1960s, when he was a junior officer in the U.S. consulate general in Alexandria and I was an assistant naval attaché in Cairo. I saw him again during a visit to Tehran in 1975, where he was the political-military officer at the embassy. We became better acquainted during the first year of the Carter administration when he returned to Washington to assume a key post in the Bureau of Political-Military Affairs and we found ourselves on the same mini-loop of the Washington diplomatic circuit.

Henry enjoyed portraying himself as "just a country boy from Georgia" and I found his plain-spoken irreverence refreshingly reminiscent of my own small-town origins in Kansas. My wife took an instant liking to Marian Precht, and they would seek each other out at receptions to take refuge from the sterile small talk and office gossip that too often pass for conversation in Washington. It was at a small dinner party at the Precht home where I first met Richard Helms, the former director of central intelligence and the previous ambassador to Iran. When I learned in early 1978 that Henry Precht was to be appointed country director for Iran, replacing another old friend, Charles Naas, who was leaving for Tehran as Ambassador Sullivan's deputy, I was personally and professionally delighted.

It is a measure of the emotions aroused by the Iranian crisis that even this warm personal relationship could not transcend the institutional rivalries and policy disputes. I had been in government long enough to know that staff members can and do work together even when they represent opposite institutional or personal perspectives. Often that is the invisible glue that holds the system together, even in times of great stress. In this case, however, it did not work, perhaps because Henry Precht was not only a staff officer but also the leading proponent of a policy position. During this period he became passionately committed to a single policy line and just as passionately convinced that Brzezinski was the malevolent force thwarting him at every turn. It was Saint George and the dragon.

Henry Precht was among the first in the government to conclude that the shah was unlikely to survive the revolution. He also believed that the revolution would bring to power the moderate constitutionalists of the National Front, who had for years represented the lonely voices of democracy and human rights in Iranian society. Based on these two judgments, he viewed U.S. declaratory policy of support for the shah as utterly misguided and counterproductive. In his view, such a policy would only succeed in alienating those who would be our natural allies once the shah had fallen.

My position on the NSC staff inevitably located me in the opposite camp, and that perception was no doubt reinforced by my personal view that the "moderates" in Tehran were too weak to provide an effective alternative to Khomeini's extremism. Whatever the reasons, the result was not the lively discussion of policy that might have been expected, but rather the gradual choking off of any useful communication at all.

I began to discover in late October and early November that a telephone call to Henry Precht, even on the most mundane issue, inevitably resulted in an extended lecture in which he unburdened himself in tones of rising exasperation of his considerable frustrations and complaints about the course of U.S. policy. While I respected his views and the depth of his personal commitment, after about the third lecture I began to find the process both repetitious and unproductive. So I began to search for other avenues to coordinate the many issues that required a measure of cooperation between the White House and the Department of State. During this period I relied heavily on Precht's superior, Harold Saunders, the assistant secretary of state for Near East and South Asian affairs, or else on Henry's colleagues on the Iran desk to transact the necessary day-to-day business of government.

This near-breakdown of communications was personally painful to me. My failure to bridge the gap was more acutely disappointing in human terms than any other aspect of the entire crisis. Unfortunately, its effects were not confined to the level of personal relations. It obviously complicated the conduct of routine policy coordination, but more important, it closed a potentially useful channel of policy dialogue just at the moment when it could have been most valuable.

This failure of communications at the staff level was, of course, a symptom of some of the problems at higher levels. Brzezinski took an avowedly hard line, which meant, in practice, encouraging the shah to take much tougher actions toward the opposition forces with the assurance of full U.S. support. Vance's position was considerably more enigmatic. Curiously, Vance left few enduring imprints on U.S. policy during the Iranian episode. His absence from the original policy meeting on November 2 established a pattern that became familiar as the crisis wore on. Although the secretary of state regularly conferred with the president and Brzezinski by telephone or in private meetings on key policy decisions, he seldom attended policy meetings and generally delegated authority to his deputy, Warren Christopher.

The basic reason for this was clear. Vance had a very full plate. Throughout the fall of 1978, Vance was deeply and personally engaged in the delicate negotiations with the Soviet Union on the SALT II treaty and with the complex, time-consuming negotiations between Egypt and Israel, which resulted in a peace treaty the following spring. President Carter's fundamental policy objectives—and his personal prestige—were at stake in each of these undertakings, and Secretary Vance was carrying a heavy burden of responsibility for their success or failure.

Nevertheless, Vance's conspicuous absence from interagency meetings on Iran aroused some curiosity about his position on the developing policy debate. At least in the initial stages of the policy-making process on Iran, Vance appeared to share—or at least to acquiesce—in policy positions that were compatible with, if not identical to, those being promoted by Brzezinski and endorsed by the president. It must be remembered that, in the second year of the Carter administration, the rivalry between Vance and Brzezinski was still quite muted, and Vance enjoyed a measure of influence second to none on those foreign policy issues on which he chose to assert himself. If he differed strongly from the policy that was beginning to take shape, it was not evident. On the contrary, he appeared to endorse it while tacitly removing himself from the day-to-day policy process.

In his memoirs, Vance described in some detail the views of some of his colleagues in the State Department during this period that the "shah's autocratic reign was over" and that the Iranian monarch should be advised to relinquish power to the "secular political opposition." While acknowledging that these arguments were "powerful and persuasive," Vance carefully dissociated himself from these views and indicated his support for the policy of continued U.S. support to the shah. He observed that "an estrangement grew up between the White House *and my key advisors.*"[2]

Thus, those in the Department of State, such as Henry Precht, who were attempting to change U.S. policy toward the shah, found themselves constantly frustrated. Without the support of the secretary of state they were unable to argue their views at the highest level. Moreover, Vance's absence from day-to-day policy making left the field, by default, to Brzezinski.

Opposed by many of their department colleagues, and unable to muster the support of their own Seventh Floor, Henry Precht and his colleagues were reduced to conducting a kind of bureaucratic guerrilla warfare while focusing their ire on the person and policies of Zbigniew Brzezinski. Brzezinski, who thrived on conflict and who was not noted for his sensitivity to the feelings of political adversaries, seemed not at all perturbed at being singled out as the *bête noire* and almost seemed to go out of his way to twist the knife. As the level of frustration mounted in some quarters of the State Department and the Tehran embassy, the degree of personal animosity toward Brzezinski assumed nearly pathological proportions.

Brzezinski's relationship with Ambassador Zahedi was a prime target. Zahedi's father was the army general who became prime minister when the shah was restored to his throne in 1953. Young Ardeshir himself had been a prominent participant in the heady events of those days. Now ambassador to the United States, Ardeshir Zahedi did not disguise his interest in becoming prime minister himself, and the prospect of history repeating itself, with the younger Zahedi playing his father's role as the rallying point for pro-shah forces, must have been tantalizing in the extreme.

Ambassador Zahedi exuded raw energy and brash self-confidence, commodities that were in rare supply among the Iranian elite in those days. They were also characteristics certain to appeal to Brzezinski, who was seeking an appropriate *point d'appui* to stem what he saw as the progressive deterioration of leadership in Tehran. Ambassador Zahedi, in turn, viewed his relationship with Brzezinski as his trump card. It lent weight and a valuable air of mystery to his activities, which Zahedi was not reluctant to exploit. Inevitably, it also created doubts whether in each instance Zahedi was speaking for himself or for the White House—doubts that Zahedi did nothing to dispel.

Aware of this burgeoning relationship, the Iran desk and Ambassador Sullivan attempted to spike Zahedi's influence. Late on the night of November 1, a State Department message was sent to Tehran reporting that Ambassador Zahedi was telling Americans privately that his advice to the shah was to bring out pro-government groups to demonstrate and, if necessary, to do battle, even if that meant civil war. The Iran desk commented acidly that Zahedi had "clearly learned at his father's knee" how the day was won in 1953 but wondered if the same potential for pro-regime mob support existed today. The message asked for Ambassador Sullivan's views.

Within hours a reply came back from Sullivan saying that Zahedi had telephoned the shah while Sullivan was meeting with him on November 1, making the same suggestions. Sullivan said the shah had cut Zahedi off short, with a statement that "this is not 1953 and is not even the same situation that existed two weeks ago" (when Zahedi was in Tehran). Sullivan noted that there had been a recent spate of provincial and tribal attacks on mosques and anti-government demonstrators that some attributed to Zahedi's instigation. Sullivan was certain that Zahedi could not rally the mullahs and bazaar to the support of the shah, as was done in 1953. Instead, he reiterated that only a political solution capitalizing on the "moderates of the center" could succeed.

This quick exchange of telegrams was clearly intended to demonstrate that the shah did not share the views of some of those in Washington who were inclined to place great faith in Zahedi's views. However, it had no visible effect on Brzezinski.

Advising the Shah

At nine o'clock in the morning of November 3, Brzezinski placed a telephone call to the Iranian embassy in Washington and spoke with Ambassador Zahedi. The call was then relayed to the palace in Tehran, and Brzezinski spoke directly to the shah, as the president had directed in the course of the SCC meeting the previous evening. Using the guidelines of the November 2 policy message, Brzezinski assured the shah of the unshakable support of the U.S. government for whatever decisions he took with regard to the formation or composition of a new government. Brzezinski stressed that the United States did not encourage any particular solution but that, in his view, concessions alone would only make the situation more explosive.

In every way possible, Brzezinski attempted to convey a sense of U.S. steadfastness and the need for the shah to exert tough leadership. However, an Iranian embassy official commented to me years later that the shah's voice was "not good."

On November 4, Ambassador Sullivan again met with the shah for what he termed "a long prayer session." According to Sullivan's report, the shah began by referring to the Brzezinski telephone call. He said that he appreciated the president's willingness to support him in any decision, including a decision to form a military government; however, he wondered why the president thought a military government would be successful. He cited the outbreak of violence earlier the same day when troops had confronted demonstrators at the University of Tehran, only to have hit-and-run demonstrations break out all over town.[3]

While he was pleased to have the president's statement of support, the shah said he could not see what the president would actually do in tangible terms. The shah noted that the situation was vastly different from 1953, when U.S. assistance had been helpful. He said he felt that the only hope for law and order would be in the formation of a government that would on the one hand accept the constitution (i.e., the monarchy) and on the other hand would have the support of the moderate clergy. However, to form such a coalition, the National Front and the moderate clergy would have to have the courage to make an open break with Khomeini. If the government or the military faced a coalition of Khomeini, the National Front and the moderate clergy, he believed Khomeini would call for a holy war and there would be a bloodbath. Even some of the military would take their obligations to Islam ahead of their obligations to the shah.

Ambassador Sullivan further reported that the shah felt that public statements of support for him by U.S. officials were becoming counterproductive. It was evident that the shah's concern related in this instance to Secretary Vance's press conference which, almost simultaneously with the Brzezinski telephone call, had publicly declared U.S. support for the shah's efforts to restore order before continuing the liberalization program. When that statement was broadcast in Tehran, the military had sent extra troops to protect the U.S. embassy, in anticipation of popular reaction.

The Vance statement was intended as part of a carefully orchestrated effort —a formal message, a telephone call from the White House and a public statement by the secretary of state—to ensure that the fundamental policy message decided on November 2 was delivered with the full authority of the U.S. government. If ever there was a case of the U.S. government speaking with a single voice, this was it. The results of this effort, however, served only to demonstrate the peculiarities of public communications between Washington and Tehran.

In his memoirs the shah complained that "The messages I received from the United States while all this was going on continued to be confusing and contradictory. Secretary of State Vance issued a statement endorsing my efforts to restore calm and encouraging the liberalization program. Such Herculean fantasies left me stunned."[4]

Vance had faced stiff questioning during his press conference about whether the United States was backing away from its support of liberalization in Iran. He had replied, quite accurately, that there was no inconsistency in re-establishing stability within the nation and then moving on subsequently with elections in accordance with the liberalization program. The shah evidently fixed on this exchange and drew the conclusion that Vance was pressing for additional liberalization measures while the nation was in flames.

With regard to the Brzezinski message, the shah commented that in his meeting with Sullivan on November 4, he sought confirmation of the message. "As usual," the shah observed, "the American envoy promised to cable Washington, but when I next saw him, he said gravely that he had received no instructions. This rote answer had been given me since early September and I would continue to hear it until the day after I left the country."[5] Sullivan's extensive cable reporting on the November 4 conversation provided no indication that the shah had any doubt about the accuracy or authoritative nature of the message, which would have been odd in any event, since Sullivan had a fully coordinated policy cable from Washington confirming its key elements.

This discrepancy could be dismissed as the vagaries of memory, since the shah was writing in exile long after the event. In his own later account, Ambassador Sullivan failed to mention this particular meeting; however, he gave substance to the shah's complaint by citing his constant inability to get Washington to respond to specific policy questions or to confirm the statements of various spokesmen or emissaries.[6]

Sullivan's message of November 2 was important precisely because it was the very first time the ambassador had asked for policy guidance from Washington. It resulted in an emergency SCC meeting, a policy cable, the Brzezinski telephone call and the Vance statement within thirty-six hours. It is evident that the policy guidance emanating from Washington was not what the ambassador may have anticipated nor perhaps what he wanted to hear,[7] but that is very different from the charge that Washington consistently failed to provide policy guidance in response to direct requests from the ambassador in Tehran.

Both the shah and Ambassador Sullivan later asserted unequivocally that the ambassador repeatedly found himself in the position of answering the shah's queries with the same response: "I have no instructions." In view of the voluminous reporting out of Tehran, it is difficult to understand why policy makers in the White House had to wait for their memoirs to learn of these exchanges.

Military Government

On November 5, the day after Sullivan's "prayer meeting" with the shah, Tehran exploded. Reacting to the clash at Tehran University the previous day, where soldiers had fired on students attempting to pull down a statue of the shah, mobs took to the streets in a coordinated attack on symbols of Western presence. Banks, liquor stores, cinemas, Western business establishments and tourist hotels were torched. U.S. advisers with the Ministry of Labor were forcibly evicted from their offices. The British embassy was overrun, and its chancery was set ablaze. At the end of the day the shah told Ambassador Sullivan, after a survey of the city by helicopter, that Tehran looked like a wasteland.

The security forces deliberately made no attempt to intervene. Some believed at the time that their lack of response was in protest against the political constraints that had been placed on them and the criticisms that had been directed at them by the Sharif-Emami government. Others suspected that the military was attempting to bring pressure on the shah to move to a military government.

That morning, as the riots were beginning, Ambassador Sullivan met with the prime minister. Sharif-Emami had sent a message to Sullivan two days earlier requesting a meeting. That message, through an intermediary, had contained the blunt assessment that the shah was incapable of making any decision and sounded an almost desperate appeal for guidance. By the morning of November 5, the prime minister had concluded that order was evaporating and that a military government was required.

Ambassadors Sullivan and Parsons rehearsed for the prime minister the discussions they had had with the shah about the possible formation of a coalition government, including moderate elements of the clergy and the National Front. The prime minister thought that would be fine if these individuals would agree openly to break with Khomeini; however, he doubted they would ever have the courage to do so, citing the public statement by the leader of the National Front in Paris that he would cooperate with Khomeini to bring down the shah's government.

On the way home from this meeting, the two envoys were nearly trapped by the rampaging mobs and had to take refuge in a bank.[8] Later that evening the shah called Ambassador Sullivan and his British colleague to the palace to inform them that he had no choice but to establish a military government. In fact, his contacts with the National Front and other political leaders had convinced him that there was no realistic prospect of enticing civilians of almost any stripe into a new government at this juncture.

Sullivan, armed with the policy statement of November 3, was able to offer the shah immediate assurances that the United States government would support his decision. Ambassador Parsons had no instructions and could not seek guidance from London, since his communications equipment had been destroyed in the attack on his embassy. As the two ambassadors left the Niavaran Palace they passed General Gholam Reza Azhari, the Iranian chief of staff and prospective new prime minister, waiting forlornly in the foyer.

On November 6 the shah announced the new military government in a nationwide address. Those observers in Washington who had argued in favor of a military government in Iran to restore order were stunned when they read the text of the speech:

In the climate of liberalization which began gradually two years ago, you arose against oppression and corruption. The revolution of the Iranian people cannot fail to have my support as the monarch of Iran and as an Iranian. . . . The waves of strikes, most of which were quite justified, have lately changed in their nature and direction, causing the country's economy and the people's daily lives to be paralyzed. . . . We exerted all our efforts to establish the rule of law and order and peace by trying to form a coalition government; but when it became apparent that there was no likelihood of such a coalition, we had to appoint a caretaker government. . . . I once again repeat my oath to the Iranian nation and undertake not to allow the past mistakes, unlawful acts, oppression and corruption to recur but to make up for them. . . . I heard the revolutionary message of you people, the Iranian nation. I am the guardian of the constitutional monarchy, which is a God-given gift, a gift entrusted to the shah by the people.

The apologetic tone of the speech and its almost pathetic attempt to align the shah with the revolution was not the tough message of a sovereign who had just appointed a military government. The enumeration of past abuses, coupled with the unexpected reminder that the shah's position in effect derived from the consent of the governed, was virtually an invitation for the disaffected to persevere in their efforts to withdraw their "gift" to the shah.

In purely human terms, this speech captured the sense of the shah's agonizing personal dilemma as well as any public document to emerge from the revolution. Whatever the shah's enemies or his historians may say, the shah considered himself a genuine Iranian patriot who had sacrificed and overcome enormous odds to lead his country and his people into a promising new era. He believed deeply that the people of Iran, with the insignificant exception of the extreme fringes of the left and right, which he dismissed as the "unholy alliance of the red and black," shared his vision and loved him for his wise leadership.

When he discovered, in August and September 1978, that this comforting image was grotesquely at odds with the rage of the burgeoning mobs, he reacted as any human being might react to an overwhelming personal loss. He denied it was happening. He blamed sinister external forces beyond his control. And in this speech he seemed to suggest that it was a monstrous misunderstanding by attempting to dissociate himself from his own thirty-seven years on the throne.

In the days that followed, this process produced some of the ugliest spectacles of the entire revolution. General Nematollah Nassiri and Amir Abbas Hoveyda were arrested, with more than a dozen other former high officials. General Nassiri had served for fifteen years as the shah's hand-picked director of SAVAK. Amir Abbas Hoveyda had served the shah faithfully (and honestly) as prime minister for nearly thirteen years and as minister of court for one year more. These men were extensions of the shah himself and instruments of his rule. Nassiri was perhaps the most hated and feared man in all Iran. But their sins and failings were the sins and failings of the shah himself, and their imprisonment would persuade no one to believe otherwise. On the contrary, the arrest sent an unmistakable message to the opposition that the shah was on the run, while the shah's associates could only conclude that it was every man for himself.[9]

Both Nassiri and Hoveyda remained in prison until the Khomeini regime took power in February 1979. Then both were brutalized, interrogated in mock trials on public television and summarily executed, with grisly photos of the bodies publicly displayed as one of the early triumphs of the new "Islamic" justice.

The events of the first week of November 1978 should have been sufficient to put to rest the notion that a moderate alternative government could be constructed to bridge the revolutionary abyss. Similarly, the shah's speech of November 6 and the actions that followed should have provided incontrovertible evidence that the shah was incapable of adopting and sustaining the kind of hard line that many were pressing on him. Neither lesson, as we shall see, was absorbed, much less acknowledged, at the time. Talk of a coalition government persisted to the end; and Ardeshir Zahedi's embassy in Washington circulated a text of the shah's November 6 speech that simply edited out those parts of the text that proponents of a hard line did not want to hear. In a memo to Brzezinski I pointed out Zahedi's *post hoc* rewriting of the shah's speech, but Brzezinski declined to comment.

The Intelligence Gap

On the day of the shah's speech, a long-scheduled policy meeting was held in the White House to review the situation in Iran. The meeting was unique in two respects: it was the only use of the Policy Review Committee (PRC) during the revolution, and it was the only interagency meeting on the crisis chaired by Secretary of State Vance.[10] The fact that it took place on the day the shah announced his military government was totally coincidental. The meeting focused on the quality of intelligence available to the United States about the situation in Iran and on some limited contingency steps that might be taken in response to specific problems that were developing.

Secretary Vance said he had talked that morning to President Carter, who was interested in getting a better understanding of the loyalty of the Iranian military. Vance also felt it was important to get better information on the attitudes and activities of the opposition groups. Brzezinski agreed, noting that Washington had received very little intelligence information on the events in Iran. He suggested that once this was over, it might be useful to have a post-mortem to identify the problems.

Admiral Turner responded that U.S. capabilities to follow domestic events in Iran were extremely limited, in large part because in the past there had been the concern that U.S. contact with opposition elements would be seen by the shah as an unfriendly act. Vance observed that in our efforts to improve our information, we should avoid giving the shah the impression that we did not support him.

Deputy Secretary of Defense Charles Duncan, who had recently returned from a visit to Iran, believed that the United States could be helpful in the present circumstances by providing training for Iranian forces in non-lethal crowd-control techniques. Vance noted that we were providing tear gas and other non-lethal equipment. There were statutory restrictions on our ability to provide police-type training to foreign military forces, and it was Vance's understanding that the British were taking the lead on this. Duncan was not persuaded, and he asked that the State Department query Ambassador Sullivan on the desirability of some U.S. assistance in that area.

Assistant Secretary Harold Saunders reported on an initial examination of the problems that might be encountered in the event an evacuation of U.S. citizens was required. He noted that the very large number of Americans in Iran would make such an operation extremely complicated and lengthy. It was estimated that, using military airlift, it would require more than three weeks to complete a total airborne evacuation. The embassy, he observed, believed that Americans should remain if at all possible, since a mass departure would have severe political and economic implications for Iran.

There was a brief discussion of steps that could be taken to improve communications with the embassy in Tehran, and it was decided to install a satellite terminal on the embassy grounds to provide additional channels for voice communications. Concern was also expressed about the security of sensitive items of military equipment in Iranian hands as order deteriorated. The Defense Department was to examine this problem.

The level of U.S. military forces in the region was also reviewed. These consisted only of the noncombatant flagship of Middle East Force plus the routine presence of a destroyer and a frigate attached to that force. The annual CENTO naval and air exercise was scheduled to begin on November 15, and Duncan noted that the carrier U.S.S. *Constellation* could be added to our participating forces if desired. (Ambassador Sullivan subsequently recommended against any augmentation of U.S. military presence in the region. He also opposed Duncan's suggestion of U.S. training for Iranian forces, on the grounds that the British were providing as much training and support as the Iranians could absorb. Both recommendations were accepted in Washington.)

One further issue that was raised briefly in the November 6 meeting was the prospect of a world-wide oil shortage resulting from the continuing strikes in Iranian oil fields. Until the strikes began, Iran was the second largest oil exporter in the world, after Saudi Arabia, supplying some 5 million barrels per day to the international oil market, in addition to the 500,000 to 800,000 barrels per day consumed within Iran itself. The stability of Iran was also intimately linked to oil. Internally, the budget was based on anticipation of continued high oil revenues, and a prolonged drop in exports risked severe dislocations in such fundamental areas as food, since Tehran relied on massive imports of foodstuffs that required a constant source of hard currency.

Internationally as well, Iran's credit position was directly related to its lucrative oil revenues and to its reputation as a reliable supplier of oil. By early

November, strikes and political turmoil in the oil fields had reduced Iran's exports to less than a million barrels per day, effectively withdrawing up to 4 million barrels a day from world supply just as the heavy winter demand was beginning. The international oil companies had not seen this coming, and they had failed to build up their reserve stocks in advance. With world oil demand running very near available supply, the unexpected shortfall in Iranian production risked setting off an international oil shortage.

Because of the importance of the oil industry for Iran, the level of oil production constituted a rough barometer of the political health of the regime. In a memorandum to Brzezinski in advance of the PRC meeting I offered the view that "the touchstone of the military government will be its ability to stop the strike in the oil fields and restore production. If they fail to accomplish this rather promptly, they will not survive." The regime's record to that point had only underscored its weakness. When the strikes began, the government had responded with sizable pay increases and benefits; thereupon demands escalated from the economic to the political. Strikers were not arrested and were not penalized for their actions. As the organizers in the oil fields discovered they could act with impunity, they rapidly increased both their following and the scope of their demands. By early November, the situation was becoming critical.

Military Rule Falters

The new military government that the shah installed on November 6 was just as equivocal as the shah's address to the nation. Although General Azhari, as the chief of staff, was an obvious choice to head the government, he was personally a mild man who had no stomach for politics or repressive violence. He was not among the generals who had been pressing the shah to crack down, and he went out of his way from his first day in office to let it be known that he had accepted his new post with the greatest reluctance and wanted nothing so much as to be rid of it again. If the shah was primarily concerned about avoiding a possible military takeover or the emergence of a military rival to himself, Azhari was the perfect choice. If he was, instead, intent on installing a tough and vigorous military government that would restore some measure of discipline to the country, Azhari was an unlikely selection.

Of the eleven cabinet ministers appointed by Azhari, only six were military, and even this number was whittled down in the following weeks. The military cabinet ministers, for the most part, had no experience in their respective areas of responsibility. What is more, most of them retained their original military responsibilities in addition to their cabinet posts. As a result, most of the new nominees quickly came to depend on their civilian subordinates. In short, the hotly debated change to a "military" government was, in practice, more cosmetic than real.

Nevertheless, the opposition forces initially responded with great caution.

The military was their most dangerous enemy, and they took the threat of a military government with the utmost seriousness. For several weeks there was a noticeable reduction of street violence, most of the strikers returned to their jobs, oil production rose to 4 million barrels a day, and there was a deceptive lull of several weeks as the opposition tested the new waters.

They soon learned that the constraints placed on the new military governors were virtually the same as those applied to their civilian predecessors. After an initial burst of activity, the new government settled down to the same tactics of bargaining and concessions that had proved futile in September and October. As that fact became increasingly obvious to the opposition, the cycle of strikes and street violence resumed. By the end of November, the revolution was once again in full cry.

V

THINKING
THE UNTHINKABLE

On November 9, Ambassador Sullivan submitted a long telegram to Washington incorporating his thoughts about the situation in Iran and the possible course of future events. This analysis, which Sullivan entitled "Thinking the Unthinkable," was one of the most important U.S. policy documents to be produced in the course of the revolution and deserves to be considered in some detail.

Sullivan began by saying that he wished to take advantage of a holiday weekend to engage in some fundamental reflections on the situation in Iran and to "examine some options which we have never before considered relevant." He noted that the authority of the shah had shrunk considerably, to the point where his support among the general population had become almost invisible. In fact, the only tangible evidence of support for the monarchy came from the armed forces, and even there the events of recent days might have produced a subtle change.

He identified two key elements in the revolutionary situation: the clerics and the military. The clerics, he noted, had called for passive resistance, including strikes in strategic areas of the economy. If the military succeeded in returning key sectors of the economy back to full production peaceably, it would probably, in Sullivan's judgment, prevail. However, if it should fail, the military would have to make a fateful decision either to enforce production by a bloodbath or else reach an accommodation with the clerics. Since the religious forces were dominated by Khomeini, one had to assume that a precondition for accommodation would be acceptance of Khomeini's demand that the shah must leave and that the monarchy be abolished in favor of an Islamic republic.

Sullivan found it difficult to believe that a man like Prime Minister Azhari would willingly plunge the nation into a bloodbath. Likewise, it was difficult to imagine him or most other senior officers inviting the shah to abdicate. However, if both the shah and the military shied away from a bloodbath, both the shah and the more senior military officers might eventually depart, leaving the armed forces under the leadership of younger officers who would be prepared to reach an accommodation with the religious forces. It was this eventuality that Sullivan wished to evaluate in terms of its consequences for the policy of the United States and its allies.

With that general background, Sullivan proceeded to set forth a series of propositions about the political factors that might be expected to influence the nature of a future accommodation. Both the Iranian armed forces and Khomeini's forces were strongly anti-Communist and anti-Soviet, he felt, and the younger officers had a genuine pro-West orientation, having been trained in the West. Furthermore, despite opposition claims that the West was stealing Iran's oil, the logic of Iran's economic ties with the West would have to assert itself in any realistic appraisal of Iran's economic survival. Sullivan felt that the Iranian military ought to be able to preserve its integrity and not evaporate, while the religious forces would find it useful for the military to remain intact, since they had no Islamic instruments for maintaining law and order.

This being the case, Sullivan postulated that as a consequence of any military-mullah accommodation, Khomeini could be expected to return to Iran in triumph and hold a "Ghandi-like" position in the political constellation. Sullivan anticipated that Khomeini would have to choose a candidate for political leadership who was acceptable to the military, rather than a more extreme individual of the "Nasser or Qadhafi" type who might be more to the ayatollah's preference.

Thus, if non-Communist, moderate political figures emerged in positions of responsibility, they could be expected to call for elections to a constituent assembly to draw up a constitution for an Islamic republic of Iran. Furthermore, if elections were held in any atmosphere other than one of frenzy, the resulting constituent assembly ought to contain a strong presence of non-Communist, non-fanatic Islamic and pro-Western moderates who would have considerable influence in developing a responsible constitutional document.

While recognizing the difficulty of predicting the sort of government that might emerge from the subsequent general elections, Sullivan felt there were reasons to hope that it would maintain Iran's general international orientation, except that it would cease its ties with Israel and associate itself with the Arabs, probably closer to the hard-line views of Syria and Libya than to Saudi Arabia. In its general orientation, it would probably be a "Kuwait writ large."

Finally, although U.S. involvement would be less intimate than with the shah, Sullivan speculated that it could be an essentially satisfactory one, particularly if the military leadership preserved its integrity. There would presumably be fewer Americans and they would have a reduced status, but they could probably stay if they chose.

In concluding this analysis, Ambassador Sullivan noted that this scenario could come about only if every step along the way turned out well. Any single misstep anywhere could destroy it and lead to unpredictable consequences. Therefore it should not be regarded as the embassy's prediction of future events.

The existing U.S. posture of trusting that the shah, together with the military, would be able to face down the Khomeini threat was "obviously the only safe course to pursue at this juncture," Sullivan acknowledged. However, he added, "if it should fail and if the shah should abdicate, we need to think the unthinkable at this time in order to give our thoughts some precision should the unthinkable contingency arise."

As a piece of analysis, the telegram had several deficiencies. It identified the two contending poles in the power struggle as the military and the religious forces, but it made no effort to weigh their relative strengths or to consider how they might interact in a fluid and dynamic situation. Curiously, the shah was relegated to the role of a minor participant in this unfolding drama. More important, the message did not address the role U.S. policy might play in structuring an accommodation between the contending forces. It did not identify what new decisions, if any, might be required to position U.S. policy in advance of the shah's possible departure, and it asked for no authority or guidance from Washington to pursue contacts beyond those already under way with the various power centers.

Nevertheless, this message was a unique and important contribution to the policy debate, if only because it spelled out clearly and explicitly the assumptions underlying one school of thought. With great clarity, this telegram identified the necessary sequence of events that would be required to achieve an outcome in Iran that would be compatible, on the one hand, with U.S. liberal, democratic values and, on the other, with U.S. national interests in maintaining an independent, Western-oriented Iran.

There can be no doubt that from a U.S. point of view, the emergence in Iran of a coalition of non-Communist, non-fanatic Islamic and pro-Western moderates operating within a responsible constitutional framework was profoundly to be preferred to the virulently anti-Western theocracy that ultimately assumed power. The question that will occupy future historians is whether such an outcome was ever feasible and, if so, what preconditions were necessary to transform the wish into reality.

There is never a definitive answer to any historical question that begins "What if . . ." Yet in this instance we at least have benefit of a rigorous set of necessary conditions provided by Ambassador Sullivan that offer a useful starting point. The key points are as follows:

- Iran's younger officers were genuinely pro-Western in orientation as a consequence of their training experiences in the United States and other Western states.
- The military would be able to maintain its integrity and cohesion as an

independent power center through the turmoil of the shah's abdication and the departure of its senior leadership into exile.

- The religious forces would be compelled to rely on the Iranian military to maintain civil order, since they lacked any Islamic institution to perform that function.
- Khomeini would play a relatively passive or benevolent role in government affairs after a triumphal return.
- The combination of the military and the moderate political forces would be able to contain the forces of extremism in a post-shah Iran and manage the transition to a responsible constitutional government.

In the tumultuous months that followed, none of these assumptions proved valid. The pro-Western veneer of the younger military officers was stripped away by the revolutionary, Islamic fervor of Khomeini's religious movement. The departure of the shah and the subsequent collapse of the senior military leadership proved to be profoundly demoralizing to the military hierarchy and left it in disarray. Khomeini and those around him acted swiftly to neutralize the military and all other institutions of the shah's period and to replace them with new, popular forces drawn from the ranks of the revolution. Not only did Khomeini himself prove to be a formidable political force, but he surprised even many of his close followers with his implacable determination to implement the provisions of the theocratic government that he had outlined years before in his lectures in Najaf. The moderate political forces of the National Front, who sought a return to the constitution of 1906, proved to be no match for Khomeini and the Islamic hard-liners.

Could these negative developments have been foreseen in November 1978 and could a different U.S. policy have produced the outcome projected by Ambassador Sullivan? On balance, it is probably safe to say that in November 1978 none of the key participants—the shah, the senior military leadership or the religious opposition, let alone the United States—could confidently assess the loyalty of the military in a final showdown, although everyone was aware of the steady erosion that was taking place.

The shah had been aware of problems within the military since at least early October when he raised the subject with Ambassador Sullivan, and the number of desertions and isolated mutinies were observed with growing apprehension as the revolution gathered force. Nevertheless, soldiers continued to obey orders—including firing on demonstrators—and displayed remarkable discipline well beyond the point when they might have been expected to become demoralized. Even in mid-December 1978, Mehdi Bazargan and other revolutionaries within Iran were deeply concerned that the army would perpetrate a massacre.[1]

There is evidence that Khomeini had difficulty reconciling the fact that "good Iranian boys" in the army were willing to fire on their "brothers and sisters" in the revolution. He told a visiting American in all apparent seriousness that the troops who had fired in Jaleh Square were not Iranian at all but rather Israeli troops imported by the shah. According to the prominent Egyptian journalist Mohammad Hassanein Heikal, who visited Khomeini in Paris, the ayatollah shared the view of Brzezinski and others that the army was the key to the success of the revolution—not the shah, not SAVAK and not the opposition politicians.

Khomeini's tactics for dealing with the army was martyrdom for his followers in whatever numbers were required to break its link with the shah. "Do not attack the army in its breast, but in its heart" was his message. "You must appeal to the soldiers' hearts even if they fire on you and kill you. Let them kill five thousand, ten thousand, twenty thousand—they are our brothers and we will welcome them. We will prove that blood is more powerful than the sword."[2]

Although none of the participants could make a confident judgment about the reliability of the military, an assessment of the role of the "moderates" was less problematical, even in November. The widespread perception of Khomeini as a benign figure—the "Gandhi" of Iran, to adopt Ambassador Sullivan's simile—was from the beginning more the product of wishful thinking than of dispassionate analysis.

Khomeini, like most extremist political leaders, was remarkably candid in describing his objectives. His lectures in Najaf, collected under the title *Islamic Government,*[3] described in some considerable detail the nature of the government that eventually was established in Iran. Those who were committed to a secular, liberal, constitutional outcome—including many who allied themselves with Khomeini—were either unaware of these writings or else chose to explain away Khomeini's extreme views as the distortions and exaggerations of those who were ignorant of, or hostile to, Iranian culture and traditions. Khomeini and the clergy, they insisted, would serve as the transmission belt of the revolution but would then retire to serve as the conscience of the new government, rather than its masters. It is not difficult to understand why they would want to believe that their own reformist views, rather than Khomeini's radical medievalism, would shape the Iran of the future. But the contrary facts were there for those who wished to see them.

Similarly, the effective strength of the old-line moderates, who traced their lineage to Mossadegh's nationalistic movement, was not difficult to gauge, even in November 1978. Although they saw themselves as the legitimate representatives of the constitutional reform movement that had transformed Iranian politics in the early 1900s, they were late in recognizing the revolutionary appeal of Khomeini's incendiary rhetoric. Initially, they attempted to capture the burgeoning opposition to the shah under their own banner but failed to forge an effective political organization.

When their representatives finally arrived in Paris in October seeking an alliance with Khomeini, the most they could offer were the talents of their own loose association of political leaders. Presumably, leadership was one commodity of which Khomeini was not in short supply, and he quickly let them know that if they wished to join him, it would have to be on his terms and under his leadership. They quickly yielded and in a public statement confirmed their acceptance of Khomeini's leadership. Although they unquestionably harbored visions of themselves as the logical inheritors of the revolution, they were never able to exercise an influence on policy commensurate with their own self-image. They were simply no match for Khomeini.

Although Ambassador Sullivan's long telegram received a careful reading in Washington, there seemed to be less to it than met the eye. Taken at face value as a political analysis, its failure to assess the relative strength of the contending forces in Iran robbed it of analytical power. If it was intended as a prescription for U.S. policy, why did it make no recommendations? The answer seemed to lie more in what was *not* said than in the words of the cable itself.

Washington's policy was based squarely on the premise that the shah (and his new military government) would be able to prevail over the revolutionary forces. Sullivan did not challenge this approach; he even gave it a lukewarm endorsement. Nevertheless, by focusing his attention on the "unthinkable" consequences if the policy should fail, he signaled his own lack of confidence about its prospects. He then identified two elements of a possible future coalition: the younger military officers and the aging leadership of the moderate opposition. The first was arguably a wasting asset, the second a demonstrably weak reed. If the situation continued to drift, the military might melt away, while the "moderates" would have to be propped up if they were to exercise any significant independent influence on events.

So there were two implicit conclusions to be drawn from Sullivan's presentation. First, if the younger military were to be preserved as a moderating influence, it would be preferable for the shah and the senior leadership to leave sooner rather than later, and with a minimum of turmoil. Second, some steps should be initiated, presumably by the United States, to enhance the credibility of the moderate political forces as an alternative to Khomeini's extremism.

If this was, indeed, the message that Ambassador Sullivan intended to convey to Washington, he would have been much better off to have said so directly. Washington was directing all its efforts toward bolstering the shah and persuading him to act with more decisiveness. The president and his top advisers were far from concluding that the shah was doomed, and they wished to avoid at all costs the appearance or reality of abandoning a close ally.

The kind of steps that Sullivan seemed to be suggesting—preparing the way for easing the shah and his senior command out of the way as painlessly as possible while beefing up the position of the moderate opposition—could not be concealed and would inevitably be recognized in Tehran, in Riyadh, in Washington and elsewhere for what they were. There was simply no high-level support for such a policy shift—from the president, from Brzezinski, from Brown or from Vance. The official policy of total support for the shah was based on the assumption that the shah was capable of acting vigorously and decisively—an expectation that also proved to be unfounded and based largely on wishful thinking. However, Sullivan did not challenge the conventional wisdom or present a case that might have changed official thinking in Washington.

The elliptical nature of Sullivan's message permitted him to ruminate about policy without committing himself to any controversial positions. Did he think the shah and the military government were likely to fail? He did not say. Were there immediate steps that should be taken to hold the military together and enhance the position of the moderates? He did not say. Moreover, Sullivan's cautious disclaimer that his scenario would work only if every intermediate step turned out well was not calculated to induce a high-risk policy shift in Washington. The message was cleverly written, but it may have been too clever by half.

Contrary to some reports, the message did not create much of a policy stir in the White House.[4] It was widely read, and the catchy title became part of the essential vocabulary of the crisis. However, it made no concrete proposals and asked for no reply. It was never the subject of a high-level policy meeting, and its implicit policy recommendations became the subject of heated debate only much later. Sullivan himself made no further reference to it.

Rightly or wrongly, this message was regarded—at least within the White House—as a veiled attack on existing policy and as a signal that the ambassador in Tehran was at best equivocal in carrying out the instructions he had been given. That suspicion may say more about the atmosphere of rivalry and mutual distrust breeding within the Iran policy community than about Sullivan's motives. However, it is a measure of the times that the telegram only served to further erode Sullivan's dwindling credibility.

Private Emissary

The concern about Ambassador Sullivan's reporting led Brzezinski to seek an independent reading on the state of events in Tehran. On November 9, Brzezinski met with a U.S. businessman who had served as the CIA station chief in Tehran many years earlier. Brzezinski asked him to travel to Tehran to meet with the shah and any other individuals he considered useful to provide an independent reading on the situation. Brzezinski was particularly interested in getting his personal assessment of the prospects for the shah's survival, a reading on popular attitudes inside Iran, and any ideas about what the United States could or should do. He was specifically directed not to attempt to offer advice to the shah about how to handle the situation, although he could say that Washington would like to be as helpful as possible.

Secretary Vance approved the trip, and a message was sent to Ambassador Sullivan. The emissary was expected to check in with the embassy on arrival, and the extent of his discussions with Ambassador Sullivan and other embassy officials was left to his discretion. Although there were many other visitors in Iran over the next several months—public and private—this was the only instance of a personal emissary of which I was aware.

This individual met with the shah on November 14 and reported back to Brzezinski on the seventeenth. The shah expressed appreciation for Brzezinski's phone call. He said the only thing he could think of that the U.S. government might do would be to "tell the leaders of the political opposition what you are telling me, that at the highest levels you support me fully in my efforts to restore order and stability and that you look towards me as the key to continued strength, stability and prosperity for Iran."

As usual, the shah was suspicious about U.S. intentions and was well informed about the media. Presidential assistant Hamilton Jordan, appearing on a television talk show, had mentioned that the United States had to be considering possible contingencies. The shah wondered if that meant America was preparing to deal with an alternative government. (He was later assured that this was not the meaning of Jordan's comments.)

When asked for his own assessment, the shah said that he found it hard to understand how this "terrible situation" had come about. Perhaps it was his fault. Maybe some of the fault was from the outside, specifically Western media attention to Iranian failings. He felt the Iranian press and television were completely penetrated by enemies of his government, and he said he was unable to control even what the TV stations were broadcasting.

The shah would not be drawn into a broad assessment of the situation, and the emissary had the impression that the shah found it "baffling, incomprehensible and almost overwhelming." Furthermore, the shah seemed to trust no one, and his earlier confidence in his own judgment seemed deeply shaken. The shah once again alluded to the persistent rumors that the British and Americans (i.e., the CIA) were somehow behind the present troubles in Iran.

The emissary prepared a handwritten report during the lengthy flight back from Tehran; this memorandum was sent to President Carter in its original form, with a brief cover note. Ambassador Sullivan in a private message complained bitterly to Brzezinski about this mission; however, the visitor had punctiliously observed embassy protocol, meeting with Ambassador Sullivan both before and after his interview with the shah. In his written and verbal reporting, the emissary tactfully avoided any comments about the operation of the embassy or judgments about the performance of the professionals in the field. Although President Carter reviewed the recommendations in the report in considerable detail, the overall effect of the mission was to confirm the existing course of policy rather than to alter it.

Two other official visitors were scheduled to go to Tehran shortly thereafter. Secretary of the Treasury Michael Blumenthal had a long-scheduled trip planned to the Middle East, including Iran. (It had been the practice for some years for the secretary of the treasury to visit Iran and the Gulf annually.) The majority leader in the Senate, Robert C. Byrd, was also scheduled to travel to the Middle East. Senator Byrd's daughter was married to an Iranian, and it was felt that he might have access to a body of opinion not ordinarily available to official visitors to Tehran. Neither man was particularly enthusiastic about traveling to Iran in view of the continuing riots and civil disorder. Moreover, some individuals in the Department of State believed that the Tehran circuit was being overworked. But Ambassador Sullivan was consulted and approved the visits, so planning proceeded.

A Policy Review Committee meeting was held at the White House on November 9 to brief Secretary Blumenthal. Discussion of Iran focused, appropriately, on the economic situation and on the practical aspects of security. With regard to the latter point, the representative of the Joint Chiefs of Staff reported that the embassy and the Military Advisory Group in Tehran were both convinced that the army remained loyal to the shah and to Iran as a nation. Conscripts, he reported, were not being used for riot control, and it was estimated that the Iranian military had the ability to act under stress. With regard to the ability of the military to run the government, it was clear that they needed help, and we should offer to assist wherever possible. Secretary Blumenthal agreed to sound out the shah and his economic advisers about ways the international financial system might be helpful in assisting Iran through a difficult period.

Holiday weekends in both Iran and Washington on November 10–12 provided an opportunity for taking stock after the first week of military government. Most of the reporting was upbeat. A threatened general strike did not materialize; oil-field workers seemed to be going back to their jobs; public services and airports went back into operation; and the public respected the rules of martial law. There was a cautious sigh of relief as some semblance of order began to reappear in Tehran. Both sides began to think about the religious month of Moharram.

Moharram is the first month of the Islamic calendar year, and it has very special significance for Shi'i Moslems. On the first of Moharram in the sixty-first year of the Islamic era (A.D. 680), Husayn, the grandson of the Prophet Mohammad whom Shi'is regard as the legitimate successor of the Prophet ("Imam"), arrived with a band of supporters at Karbala (in modern Iraq) to confront the False Caliph Yazid. On the tenth of Moharram ("Ashura"), Husayn was martyred and his body desecrated. Those ten days of struggle and martyrdom against an unjust tyrant are commemorated each year by Shi'i Moslems in a frenzy of mourning and self-flagellation. In 1978 the dates fell on December 2 to 11, and the symbolism of the revolt against the shah combined with the religious drama of Moharram was widely expected to provide the setting for the first major test of the military regime.

The Intelligence Failure

During the short breathing spell before Moharram, attention shifted from Tehran to Washington, where the question of the U.S. "intelligence failure" in Iran was exploding into a major public issue. I may have been partly responsible for setting off this contentious debate, although it quickly escalated and assumed a life of its own.

In preparation for the Policy Review Committee meeting of November 6, I had written a briefing paper for Brzezinski noting that "the most fundamental problem at the moment is the astonishing lack of hard information we are getting about developments in Iran." I commented that "this has been an intelligence disaster of the first order. Our information has been extremely meager, our resources were not positioned to report accurately on the activities of the opposition forces, on external penetration, the strike demands, the political organization of the strikers or the basic objectives and political orientation of the demonstrators." President Carter was also concerned about the lack of information about the Iranian military, and he raised this issue with Secretary Vance in advance of the PRC meeting. Most of the meeting was devoted to a discussion of the intelligence problem. The director of central intelligence, Admiral Turner, acknowledged the problem but said he was unable to respond to the questions that were being raised, since U.S. intelligence capabilities in Iran had been allowed to atrophy in recent years.

On November 8, I prepared a memorandum for Brzezinski summarizing the follow-up measures that were being taken in response to the November 6 meeting. The memo recommended overhauling and beefing up the reporting capabilities in Tehran, which "were designed to deal with an entirely different world, and [had not] performed adequately when put to the extreme test of the past nine months." As a first step I drafted a proposed directive for Brzezinski's signature to the secretary of state and the director of central intelligence, asking them to prepare for the president an examination of the political reporting capability of the embassy and the intelligence community, with recommendations for changes that should be undertaken. Brzezinski signed this memo on November 10.

I was unaware that, in addition to signing the memo to Vance and Turner, Brzezinski also sent a memo to the president complaining about the quality of political intelligence that the White House was receiving. It was evidently that memorandum which prompted President Carter to prepare a handwritten note on November 11 to "Cy, Zbig, Stan" informing them that he was "dissatisfied with the quality of political intelligence" and directing them to correct the situation. This note was subsequently leaked to the press, setting off a public debate about U.S. intelligence capabilities that continued for more than a year.

The Iranian crisis was the proximate cause for this re-evaluation of U.S. intelligence procedures. However, the issue went far beyond the quality of reporting on Iran. There were many in Washington at that time who were deeply dissatisfied about the management of intelligence by Admiral Turner. The Iranian situation provided an exceptionally clear example of intelligence malfunction, and those who opposed Turner were quick to take advantage of the situation to embarrass him and to raise doubts about his handling of other major issues, such as SALT and Soviet policy. The immediate leaking of President Carter's note was undoubtedly motivated by the desire to undercut Turner's relationship with President Carter.

Although this maneuver was squarely in the tradition of hard-ball Washington infighting and provided some raw meat for the gossip-hungry Washington press corps, it contributed nothing to effective policy making on Iran. On the contrary, by initiating a public attack on Turner, the CIA and the intelligence community in general, it set off a scramble of defensive countermoves and self-justifications that seriously detracted from the fundamental problem of trying to gain some genuine understanding of what was happening in Iran. The quality of information available to U.S. policy makers on Iran was indeed dreadful, and that unpleasant fact only became more apparent as the crisis progressed.

Embassy Reporting

As one element of the internal government investigation following President Carter's directive, Brzezinski asked me to review all of the reporting from the embassy in Tehran over the previous year. The National Security Council does not maintain comprehensive files on each country or issue, relying instead on the various Washington agencies. Consequently, I spent a full day at the Office of Iranian Affairs at the State Department, reviewing a stack of thick file folders under the baleful eye of Henry Precht. I summarized my findings in a memorandum on November 17.

I concluded that the embassy had done a good job of reporting on the basic facts, keeping Washington aware of the daily news about strikes, demonstrations and the like. However, there was very little digging below the surface. The most interesting reporting occurred in accounts of conversations with the shah and other high political figures. These provided insights into the political situation not available from other sources and occasionally sparked revealing comments and asides from the ambassador and other officials.

There was, I found, little questioning of official Iranian government pronouncements. There was a general tendency in the embassy's reporting to explain away the "exaggerations" and "distortions" in non-official news reports and local rumors, although many of these reports and rumors later proved to be more accurate than the government's official line. There was a notable absence of reporting on conversations or contacts with unconventional sources or outsiders, including visiting journalists or others who might have views contrary to the conventional wisdom.

Deputy Chief of Mission Charles Naas and the political section of the embassy wrote a long piece of political analysis in August which identified the sources of dissent and the key issues that motivated the opposition. The authors recognized that there was serious trouble ahead, although they were studiously non-alarmist and clearly did not anticipate just how serious the troubles would be. From this single report it seemed evident that the embassy was not unaware of what was happening. I was struck by the fact that this was virtually the only example of such reporting in the huge volume of messages that I reviewed. Ironically, it was written and sent during the period when Ambassador Sullivan was on his extended home leave.[5]

A similar but much more comprehensive review of the intelligence problem was also initiated in November 1978 by the Select Committee on Intelligence of the House of Representatives, resulting in a public report in January 1979.[6] This study concluded that intelligence collection and analysis were weak and that the confidence of policy makers in the shah, which intelligence reporting did not challenge, further skewed the U.S. reading of the situation in Tehran and contributed to the warning failure.

The CIA, it noted, had produced two separate analytical pieces about Iran over the previous year that entirely failed to prepare Washington decision makers for the problems they encountered in late 1978. In August 1977 a 60-page study entitled "Iran in the 1980s" was based on the assumption that "the shah will be an active participant in Iranian life well into the 1980s," and that "there will be no radical change in Iranian political behavior in the near future."

The other, a 23-page study entitled "Iran after the Shah," was published in August 1978. Despite its provocative title, this study was limited to an examination of the conventional power structure of the Iranian elite—the royal family, senior political figures and the military—as possible participants in what was expected to be a smooth transition of power at some future date. The study was prefaced with the judgment, just one month before the Jaleh Square incident, that "Iran is not in a revolutionary or even a 'prerevolutionary' situation."

The Senate study also traced the hapless course of the National Intelligence Estimate (NIE) that the NSC had requested in June. The NIE process is cumbersome and time-consuming, and this official evaluation of the situation in Iran had wound through a labyrinthine review process throughout the summer. The official views of the CIA were on the record as of the August report mentioned above, and the basic drafts of the NIE reflected those judgments.

The Department of State during this period had no Iranian analyst in its Bureau of Intelligence and Research (INR). Nevertheless, the INR division chief for South Asia, George Griffin, was less sanguine than the CIA analysts about the situation in Iran and objected repeatedly to optimistic interpretations in the draft NIE. Failing to achieve consensus, and with the situation in Iran deteriorating rapidly, the NIE was quietly shelved by Admiral Turner in September. I requested and received a copy of the unpublished draft but found it singularly unhelpful in attempting to understand the nature of the forces at work in Iran.

Unfortunately, the CIA did very little to improve its zero batting record on Iran even after President Carter's sharp jibe. On November 22, eleven days after the president's note, CIA analysts distributed a paper that attempted to explain the shah's response to the crisis. This paper concluded that the shah was "not paralyzed with indecision," and for the most part was "in accurate touch with reality." His vacillation, according to this analysis, probably meant that he was "continuing to cope with the problems of his regime" in a situation that had no clear solution.

I was appalled to be informed that as long as the shah failed to make up his mind, it was evidence that he was coping. What were we to think if he suddenly became decisive? In my opinion, in terms of sheer gobbledygook masquerading as informed judgment, this report had no peer in the entire history of the Iran crisis. Quite unwittingly, the authors of this paper confirmed the validity of President Carter's concern about the quality of intelligence he was receiving on Iran.

Rumbles from the USSR

Ambassador Sullivan and his British colleague again met with the shah for two hours on the evening of November 18. Sullivan reported that the shah "seemed tired, rather tense, but in a positive frame of mind." The shah expressed alarm about an article by Iraj Eskandari in the Parisian Communist newspaper *L'Humanité* in which the exiled Tudeh Party leader praised the religious side of the anti-shah movement, specifically Ayatollah Khomeini, and called for a popular front of all "democratic forces," including the Tudeh and the religious forces. The shah interpreted this as a signal that the Soviets were preparing to back Khomeini by sending weapons into Iran and promoting civil war. It confirmed his view that the demonstrations in Iran were the product of an "unholy alliance" between Communists and clerical reactionaries.

The shah had experienced a difficult two weeks. He complained to the two ambassadors that he was spending most of the day on the telephone directing the details of the current government, since his military officers were in the habit of seeking his approval for their every step. To add to his problems, he had just received a hoax telephone call, purportedly from Senator Edward Kennedy in Washington. When he picked up the phone, he heard only a quiet voice repeating, "Mohammad, abdicate. Mohammad, abdicate."

The shah felt that the military government was doing reasonably well, and he expected no significant changes in the situation before Moharram. For the moment, his instructions to the military government were to move steadily but slowly, and to avoid confrontations. He hoped that this policy of caution would not be interpreted as weakness.

He indicated that he was receiving numerous messages from Americans, through Ambassador Zahedi, urging him to be "tough," to assert control and to face down the opposition. He said he had also heard that he was getting old, that he was no longer able to make decisions and that he was lacking in "guts." He asked Ambassador Sullivan to tell these people that he had guts, but he also had a heart and a brain. He did not intend to murder the youth of his nation in order to rule it.

He said he had been meeting with former Prime Minister Ali Amini and had agreed to the formation of a consultative council that would serve as an intermediary to bring in opposition elements for discussion. This council would attempt to develop a dialogue that would eventually produce a coalition government to supervise general elections. The shah confirmed that he had been in touch with the leader of the National Front, Karim Sanjabi.[7] As a result of his contacts, the shah had concluded that Sanjabi had so firmly aligned himself with Khomeini that cooperation with the monarchy was no longer possible. He believed that there were others who would be more cooperative, although he commented wryly that Amini had as yet failed to produce any "warm bodies." (I was informed years later by an Iranian official with excellent credentials that the Amini initiative was ultimately blocked by Ambassador Zahedi, who saw Amini as a potential competitor in his efforts to become prime minister.)

The shah indicated that the anticipated demonstrations during Moharram would be a true test of strength. During that time he planned to place the armed forces on full alert and allow no public processions or religious manifestations outside the mosques. Gatherings would be broken up before they could get started.

With regard to the nascent bargaining with the moderate opposition, the shah spelled out his position with some clarity. He was prepared, he said, to accept the exact letter of the constitution and to recede from all direct involvement in the affairs of government. However, he would insist that he not only retain his function as commander in chief of the armed forces but also retain control of the military budget, which would not be subject to the vote of the Majles. From this comment, the shah left no doubt about his own view of where real power resided in Iran, but it also suggested that negotiations with opposition elements on this fundamental issue were likely to be prolonged and contentious.

By this stage of the crisis, most observers had concluded that the army was the key to the ongoing power struggle. On the same day as Sullivan's meeting with the shah, I contacted a U.S. academic specialist on Iran who had been following closely the activities of the religious opposition. I was surprised to hear him say that the outcome relied entirely on the army. He warned me that the National Front was making a major effort to convince everyone that it was the only real alternative to the shah. Although the National Front was making progress, he felt that it could not in itself provide a viable alternative. Likewise, he insisted that the religious leadership could not possibly assume direct authority for running the government.

He warned me not to underestimate the shah, who he felt was very much on top of the situation and was "calling the plays." The shah, he believed, would have to make a bold, dramatic move before Moharram if he wished to retain power. If that failed, he was convinced there would be a power struggle within the military, with the younger officers taking control and then working out a political relationship with the National Front to provide leadership for the country. He would not be drawn into speculation about what role, if any, the United States should play in that scenario.

Also on November 18, the White House received a message from the Soviet leader, Leonid I. Brezhnev, warning against any U.S. interference in Iran's internal affairs. This message set off an intense bureaucratic battle between Zbigniew Brzezinski at the White House and Secretary Vance at the State Department about the tenor of the U.S. reply. Brzezinski and Vance, it is important to recall, had worked in surprising harmony during the first two years of the Carter presidency; however, they differed fundamentally about U.S. policy toward the Soviet Union, and by the end of 1978 those differences were beginning to harden into the bitter dispute that was to dominate U.S. foreign policy for more than a year.

Brzezinski found the draft reply prepared by the State Department unduly apologetic, and he argued strenuously in favor of a stiff warning to the Soviets not to interfere in Iran. At a press conference the following day, Secretary Vance gave public expression to the U.S. position. The United States, he declared, did not intend to interfere in the internal affairs of any other country, and reports to the contrary were totally without foundation. "We expect other nations to conduct themselves in similar fashion," he went on, pointedly noting that "the Soviet Union has said yesterday that it will not interfere in the affairs of Iran and will respect its territorial integrity, sovereignty, and independence." He reiterated that the United States "firmly supports the shah in his efforts to restore domestic tranquillity in Iran. . . . We intend to preserve and pursue with Iran our strong bilateral political, economic and security relationship."[8]

For the most part, this exchange left things very much as they were. American policy remained unaltered, and the situation in Iran was unchanged. Nevertheless, this episode was regarded as extremely important in Washington since it marked a clear shift in Soviet policy. Despite the earlier Eskandari interview, Soviet reaction to events in Iran had, to this point, been cautious in the extreme. The Soviet leadership had cultivated a very satisfactory relationship with the shah, and there was evidence that the Soviets were surprised —perhaps as surprised as the Americans—at the rapid deterioration of the shah's position.

The private Brezhnev message indicated that the Soviets were revising their estimates. The fact that Brezhnev chose to publish his "warning" in *Pravda* at the same time it was being delivered to the White House suggested that the USSR was beginning to position itself as the "protector" of the revolutionary forces against U.S. intervention. Lest that interpretation slip by unnoticed, the Soviet-based clandestine radio (the so-called National Voice of Iran, broadcasting in Persian from the vicinity of Baku) commented on November 20 that "In their current battle to oust imperialism, particularly U.S. imperialism and its supporters, the people of our homeland [i.e., Iran] enjoy the support of progressive humanity and all peace-loving nations, particularly our northern neighbor."

Although Khomeini immediately denied any cooperation with Marxism and criticized the Soviet Union for its oppression of Moslems, the essential lines of Soviet strategy were established. The Soviet effort to ingratiate itself with the revolutionary forces and to encourage religious cooperation with the Tudeh Party was pursued quietly but relentlessly over the next several years.

Analyzing the Shah

On November 21 the first of a continuing series of "mini-SCC" meetings was convened by David Aaron, Brzezinski's deputy. Primarily concerned with policy coordination and implementation, these meetings provided a useful opportunity for a regular exchange of views and ideas at the senior staff level. At this meeting two senior State Department representatives commented that the shah seemed to be experiencing psychological problems and lapses of attention. All agreed that greater contact with opposition elements was needed. There was general consensus that the shah seemed to be attempting to persuade the United States to take decisions and responsibility that he was unwilling to take for himself.

Some of those views were reflected in a message from Secretary Vance to Ambassador Sullivan later in the day that directed Sullivan to continue to provide counsel "frankly and constructively" but to emphasize to the shah that the decisions were his and that the leading role in the crisis could not be shifted to another party. The message also expressed continuing concern about the shah's failure to exert public leadership and his apparent belief that the CIA was somehow involved in encouraging opposition forces. Secretary Vance raised the possibility of a private U.S. emissary who could discuss these issues on a personal basis with the shah.

The proposal for sending another emissary never materialized, but there was no shortage of visitors to Tehran during this period. On the same day of this message, November 21, Secretary of the Treasury Michael Blumenthal arrived in Tehran and met at length with the shah. Secretary Blumenthal was startled at the change in the shah's appearance since his visit a year earlier. Then he had been self-confident and "imperial." On this occasion, Blumenthal reported, he appeared distracted and thoroughly depressed. His conversation was punctuated by long pauses, during which he stared despondently into space. In Blumenthal's view, the shah appeared to be out of touch with, and unable to grasp, the situation around him.

The shah referred to the Brezhnev letter and public statement, commenting that this probably meant the Soviets thought things were going their way in Iran. He recalled Khrushchev's comment to Walter Lippmann many years before that Iran would be like a "ripe apple" falling into Russia's lap. The statements of the Tudeh Party suggested that the Soviets were positioning themselves. The shah believed that if the revolution led to his overthrow, the Iranian intelligentsia would not accept the role of the mullahs, and the mullahs would be incapable of ruling. The outcome would be that the country would "turn red."

One of the congressmen in Blumenthal's party asked if the shah was still committed to moving Iran toward democracy. The shah said he saw no other way. In a monarchy like Iran's, he said, it was not possible to transfer full power and authority to your heir. Only institutions could be transferred. He wondered if he had not moved too fast in that direction. He said he was astonished by the reaction he was witnessing. A great many people who had benefited from his programs had now joined the opposition. He could not understand it. With this he fell into a long silence, staring dejectedly at the floor.

On the following day, at Brzezinski's request, the NSC hosted an all-day meeting on Iran, bringing together a small group of academics and others outside the government who might be able to offer fresh insights and perspectives on the crisis. The State Department had hosted two earlier conferences on Iran that had been useful in stimulating views of individuals not associated with the government. The meeting on November 22 was held entirely without publicity in the windowless Situation Room in the basement of the White House. The intention was to go beyond an evaluation of the situation to formulate some specific policy suggestions for consideration by the president.

All of the participants agreed that the month of Moharram would be critical, possibly decisive, in determining whether the shah would survive. Contrary to the shah's stated intentions, the group believed that the Iranian government should not attempt to forbid religious processions during Moharram; rather, it should draw a firm line between religious activities and political demonstrations, backing up its position with a massive show of force if necessary. Most of the group felt that the shah should be able to survive Moharram, but if the mob gained the upper hand or sensed imminent victory, he might not be able to stem the revolutionary tide.

Once Moharram was over, the United States would have to reassess the situation and to assist the shah in addressing the economic and social root causes of the rebellion. There could be no return to business as usual, whatever the outcome. The shah had succeeded in alienating virtually every element of Iranian life, and he should concentrate on winning back those who had the most to gain from his continued rule: the merchants, the middle class, the technocrats. Rebuilding support would require more flexibility and political acumen than the shah had demonstrated to date.

Some devolution of power was considered inevitable, although the group was convinced that the shah would fight change every step of the way. If the shah was to have any chance of rectifying the situation, he would have to be perceived as accommodating from a position of strength, not caving in under pressure. Thus far he had failed to project an image of decisiveness, and many in the group felt he was fundamentally a weak man who had succeeded in portraying himself as a strong leader only because he was riding the crest of an economic boom.

The group split three ways on the question of the shah's future prospects. Some felt he would abdicate in the face of the continuing pressure. Others thought he would make it through Moharram but would have only a fifty-fifty chance of surviving politically through 1979. Others felt that if the shah survived Moharram, he would be able to stick it out and would probably continue to rule for several years at least. The outcome, in the view of the group, depended heavily on the shah himself. Whatever the outcome, the group agreed that Iran was in for a prolonged period of instability that would make it an uncertain ally and render it more vulnerable to Soviet influence and subversion than in the past.

Brzezinski met with the group briefly during the course of the day, but left it to me to chair the discussion and to prepare a written summary of conclusions. When I discussed the group's findings with him the following day, Brzezinski made no secret of the fact that he was disappointed. My summary, he said, read "like an editorial in the New York *Times.*"

He had hoped we would produce some clear recommendations for U.S. policy that went beyond the existing conventional wisdom. He obviously favored a much more active U.S. involvement, and the meeting of November 22 can be seen as the first in a series of bureaucratic maneuvers by Brzezinski in an effort to generate alternative policy views that he could use as ammunition with the president, the secretary of state, and others who were reluctant to pressure the shah to take controversial decisions that he seemed determined to resist.

Zahedi Redux

Unknown to me, quite a different initiative was being launched at approximately the same time. On November 21, Ambassador Zahedi came to the White House and met with President Carter, Secretary Vance and Zbigniew Brzezinski before returning to Iran. The shah learned of this meeting from Zahedi, and he called Sullivan in on November 23 to discuss it. The shah said that according to his reports, the meeting was basically a session devoted to the state of his morale, and he was surprised that the entire high command of the United States would be gathered for such a purpose.

Sullivan alluded to U.S. concern about the need for a more vigorous leadership role on the shah's part. The shah replied that leadership had to be tailored to the circumstances, and people had to live in Iran to understand those circumstances. Zahedi had told him that the U.S. leaders had urged him to return to Iran to buck up the shah's morale. According to Sullivan, the shah indicated "no great desire" to have Zahedi in Tehran during a delicate period such as Moharram. Sullivan completed his report with the observation that the shah seemed much better in this meeting than in the meeting with Blumenthal two days earlier.

Whatever the shah's apprehensions about having a hard-line activist such

as Zahedi in Tehran at that delicate juncture, they were more than reciprocated by Ambassador Sullivan, who regarded Zahedi as a direct rival. Sullivan's concerns were not without justification. President Carter had supported
Zahedi's plan to return to Tehran and had encouraged him in his intentions
to urge the shah to exert more decisive leadership.

Zahedi was not at all reluctant to advertise his "special relationship" with
the White House and to leave the impression that every move he made was
secretly authorized—or even initiated—by Washington. However, his telephone conversations with Brzezinski from Tehran were much less frequent
than he suggested to Sullivan and others—not more than five or six calls over
the following month. In each case, Zahedi initiated these calls, and he used
them to brief Brzezinski on what was happening in Iran. Although there were
frank discussions about the security situation and plans for dealing with the
Moharram demonstrations, these conversations were not decision-making sessions. Despite Zahedi's best efforts and insinuations, his direct impact on U.S.
policy-making was not great.[9]

Nevertheless, Sullivan was correct in regarding Zahedi as a threat to his
own position. Zahedi was in contact with a group of generals—specifically
General Gholam Ali Oveissi, the martial-law administrator for Tehran; General Manuchehr Khosraudad, the paratroop commander; and General Abbas
Ali Badrei, the commander of the Imperial Guard—who had been urging the
shah for months to crack down on the opposition. This group wanted to form
a military government with much greater latitude to use force against the
opposition. The shah's resistance to this solution was reflected in the fact that
he had by-passed these officers when he established the military government
on November 6. Zahedi's presence in Tehran meant that the advice of this
group would be heard in the palace, and the telephone connection also ensured
that these views would be transmitted directly to the White House.

Zahedi's influence in Tehran was probably as overestimated by Brzezinski
and the president as his influence in Washington was exaggerated by Sullivan.
Zahedi had been out of Iran for more than five years, and he had no real base
of support in the country. He was not personally close to the shah, nor
especially trusted as an adviser. His relationships within the military did not
run deep, and the generals tended to be suspicious of his motives. Zahedi's
political ambitions were quite well known but not widely shared. His independent pipeline to Brzezinski was evidence that the White House had begun to
have serious doubts about the completeness and accuracy of the ambassador's
reporting; however, given the level of support Zahedi received in Washington,
it is surprising how little effect he had on policy.

Two additional sets of visitors from Washington met with the shah in late
November. Lieutenant General Eugene F. Tighe, Jr., director of the U.S.
Defense Intelligence Agency, and Robert Bowie, deputy director for estimates
in the Central Intelligence Agency, met with the shah to provide a briefing
unrelated to the crisis.

The shah also met on November 27 with Senator Robert C. Byrd, the Senate majority leader. In the course of his briefings prior to departure, Senator Byrd had become familiar with the belief—then popular in Washington—that the shah should take his case to the Iranian people more directly by making greater use of radio and television. This idea had originated with Ambassador Zahedi and it had been relayed to Tehran. Ambassador Sullivan had personally raised the idea with the shah during his meeting of November 23.

Senator Byrd had gone to Tehran prepared to make this recommendation more strongly to the shah, but after talking with his son-in-law and other Iranians in Tehran, he changed his mind. He concluded that the shah's personal identification with every aspect of the nation's life over the last several decades was the major reason why his subjects held him responsible for every flaw and failure of the past. Additional public exposure would only be counter-productive.

Senator Byrd found the shah dispirited. Although the shah gave a lucid description of the difficulties facing his regime, he seemed to have no answers to the problems and no clear plan for dealing with them. During the luncheon that he hosted, he withdrew almost totally from conversation and gave the impression of being under sedation.

The shah admitted once again that he had been taken by surprise by the demonstrations. Only a year before, he lamented, the country seemed solid as a rock. He was trapped, he said, in a vicious circle. He wished to establish the machinery for democracy, but at each step he found himself confronted with a breakdown of law and order. He expressed appreciation for the words of support that the senator brought from President Carter, but he recognized there was little other countries could do. "It is a deep and internal matter here," he said, "and all the best statements from Washington, London and Bonn cannot change that."

Preparing for the Worst

With the religious celebrations of Moharram to begin on December 1, both Washington and Tehran began battening down the hatches for what was expected to be the climactic confrontation between the military government and the religious forces.

David Aaron convened another of the mini-SCC meetings to review the progress of contingency planning by the various agencies. Anti-American incidents were becoming more frequent, and there was a growing concern about the safety of the many Americans living in Iran. Ambassador Sullivan was treading a fine line in his attempts, on the one hand, to encourage Americans in Iran to exercise maximum caution without, on the other, generating a sense of panic that might lead to a mass departure. A mass exodus of the U.S. community, it was feared, would be interpreted as a loss of U.S. confidence in the Tehran government, possibly leading to its collapse. It was decided to take no new precautionary steps for the moment, on the assumption (which proved to be valid) that companies and individuals would gradually reduce their representation in Iran without further prodding from Washington.

In the meantime, contacts had increased between the U.S. embassy and some elements of the opposition. By the end of November the opposition political and religious leadership in Tehran was becoming very nervous about the possibility of a bloodbath during Moharram. In a series of meetings with embassy representatives they outlined a proposal to form a Regency Council of nationally respected political and military leaders. The shah would step back, perhaps on the pretext of a "vacation," and the council would appoint a coalition government to rule during the preparation for national elections.

The U.S. representatives made it clear that they could not strike a deal of this nature; only the shah could approve or disapprove such a plan. Nevertheless, the Americans listened and reported the conversations to Washington and to the palace. In the end, Ayatollah Husayn-Ali Montazeri was nominated to go to Paris to present this plan to Khomeini as a means of avoiding a bloody confrontation. Khomeini refused to consider it, reportedly considering the talks a trick aimed at aborting the revolution. Without Khomeini's support, the effort collapsed.

On the eve of Moharram, Khomeini underlined his uncompromising position by issuing a proclamation that called on the people of Iran to "unite, arise and sacrifice your blood." He called for disobedience of the government's order banning demonstrations. The month of Moharram, he stated, would be the month when "blood will triumph over the sword, the month of the strength of right, the month the oppressors will be judged and the satanic government will be abolished."

The stage was set.

VI

THE END
OF A BAD YEAR

O n Thursday, the last day of November 1978, two days before the crucial
month of Moharram began in Iran, Zbigniew Brzezinski telephoned
and asked to see me immediately. During that brief and familiar trek
—the elevator ride down from the third floor of the Old Executive Office
Building, across the drive to the White House and up the cramped stairway
in the West Wing—I rehearsed in my mind all the current strands of policy.
In two years I had learned that Brzezinski delighted in popping the unexpected
on his staff, partly to see how they would react but also out of genuine
amusement at watching his "experts" trying furiously to adjust to a new piece
of information while he looked on. What would it be?

As I came into his office, with the sun streaming through the high windows,
he got up from his desk and handed me a paper—a totally mundane report
I had written a day or two earlier. We discussed it for a moment. When I took
the paper to leave, he said with elaborate casualness, "Oh, by the way, there
is one other thing." His eyes narrowed, giving him away, and I thought to
myself, Here it comes. "George Ball," he said, "is coming down to Washington
to take over the Iran business for a while. You ought to be thinking about
finding him a place to work." My reaction, no doubt, was exactly what he had
hoped.

Secretary of the Treasury Blumenthal had returned from Tehran worried
about the state of the shah and the policy drift in Iran. He had spent much
of the previous weekend with former Undersecretary of State George Ball, an
old friend, discussing the situation. Reviewing his trip later with Brzezinski,

Blumenthal had suggested bringing Ball in to take a fresh look at the Iranian situation. Brzezinski, who had worked briefly for George Ball in the Policy Planning Staff at the State Department many years earlier and who had a deep respect for him as a man of independent views, agreed with Blumenthal and secured President Carter's approval.

Iran was approaching a critical moment. At the same time, the Middle East bureaucracy was immersed in the continuing negotiations between Egypt and Israel on a peace treaty, and the SALT II treaty and normalization of relations with China were all coming to a head. Moreover, there were deep divisions within the government about the proper course of U.S. policy in Iran. So the idea of enlisting a seasoned statesman for a high-level review was appealing. Mr. Ball had already been contacted, Brzezinski told me, and would arrive in Washington over the weekend.

Once I had absorbed the news, I volunteered to relinquish my office for his use. I suggested that it might be useful to provide some advance briefings so there would be a minimum of lost time. Brzezinski agreed. I contacted George Ball's secretary, and the next morning I found myself on the shuttle to New York.

I had never met George Ball, although I had read one of his books and a number of his articles and commentaries. I knew him as one of the great names of modern U.S. foreign policy, a member of the elite band of "Europeanists" who had put an indelible stamp on world politics during the period of the Marshall Plan and the early stirrings of the European Community. I was aware that he had dissented with dignity and vigor over the Vietnam policies of Presidents Kennedy and Johnson from his position at the Department of State, and that he held principled but politically unfashionable views about Israel's occupation of the West Bank.

I was soon to learn that he was a mountain of energy, a veritable encyclopedia of U.S. politics, and a man of great wit and charm, with a healthy appetite for fine French food, good drink and good company. Over the succeeding fourteen days I had ample opportunity to see the man whole, for I was with him constantly except for those occasional brief hours that he reluctantly conceded to the human frailty of sleep.

As I arrived at his Wall Street office I was intensely conscious that George Ball would be familiar to the point of boredom with the *genus* of eager young aide packing a briefcase of papers and data. Was this trip worth the effort? I need not have been concerned. I was received not so much with courtesy as with an insatiable curiosity to understand exactly what was happening in Iran and Washington. Within ten minutes we were engrossed in the most far-ranging discussion of the Iranian crisis I had had with anyone inside or outside the government.

He had drinks and a substantial lunch brought to the office, and we continued without missing a beat. Four hours later I had also learned a great deal. George Ball, whose acquaintance with the shah went back several decades, did not share the optimism of the Washington bureaucracy that the shah's weaknesses were merely temporary and remediable by a dose of U.S. assurances.

His personal acquaintance with members of the Iranian intelligentsia and his periodic business trips to Tehran had given him a keen appreciation of the effects of some of the shah's economic excesses and the discontent that had emerged within the middle class. Aware of the feud being waged between Brzezinski and the Iran desk at the State Department, he requested that his first Washington appointment, at his hotel on Sunday night, be set up with Henry Precht and Harold Saunders.

On the flight back to Washington I began to realize that I was in for a ticklish time. I was Brzezinski's assistant, but I had also been freed to work full time with George Ball. After only four hours it was blindingly clear that Ball would produce some fresh insights about the situation in Iran but that they would not be what Brzezinski wanted to hear. I decided that the only honorable course of action for me was to be as honest and frank with both men as I was able and let the chips fall where they might. In the meantime, I rather looked forward to the fireworks.

The next two weeks were a whirlwind. Ball described his procedure as "total immersion," and from the moment of his arrival he began a furious round of meetings with everyone in Washington who might have special knowledge or views on Iran. Protocol and status were irrelevant. He met with all the key cabinet officials, but he also sought out staff officers at all levels in addition to journalists, academics, former Iranian officials and anyone else who might have something interesting to offer.

Ball did not require much of the formal "care and feeding" that Washington staff aides know so well. Talking papers, memoranda of conversations and elaborate schedules were discarded when they interfered with the business at hand, although I kept handwritten notes of all the conversations and a running tally of significant points that might be useful for his report to the president. He also did most of his own drafting, often late at night. What he seemed to want most was someone to bounce ideas off, a role I accepted with relish.

We normally met at his hotel for breakfast and a discussion of the previous day and the day ahead, followed by a full schedule of meetings interrupted only for an elaborate lunch, ending the day with a good dinner and discussions over drinks that often went well into the night. It was exhilarating, exhausting and fattening. It was also never boring. Although the focus was Iran, George Ball's range of interests were as wide as his anecdotal supply was limitless, and conversation never flagged.

The Book of Job reminds us that "Great men are not always wise," and even my limited encounters with the famous, the rich and the powerful had led me to conclude that sustained contact all too frequently revealed feet of clay. Wisdom may be more than an open mind, a zest for the truth, a lively intelligence and the absence of pomposity, but that is a very good start. Those were the qualities I came to appreciate in George Ball during those hectic two weeks.

The Moharram Crisis

The beginning of Moharram in Iran was marked by widespread public disobedience to the military government's order prohibiting demonstrations. Enormous crowds flocked to the mosques for religious observance, spilling over into the streets and ignoring the early-evening curfew. At night the citizens of Tehran, now including middle- and upper-class residents of northern Tehran in addition to the "sans culottes" of the southern slums, climbed to their roofs at night and chanted religious and revolutionary slogans.

The authorities recognized that it would be impossible to sustain the ban against demonstrations during the high holy days of Tasua and Ashura (literally, the Ninth and Tenth of Moharram), commemorating the martyrdom of Imam Husayn at Karbala in the seventh century at the hands of the False Caliph, Yazid. Husayn's martyrdom is the central symbolic event of Shi'i Islam and is marked annually by mass processions of young men rhythmically striking themselves with fists and chains in sorrow and exultation. The antiestablishment theme of resistance to the death against an illegitimate tyrant provided a rich backdrop for Khomeini's revolutionary rhetoric, which whipped the crowds into a state of intense fervor.[1]

Negotiations between the opposition and the military government continued throughout the first week of Moharram, while the level of street violence steadily increased. Clandestine urban guerrilla bands began to operate much more openly, conducting hit-and-run attacks against police stations and even small military units. Harassment of Americans began to become commonplace. By December 8 the military government agreed to withdraw the ban on processions in return for pledges that the marches on Tasua and Ashura would be orderly and nonviolent.

Ambassador Zahedi and his hard-line military allies monitored these discussions closely, keeping Brzezinski informed by telephone. In the end, the hard-liners chose accommodation rather than provoke an all-out confrontation that would place severe strains on the loyalty of the army and that would give Khomeini the "torrents of blood" he seemed to welcome.

Is It Really the Left?

The situation in Iran was reviewed at a mini-SCC in the White House on December 5. David Aaron chaired the meeting, with George Ball sitting on his right. Robert Bowie of the CIA had returned from Tehran persuaded that the forces of the left were playing an important organizing and management role behind the scenes. George Ball wondered if it was not perhaps the work of the National Front, which was beginning to get itself organized. Henry Precht remarked that there was a tendency to underestimate the capacity of Khomeini and his religious followers to organize sophisticated opposition activities.

This inconclusive discussion about who was responsible for the impressive organizational feats being observed daily in Iran was part of a debate that ebbed and flowed in Washington throughout the course of the revolution. The answer seemed to depend far more on the attitude of the observer than on any hard evidence. Many old hands were conditioned to look for the hand of Moscow in any Third World revolutionary situation.

The case for such an interpretation in Iran was presented in some detail by a British journalist, Robert Moss, in an article entitled "Who's Meddling in Iran?"[2] Moss, who was described to me by a British diplomat as a "professional anti-Communist polemicist," reviewed the long-standing Soviet interest in Iran and detailed the many facilities available to the USSR for penetration of Iranian society and the revolutionary movement. In his view, since the Soviets had sufficient motive and adequate means, they *must* be guiding events in Iran. That view found a ready audience among many policy makers in the United States and elsewhere. Certainly the shah was a strong proponent of this explanation, as were most educated Iranians, who regarded the mullahs as incompetent. When I disputed this point with one of my colleagues, he dismissed my arguments with an impatient wave of the hand. "The Soviets are there," he insisted, "but they know how to cover their tracks. By the time you get proof, the Russians will be in control of Tehran."

Brzezinski did not use these words, but he reproduced the Moss article, circulated it to the president and other top policy makers, and cited it in policy meetings for weeks. Although Moss cited no real evidence and had no apparent qualifications as a specialist on Iran, his article attained the status of a major document in U.S. policy-making circles at a key moment. Moss stated explicitly what many in the government instinctively feared, and they seized on this statement as an expression of their own suspicions. It demonstrated the power of a well-timed bit of political propaganda in a crisis situation.

In retrospect it is clear that Moss was wrong. The pro-Soviet left, the religious left, the National Front and the merchant guilds of the bazaar all contributed in various ways to the revolutionary movement; but the central organizing force of the revolution, as Henry Precht suggested, was the religious network operating out of the mosques under the strategic control of Khomeini. The Iranian revolution, like other major revolutions before it, refused to conform to the conventional wisdom of the day, and contemporary analyses often had more to say about the prejudices and assumptions of the observer than about the new reality being created in the mosques and streets of Iran.

The December 5 mini-SCC also reviewed the problem of the U.S. community in Iran, which was finding itself increasingly beleaguered. Many U.S. companies in Iran were quietly weeding out dependents and unnecessary personnel and sending them home. The embassy was still opposed to such a policy for the official U.S. community out of fear that it would set off a panic exodus. The matter was brought to a head by a letter to the editors of the Washington *Star* from the wife of a U.S. military official in Tehran. She complained that dependents were being held hostage to U.S. policy in Iran, since they could leave Iran only at their own expense.

George Ball took advantage of this chance letter in much the same way that Brzezinski used the Moss article, arguing very strongly that some means should be found to reduce the size of the large U.S. official community. On this issue, Brzezinski and Sullivan for once found themselves in accord; both of them were worried that the Iranians would see such a reduction of U.S. presence as a fundamental shift in policy. However, once Ball had questioned the policy, he discovered a considerable body of support within the various Washington agencies whose personnel were threatened by the swirling turmoil in Iran. Robert Murray, the deputy assistant secretary for Near Eastern affairs in the Pentagon, suggested a voluntary program that would give official dependents the option of returning home for a paid holiday leave, and this policy was quietly adopted.

The Council of Notables

Finally, the December 5 meeting turned to consideration of U.S. options to end the growing impasse in Tehran. By chance, just at this moment David Aaron was called away from the meeting, and he asked George Ball to chair the remainder of the meeting in his absence. Thus, on his second full day in Washington on the Iranian crisis, Ball found himself in charge of what turned out to be one of the most far-reaching policy discussions to date. Although the participants were mostly of assistant-secretary level or lower, this provided a unique opportunity for Ball to try out some of his own ideas on a very knowledgeable group representing all the key Washington agencies. Responding like an old war horse who has caught the scent of battle, he launched into the fray.

As soon as Aaron left, Ball remarked that in his view, the United States could not ask the shah to form a new government. It would not be credible. Instead, he suggested, we should make an effort to produce a list of names of key individuals in Iran who were respected but not extremist. With such a list in hand we could suggest to the shah that a "Council of Notables" be convened to choose a government. Under such an arrangement the shah could remain, although he would obviously have to relinquish some power. The objective would be to provide a breathing spell during which the focus could be redirected toward the search for a political solution.

Assistant Secretary of State Harold Saunders immediately picked up on the suggestion as compatible with the ideas being raised by many of the moderate opposition figures who were in contact with the embassy in Tehran.[3] Clearly, the shah would exercise his own judgment in selecting such a council, and there were many unanswered questions about the actual exercise of power, particularly with regard to control of the military. Nevertheless, Ball's proposal was regarded as a useful starting point. After some discussion it was decided that each agency would prepare a list of possible names that might be raised with the shah, and the group would meet again in a few days to compare notes and possibly to draft new instructions to Sullivan.

Ball had been considering the idea of a Council of Notables from the time of my first meeting with him, and he had tentatively tried it out on several cabinet members during his meetings. The basic concept of an interim regime leading to a new government was very much alive at the time. It had been incorporated in a draft State Department policy paper Harold Saunders had sent to Ambassador Sullivan several days earlier. As indicated previously, the lower echelons of the State Department were having a difficult time getting a hearing for their views at the policy level. Ball's intervention was therefore a godsend to them. At last they had a senior figure who was receptive to their general approach and who appeared willing to carry it vigorously to the White House.[4]

At approximately the same time that the mini-SCC took place in the White House, Ambassador Sullivan was preparing a reply to Harold Saunders' draft policy paper. He noted that the shah's "game plan" was to weather the period of Ashura, relying on a mixture of firmness and moderation, then to attempt to form a coalition government that would be able to supervise elections for a new parliament. Sullivan did not think the plan had much prospect for success, given the army's apparent inability to cope with daily violence in the streets and the shah's apparent inability to forge an effective moderate coalition.

In this paper Saunders had also raised once again the possibility of a more active political role for the ambassador. Sullivan again demurred. All of the parties, he noted, would like to see the United States more actively engaged, but for all the wrong reasons. The shah would see the United States coming in as his ally to support his position; the moderate opposition would see the Americans as able to tell the shah some of the more candid truths that they hesitated to put to him directly; the military would see the United States either as a "stiffener" for the shah or as their own close companions in a new power equation; even Khomeini, Sullivan observed, might welcome U.S. participation if that would encourage the shah to abdicate. Sullivan feared that if the United States were so engaged, then the United States—rather than the shah, the armed forces, the Shi'i clergy or the bazaar—would become the focus of everyone's attention. An active U.S. intervention into the center of the negotiating process, he felt, would send a signal that America was prepared to accept some solution other than that being offered by the shah.

With that very substantial disclaimer, Sullivan then went on to outline the steps he would propose in the event U.S. policy changed to more active involvement. He would first wish to consult with the shah, make sure that the military was party to future discussions, consult with moderate oppositionists, and finally go to Qom himself to meet with some of the senior moderate clergy. If those contacts should open up real prospects, he observed, then the United States would have to consider the desirability of a direct approach to

Khomeini. Sullivan doubted that Khomeini would be prepared to accept an accommodation even if the shah agreed.

Saunders had asked Sullivan for his candid evaluation of the shah's capacity to lead. "I see nothing wrong with his physical capabilities," Sullivan responded. "He is a strong man who keeps himself in good condition. His psychic condition is something else. He has rationalized himself into passivity. He lacks self-confidence, but he remains stubborn. If, after Ashura, he shows no better talent for political compromise than heretofore, it may prove very difficult to help him save himself." Sullivan believed that the shah would have roughly until the beginning of January to show some progress. Otherwise "some more dramatic move would be necessary to prevent the country from chaotic collapse."

Even before this message had been received in Washington, Saunders had sent off another message to Sullivan outlining George Ball's ideas about a Council of Notables. Sullivan replied with a very negative assessment on December 7. He did not believe the shah would accept it. Moreover, Sullivan believed that any large grouping, in the existing emotional climate, would quickly be stampeded into calling for the shah's abdication. "In short," he concluded, "I feel we should avoid suggestions which involve relatively large, uncontrollable groupings unless we are preparing a posture which is designed to dissipate the locus of responsibility for actions which will lead to the early abdication of the shah. I assume that is not our purpose."

On this issue, as in the case of the withdrawal of U.S. dependents, Sullivan and Brzezinski found themselves unwitting allies. Brzezinski did not believe that the Iranian revolution could be stopped by a coalition of moderate centrists or a conclave of notables. He viewed such proposals as exercises in wishful thinking whose practical effect would be to shove aside the monarchy, undermine institutions of authority and start a slide to the left, as had been the case with Kerensky's ill-fated government during the Russian Revolution. Faced with George Ball's unanticipated campaign in favor of an interim council to assume many of the shah's powers, Brzezinski now found himself citing Sullivan's telegrams as evidence that such a scheme was unworkable. In the end, Brzezinski in Washington and Sullivan in Tehran, operating quite independently, succeeded in blocking the Ball proposal, although, as we shall see, it was a very close thing.

A Costly Slip

A major new factor was introduced into the U.S.-Iranian relationship on the morning of December 7. On that morning President Carter held one of a series of breakfast meetings with reporters. President Carter excelled in these small group meetings, not only because of his personal charm and his easy mastery of an array of complex issues, but also because he conveyed a sense of disarming candor. The candor was genuine, not contrived, and it often served him well. But presidential candor has its risks, as every administration can attest, for even the most casual remark by the president of the United States can have unexpected policy implications.

In answer to a question, President Carter gave a concise summary of the strategic importance of Iran in U.S. policy toward the Middle East and the Persian Gulf. He was then asked whether he thought the shah could survive the present revolutionary turmoil, and he replied:

> I don't know. I hope so. This is something that is in the hands of the people of Iran. We have never had any intention and don't have any intention of trying to intercede in the internal political affairs of Iran. We primarily want an absence of violence and bloodshed, and stability. We personally prefer that the shah maintain a major role in the government, but that is a decision for the Iranian people to make.

There is no reason to doubt that this was an honest reading of the president's mind as Iran approached the critical moment of Ashura. No one, including the shah, could be sure that the monarchy would survive the coming demonstrations. But it was the wrong signal for the president to send at that critical moment.

The media understandably seized on the president's expression of doubt that the shah would survive, and the story created a sensation. The following morning Ambassador Sullivan reported, after a meeting with former Prime Minister Ali Amini, who had been acting as an intermediary between the shah and the opposition, that the shah interpreted President Carter's remarks as calling for a popular referendum on the fate of the monarchy and that the remarks had plunged him into a deep depression. As luck would have it, these offhand remarks happened to coincide with the departure on "holiday" of large numbers of U.S. official dependents. The Iranians concluded that the two events were linked and that they signaled a dramatic shift in the U.S. position with regard to the shah.

The State Department immediately issued a "clarification" denying any change of U.S. policy toward Iran. Brzezinski telephoned Zahedi to make the same point. Several days later President Carter took advantage of another public occasion to reiterate strongly his support for the shah, but the damage had been done. Even years later, this statement would be identified by many as the key turning point in U.S. policy, when it was decided to "dump" the shah. The fact that no such decision was taken—then or later—was less important than the impression created by the unguarded comment.

U.S. Public Opinion and Khomeini

The marches of Tasua and Ashura were massive, as expected, but relatively free of violence. The negotiations between the military authorities and the opposition had successfully avoided a bloody showdown in Tehran, although demonstrations got out of hand in Isfahan. The Khomeini forces regarded the marches as a street referendum against the monarchy, and their claims were buttressed not only by the sheer numbers of participants but also by the extraordinary discipline they demonstrated at a time of high religious and political emotion. Concurrently, there were signs of a breakdown of discipline within the military. On Ashura, two enlisted men of the hand-picked Imperial Guard attacked the officers' mess with automatic weapons, killing twelve officers and wounding up to fifty others before they were overcome.

On December 12, the day after Ashura, Ambassador Sullivan met with the shah. The shah briefly reviewed the situation, concluding that the marches indicated that Khomeini commanded enormous power. In the weeks before Ashura, he said, he had been told that the people were getting tired of Khomeini, but this had been disproved by the banners and slogans, all of which seemed to name Khomeini as the only leader.

The shah was continuing his efforts to develop a compromise solution. He had recently talked with National Front members Gholam Hossein Sadiqi and Shapour Bakhtiar, he said, and he was scheduled to meet in the next few days with Karim Sanjabi, the National Front leader who had recently been released from prison. However, he expected Sanjabi to insist on the shah's departure, since that was Khomeini's demand.

The shah saw three options: one, to persevere with the effort to form a national coalition; two, to surrender to the opposition demands and leave the country to chaos and a regency council; and three, to form a military junta that would apply an "iron fist" policy. His key military officers were urging the latter. The shah believed that a surrender to Khomeini would mean disintegration, but he also felt that an iron-fist policy "could never be executed by a king." Moreover, if he turned the task over to a military junta, its members would probably soon begin to have their own coups and countercoups that would also lead to disintegration. It was apparent from his comments that the shah did not believe any of these three options provided a realistic or acceptable basis for a solution.

Sullivan urged the shah to continue with his negotiations and even suggested that he might form a Council of Notables that could act as a guarantor for whatever agreement was reached with the opposition politicians. This suggestion was a bit surprising in view of Sullivan's expressed opposition to the concept only a few days earlier. The shah's reaction to the idea was not reported.

On the same evening, the long-delayed encounter between Washington officials and Ibrahim Yazdi, Khomeini's representative in the United States, finally occurred. Henry Precht and Yazdi appeared together for a televised discussion of Iran. After the program the panelists had dinner together. Yazdi denied that Khomeini had called for "torrents of blood" and stressed the peaceful nature of the Ashura demonstrations. He also denied that Khomeini had expected the shah to fall on Ashura, despite statements that suggested the opposite.

Yazdi painted a rosy picture of what would happen if and when the shah departed. At that time, he said, Khomeini would designate a cabinet that would serve as a transitional government until elections could produce a lasting government. Elections would be absolutely free. The Islamic Republic, he insisted, would enjoy full freedom of speech and the press, including the right to attack Islam. In foreign relations they would seek good ties with all countries. He expressed confidence in the support of the army and claimed that a number of officers had secretly come to visit Khomeini. He dismissed the importance of Sanjabi and regarded the negotiations with the shah about a compromise government as unrealistic.

Yazdi had returned from Paris to the United States for a series of public appearances intended to demonstrate that Americans had nothing to fear from the Khomeini regime. His themes were simple. The revolution was peaceable, employing the techniques of nonviolence against the murderous assaults of the shah's forces. The objectives of an Islamic republic, once the shah was gone, were fully compatible with U.S. ideals of personal freedom and human rights. Iran was in no danger of being taken over by Communist elements, and an Islamic republic would not be interested in aligning itself with the Soviet Union. On the contrary, nothing would prevent the continuation of mutually satisfactory relations with the United States. Since the fall of the shah was now virtually certain, he argued, the United States should give up its fruitless policy of support for his regime and make peace with the new revolutionary leaders who were about to take over.

These reassuring words inevitably found a wide audience in the United States. Many Americans were uncomfortable in alliance with a monarch who was widely viewed as autocratic, repressive and infatuated with military technology at the expense of social progress. Yazdi's message, with its undertones recalling the U.S. civil rights movement and the anti-war protests of the 1960s, was perfectly pitched to appeal to a wide spectrum of U.S. opinion. It was picked up by activists and many U.S. specialists on Iran, some of whom had by now made pilgrimages to Nauphle-le-Château to meet with Khomeini and to discuss the aims of the revolution with Western-educated aides such as Bani-Sadr, Ghotbzadeh and Yazdi. Many came away convinced that Khomeini was being unfairly maligned in the West and that the revolution offered the best hope in fifty years for the triumph of human rights and free political expression in Iran.

James Bill, the Iranian expert from the University of Texas who had first warned me about the brewing troubles, wrote an important article in early December 1978 that examined the origins of the revolution and addressed policy options for the United States.[5] His underlying assumptions were plainly visible. The clergy, he said, were "the guardians of social justice and morality" in Iranian society. They were calling for the "restoration of the [liberal, Western-inspired] constitution of 1906" (no mention of an Islamic republic). The dominant element in the revolution and in Iranian political life was the "professional middle class," which, implicitly, shared many Western values. "The backbone of the new political system could be provided by the National Front." These "progressive-nationalist" leaders would require the "tacit support" of the clergy, but the clergy "would never participate directly in the formal governmental structure." The United States "need not fear that a future government in Iran will necessarily be antithetical to American interests."

The appeal of such an analysis was powerful. The United States, it seemed to say, could have its cake and eat it too. If only we would disengage ourselves from the evils of the shah's rule, we could have a progressive, nationalist regime run by moderate, middle-class professionals whose respect for individual freedoms and human rights was closer to U.S. values than the manipulative and repressive rule of the shah. The popularity of this line was not restricted to human rights activists and the academic community. As we shall see, it also came to be accepted by many within the U.S. government, particularly as alternative political options receded or became too costly.

Unfortunately, this analysis almost studiously overlooked the desperate weakness of the National Front, the dominant role of the mosques in orchestrating the revolutionary activity, the religious fundamentalism of the urban dispossessed who had been stirred into action, and—inexcusably—Khomeini's own writings that spelled out his unique vision of an Islamic republic.

It is all too human to imagine that the alternative to an unpleasant situation will somehow be an improvement, and the emergence of a rose-colored-glasses school of thought about the Iranian revolution was probably inevitable. However, by the time of the shah's departure and Khomeini's triumphal return, the views of some "experts" had solidified into a body of rosy doctrine which, in its determined rejection of unpleasant realities, could only be compared with the institutional myopia of the U.S. government in persuading itself of the "stability" of the shah in the years immediately prior to the revolution.

The Schlesinger Initiative

During the critical days of Tasua and Ashura, two separate policy strands had been developing in Washington. George Ball had completed his whirlwind of consultations and was putting the finishing touches on his report to the president. The Special Coordination Committee was scheduled to review his findings on December 13. At the same time James Schlesinger, the former director of the CIA and secretary of defense, now secretary of energy in the Carter administration, had been pursuing his own course.

Schlesinger had come to know the shah well in the mid-1970s, when he attempted to introduce some order into the shah's military planning and procurement. He did not share Henry Kissinger's view of the shah as a great strategic thinker, but he was intensely aware of the catastrophic consequences for U.S. strategic interests if the shah should fall. Throughout 1978, Schlesinger had been totally preoccupied with the problems of trying to shepherd complex and controversial energy legislation through the Congress. The vote did not come until mid-October. On November 6, when the shah announced his martial-law government, Schlesinger was in China. He was so alarmed at the news that he considered flying on directly to Tehran to talk to the shah.

When he returned to Washington for the signing of the energy bill, he began a one-man lobbying effort with President Carter's closest associates: Hamilton Jordan, Jody Powell, Charles Kirbo and others. His objective was twofold. First, he wanted to alert them to the strategic implications for the United States if the shah's regime should collapse. As he put it, "The linchpin of the Northern Tier [Turkey, Iran, Pakistan] would be removed." He also stressed to the president's men that such an event would be a political as well as strategic disaster. He also met privately with Brzezinski, who shared his views totally, and with Brzezinski's support began to introduce himself into the policy-making machinery.

Schlesinger believed it was essential for someone with great credibility to go to Iran to talk to the shah. The object of such a visit would be to assure him of unflagging U.S. support and to urge him to take more decisive action. Because of his past acquaintance with the shah, his experience in both defense and intelligence, and his association with the Nixon administration, Schlesinger believed, with considerable justification, that he was a logical choice for the assignment. However, in policy meetings he confined himself to recommending that either he or Brzezinski undertake such a mission.

Schlesinger was at a considerable disadvantage in this process. He had not followed the Iranian situation in detail over the previous months, and he did not see the highly restricted message reporting from Tehran on a regular basis. He had no staff to act as his eyes and ears in a dynamic and volatile set of circumstances, and he participated in policy meetings only on a sporadic basis. He was unaware of much of what had happened before he introduced himself into the process. Under the circumstances, it is not surprising that he would later remark that this period was the most frustrating of all his time in government. He had very strong feelings about the need for an active U.S. policy, but he was not well positioned to influence the process.

The concept of using a high-level emissary was, of course, nothing new. Brzezinski's telephone call in early November to the shah, Brzezinski's personal emissary shortly thereafter, the visits of various senior U.S. officials, and the presence of Ardeshir Zahedi in Tehran had all been variations on that theme, and none of them had significantly altered the shah's Hamlet-like approach to his personal and political dilemma. However, there was a dearth of fresh policy ideas as Moharram approached, and Schlesinger's proposal that either he or Brzezinski go to Tehran was presented to President Carter for consideration.

The Ball Report

On Wednesday afternoon, December 13, Brzezinski chaired a meeting of the SCC to review the results of George Ball's ten-day mission to Washington.

Secretary Vance was in the Middle East and was represented by his deputy, Warren Christopher. Otherwise, the representation was all cabinet level: Defense Secretary Harold Brown and his deputy, Charles Duncan; Treasury Secretary Blumenthal; Director of Central Intelligence Turner; the chairman of the Joint Chiefs of Staff; and Secretary of Energy James Schlesinger; as well as George Ball, David Aaron and myself as note taker. Brzezinski opened the meeting by inviting George Ball to summarize the conclusions of his report.

Ball said the report had a very simple thesis: the shah was irreparably damaged by the events of recent weeks. The belief that he could be restored to his previous position without the army's taking repressive measures was simply not feasible. However, it was useful to support the continued presence of the shah, since he had the backing of the army and because withdrawal of U.S. support would seriously affect our relations with other important regional states, particularly Saudi Arabia. There was, he commented, no easy or risk-free way to deal with the situation, which was working up to an ultimate collision. There was doubt that the army could hold together. Some cracks had already appeared.

One alternative, Ball observed, would be to work out a transfer of power, convincing the shah to become a constitutional monarch within the existing meaning of the constitution. This also had its risks, since a successor government would have anti-American aspects to it, though probably less than there would be later on if nothing was done. Ball said it was his feeling that we should make it clear to the shah that we were as interested as he in preserving the monarchy, but that the minimum required would be a transfer of power in a constitutional framework.

Ball was not persuaded that the National Front's efforts to put together a Regency Council would work, since it would require abdication. He suspected, however, that the shah would accept a constitutional role if that was the choice. The continual bucking up of the shah was all right for public policy, but in private we should be tough. There might be some advantage in placing a group between the shah and a new government. To that end, some names had been collected of respected individuals who might be able to perform such a function if they were given real authority.

Harold Brown wondered if the list included any military men. Ball said that it did, but that he did not see an army man as the future prime minister, since that would connote a military government. Brzezinski wondered what would be wrong with that. Ball replied that in his view a military government would only prolong the uproar and that continued repression would lead to civil war and the danger of Soviet intervention. If the various individuals chosen for a Council of Notables could not work together, his second choice would be a Regency Council. He thought that if the United States moved quickly, it could have considerable influence in shaping a relatively moderate government. The longer we waited, the harder it would be.

Brzezinski said that we should not overlook the fact that Iran had its own traditions. It was not South Vietnam. We should carefully pick the outcome we would prefer; however, we did not know enough about the situation to be sure which was correct. Brzezinski believed that it would be useful to put in motion a process of political change, but he was not confident that the outcome proposed in the paper was necessarily the right one.

Perhaps others were preferable, Brzezinski suggested, such as a military government that became progressively "civilianized," as in the case of Turkey or Brazil. It would also be possible, for example, for a Council of Notables to be created to select civilian members to enter the existing government. Harold Brown added that the extent, tone and pace of political change should not be up to the United States; he was also concerned that too rapid a move toward a civilian regime would risk radicalizing and splitting the Iranian military. Ball responded that, in his proposal, the shah would remain as commander in chief, and he thought the shah would best be able to obtain the kind of agreement necessary from the military commanders.

Brzezinski commented that, in his view, Ball was asking for the shah to hand over power to the opposition. He thought the shah was willing to compromise some, but that was more than he had in mind. Ball said he believed that a dramatic move by the shah was necessary to change the political situation. Brzezinski felt that it was necessary to move in stages.

Warren Christopher thought that there was a very narrow period of time available for some kind of action, not more than two weeks. He felt that at this point the shah had less than a fifty-fifty chance of survival.

Brzezinski said that he sensed in the group no agreement about how far or how fast the United States should go in pressing for fundamental political changes in Iran. Secretary Schlesinger remarked that it was not wise to push things to a confrontation at this point. Ball responded that, in his view, time was running out; the shah had to re-establish some degree of trust with the people if he was to continue as monarch.

The discussion terminated on that ambiguous note and the meeting turned to a variety of other issues. A memorandum was prepared for President Carter that evening, summarizing the key judgments and points of disagreement.

George Ball met with President Carter the following afternoon to present his report and his recommendations.[6] By the time of the meeting, Carter had read Ball's report and the summary of the SCC meeting the previous day. Carter indicated that he was not prepared to "tell another head of state what to do," and while he agreed with much of the report, he did not fully accept its recommendations. The president mentioned that he intended to send Brzezinski to Tehran, an idea that Ball vigorously (and successfully) opposed. That evening George Ball left Washington and had no further direct involvement with policy developments.

In his memoirs Ball concludes that he had relatively little effect on the course of U.S. policy toward Iran. It is true that his intervention resulted in no dramatic shift of policy. Nevertheless, his presence at a critical moment may have had more effect than he realized. His forthright advocacy of a policy permitting U.S. dependents to leave Iran helped break a policy impasse. Although that decision was not without its costs, it contributed to the reduction in size of the very large U.S. community in Iran before Ashura and thereafter. With the exception of one assassination, no U.S. lives were lost in the Iranian revolution.

George Ball also served to introduce some fresh policy ideas into the highest levels in Washington. His concept of a Council of Notables probably came too late to change a rapidly deteriorating situation in Iran. Nevertheless, he provided a focal point for some original thinking about Iranian politics. In fact, as a result of Vance's preoccupation with other matters, George Ball during his brief appearance functioned almost as a surrogate secretary of state. He actively consulted with all levels of the bureaucracy and stimulated the first formal, high-level assessment of U.S. policy options in Iran since early November.

Questions for the Shah

Despite the inconclusive nature of the December 13 SCC meeting, it resulted in an illuminating exchange with the shah of which Ball was unaware. President Carter was not prepared to tell the shah how to run his own country. On the other hand, after listening to Ball, he was persuaded of the urgency of the situation and the need to sound out the shah on a more active U.S. role. As a result, on Saturday, December 16, a very private message was prepared and sent to Tehran for the ambassador's eyes only, posing a set of pointed questions to be raised with the shah.

In the message President Carter asked Sullivan to see the shah at the earliest opportunity and tell him that the president had continued to follow events in Iran with deep concern in the context of U.S. support for the shah and his courageous effort to restore peace and stability. It requested the shah's own considered judgment on a number of important questions to assist President Carter to offer helpful suggestions or comments. Several of the questions, which covered the gamut of major issues in Iran (economic, political and military), were specifically generated by Ball's report. In addition, Sullivan was provided with a list of twenty-one names compiled from the dossiers assembled during Ball's visit. Whether or not to present this list was left to Sullivan's discretion, depending on the shah's reaction.

Sullivan met with the shah on December 18, and relayed the president's questions. Among other things, the shah said he hoped to be able to replace the current government with a government of national unity within two weeks. He had met the day before with Gholam Hossein Sadiqi,[7] who had accepted the task of forming such a government. Both he and Sadiqi wished to return the military to its normal functions. The shah said he envisaged a purely constitutional role for himself. He would continue to be commander in chief of the armed forces, but budget authority would have to be "worked out" with particular attention to the diminished revenues of the state.

The shah insisted that the United States could not be helpful in the process of negotiating with the opposition beyond the limited role being played at the present time. He believed that U.S. statements to members of the opposition had had a constructive effect, and he thought that was all any outsider could do. If the United States entered into negotiations as a mediator, it would be seen as preparing something less than a constitutional role for the monarch. If the constitution was to be abandoned, the future would be "full of surprises."

The shah recognized that Sadiqi would have difficulty putting a cabinet together because most opposition politicians did not dare offend Khomeini. There was a real risk that Sadiqi would fail, in which case the shah would probably turn to Shapour Bakhtiar.[8] If both should fail, he was considering former Prime Minister Ali Amini's proposal for the creation of a Regency Council that would be formed while he was still in the country, rather than leave the country as Sanjabi had proposed. He said he would rather quit than be "clipped like a bird and put in a cage."

Sullivan commented that the shah seemed well informed about current economic developments and gave the impression of more active interest in governmental affairs than had recently been the case. In general, Sullivan remarked, the shah seemed less depressed and more confident.

In view of the shah's responses to the president's questions, Sullivan chose not to mention the list of possible names (which he personally dismissed as composed of individuals "who would not be found in the same room with each other"). This judgment was welcomed in the White House by Brzezinski, and it sounded the death knell for George Ball's concept of a Council of Notables.

The shah told Sullivan that he suspected the president's questions were the result of George Ball's report, and reading between the lines, he detected an inclination toward a more active U.S. role in internal Iranian politics. What advice, he asked Sullivan, would the ambassador give him personally if that was the case? "Steady nerves," Sullivan replied. The shah reportedly thought that was good advice and asked the ambassador to convey the same to Washington.

In the interest of snappy message titles, this report could appropriately have been labeled "What—Me Worry?" Iran was in truly desperate straits as this conversation took place. The mass demonstrations of Ashura had occurred only a week before, and a nationwide general strike was in progress as the shah and the ambassador spoke. There was disturbing new evidence of a breakdown in military discipline, including growing reports of sabotage on military bases. At one base a senior military officer had confided to his U.S. counterpart that "The shah must go." At the same time, pro-shah military commanders were becoming openly rebellious. In the wake of the Ashura marches, when the Azhari military government was stressing moderation, a number of local commanders had launched their own pro-shah demonstrations, sweeping through cities such as Isfahan smashing windows, attacking hospitals, forcing the population to shout pro-shah slogans, and shooting anyone who got in their way.

In this context, the shah's essentially upbeat assessment of the situation had a dreamlike air of unreality. The time was long past when manipulation and clever political maneuver could save the day. Yet the shah, in his negotiations with Sadiqi, was bargaining on the margins, making tactical concessions as necessary to bring Sadiqi into the process but stopping short of commitments that would permit Sadiqi to form a credible government. Given the shah's own political background and his performance throughout the crisis, this perhaps should have come as no surprise. But it was disappointing to find the U.S. ambassador apparently going along for the ride.

On three occasions in seven weeks, Washington had raised with Ambassador Sullivan the possibility of a more active U.S. role in attempting to halt the political deterioration. In each case he had flatly rejected the idea. Reading this latest message, despite my normal immunity to conspiracy theories, I was forced to ask myself whether Sullivan, in line with his scenario outlined in early November, was saving all of his efforts for a last-second deal between the opposition and the military *after* the shah was finished. In the meantime, he was prepared to wait and watch as the shah went down for the third time.

A Personal Intervention

On Thursday afternoon, December 21, all of the policy concerns of the past weeks came to a personal climax for me. A Christmas party was going on in the administrative offices across the hall, and I was preparing to join it when I learned from the Situation Room that an urgent message had been received.

Ambassador Sullivan had just been informed that General Azhari had been relieved of his military command (though he remained as prime minister), and Sullivan had been asked to meet with the shah at noon the following day. We were aware that Azhari had suffered a mild heart attack and had been confined to bed for several days. It appeared that a fundamental reshuffling might be under way, and Sullivan should be equipped with instructions for his meeting with the shah the following day. I was convinced that the last act of the drama was beginning.

I took the message across the hall, where Brzezinski had joined other staff members for the party, and—much to the annoyance of several of my colleagues—I buttonholed Brzezinski in a corner of the room to show him the cable and express my own view that we were at a critical turning point. He listened, then asked me to put my views in writing.

I went back to my desk and dashed off a rough memo that I delivered to Brzezinski less than an hour later. My central thesis was that unless an effective government was established in Iran by the first week in January, "the shah and his dynasty are going to be swept away." I did not believe that the negotiations with Sadiqi would succeed in forming such a government, and I recommended that we inform the shah that these talks were only letting precious days slip away at a time when there was no time left. The only chance to avoid a complete breakdown of order would, in my view, be for the shah to make a dramatic announcement to the nation, proclaiming an immediate return to the constitution of 1906 and the supplementary law of 1907, which had spelled out a purely constitutional role for the monarch and provided for Islamic review of the legislative process. At the same time, the shah should call on a recognized leader of the opposition to form a government of national salvation. The announcement should stress the progressive deterioration of the economic situation and the threat posed to every Iranian citizen if chaos should prevail.

I did not think that a transition to a harshly repressive military regime would work. First, I believed that the Iranian military was itself too fragile to sustain such a policy for any prolonged period of time without an accompanying political solution. Second, I believed that a policy of simple repression would prove impossible for the United States to support for any length of time unless it was accompanied by a new political framework. Any policy adopted by the shah would have to be supported by a firm determination to maintain order; however, repression alone, without significant political change, offered no answer.

The constitution of 1906, which the shah and his father had systematically subverted, was widely regarded as an acceptable political goal by much of the opposition. It provided for constraints on the power of the monarch that the shah might be reluctant to accept, but it had the benefits of historical legitimacy and the undeniable advantage that virtually any other possible outcome would be worse for the monarchy.

This proposal, like a number of other suggestions during the crisis, may have come too late to have any real prospect of stemming the tide. However, I felt very strongly that this was the last clear chance to avoid a total collapse of order in Iran, and I argued heatedly with Brzezinski that the shah would go on frittering away opportunities unless the United States pressed him hard. The condition for continued U.S. support should be a fundamental political change toward a moderate constitutional solution.

Brzezinski listened to me carefully and with a touch of surprise at my uncharacteristic display of emotion. By this time—the end of 1978—I was well aware that Brzezinski had little respect for yes men. He much preferred someone who would stoutly defend his own convictions, even if those were contrary to his own. Nevertheless, I did not feel entirely comfortable adopting a strong advocacy role. My twenty years as a military officer had imbued in me a strong sense of the importance of institutional and personal loyalty, as well as the traditional view deeply ingrained in U.S. values that the military should remain aloof from policy matters. My position on the NSC staff rendered my inhibitions pointless, even counterproductive. Still, in addition to the perfectly natural apprehensions associated with picking an argument with one's boss, this sudden leap into advocacy had for me the added discomfort of violating a cultural taboo.

Although I did not know it at the time, a similar personal drama was being played out almost simultaneously at the Department of State. On December 19, Henry Precht decided it was finally time to put his career on the line with a formal statement of his views on our Iranian policy. In a six-page memorandum to Harold Saunders, Precht argued that there was no longer more than a marginal chance that the shah would survive, and he spelled out a series of proposed steps the United States could take to preserve its interests in the transition to a "post-shah future in Iran."

He sent this memorandum not only to Saunders but also to Ambassador Sullivan in Tehran, with a personal letter explaining his views. Precht knew that he was bucking the tide of official policy, and he was aware of the dangers for his own career. After unburdening himself of his frustrations and concerns, he remarked to Sullivan, "I have probably confided more than I should to a piece of paper, but I doubt I have much of a future anyway."

In this poignant letter Precht noted that he had held these thoughts for a long time, "but as we come nearer to the day of investigations, I have decided to put a few of them down on paper. You may not agree with my outlook or analysis," he wrote to Ambassador Sullivan, "but the task seems to me to be one of finding a graceful exit for the shah while gaining a fair amount of credit in doing so for the U.S." Precht did not believe that the United States ought to name ministers to a new Iranian cabinet, but he thought U.S. "midwifery" could be very active. He favored convoking a balanced six-to eight-man committee of notables to work out a solution. The U.S. government, he thought, should back the recommendations of this group, whether they proposed "a constitutional monarchy or a regency substitute."

There are several remarkable elements of this letter and memorandum. The first is that Henry Precht, the country director for Iran in the State Department, was unaware that George Ball's Council of Notables idea had already been floated to Sullivan and that he had rejected it. This is a measure of the degree to which the circle of information had contracted. Critical policy messages were no longer being distributed below the level of the assistant secretary.

Second, despite Henry Precht's verbal criticism of continued U.S. support for the shah, which was quite well known throughout the policy community and which he had presumably expressed directly to Brzezinski several weeks earlier,[9] Precht had waited until December 19 to put his thoughts on paper. Moreover, he wrote the memorandum and letter with a fatalistic sense of sealing his own doom. This fact, more than any other in the history of the crisis, demonstrates the overwhelming reluctance of officials at all levels to be perceived as backing away from support of the shah. The U.S. relationship with the shah was so deeply ingrained in the minds and policies of everyone responsible that even a carefully reasoned expression of doubt was regarded as a heresy that could destroy a career—hence the immense reluctance to "make the call" by proclaiming the shah irreparably wounded.

A third remarkable aspect of this letter and memorandum was the fact that Precht clearly expected Ambassador Sullivan not to agree with his "outlook or analysis." Despite months of messages, memos and telephone conversations, Precht was as uncertain as the White House about Sullivan's attitudes toward the shah and the prospects for his survival.

Finally, the sheer coincidence of Precht's letter of December 19 and my own impassioned intervention with Brzezinski two days later deserves mention. Henry Precht and I were the two most senior policy analysts on Iran—he at the State Department, and I at the White House. Quite independently and almost simultaneously, we both chose to argue for a substantial change in U.S. policy, recognizing that our actions could destroy our careers. Ironically, I learned of Precht's intervention only years later, after President Carter had left the White House. Precht, I am sure, was equally unaware of my actions. Communication between the White House and State Department on such "internal" matters had long since ceased.

Although this episode had great emotional importance for me (and presumably for Henry Precht), it had no visible effect on policy. On the contrary, both recommendations were simply ignored. Late on the night of December 21 a message was sent to Sullivan from the acting secretary of state (Vance was in the Middle East) telling the ambassador to maintain the position of continued U.S. support for the shah's efforts to re-establish order, to convey U.S. concern that continued political uncertainty would result in demoralization of the army, and to report any indication that the shah was moving to adopt an iron-fist policy.

Sullivan met for an hour with the shah on December 22. The shah, who had just seen Zahedi, downplayed the importance of Azhari's removal as military chief of staff, claiming disingenuously that the constitution did not permit him to be prime minister and chief of staff simultaneously. On the political situation, the shah said that Sadiqi was to produce a cabinet list by December 25. He thought Sadiqi had only a limited chance to restore stability, and the shah anticipated that martial law would have to be imposed and the military take things in hand. If Sadiqi could be installed, the shah would "take a well deserved vacation," possibly aboard the imperial yacht in the Persian Gulf. If Sadiqi succeeded in restoring order, well and good; if he did not, the shah implied it would be up to the military to take over. If Sadiqi failed to produce a cabinet, the shah indicated that he would probably give up further political efforts and settle in for a long battle of attrition, with Azhari continuing as prime minister. Sullivan reported that the shah looked more resolute and talked more defiantly than he had for months.

Late that same night the State Department sent a further message to Sullivan asking him to inform the shah that Washington believed that the shah's continued presence in Tehran would enhance the chances of success for whatever government Sadiqi might be able to form, as well as lending legitimacy and moderation to whatever might follow in the event he failed. During this period, there were increasing reports of desertions throughout the Iranian military. An army division in Mashhad totally broke down, and the commander of the unit had to be replaced.

Newsom's Working Groups

On the day after Christmas, Secretary of State Vance, recently returned from the Middle East, held a staff meeting to consider U.S. Iranian policy. He concluded that the Department of State had not been giving sufficiently sustained and high-level attention to the issue. He directed David Newsom, the undersecretary of state for political affairs and the third ranking official in the department, to establish a new working group to deal with day-to-day problems such as the safety of U.S. citizens, as well as addressing the longer-range problems of the political future. The first meeting of the group was held that same afternoon.

The need for systematic coordination between the various government agencies was clear. The progressive deterioration in Iran required adjustments and mundane decisions on energy, commerce and personnel matters almost on a daily basis, quite apart from considerations of high policy; and there was no framework for relating these decisions to overall U.S. policy. The mini-SCC was originally intended to deal with these problems, but it had met only sporadically and had concerned itself mainly with larger security and policy issues.

However, at this advanced stage of the crisis, the establishment of a new coordinating structure entailed some very special problems. If the working group was to have any significant effect, it would have to be restricted to a small group of individuals who were intimately familiar with the evolving situation in Iran and who could speak freely and frankly with one another. Unfortunately, by the end of December, contradictory leaks and comments to the media by "informed sources" had degenerated into a virtual torrent. Every senior official was convinced that the leaks originated in other departments or among individuals opposed to their own policy views; consequently, each official tended to keep his own views to himself and to confine his own policy consideration to the smallest circle of trusted advisers. Similarly, distribution of sensitive policy messages had been severely restricted, and each agency had begun to rely increasingly on its own "back channel" communications. This had evolved to a point where literally no one in the government could be entirely certain he was seeing the whole picture.

In this atmosphere of suspicion—if not paranoia—the Department of State faced some difficult procedural problems in attempting to launch a new coordinating body. The traditional process for managing a policy issue in the State Department was for one bureau to take the lead in framing a paper, then to coordinate it with all other elements that had a substantive interest. In the case of Iran, where the policy ramifications cut across the entire spectrum of U.S. interests, there was scarcely an office that could not argue that it had a direct interest in the problem. Moreover, since the message traffic was being restricted to such a small group, there was irresistible curiosity to find out what was actually going on. Although Secretary Vance and his key advisers were well aware of the need for security, they were either unable or unwilling to deny their colleagues access to these meetings.

When I arrived for the first meeting in the large conference room in the State Department Operations Center, I found at least twenty officials assembled, including some I had never seen before in my life. From the first moments it became obvious that most of the people in the room had very little acquaintance with recent policy developments and intended to use the meeting as a briefing session to satisfy their own curiosity. I immediately concluded that nothing very significant was likely to come of this group, and I confined my role as the "White House representative" to listening and uttering only the most bland generalities. My fears were not exaggerated. Almost from the first day, the Washington *Post* began carrying such detailed reports on the meetings that I remarked jokingly to Hal Saunders that it saved me the trouble of taking notes.

By the third meeting, as word got around, there were representatives of twelve different State Department bureaus, in addition to officials of eight other agencies. David Newsom, surveying the overflow crowd in the Operations Center conference room, opened the meeting with the wry comment that "We may have to hold our next meeting in the State Department auditorium."

Not surprisingly, there was no next meeting. Instead, Newsom appointed five subcommittees to examine various aspects of the issue. These committees, which quickly assumed the function of technical adjuncts to the cabinet-level meetings of the SCC, met regularly and were quite helpful in dealing with the many complex issues that arose over the next eight weeks or so. Although Brzezinski had originally feared that the working group was an attempt to shift the locus of policy making away from the White House to the State Department, that concern gradually faded as the value of the committee system became apparent.

The Shah Turns to Bakhtiar

Sullivan again met with the shah on December 26 for a "tense, pregnant" audience. Sadiqi had reportedly located seven or eight prospective ministers but had told the shah he needed up to six weeks to form a government. Sullivan exclaimed that Sadiqi was badly informed if he thought he had six weeks. The shah said that his options seemed to have narrowed to two: either surrender or apply the iron fist.

He repeated his conviction that, as a king, he could not preside over a bloodletting among his own people. The shah said he was not sure that General Azhari had the physical stamina to act after his recent heart attack, and he wondered aloud whether Iranian troops would be willing to execute a harsh policy. What did the United States want him to do? the shah asked. Sullivan repeated Washington's assurances that the United States fully supported the shah's efforts to restore order and stability. The shah asked if he was being advised to use the iron fist even if that meant widespread bloodshed and even if it might fail to restore law and order. Sullivan replied that if the shah was trying to get the United States to assume responsibility for his actions, he doubted that he would ever get such an instruction from Washington. "You are the shah," Sullivan observed, "and you must take the decision as well as the responsibility."

As Sullivan returned to the embassy to prepare his report on this fateful conversation, the city was "echoing the sounds of gunfire as troops fire into the air to break up swirling groups of demonstrators which form and re-form . . ." On the following day, at the urgent request of the palace, the U.S. consulate in Tehran issued visas to the Queen Mother and her entourage, who listed their destination as Los Angeles.

Brzezinski called a meeting of the SCC on December 27 to review policy in light of Sullivan's latest meeting with the shah. In preparation for the meeting, I wrote still another lengthy analysis of the situation, stressing that, in my view, the policy choices of a harsh military regime and political movement were not mutually exclusive. "If we are to back the shah in a series of repressive moves to restore law and order," I wrote, "it should be with the clear understanding that repression is no substitute for political concessions on his part, leading to a new government which will have some real credibility. . . ."

By the time the meeting convened, word had been received from Tehran that Shapour Bakhtiar had been designated by the shah to form a new government. Consequently, no further instructions were prepared pending some clarification of Bakhtiar's understanding with the shah. Most of the discussion among the participants at the meeting (Vance, Brown, Schlesinger, Turner and Aaron, plus myself as note taker) focused on contingency planning in the event a total collapse of order should threaten the lives of Americans in Iran.

The group agreed that the secretary of defense should order the Seventh Fleet carrier U.S.S. *Constellation* and its task force to take a position close to Singapore so it would be available on short notice for deployment to the Indian Ocean, should that prove necessary or desirable. Further, because of the deteriorating security situation and growing fears in the region of a possible Soviet intervention in Iran, the secretary of state was to explore with the government of Saudi Arabia the desirability of a visit by a squadron of U.S. Air Force F-15 fighter aircraft as a symbolic gesture of support. A series of steps was outlined for progressively thinning out the remaining American presence in Iran.

The following morning Vance, Brown, Turner and Duncan met with Brzezinski in his office. Secretary Brown reported that it would require two days for the Seventh Fleet Carrier Task Force to be readied to move from its present location in the Philippines toward Singapore, and he had instructed it to proceed with preparations.

Much of the meeting was devoted to discussion of a draft cable of instructions to Sullivan. The policy issue had by now been reduced to a single question: Would the United States support or reject an "iron fist" policy in Iran? Vance wanted Sullivan to inform the shah that the United States would not support such an option. Instead, he proposed authorizing Sullivan to open

discussions with the various factions to create a civilian government. Brzezinski, with Brown's support, argued in favor of a strong statement of U.S.
support for the shah, leaving open the distinct possibility of a military crackdown. The result was a compromise. President Carter was at Camp David, and
Secretary Vance was to seek the president's concurrence on the draft when he
saw him that afternoon.

The message was sent to Sullivan from Camp David later that afternoon
(December 28). It asked Sullivan to convey a four-part message to the shah
as soon as possible. First, it was the president's view that continued uncertainty
was destructive of army morale and of political confidence. Second, if a civilian
government could be formed soon that was moderate and could maintain
order, then that would obviously be the preferred alternative. Third, if there
was uncertainty either about the underlying orientation of such a government
or its capacity to govern, or if the army was in danger of becoming more
fragmented, then the shah should choose without delay a firm military government that would end the disorder, violence and bloodshed. If it was the shah's
judgment that these alternatives were not feasible, then a Regency Council
supervising the military government should be considered. Finally, Sullivan
was to inform the shah that U.S. support was steady and that it was *essential*
to terminate the continuing uncertainty. Sullivan was to make it clear to the
shah that, in any case, it was Washington's judgment that it would be impossible to restore his absolute power.

Both Brzezinski and Vance, focusing on different elements of this carefully
crafted statement, saw it as a victory for their respective positions. Brzezinski
later said that it "represented the clearest and most direct effort to get the Shah
to do what needed to be done . . ."[10] Vance, on the other hand, believed that
"The shah could not fail to see from this message that we would support a
military government only to end bloodshed, but not to apply the iron fist to
retain his throne."[11]

Ambassador Sullivan relayed this message to the shah at noon the following
day. When he had finished his presentation, the shah remarked that the scale
of preferences in the message was the same as his own. However, his efforts
to form a civilian government had suffered a setback when Sadiqi withdrew
the previous day. The shah had called in Bakhtiar and offered him the charge,
and Bakhtiar had agreed to try. Both the shah and Sullivan were pessimistic
about Bakhtiar's chances.

The shah then turned to the "iron fist" option. He said that the military had
not asked him to be allowed to use the iron fist,[12] and as far as he knew, they
had no articulated plan of how to go about it. He thought Washington's
formulation of a military government to "end the . . . bloodshed" was unrealistic. There would be enormous bloodshed, and even then it might not succeed.
He said he "did not have the heart" for this option. If it were to be tried, he
would in any event leave the country because he "would not wish to be
associated with it."

With respect to a possible Regency Council, he wondered if Washington expected him to go abroad, since such a council would normally act only in the monarch's absence or incapacitation. Sullivan replied that the issue was not addressed in the message. The shah remarked rather philosophically that everyone seemed to be telling him that a Regency Council was the only way to save the monarchy. If he chose this route, he commented, he would have to explain his actions carefully, particularly to the military.

The shah then said there was the problem of where to go, and Sullivan related that "there was a long pregnant silence while he stared at me." Finally Sullivan said that he had no instructions but that he was confident the shah would be welcome in the United States. The shah seemed enormously relieved to hear this, and indicated his intention to discuss all these matters with his advisers.

The Constellation Fiasco

At approximately the same time that this conversation was taking place, the Joint Chiefs of Staff were transmitting a movement order to the Seventh Fleet Carrier Task Force, which was in port in the Philippines. The message notified the task force to position itself in the vicinity of Singapore (at the entrance to the Indian Ocean) and to make preparations for a possible deployment to the Arabian Sea if an augmented naval presence proved necessary. It was later determined that a sailor telephoned his home in a small town in Nebraska to say that he was going to the Indian Ocean. That information was picked up by the United Press stringer in the town, and literally within hours a story moved on the wires.

To the everlasting chagrin of the president's advisers, the story was broadcast even before President Carter learned of their decision the previous day. Normally, presidential approval would have been obtained before ordering a naval movement of that magnitude at such a critical moment. However, they considered this only a precautionary move to position the carrier to be able to respond if the situation required. Any subsequent move to the Arabian Sea would have to be considered in light of the situation in the Persian Gulf and the risk that it would be perceived as a U.S. intent to intervene militarily in Iran.

However, once the incorrect story had been trumpeted by the media, this episode permanently entered the folklore of the crisis. Denials by administration spokesmen only made things worse. Commentators seized on the denials as evidence that the Carter administration had changed its mind under pressure, and the incident became enshrined as an example of President Carter's "vacillation."

Within the government, the incident led to some very different conclusions. The almost instantaneous leak of a classified movement order to U.S. forces was regarded by senior officials in Washington as distressing evidence that normal military channels could not be trusted in matters of any political sensitivity. The military, in turn, was intensely embarrassed at its failure to maintain security. Both of these "lessons" would be remembered vividly more than a year later when planning was under way for the attempted rescue mission of the hostages in Tehran. Ironically, partly as a result of this episode, extreme and unorthodox security measures were adopted during the planning and execution of the rescue mission which may have contributed to its failure.

On December 29, David Aaron convened another mini-SCC meeting which, not surprisingly, included some angry exchanges between Aaron and the representative of the Joint Chiefs of Staff about the inaccurate and very damaging report of the carrier's movements. Aaron said that no decision would be taken about further deployment of the carrier until early January. The U.S.S. *Constellation* was not expected to arrive in the vicinity of Singapore until at least January 2.

The remainder of the meeting was devoted to discussing the proper role for Ambassador Sullivan in the delicate political negotiations under way in Tehran. Curiously, Harold Saunders was quite critical of the "options" message that had been sent to the shah the previous day, arguing that it failed to clarify the role the United States and the ambassador would play. As the discussion went on, it became apparent that Saunders and the director of the State Department Policy Planning Staff, Anthony Lake, both close advisers to Vance, were unaware that Vance had personally redrafted the message at Camp David with the president.

Saunders was quite insistent that the key issue was to get Sullivan more actively engaged with key opposition figures (a process he had thrice recommended to Sullivan, only to be rejected). Aaron was sympathetic to the need for better information about the opposition leadership, and he said he would raise the idea with Brzezinski while Saunders raised it with Secretary Vance. In any event, late that evening Vance sent a message to Sullivan recommending that he contact more prominent opposition leaders to get better information about their views.

To this Sullivan replied that he was already "moving in that direction." However, Sullivan claimed that contact with opponents of Bakhtiar would risk undercutting his efforts and that direct contact with senior ayatollahs would be perceived as intervention. Consequently he preferred to keep those options "on the back burner" for the moment. As we shall see in the next chapter, Sullivan had already progressed far beyond the "back burner" in his contacts with the opposition, but Washington did not know that and Sullivan was doing nothing to enlighten them.

Auld Lang Syne

On December 30 the Department of State approved Sullivan's recommendation to encourage all remaining U.S. dependents to leave Iran. This decision, however, was complicated by striking Iranian civil air personnel who terminated air traffic control services at the Tehran airport and announced that Israeli and U.S. aircraft were no longer permitted to land in Tehran. Pan American immediately ceased its flights to Tehran, and planning began for possible use of military transport aircraft to assist Americans to leave.

The embassy reported that conditions in Tehran were approaching a state of anarchy, with troops totally ineffective in their efforts to control roving gangs and mobs that had begun looting. Americans were increasingly finding themselves the targets of personal attacks, and U.S. companies were scrambling to arrange charter flights for their people. Tehran Radio reported that the shah would soon leave Iran for a prolonged period of "medical treatment." Oil production had dropped below the level necessary to supply internal Iranian needs, and stocks of household kerosene were running low.

In this condition of mounting chaos, a standard message arrived from the shah offering his best wishes to President and Mrs. Carter for the New Year. It was a melancholy reminder of the fact that, exactly one year earlier, President Carter had been in Tehran offering a toast to the stability of the shah's regime.

It had not been a good year.

VII

LAST GASPS

On New Year's Day, 1979, Shapour Bakhtiar addressed the Iranian nation. He outlined an ambitious reform program that he said would lead to a truly "social democratic" society. He reminded the people of his service in the cabinet of Mohammad Mossadegh nearly thirty years earlier, and he managed to complete his twelve-minute speech without once mentioning the shah.

Two questions were much on the mind of political leaders in Tehran and Washington. First, would Bakhtiar be able to attract a credible group of ministers? Second, when and under what circumstances would the shah actually leave the country? Both questions were raised immediately when the ambassador met with the shah the following day for what Sullivan described as a "long, doleful audience."

The appointment of minister of war was widely regarded as the key to a viable new government, and Bakhtiar had let it be known that his choice for this position was retired General Fereidoun Jam. Jam, who was living in exile in London, had resigned as chief of staff many years earlier after a dispute with the shah over use of the army to put down domestic dissent. He was unique among Iranian military leaders as a man who was highly respected by the professional military but who had dissociated himself from the shah's policies of repression. His acceptance of the military portfolio would constitute a powerful vote of confidence for Bakhtiar.

The shah dashed these hopes. General Jam, he told Sullivan, had declined the position. This was very bad news indeed, for it would be interpreted as a signal that Jam did not believe the Bakhtiar government would succeed. What the shah did not tell Sullivan was that he had refused Jam's request to have full control over the military, thus leading Jam to the conclusion that the Bakhtiar government would not have the necessary authority to function effectively.

This fact became clear only weeks later, after the shah was already out of the country, but it was wholly consistent with the shah's tenacious refusal throughout the crisis to transfer any real power from himself to the government. The result in this case—as previously—was to cripple the government by making it appear to be nothing but a front for the real power, which continued to reside only in the monarch.

With regard to his own departure, the shah told Sullivan he intended to make a statement that he would leave the country for a rest, but he would not indicate a date of departure. He preferred to wait until law and order had been restored. The shah clearly expected Bakhtiar to fail in that task, and he again turned to an agonizing appraisal of his remaining two options: either the "iron fist" or the establishment of a Regency Council to rule while he took himself out of the country. He remained unprepared, as before, to accept either course of action.

Sullivan believed that the shah would make up his mind only if the United States weighed in forcefully, and he favored pressing the shah to accept Bakhtiar's proposal of an early departure after the new government was installed, with a Regency Council to act in his absence. If the shah continued to temporize, Sullivan expected a military coup within ten days by Ardeshir Zahedi and his hard-line military supporters.

President Carter convened a meeting of the National Security Council at noon on January 3. There was no disagreement among those present that the shah was irreparably wounded. However, there was a deep reluctance, even repugnance, to force him to step aside. Such an action, it was felt, would be viewed with alarm by other friendly states in the area, and it would probably be regarded in Iran as a disengagement on the part of the United States that could plunge Iran into civil war. Charles Duncan, who was acting secretary of defense in the absence of Harold Brown, suggested sending General Robert Huyser, deputy commander of the Supreme Allied Command in Europe, to Iran to maintain contact with Iranian military leaders as a show of continuing U.S. support. Huyser, he noted, had worked closely with the Iranian military over a period of years and was personally acquainted with many of the top generals. Duncan's proposal was accepted as part of a package that would acquiesce in the shah's almost inevitable departure while signaling continued U.S. support for the constitutional government and military loyalty to that government.

That night, two messages were sent. A presidential memo was relayed to the shah via Sullivan supporting efforts to form a civilian government under Bakhtiar and pledging U.S. cooperation to preserve the independence, stability and integrity of Iran. It concurred with the shah's suggestion that he would establish a Regency Council, and when the new government was installed, leave the country for a well-deserved rest. The president confirmed that the shah would be welcome in the United States and that security assistance would be provided. The message emphasized the importance the United States attached to the continued cohesion of the military leadership. The message included a specific request that the top military leadership remain in place and not depart with the shah.

The latter point was covered in greater detail in a separate message of presidential instructions to General Huyser, who was directed to leave immediately for Tehran. Huyser was to convey to the top military leaders that the United States regarded it as vital that the Iranian people have a strong and stable government friendly to the United States. Huyser was to urge military leaders to remain in Iran and to offer assurances that the United States would stick with them. The military-supply relationship would be maintained, and U.S. support personnel would remain as needed. Special concern was expressed about the security of sensitive military equipment.

General Huyser arrived in Tehran unannounced on January 4, at approximately the same time that President Carter was arriving on the Caribbean island of Guadeloupe for a meeting with the leaders of Britain, France and Germany. Just before Huyser arrived, Sullivan reported signs that the Iranian military was about to carry out a coup. In fact, several such reports (all spurious) were received during the first days of January after news began to circulate about the shah's impending departure. When Vance learned of this report, he immediately ordered General Huyser to postpone meeting with any Iranian generals until his instructions could be reviewed with President Carter.

Vance telephoned the president to discuss what Huyser should tell the generals. Carter consulted with Brzezinski (who had accompanied him to the Caribbean), and then reaffirmed that his original instructions to General Huyser remained valid. That night (January 4) Vance sent a message to Tehran confirming that Huyser should proceed with his meetings with the Iranian military leadership.

Sullivan Launches His Plan

In late December and early January, Ambassador Sullivan had concluded that with the shah planning to leave the country in an act tantamount to abdication, it was time to initiate the plan he had outlined in his "Thinking the Unthinkable" message in early November. Sullivan did not reveal his intentions or the details of his plans to anyone in Washington. Contrary to his message of December 29, which argued against contacts with senior ayatollahs or opponents of Bakhtiar, by the date of that message U.S. embassy officials in Tehran had in fact established contact with both, including Ayatollah Mohammad Beheshti, who was emerging as Khomeini's chief lieutenant in Tehran.

The substance of these discussions with the opposition was not shared with the White House; however, the first stage of the plan that had resulted from these contacts was worked out with the Department of State. By this time Sullivan had almost totally stopped relying on normal channels—or even on messages. As the situation became more sensitive, he used a secure telephone and a teletype line to communicate with the department.

Sullivan believed it was necessary to confirm with Ayatollah Khomeini in Paris the essentials of the tentative agreements he had worked out with the opposition in Tehran. Thus, he proposed to Vance, Newsom and Saunders a direct contact with the ayatollah in Paris. After some discussion Sullivan and the State Department developed a plan whereby Theodore L. Eliot, Jr., the inspector general of the Foreign Service who had Farsi language experience, would travel to Paris to meet with the ayatollah, the objective being to fashion an accommodation to permit a transition of power in Tehran with a minimum of bloodshed. Sullivan believed that if the plan was to have any chance of success, it was essential for contact to be established prior to the shah's departure, which could occur as soon as January 6, when Bakhtiar was scheduled to present his cabinet list to the Majles.

By January 3 Ambassador Sullivan and the State Department had developed proposed terms of reference for Eliot's demarche to the ayatollah and had set January 6 as the target date for the meeting. Then, just prior to the president's departure for Guadeloupe, the proposal of a direct contact with Khomeini was raised for the first time in very general terms with the White House. Brzezinski was unaware of the detailed planning that lay behind this proposal, but he was profoundly skeptical of the idea. He insisted that Sullivan seek the views of the shah, believing that the shah would oppose any direct U.S. contact with Khomeini.

Ambassador Sullivan met with the shah immediately and outlined the planned contact in Paris. Sullivan later recounted that the shah listened "gravely and without enthusiasm," but voiced no objections.[1] As a result, Vance again called President Carter in Guadeloupe, informing him that the shah had approved and recommending that the Eliot mission proceed. President Carter had reservations about the wisdom of an official approach to Khomeini, and he again consulted with Brzezinski. Stalling, Brzezinski argued that the matter was too important to be dealt with peremptorily on the telephone and that any decision should be postponed until it could be examined more systematically in Washington after the party returned from the Caribbean. The president agreed, and Sullivan was informed late that night that the mission was off.

Ambassador Sullivan recalls that his "surprise and anguish could not have been more complete" when he received this information.[2] His reaction was understandable. He had worked himself rather far out on a dangerous limb.

His discussions with the opposition leadership around Khomeini had passed the point of generalities. By this time he was engaged in an effort to stitch together an alternative coalition that he believed had the potential to survive after the shah's departure. He expected the shah to leave in the next few days, and he was convinced that prior contact with Khomeini was required if an accommodation was to have a chance of success. He had outlined his plan to the shah, who had almost certainly interpreted his presentation as a shift of U.S. support from himself to the opposition. Bridges had been burned, and he had no place left to turn.

Sullivan had been ambassador to Laos and the Philippines. In each case he had had exceptional latitude for independent action. He was accustomed to crises, and he was accustomed to dealing with them on his own terms, with a minimum of interference or guidance from Washington. In Iran, faced with a crisis, he responded by attempting to fashion his own independent solution, without policy communication or coordination with Washington. In this case, however, his tactics misfired disastrously.

The handling of this issue and the way it was presented to the White House virtually guaranteed that it would not be accepted. This initiative, which involved a fundamental shift in policy, was prepared without the knowledge of the president and was then presented only at the very last moment as the situation became desperate, almost as a *fait accompli.* At best, it was a high-risk bureaucratic strategy that, in effect, asked the president to buy a pig in a poke. When the president balked, with the encouragement of Brzezinski, the strategy collapsed, with the result that the plan never received the kind of serious examination that it clearly deserved.

Would the Plan Have Worked?

Quite apart from the bureaucratic management (or mismanagement) of this proposal, it is important in retrospect to examine this proposal on its own merits. Did it offer a realistic alternative for U.S. policy? Would its adoption have changed the course of events in a direction more favorable to U.S. interests? Was it, in short, the critical missed opportunity of the crisis? The answers can never be known with any certainty, but it is nonetheless possible to evaluate the underlying assumptions and logic of the plan in light of what was known at the time and what became evident only later.

The proposed direct contact with Khomeini in Paris was, of course, no end in itself but only the beginning of a process. The ultimate objective of that process was to strengthen the political position of a group of moderate, secular, nationalist politicians within the ranks of the anti-shah opposition, thereby increasing the likelihood that those forces would emerge in political control of Iran, rather than the radical Islamic forces represented by Khomeini and his entourage.

The "moderates" in this case were Mehdi Bazargan and his activist colleagues in the tiny but influential Liberation Movement of Iran. These were individuals who were passionately opposed to the shah's regime and who had fought against him for years. At the same time, they were deeply committed to principles of popular democracy and human rights, and they wished to avoid the kind of bloodshed that they feared would result from a direct confrontation with the military. They had been in contact with the U.S. embassy throughout the latter months of the crisis in an attempt to find a nonviolent political solution. They were men of great honor, integrity and talent; however, they lacked any independent power base.

Sullivan's plan was to endow these men with real power by engineering an accommodation between themselves and the military. The United States was to be the matchmaker for this alliance, using its influence to bring the army into line and prevent it from lashing out in the wake of the shah's departure. If this worked, the transition of power could be accomplished with a minimum of bloodshed, and a relatively liberal leadership would acquire the strength, through its association with the army, to moderate the excesses of Khomeini and his immediate entourage. Moreover, because of the military's continuing need for technical support and spare parts, the United States would retain at least some limited measure of influence over developments.

Could it work? If the plan was to succeed, a number of conditions had to be fulfilled:

1. Khomeini had to acquiesce in the arrangement on terms that were politically acceptable to the United States.

2. The "moderates" had to be able to keep their end of the bargain.

3. Some provision had to be made for Shapour Bakhtiar, the prospective prime minister of the new government, who did not figure in the plan.

4. The United States, for its part, would have to be prepared to offer assurances that it would use its full influence to secure the cooperation of the military.

It is worth examining each of these in turn. First, Khomeini might have been tempted by the prospect of the army being "delivered" into the hands of the opposition by the United States; however, Khomeini was never as worried about a direct clash with the military as Bazargan and others were. He would almost certainly have demanded a renunciation of U.S. support for the shah and a pledge of noninterference in Iranian affairs. Although the shah was politically crippled, it would have been extremely difficult for the United States to renounce his claim to authority unilaterally.

Even assuming that the U.S. government was willing to meet Khomeini's essential demands, what kind of assurances would be expected of Khomeini in return? Would the United States negotiate with Khomeini about political posts in a new revolutionary government? Would we ask for assurances about Khomeini's own political role? Would we try to define the political outlines of the new regime? It stretches the limits of credulity to imagine Theodore Eliot sitting on the floor at Nauphle-le-Château driving such a bargain with Khomeini. More likely we would have to settle for some general assurances of a peaceful transition and "correct" bilateral relations after the transition was complete, with Khomeini to determine how those assurances were implemented later.

Second, there was the question of the "moderate" leadership on whom

Sullivan was relying. Bazargan and others had been totally ineffective in attempting to moderate Khomeini's tactics throughout the crisis to this point. There is very little substantive evidence to suggest that they would have been more successful in pressing their demands on Khomeini after he had eliminated the shah. In fact, Bazargan and many of the other "moderates" were eventually appointed by Khomeini to run the provisional government. They did fight courageously for civil rights and secular rule during the summer of 1979, but they proved no match for Khomeini's charisma and dogged insistence on theocratic rule and were eventually dismissed. It was simply inconceivable that these gentle proponents of human rights and nonviolence would have been willing or able to use the military as an effective lever of influence against Khomeini's driving vision.

Moreover, even at this late stage, as the revolution approached its climax, the moderates themselves were far from united. At the same time that Sullivan was negotiating terms with the leaders of the Liberation Movement, leaders of another major political grouping were establishing contact with the State Department and the White House with a different set of proposals. Specifically, they discouraged direct U.S. contact with Khomeini, since it risked undercutting their own bargaining position with the ayatollah.

Third is the question of Bakhtiar. Sullivan made it unmistakably clear in his dialogue with Washington that he regarded Bakhtiar as a vehicle for the removal of the shah and nothing else. Perhaps that was a realistic judgment, but it was by no means certain that Bakhtiar—an ambitious, proud and tenacious man—would meekly step aside when the U.S. ambassador determined that he had fulfilled his limited function. What if Bakhtiar decided to make common cause with some or all of the top generals who were slated for replacement?

That leads to the fourth question: Could the United States carry out its end of a promise to deliver the Iranian military? Unbeknownst to anyone in Washington, Ambassador Sullivan had progressed quite far in this direction in his negotiations with the opposition leaders. By January 3 he had in his possession a list of more than one hundred senior Iranian military officers who would be expected to leave the country with the shah, with replacements to be selected by the revolutionary leaders. In return for this favor, the leaders of the moderate opposition were prepared to pledge that there would be no arrests or other acts of revenge against the military.[3]

This was scarcely a trivial issue; however, the president, the White House, the State Department and the Defense Department were unaware of the nature of this prospective bargain. It does help to explain why Sullivan was so upset by the arrival of General Huyser, whose instructions from the president specifically directed him to "urge military leaders to remain in Iran and to assure them that the United States would stick with them," and it explains Sullivan's last-minute effort through Vance to stop Huyser from initiating talks with the Iranian generals. It also helps to account for Sullivan's sense of urgency in initiating contact with Khomeini before the shah departed. Among other things, he had to have time to find room on the shah's plane for a hundred Iranian officers.

Very simply, not only was Sullivan operating entirely on his own without instructions from Washington, but he was acting in direct contradiction to U.S. national policy. Over a period of months, President Carter had been coming to the view that Sullivan was not faithfully representing U.S. policy to the shah and others in Iran. In this case, the president's suspicions proved to be entirely justified.

Quite apart from the question of loyalty, Sullivan's plan suggested a flight from political reality. It is very unlikely that any U.S. president would ever have associated himself with a plan that called for the United States to dismiss peremptorily the entire top military leadership of a foreign nation and then delegate responsibility for selecting replacements to a group of revolutionary leaders. Quite apart from the propriety and feasibility of such an action, what was supposed to happen when one or more division commanders decided they did not want to go into exile? Was the United States supposed to join the rebellion to force them out?

In a world of total *Realpolitik*, where nations have no friends but only interests and where alliances are made and broken according to an iron law of tactical advantage, a case can be made that the United States should have leaped aboard the revolutionary juggernaut in a frantic effort to preserve some measure of influence with the new regime. But in the real world, where the United States carried with it the heavy weight of more than three decades of historical association, there was never any practical possibility that such a cynical reversal of roles would or could have been sustained by a U.S. president. The best evidence that Ambassador Sullivan sensed this inevitable clash was the almost clandestine manner in which the details were worked out and the fact that key elements of the plan, such as the list of Iranian officers to be removed, were withheld at the same time that President Carter was being urged to authorize the seemingly innocent first step of an emissary to Khomeini. As it happened, President Carter was unwilling even to go that far.

On the morning of January 10, after his return from the Caribbean, President Carter met in the Oval Office with Vice President Walter Mondale, the secretaries of state and defense, Zbigniew Brzezinski and David Aaron. In this meeting, after rancorous argument, Sullivan's plan was definitively rejected. Instead, it was decided to approach Khomeini indirectly through the French, urging him to give the Bakhtiar government a chance to restore order and to avoid further disintegration of the situation in Iran. Ambassador Sullivan was directed to support Bakhtiar's efforts to get parliamentary approval of his cabinet. General Huyser, who had originally anticipated remaining in Iran only a few days, was ordered to remain and pursue his contacts with the military leadership. The discussion made clear that the overriding U.S. objective was the preservation of the military, and the possibility of a military government was again not excluded. Sullivan was to urge the shah to speed the process of forming a civilian government and a Regency Council and then to leave the country as agreed.

Sullivan received this message in the middle of the night. He dashed off an outraged message which, among other things, characterized the president's decision as "insane." With that message, he burned his last bridge. Washington was fairly on notice that the rebellion in Iran now extended to the person of the U.S. ambassador.[4]

Carter directed Secretary Vance to "get Sullivan out of Iran," but Vance persuaded him that it would be a mistake to put in a new ambassador at such a critical moment. Carter reluctantly agreed to leave Sullivan in Tehran. However, since the president had lost confidence in his ambassador, he began to rely primarily on General Huyser's reports. Thus, the decision to leave Sullivan in place resulted in the progressive development of alternative and competing channels of communication between Washington and Tehran, compounding the already existing confusion and distrust.

The New Conventional Wisdom

On January 11, David Aaron chaired another mini-SCC meeting for a general review of the situation in Iran. The participants included the senior staff of all the major agencies who worked on Iran policy. As one after another spoke up around the table, a remarkable consensus began to develop.

Khomeini, it was felt, was no great threat; he did not understand how to run a government and he was uninterested in foreign affairs. The National Front and the moderates in the opposition provided the natural source of leadership for a future government, and the military would go along, since it had careers to protect. Khomeini would not reverse the beneficial and popular elements of the shah's program and, in fact, would probably not change things very much, although the faces at the top would be different. Henry Precht commented that although there would be tensions, Iran under Khomeini might well be more stable than in the past. It was generally agreed by this group that the real obstacles to this happy state of affairs were the shah and Bakhtiar. As we left the meeting, David Aaron and I merely looked at each other in mutual astonishment.

That night I wrote a report for the president describing this new conventional wisdom. I commented that we seemed to have become captive to the demonology of the Iranian mobs who believed that once the exorcism (the shah's departure) had been performed, all would be well. I felt that nothing could be further from the truth. It was possible to recognize that the shah had let the situation drift beyond the point of no return and still understand that the prognosis for any successor regime was extremely poor.

The National Front, in my view, was composed of aging idealists who could agree on nothing, whereas Khomeini knew very well what kind of Islamic republic he intended to create. Khomeini would be as uncompromising on that subject as he had been in the past. The United States was giving up on the shah only after being forced to conclude that he was incapable of decisive action; however, after the shah's collapse we might soon face a situation that "would make the shah look very good indeed by comparison."[5]

Ambassador Sullivan and General Huyser spent two hours with the shah on January 11. The shah expressed deep concern about the suffering of the Iranian people and urged the United States to approach Khomeini to stop the potential bloodshed and to give the Bakhtiar government a chance. The shah reviewed the list of names for the Regency Council that was about to be formed. Much of the meeting was occupied by a discussion of planning about the shah's impending departure and arrangements for his reception in the United States. The shah planned to leave no later than January 17, after the Majles vote on the Bakhtiar government, and planned to fly direct to the United States.

General Huyser later spoke by secure telephone to Secretary of Defense Brown. He had spent endless hours in talks with each of the key military leaders, and he was not convinced that the generals were prepared to throw their full support behind Bakhtiar when the shah departed. They wanted to see Bakhtiar succeed, but if he failed, they were preparing contingency plans for the military to take over essential functions and avoid a total breakdown of order.

Brown reconfirmed that this two-pronged strategy was consistent with the instructions sent to Sullivan on December 28 and to Huyser on January 3 and 4. Subsequently this position was further developed into three sequential options:

A encourage the Iranian military to support Bakhtiar's civilian government;
B plan for possible direct Iranian military action if required to bolster the civilian regime
C support a military takeover by Iranian forces if public order collapsed.

As the situation developed over the following weeks, the shorthand of "Options A, B, and C" was used to refer to alternative policy choices within a small circle of advisers in Washington, consisting essentially of Vance, Brown and Brzezinski.

By this time the telephone had almost entirely replaced written messages between Tehran and Washington, and it assumed a curious dual track. Each evening in Tehran, Sullivan and Huyser would repair to the communications center in the embassy, where each would report—Sullivan to the Department of State and Huyser to the Department of Defense—describing what had transpired during the day and seeking instructions. Comparing notes after their respective conversations, Sullivan later commented that "There were times when we felt we must have been talking to two different cities."[6]

Contact with Khomeini

Sullivan continued to press for a contact with Khomeini, and the French were unwilling to act as intermediaries. So on January 14 the president authorized a meeting between Warren Zimmerman, the political counselor at the U.S. embassy in Paris, and Ibrahim Yazdi, the Khomeini aide who had earlier represented the ayatollah in the United States. At the same time, General Huyser was encouraging the military in Iran to establish direct contact with the religious leadership in order to ensure that lines of communication were available and to provide at least a limited forum for clarifying the intentions of the two opposing forces.

Both the shah and Bakhtiar were aware of these moves and approved of them as a means of avoiding misunderstanding and potentially preventing unnecessary bloodshed. General Abbas Gharabaghi, who had replaced General Azhari as chief of staff, impressed General Huyser as a fine professional soldier who deserved the full confidence of the United States. It was Gharabaghi who emerged as a natural leader within the group of Iranian generals, and he was instrumental in opening the lines of communication to the religious forces. As we shall see later, Huyser's confidence in Gharabaghi may have been a bit naïve.

Huyser also reported that the desertion rate within the military was as high as 500 to 1,000 per day. Although Huyser minimized the importance of this trend, noting that it was a small fraction of a total military force of nearly half a million, it was disturbing evidence of the constant erosion taking place within the military ranks. In Paris, Khomeini drew attention to the reports of desertions and proclaimed, "The shah will definitely lose the army, and with it his last hope." In Tehran, Ayatollah Mohammad Beheshti, who was emerging as one of the key organizers of the religious opposition, told a U.S. embassy officer with absolute confidence that he did not fear a direct confrontation with the military, since "we control everyone below the rank of major."

On January 14, Khomeini was interviewed on CBS television. Again he claimed that "a great part of the army" was loyal to the opposition forces. When pressed about his own role, Khomeini said he would not assume a governmental position but rather would supervise and guide the government's activities. "You will be in effect the strong man of Iran?" he was asked. Without a flicker of emotion, the ayatollah replied, "You may assume so."[7]

The shah had finally settled on January 16 for his departure. On the day before the scheduled departure, Sullivan was informed that the shah would not fly direct to the United States but would instead stop for a day or two in Aswan, Egypt, at the request of President Sadat. This late change of plans completely disrupted the complex arrangements that had been developed for the shah's reception in the United States and gave rise to concern about the shah's real intentions.

No explanation for this change of plan was ever provided, but there were persistent reports that the shah was persuaded by some of his advisers to remain as close as possible to Iran in case of a sudden turn of events. It was recalled that in the course of Operation Ajax in 1953 the shah had fled the country briefly, only to be recalled in triumph a few days later when the mobs reversed themselves overnight. Perhaps he anticipated a similar reversal in 1979.

Washington still expected the shah to come to the United States, so plans for his reception were revised, awaiting his next move. However, as we shall see, this final act of equivocation vastly complicated the problem of providing a secure political refuge for the shah and his entourage. In the ensuing months, the shah became a political burden for a series of host governments, culminating in his admission to the United States under very different circumstances, thereby triggering the second great crisis in U.S.-Iranian relations.

On the day before the shah's departure, Zbigniew Brzezinski joined Harold Brown for the daily telephone conversation with General Huyser. Huyser reported extreme nervousness and uncertainty within the armed forces as the moment of the shah's departure approached. Brzezinski asked whether the military had developed a plan in the event the Bakhtiar government should falter. Huyser said that earlier reports of such a plan had no basis in fact. The military had only begun serious work on such a plan within the previous four or five days and had only a marginal capability.

Huyser was having enormous difficulties in getting the various military leaders to work together on anything. In the entire modern history of the Iranian military, each service chief had always reported independently to the shah, with virtually no coordination between themselves. The shah had perpetuated such a system as a form of political insurance, but it meant that any form of joint planning was totally contrary to more than a generation of military experience. Old habits of mutual suspicion and personal rivalry died hard.

One of the major obstacles the military encountered was the growing shortage of gasoline and diesel fuel. Oil production had plummeted almost to zero after a U.S. oil executive, Paul Grimm, was assassinated on December 23, prompting the mass departure of all foreign technicians. Mehdi Bazargan, with Khomeini's blessing, had gone to the oil fields to attempt to get oil production started again on a sufficient level to provide for the daily needs of the population. He was astonished at the extent of leftist influence among the oil workers, and his mission was extremely stormy. Nevertheless, limited production resumed, but the oil workers refused to provide fuel to the military. The military, in turn, lacked the technical capacity to operate the oil fields, and the situation turned into a standoff. In response to Huyser's request, a U.S. tanker was diverted to Iran to provide the badly needed fuel supplies.

At the same moment that Brown and Brzezinski were talking to Huyser, a very different conversation was under way in Paris. In a small inn outside the city, Warren Zimmerman sat down for the first official U.S. meeting with a member of Khomeini's entourage. Zimmerman gave Yazdi the latest official statements of the U.S. position concerning Iran, and Yazdi reciprocated by providing a Khomeini statement issued the night before. Yazdi said that a Revolutionary Council was already at work in Iran preparing the way for a transitional government that would organize elections for a constituent assembly.

Yazdi was interested in learning about U.S. contacts with the Iranian military. He was very concerned about reports that the military was preparing a coup to take place either at the time of the shah's departure or shortly thereafter. He said it would be difficult for the Iranian people to accept that such a coup could be carried out without U.S. support, and he suggested that it would radicalize the situation and increase the risk of violence against Americans in Iran. Speaking for Khomeini, he urged the United States to do everything possible to prevent such an action. Yazdi also asked for any late information about the shah's travel plans, but Zimmerman had none. The meeting broke up amicably after twenty minutes.

After the Shah

Shortly before noon the following day, the shah boarded an airplane at Mehrabad Airport in a tense and emotional scene and departed his country. The news was greeted in Iran by noisy and widespread popular celebrations. According to Huyser, the military was close to a state of shock. There was widespread talk about a possible coup, but the military leadership seemed more concerned about what would happen if and when Khomeini accepted the invitation that Bakhtiar had issued and returned to the country. They feared it would split the military and prompt a violent reaction that no one could control.

Brzezinski stressed to Huyser the continued importance of planning to make sure that the military option remained open. Brzezinski argued that the credible threat of a coup would discourage any rash actions by Khomeini's supporters and would buy time for Bakhtiar to consolidate his position. These conversations were reported fully to President Carter, and such planning was explicitly authorized in three separate presidential messages of instructions to Sullivan and Huyser. On several occasions President Carter made it clear that he shared the view that the *threat* of a military coup was the most effective leverage available to forestall a revolutionary power grab and was an essential element in buying time for a possible constitutional solution under Bakhtiar. Yazdi's comments to Zimmerman in Paris indicated that that judgment was not without validity.

Ambassador Sullivan came to the same conclusion. After reading the account of the first Yazdi-Zimmerman meeting, he drafted some proposed guidelines for the second encounter that called for Zimmerman to stress quite candidly that the Iranian military had seriously discussed conducting a coup, that they had deferred their plans at General Huyser's urgings, but that continued calm depended on the absence of new provocations by the Khomeini forces. The reaction of the military could not be predicted if Khomeini should return suddenly to Iran, for the military leadership had indicated that in such an event they might act "to protect the constitution." Zimmerman was to urge Khomeini to refrain from actions that would precipitate the collapse of the Bakhtiar government and to support the dialogue between representatives of the military and the religious forces that were beginning to be worked out in Tehran. The White House approved this approach immediately and it was cabled to Paris.

Zimmerman delivered this message to Yazdi during a fifty-minute meeting on the evening of January 16, with Yazdi taking it down word for word in Farsi translation. Yazdi said that as far as he knew, Khomeini had no plans for an imminent return to Iran. He wondered whether a military reaction would be provoked by the fact of Khomeini's return or by the "excitement of the people" that would follow. Zimmerman offered his own view that the return itself, if not carefully prepared by prior arrangement with the military, could well prompt a reaction.

Yazdi wondered what was meant by the phrase "to protect the constitution." If it implied saving the monarchy, that would be a major problem. If it only meant preserving the integrity of the army, then it would not be a problem. Yazdi insisted that the revolution did not want to destroy the army. Finally, Yazdi alluded to reports that Americans in Iran were destroying or removing sophisticated military equipment. Khomeini had stated publicly that this equipment belonged to Iran and that the Iranian military should protect it. What was U.S. policy? Zimmerman said he would refer all three questions to Washington.

The two representatives met again on the morning of January 18. Yazdi was provided with a lengthy statement stressing the importance of contacts between the two sides and reliance on constitutional procedures. It warned of the dangers of the growing power of the Tudeh Party, and the risk that the left would be the only force to gain from a religious-military clash. The first two questions, the message noted, could only be answered by Iranians, not Americans, though the United States shared an interest in stability and the observance of constitutional processes. The message reiterated U.S. interest in Iran's ability to defend itself and firmly denied any destruction or dismantling of military equipment.

Yazdi again took copious notes. He commented that the Tudeh threat was fully appreciated but that the Islamic movement was too strong to be taken over by "Bolsheviks." He indicated that Khomeini had passed the word to his supporters in Tehran to get in touch with the army. With regard to the constitution, he noted that Khomeini demanded a new constitution, not just a revised document; however, clauses such as those providing for the rights of religious minorities (Jews and Christians) would be preserved.

Vance, Brown and Brzezinski met for one of their weekly lunches (the so-called VBB lunches) on January 18. The following day a new guidance message was sent to Sullivan and Huyser in Tehran with President Carter's approval. It reconfirmed the previous policy guidance and encouraged opening lines of communication between the religious and other elements. However, that did not mean endorsing a coalition with Khomeini. On the contrary, the message cautioned against the introduction of new elements into the Bakhtiar government that would pull it toward a more radical posture. The objective, the message explained, was an Iranian government that functioned, that was stable and that retained its ties with the West.

Zimmerman again met with Yazdi on the morning of January 19. In response to some of the questions raised by the U.S. side, Yazdi gave a lengthy description of the principles and objectives of Khomeini's Islamic revolution. On the economic side, apart from restoring stability to Iran, the primary concern would be the revitalization of agriculture, perhaps with U.S. cooperation. Iran would sell oil to whoever would purchase it at a fair price, though Israel and South Africa would be excluded.

In foreign affairs, Yazdi outlined a policy of strict nonalignment, which he compared to U.S. isolationism of the past. They would not seek stability through a military buildup. He stressed the deep popular resentment and hatred toward the United States for its unconditional support of the shah since 1953, but he felt that friendly future relations were possible if America stopped interfering in Iranian affairs. He said Iran had "no better memories" of the Russians than of the Americans. They would seek friendly relations with the Soviet Union, but that process would be complicated by Soviet atheism and antireligious policies. "At least Americans believe in God," he noted, which made it easier to maintain a closer relationship.

Iran would turn inward, Yazdi said, and would not attempt to foment revolution in neighboring countries. "If they want to get rid of their corruption, they must do it themselves." Iran would favor détente and peaceful settlement of international disputes through negotiations and the United Nations.

Even in retrospect, there is no reason to doubt that these and other statements by Yazdi accurately reflected the thinking of those around Khomeini. Their position was based on two fundamental assumptions: the shah's policies had "destroyed" Iran; and the origin of those policies could be traced to external interference, particularly by the United States. Consequently, it was implied, if Iran could rid itself of the shah and of external meddling, the nation could heal itself under a popular government based on religious principles.

The appeal of this position lay in its almost innocent simplicity. Disagreeable realities and inherent contradictions would make themselves felt only later, and the leadership was supremely confident it could deal with those when the time came. In fact, the revolutionary movement may never have been so united —either previously or later—as it was in those days following the shah's departure, before its adherents were required to reconcile ideal objectives with the grubby realities of political rule. Yazdi conveyed the serene self-assurance of those days. They had drawn the conclusion, he said, that the army could no longer restore the shah and that its only interest was in preserving its own integrity.

That was not the impression being reported from Tehran by General Huyser, who recounted Bakhtiar's difficulty in persuading the military chief of staff not to end every public statement with the words "Long live the shah!" Nevertheless, a deceptive air of calm prevailed in Tehran. Religious marches on the nineteenth proceeded without violence, the military authorities had finally conducted their first meeting with the religious opposition, and the Bakhtiar government was energetically dealing with problems of production and distribution of essential commodities. This encouraging state of affairs was diminished, however, by news that the new chairman of the Regency Council, who had been sent by Bakhtiar to meet with Khomeini in Paris, had resigned and defected to Khomeini's side after talks with the ayatollah. In his public statements in Paris, Khomeini balanced a public call for Iranians to cooperate with the army in restoring calm with new attacks on U.S. policy, calling President Carter "the vilest man on earth" for his past support of the shah.

Cleavages between the two U.S. representatives in Tehran were also becoming more apparent. Sullivan and Huyser, despite "talking to different cities," had developed a useful division of labor that added an important new dimension to the reporting and analysis emanating from Tehran. But by January 20, basic differences of view were hardening.

Ambassador Sullivan regarded the Iranian military as a paper tiger, a view shared by Ambassador Parsons, who was being recalled to London for a new posting. Huyser, who was in contact with Iranian military leaders almost continuously, was convinced that the military had come through the wrenching experience of the shah's departure in surprisingly good shape, and his visits to various military installations persuaded him that basic discipline and loyalty were being maintained. Although he remained skeptical of the ability of the military to take action outside the context of the existing Bakhtiar government, he was not ready to write off its capacity to influence political events.

This divergence of views badly muddied the waters in Tehran, where antennae were tuned to every nuance of U.S. policy. Sullivan, with his bridges burned and now contemplating resignation, made no attempt to conceal his contempt for Bakhtiar. He carried out his instructions, but it was no secret in Tehran that he disagreed with them.

As usual, these differing views also played back to Washington. The State Department—at least at the lower levels—subscribed fully to Sullivan's views, while all the senior policy-making officials—including Secretary Vance—pursued a policy designed to strengthen Bakhtiar's position as the only remaining means of avoiding a total governmental collapse in Tehran. As a result, every official U.S. statement was immediately contradicted by "informed sources" expressing the view that Bakhtiar had no chance to survive. As usual, the press leaks were accorded at least equal weight with the official pronouncements by observers in Tehran and Paris, and whatever slim opportunities may have existed to play out a bargaining strategy with Khomeini eroded with every passing day.

Despite Huyser's relative optimism about the military, signs were appearing that the problems were not only the loyalty of the lower ranks but equally of reliability at the top. On January 20, Bakhtiar, in a public statement, indicated that he would either succeed or would turn the country over to the military. Within hours General Gharabaghi, the new chief of staff, indicated that he was submitting his resignation, since he would not be party to a military takeover. Huyser immediately met with Gharabaghi but failed to get a commitment that he would remain as chief of staff. Later that evening Bakhtiar and Sullivan met with the general, and the two of them persuaded him to remain. However, it was apparent that the chief of staff, who had by now held several meetings with the religious opposition, was having his own doubts about a direct confrontation with Khomeini's forces. All the talk about a coup was beginning to sound terribly hollow.

The final days of January were almost totally preoccupied with rumors of Khomeini's imminent return to Iran and speculation about what might happen. Bakhtiar made a show of closing the airports, and he let it be known that he had his own plans for dealing with the event. One of those plans was to divert Khomeini's aircraft to the remote Qish Island in the Persian Gulf, where he would be detained with his key aides while the huge phalanx of journalists would be returned to Paris. Some of the generals had their own ideas about what would happen after that, one version of which involved eliminating as many as 50,000 Khomeini supporters in a single massive counterstroke.

On January 24, Zimmerman again met with Yazdi to deliver a message that Bakhtiar had approved (and partially written). The message noted the mutual interest of the United States and presumably Khomeini in an independent and stable Iran free from outside interference. There were adequate constitutional processes, the message emphasized, through which all major forces could participate peacefully in shaping Iran's political future. If those processes were not followed, a direct, extra-constitutional confrontation could ensue, with disastrous results for all, including the religious elements and their followers. It concluded with the observation that under the circumstances, it would be "premature" for Khomeini to return to Iran.

Yazdi focused on the possible meaning of an "extra-constitutional confrontation," commenting that any action by the army would be perceived as a U.S. action against the revolution. He said Khomeini's interest in returning to Iran was based on his conviction that only he could end the turmoil and bring the country back to normal life. Yazdi denounced the Bakhtiar government as illegal and expressed the hope that the United States would cease its support of Bakhtiar.

A further complication was added to the equation at this delicate juncture. The shah again decided to postpone his trip to the United States. Instead, he announced that he was flying to Morocco on January 26 as a personal guest of King Hassan and that other members of his family would join him there.

This move was widely interpreted as a "gathering of the clan," possibly in preparation for a return to Iran. During the shah's seclusion in Aswan, the United States had no direct contact with him, and Washington was as much in the dark as everyone else about his intentions. From Egypt we learned that President Sadat had spent many hours with the shah and had come away puzzled by his seeming inability to make up his mind. I scribbled in the margin of this report: "Welcome to the club!"

Waiting for the Ayatollah

The military deterioration in Iran was getting worse by the day. On January 25, Huyser reported that a number of air force personnel, including some officers, had been arrested after participating in a pro-Khomeini demonstration in Tehran. The homafars (noncommissioned officers) in the air force had also emerged as a major threat. These technicians were enlisted on contract to serve in the military. Many of them were Western-trained, and they were much better educated than the regular military recruits, but they were never truly integrated into the military career structure. Charged with the maintenance of the most sophisticated weapons systems, these men regarded themselves as both superior to and separate from the regular military. As the political situation deteriorated they became ever more fractious and rebellious. A few weeks later they would ignite the spark that finally destroyed the old order.

On the morning of January 27, Yazdi and Zimmerman held what was to be the last of their secret meetings in Paris. Yazdi took advantage of the meeting to deliver the first personal message from Khomeini to the U.S. government. Khomeini stated that the activities of Bakhtiar and the leaders of the military were harmful not only to Iranians but also to the U.S. government and the future of Americans in Iran. Unless these activities ceased, Khomeini warned, he would be forced to issue "new orders" to Iran that could bring a "great disaster." Khomeini said that only he could bring stability to Iran, and that such maneuvers as closing the airports only destabilized the situation. He had resisted, he said, authorizing his followers to open the airports by force or to confront the military directly, preferring that the problem be solved without violence.

Bakhtiar had sent a message through an emissary proposing a meeting with Khomeini in Paris to discuss a constitutional solution to the crisis. Khomeini had refused to meet the emissary, although he had accepted the written message. According to Yazdi, Khomeini had informed Bakhtiar that he would meet him only if he submitted his resignation. If Bakhtiar did resign, Khomeini would be prepared to appoint him immediately as a member of the provisional government. Over the following two days there was great uncertainty about whether or not Bakhtiar would in fact travel to Paris, but in the end he was unwilling to accept Khomeini's terms and the dialogue broke off.

Nevertheless, contacts continued in Tehran between the military leaders, the Bakhtiar government and the religious leaders in the persons of Bazargan and Ayatollah Beheshti. On the morning of January 29, Bakhtiar told a press conference that he no longer intended to fly to Paris and that the airports would be opened to permit Khomeini to return to Iran. Bakhtiar met with Ambassador Sullivan that evening. He said that arrangements had been worked out for Khomeini's arrival, with the military to stand back and avoid a confrontation. Bakhtiar thought that the actual arrival would be peaceful, but he expected the crunch to come some days later, when he expected Khomeini to announce a rival government.

Bazargan was widely rumored to be named the head of the new Revolutionary Council, and, Bakhtiar thought, if the entire council was composed of reasonable men, there was some chance he could negotiate with them. However, if they made a grab for power, he would have them arrested and "pandemonium" would ensue. Bakhtiar was doubtful that the military could prevail against the masses, and he was very concerned that the Soviet Union might intervene if public order broke down entirely. Bakhtiar indicated that he had not fully made up his mind about what he would do in the event of a showdown with Khomeini, and he planned to discuss this with the Regency Council and his national security advisers over the next two days.

The Memorandum of Understanding

During this same period of time, a different set of problems had also been on the minds of U.S. officials in Washington and Tehran. The Iranian government had approximately $12 billion worth of military equipment on order from the United States, to be manufactured and delivered over a period of years. Regardless of how the political situation worked out in Tehran, it was evident that this massive program would be scaled back sharply. In the meantime, however, there was no effective decision-making structure in Tehran, and the program simply continued of its own momentum. The Department of Defense was responsible for managing this huge program. It held a large trust fund, which Iran routinely replenished with quarterly payments to cover costs. Payments had ceased by the end of 1978, and it was urgent to find a way for Iran either to restructure its purchases or to arrange for orderly termination of a number of contracts.

In January a senior official of the Department of Defense, Eric Von Marbod, was sent to Tehran to attempt to find a way to deal with the military program before it went into arrears. Von Marbod, it will be recalled, had served as the Defense representative in Tehran in the mid-1970s, and he was one of the small band of genuine professionals whose depth of knowledge and experience provide indispensable continuity to the department through successive political administrations in Washington. For weeks he had negotiated with defense officials in Tehran, and by the twenty-sixth he had succeeded in drafting a mutually acceptable Memorandum of Understanding (MOU) that called for a number of major contracts to be terminated and restructured, with the proceeds to be cycled back into the trust fund to pay for other Iranian obligations as they came due.

On January 29, David Aaron convened another mini-SCC to consider Von Marbod's draft proposal. I had read through the document in advance, and I anticipated pro forma approval; but I had underestimated the opacity of the bureaucratic mind. Representatives of the State Department, the Defense Department and the White House all had their own ideas about how the agreement could be improved, including the technical advantages of making it an exchange of letters rather than a formal MOU. After lengthy discussion the participants decided to go back to Von Marbod with a complex set of changes that would have required totally restructuring his original agreement.

I could scarcely believe my ears. In Iran, the entire fabric of authority was coming apart while this group debated fine points as if it had all the time in the world. It was one of the silliest meetings I had ever attended.

Predictably, Von Marbod, Huyser and Sullivan reacted to this new set of instructions with stunned disbelief, and they were all on the telephone immediately to try and impress some sense of reality on their counterparts in Washington. The Washington "experts" soon took off their green eyeshades and rather sheepishly approved Von Marbod's original plan. The mixed signals in Washington generated some nervous second thoughts among the senior military officials in Tehran who were, after all, taking an enormous responsibility on themselves by agreeing to restructure Iran's entire military procurement program. Nevertheless, Von Marbod persevered, and the MOU was signed on February 2, the day after Khomeini returned.

The MOU proved to be absolutely critical in managing the vast Iranian military program over the succeeding months of governmental disarray in Tehran. Without that agreement, the legal, financial and political tangles would have been unmanageable (and enormously costly to the U.S. taxpayer). Whatever the U.S. government was paying Eric Von Marbod—and it was not princely—it got its money's worth during those crucial days.

On January 30, I wrote a memorandum to Brzezinski warning that, in my view, the odds were better than even that Iran would be engaged in a civil war within two weeks. I thought events were likely to outrun our ability to exercise influence and that the chances for avoiding a total breakdown of law and order were not high. The logical targets for Iranian mobs would be the 10,000 or so Americans remaining in the country. We were, I noted, beyond the point of subtle signals, and I recommended that we batten down the hatches and save as many U.S. lives as possible by a total evacuation. Brzezinski scrawled "Done" across the bottom of this memorandum. On the same day, the embassy was notified to evacuate all dependents and nonessential Americans as soon as possible.

Khomeini Moves In

Khomeini's return to Tehran, aboard a chartered Air France 747 on February 1, generally followed the script worked out between the government, the military and the revolutionaries in the previous weeks. The army stood back, and security was handled by the revolutionary forces. The ayatollah was greeted by joyous mobs in the millions, and during his visit to the martyr's cemetery his helicopter was nearly swamped by the crowds trying to catch a glimpse of him. He took up residence in a small austere school building in the south of the city.

General Huyser had been briefed by General Gharabaghi the day before. Gharabaghi said that the military supported Bakhtiar and would follow his instructions in the present crisis. If Bakhtiar succeeded in negotiating an accommodation with Khomeini, the military was prepared to support it as a means of providing a peaceful way out of the impasse. However, if Khomeini refused and moved to establish a rival government, they would take up defensive positions to protect government buildings and installations to prevent their takeover. Beyond that, the officers had not formulated a course of action. They had plans to take over essential public operations if ordered, but they had no thoughts of undertaking a coup on their own.

Ambassador Sullivan asked Washington what role he should play in terms of contacts with the various parties. He was informed that U.S. policy continued to be support for constitutional processes and close consultation with the Bakhtiar government. If Bakhtiar asked him (Sullivan) to meet with Khomeini, he should do so. If Khomeini asked to see him, he should consult with Bakhtiar. He was ordered to have no dealings with the Revolutionary Council that would give the appearance of recognizing it either as a party or as a government. However, he was not precluded from maintaining contact with those elements of the opposition whom he had been seeing prior to Khomeini's return.

This guidance was received in Tehran on February 2. The following day John Stempel, the political officer of the embassy, met with a member of Bazargan's Liberation Movement. This man told Stempel that their members had met with Bakhtiar for two hours the previous evening and had secured Bakhtiar's agreement to two alternative compromise proposals. The first was for Bakhtiar to remain as prime minister and to organize an immediate referendum in which the people would choose between the monarchy or an Islamic republic. The second was for Bakhtiar to resign as prime minister but to remain in a caretaker status while a referendum was conducted.

Reportedly, these proposals were then presented to Khomeini in a long and strident late-night meeting. Contrary to the advice of virtually all his advisers, Khomeini rejected both compromises. Bakhtiar had to go, since he had received his mandate from the shah. The Regency Council was illegal. The only course of action was to name a temporary Islamic government to supervise the referendum. The military would have to go along.

Again, as on several previous occasions, Khomeini rejected the advice of his lieutenants who had remained in Iran to organize and manage the revolution. He sensed total victory, and he was unwilling to settle for anything less. Unlike many of his advisers, he was prepared to accept a confrontation with the army, apparently in full confidence that the military could not withstand such a showdown. Bazargan was to be named as the leader of the new provisional government, but it was unmistakably clear who was the boss.

Huyser Reports

Early in the morning of February 3, General Huyser and Eric Von Marbod left Iran. Von Marbod had finally obtained the necessary Iranian signature on the Memorandum of Understanding, and his job was done. Huyser's position was more ambiguous.

The military had survived the successive shocks of the shah's departure, the massive religious marches of January 19, and the emotionalism of Khomeini's return; but its strength and loyalty were in serious doubt. In the meantime, Huyser himself had increasingly become a target of opposition propaganda, and his continued presence in Tehran served as a magnet for attacks on the embassy and other U.S. installations. Therefore, at his own repeated request and with Sullivan's wholehearted endorsement, he was ordered to leave Tehran and come back to Washington to brief President Carter.

That meeting was held on Monday afternoon, February 5, in the Cabinet Room. President Carter met privately with General Huyser for ten minutes. When they joined the others assembled around the great oval table, the president looked as grimly angry as I had ever seen him. He thanked General Huyser for his efforts in Iran under the most difficult circumstances, then summarized in his own words what Huyser had told him in the Oval Office.

There was, he said, a fundamental difference of views between General Huyser and Ambassador Sullivan. Huyser interpreted his instructions as calling for support of the Bakhtiar government, up to and including action by the Iranian military if required. Ambassador Sullivan, however, thought it was better for the military forces to step aside, let the political forces fight it out among themselves, then accept whoever won. Sullivan was optimistic that the drift of an Islamic republic would be toward democracy, while Huyser felt it would be toward the left and an eventual Communist takeover.

The president said he was disconcerted but not entirely amazed. There had been some early problems in getting instructions through to Sullivan; moreover, judging from the nature of Sullivan's messages to the president via the media, he had been led to wonder if Sullivan was carrying out his instructions. Nevertheless, when the president and the secretary of state jointly drafted instructions, he had thought there would be no question about U.S. policy. President Carter confirmed that Huyser's understanding of his instructions was correct, and he wanted to make "damned sure" that there was no misunderstanding in Tehran.

General Huyser appeared to be intensely uncomfortable as he realized that his "private" remarks to the president were not going to be so private, after all, and he attempted to backtrack a little, commenting that his differences with Ambassador Sullivan were essentially a matter of degree over the use of force. But the president would have none of it. He had read the recent newspaper reports of Sullivan's comments, including references to his "ill advised superiors," and he was convinced that the differences between Sullivan's views and his own were profound.

Secretary Vance was late for this meeting because of a scheduled appearance on the Hill, and his deputy, Warren Christopher, sat glumly and silently through this uncharacteristic display of presidential anger. When Vance arrived, the president summarized the meeting for his benefit, this time in even stronger terms. Vance seemed startled but said nothing.

Zbigniew Brzezinski asked General Huyser what kind of resistance might be encountered if the Iranian military had to resort to Option C, i.e., a military takeover. Huyser replied that when he arrived the military was planning to carry out a coup if and when the shah left. However, the generals had no plan at all; they did not even know where key installations were located. He had persuaded them to focus their attention on key facilities and to ensure they knew how to make them work. Although the officers could not run Iran's complex government, he thought they were capable of restoring order at vital points and to use that as a starting point to reestablish a functioning government. Huyser was concerned not only with the religious opposition but also with the growth of the Tudeh Party and other leftist elements.

Huyser commented that he had been concerned about the reliability of General Gharabaghi when he threatened to resign, but more recently Gharabaghi had shown willingness to take action if there was an attempt to overthrow the legal government. Huyser attached little significance to the continuing reports of nervousness and uncertainty on the part of individual military leaders. He stressed that his judgments were based on repeated personal meetings with the generals, whereas those reports were based on isolated comments or events. In a crisis, the military would be reliable, he assured the president.

In response to a question from Vance, Huyser said his differences with Sullivan turned on the issue of the reliability of the military. Sullivan doubted the troops would respond to an order and would instead move to Khomeini's side. His own visits to military sites had convinced him that discipline remained strong. It was not surprising that there were differing judgments, he observed; perhaps the truth lay somewhere in between.

Admiral Turner said that Huyser's views were quite different from a number of other observers in Iran who felt that public support for Khomeini was so strong that it would defeat the military even if the military controlled key sites. Huyser said that signs of order had improved noticeably even during the period he was in Tehran. Estimates of the numbers of demonstrators were greatly exaggerated, particularly after the shah left. Huyser acknowledged that he was an eternal optimist, but he perceived cracks appearing in Khomeini's leadership. He anticipated a substantial erosion in Khomeini's popularity within days unless something happened quickly.

President Carter said that the talk of a military government, insofar as the United States was concerned, meant maintaining a strong military under Bakhtiar's orders. Bakhtiar might order the military to take over key installations, including the oil fields, but that was very different from a coup or a military takeover as such. Vance commented that that was a very important distinction.

President Carter observed that in retrospect it was clear that the shah had gone to pieces in December. However, despite that, he had never been diverted from the idea that he wished to avoid bloodshed. Even to save his own skin, the shah had been unwilling to order massive bloodshed.

A message was sent that evening to Ambassador Sullivan from Secretary Vance reiterating U.S. policy to remain firm in support of Bakhtiar as the head of the constitutional government, including encouraging the Iranian military to take action if necessary to increase Bakhtiar's chances of success. The military should not be encouraged to stand aside if action was required to preserve the constitutional government.

President Carter's anger during the meeting on February 5, although directed primarily at Ambassador Sullivan, was in fact more generalized. Throughout the crisis, discipline within the U.S. government had been deplorable at almost every level. Policy was constantly contradicted or undermined by leaks, unattributed comments by "insiders" who had a particular ax to grind, and bureaucratic sniping. Public reports from the shah's party in Egypt and Morocco increasingly blamed the shah's collapse on the lack of support he had received from Washington, and Henry Kissinger was beginning to launch a political campaign against the president based on the theme that Carter's policies had "lost" Iran for the West. The situation in Tehran was going from bad to worse, and nothing seemed to work. It was a moment of intense personal and political frustration.

On the morning after the meeting with Huyser, the Washington *Post* carried a story quoting State Department sources to the effect that the Bakhtiar government was not expected to survive more than a few days. Carter's anger boiled over. He assembled the entire top leadership of the State Department in the Roosevelt Room, across the hall from the Oval Office, and treated them to a tongue-lashing. He asked for no comments or explanations but simply informed them that the continuing leaks were intolerable and threatened to have them fired unless the practice ceased.[8]

Of course, leaks did not stop, and the dilemma in Iran remained just as frustrating as before. The real significance of this episode was its confirmation of what seems to be a universal law in Washington: when things are going badly, frustration will be transferred to the press and to persons unknown within the government who are believed to be sabotaging policy. It happens to every administration, and the Carter administration was actually quite mild in its reactions compared to some of its predecessors. Presumably President Carter felt better for getting it off his chest, but the problems in Iran remained as intractable as ever.

General Huyser's departure from Iran had not terminated U.S. contact with the Iranian military leadership. General Philip C. Gast, chief of the U.S. Military Assistance and Advisory Group (MAAG), had worked closely with Huyser while he was in Iran, and he now continued the daily contacts with the military and the daily telephone reports to Secretary Brown in the Pentagon.

By this time as well, the focus of the entire U.S. intelligence machinery had shifted to Iran. Although the quality of the information had not improved substantially, the volume of papers and reports was increasing geometrically. Brzezinski was concerned that he might miss a key item, so we began a unique experiment in communications. Each morning the White House Situation Room would present me with a large binder of messages and reports that had arrived overnight. I would go through these quickly, highlighting specific points of interest and adding my own comments in the margins. Brzezinski would review the folder during the morning, adding his own comments and questions. It was a cumbersome system, and my overworked friends in the Situation Room groaned under this additional burden, but the process worked as a short-term expedient.

On February 8, I summarized for Brzezinski my views on the "war of nerves" that was developing in Tehran. In my memorandum I said I thought Iran was undergoing a slow-motion coup that was as unique as it was fascinating. There were two power centers—the military and Khomeini's forces—represented by two front men—Bakhtiar and Bazargan. Neither power center was entirely sure of its strength, and neither was quite prepared for a decisive showdown. Bazargan's strategy of creeping up on power versus Bakhtiar's blocking maneuvers resulted in an intricate test of wills. Both men, in my opinion, were strong-willed, clever and basically moderate. The fact that Bakhtiar and Bazargan were old friends and allies from the Mossadegh era gave the contest a uniquely Persian flavor. The game, however, could be interrupted at any time by the wild cards on either side.

Things Fall Apart

As luck would have it, on the day after I wrote this memorandum, the wild card was played and the "slow motion" coup shifted into high gear. According to General Gast, at eight-thirty in the evening of February 9, Iranian television ran a special program on the events surrounding Khomeini's return to Tehran. The program stirred up excitement among the homafars (NCO technicians) at Doshen Tappeh Air Base on the eastern outskirts of Tehran. The homafars began to demonstrate, and fighting broke out with troops of the Imperial

Guard. The Imperial Guard brought in additional troops, but the fighting escalated, with shooting reported inside and outside the base. By 3 A.M., the situation had calmed down, but it resumed later in the morning. Overnight, the homafars or others broke into the base armory and seized as many as 2,000 rifles, some of which were tossed over the fence to opposition elements outside.

A curfew was imposed throughout Tehran from 4:30 P.M. on February 10, but it was ignored and the fighting continued. General Gast was pinned down in an office at the headquarters of the Supreme Command Staff and was unable to get back to the embassy. Demonstrations were spreading throughout the city, with sporadic shooting and fires. Brzezinski convened an emergency session of the SCC at 8:30 Sunday morning, February 11.

Secretary Vance was spending the weekend with President Carter at Camp David, so the State Department was represented by Warren Christopher, David Newsom and Harold Saunders. Secretary of Defense Harold Brown was also out of town, and Defense was represented by Deputy Secretary Charles Duncan. The chairman of the Joint Chiefs of Staff, General David Jones, was present, together with Generals Bernard Rogers and William Smith. The director of central intelligence, Admiral Turner, was delayed, and he was represented in the early part of the meeting by his deputy, Frank Carlucci.

As the meeting opened, Charles Duncan took a call from President Carter at Camp David for an update on the situation in Tehran. The available information was fragmentary and confused. General Gast was still at SCS headquarters, where the building was under fire. There were reports that the U.S. consulate in Tabriz was under attack and being sacked. The Iranian guards at the U.S. embassy had withdrawn, leaving only the twenty-two Marine guards for protection.[9]

There was no reliable information about Prime Minister Bakhtiar's whereabouts, and General Gast was unable to establish contact with General Gharabaghi, the chief of staff. The status of the army was uncertain.

Reportedly, the military high command had met overnight. Until about midnight the generals had been determined to stick with Bakhtiar, but in the early-morning hours, as the fighting intensified, they decided not to confront the people. Shortly after six o'clock the military withdrew to barracks, proclaiming its "neutrality" in the political conflict. As the news came in about the military collapse, Warren Christopher, recalling General Huyser's assurances to the president only six days earlier, permitted himself the wry observation that, in retrospect, he now found General Huyser's report of the military situation slightly optimistic.

The meeting dealt with two questions: first, how to secure the safety of Americans remaining in Iran; and second, what, if anything, the United States could do to affect the outcome of the situation. With respect to the safety of Americans, a decision was taken, based on Sullivan's reports, to continue with preparations for an evacuation but to send no aircraft or personnel into Iran for the time being.

On the larger question of what might be done on the part of the United

States to influence the situation, Brzezinski found himself playing a lonely hand. All the other representatives at the meeting had concluded that the army's decision to withdraw was unequivocal evidence that it was unwilling to take action into its own hands. That conclusion was reinforced in the course of the meeting when word was received that General Gharabaghi was meeting with Bazargan. The military, it appeared, had decided to make peace with the opposition, and an accommodation was in the process of being worked out.

Brzezinski did not dispute the evidence. However, he had been the leading proponent of Option C throughout the crisis, and he was not ready to admit that the plans for a military takeover had been invalidated before they could even be tried. Brzezinski said he did not know if the military—or elements of the military—had lost all will to act, but he was not prepared to accept that conclusion on the basis of the fragmentary information available. The stakes, he said, were too high. If a coup was no longer a possibility, so be it; but if it was still possible, Brzezinski insisted that the option be relayed to the president for consideration.

After lengthy discussion it was agreed that David Newsom would telephone Ambassador Sullivan, seeking his views and the views of General Gast about whether the army retained any capability for independent action. At the same time, General Jones was to call General Huyser (now back in Europe) to seek his views on the same question. These two conversations took place at about ten-thirty, after the meeting had been in progress for two hours. While they were going on, Brzezinski talked to the president to bring him up to date and inform him of what was happening.

The group re-formed at eleven o'clock for a report. Charles Duncan summarized Huyser's views. Huyser thought the military would act only if the United States was prepared to pledge full moral and political support, up to and including combat support. He did not recommend it. Warren Christopher, in turn, summarized Sullivan's views (Gast could not be contacted). Sullivan said that the military was in the process of making its accommodation with Bazargan, and it was too beleaguered to undertake any action. On the basis of these two reports, Brzezinski reluctantly agreed that the Iranian military had lost its will. As a consequence, military action was dropped as a realistic option.[10]

The best epitaph of the day's events—and perhaps of this entire period—was written by Air Force Colonel Tom Schaefer. Colonel Schaefer was the U.S. Defense attaché in Tehran, and he was later to be one of the hostages. At the end of a long message report summarizing the developments of February 11, he concluded with admirable military brevity: "Army surrenders; Khomeini wins. Destroying all classified."

VIII

THE POLITICS OF REVOLUTION

Nobody is ever ready for a revolution. Certainly the Carter administration was ill prepared for and repeatedly surprised by the rapid dissolution of the Iranian monarchy. However, the exclusive focus of this account on U.S. policy and the reactions of decision makers in Washington may have left the impression that Washington was unique in its almost willful blindness to the actual state of events in Iran. Nothing could be further from the truth.

If an equally candid account were written from the perspective of London, Paris, Moscow, Tokyo, Baghdad, Riyadh, Cairo, Islamabad, Tel Aviv or any other capital of any nation with significant interests in Iran, it would reveal uncertainties, misperceptions and failures of judgment at least as serious as those chronicled in this account. Moreover, these failings were not confined to chancelleries of foreign governments. Iranians of all persuasions were astonished at the rapidity of the collapse of central authority, and they almost universally misjudged the nature of the outcome and its effects on their own lives and interests. Needless to say, the shah and those around him had little comprehension of the events they were witnessing, and until very late, little appreciation of the implications for their continued rule.

This failure of comprehension was no freak occurrence. It is, in fact, the common experience of all revolutions. Hannah Arendt reminds us that the original meaning of the word "revolution" was "restoration." In fact, the process normally begins with relatively modest, reformist aims that are transformed into "revolutionary" goals only by events that outrun the imagination even of those most committed to change.[1] Revolutions are endowed with inevitability only after they are over, and their ultimate goals and meaning seldom become clear until long after the *ancien régime* has vanished.

In Iran, the original objective of the opposition was not to overthrow the monarchy and replace it with an Islamic republic. Even most of Khomeini's closest followers in Iran, who risked their lives organizing and managing mass demonstrations, had very little understanding or basic sympathy for the concept of clerical rule. Initially, they would have been more than satisfied by a return to the constitution of 1906, which provided for curbs on the absolute powers of the shah and for a review process to ensure that laws were compatible with Islamic principles. Even as late as February 1979, after the shah had departed and Khomeini was back in Tehran, many if not most of them were prepared to reach an accommodation with Bakhtiar in order to facilitate an orderly transfer of power within the framework of the existing constitutional order. Reportedly, it was only Khomeini himself who insisted on *revolutionary* change, i.e., the total invalidation of the previous system and the creation of a new order based exclusively on the will of the masses as demonstrated by their presence in the streets.

The eagerness for change in the Iranian body politic was a manifestation of deep social, economic and historical forces. Khomeini did not invent those feelings, but he mustered them and endowed them with form and purpose. Khomeini did not *cause* the revolution, but it is no exaggeration to say that he single-handedly transformed an inchoate reform movement with limited objectives into a genuinely revolutionary experience with its own unique ideological content.

Khomeini came to embody the revolution, but the highly personal and unconventional nature of his political philosophy was no less a mystery to those who chanted his name in the streets of Tehran than it was to perplexed statesmen and scholars in the West. Moreover, those who joined in protest against the excesses of the shah's rule did not know their own strength. They were astonished first by the relative ease of their initial successes against the regime, and then later by the seemingly inexorable imposition of a new political order that had no precedent in Iran's long history and which, indeed, was unlike any other form of government in the world. The anguish of that unexpected turn of events was more profound and more thoroughly disillusioning to several generations of Iranians than it was to anyone in Washington. However harshly one may judge U.S. performance, its shortcomings and errors of judgment about the nature and meaning of the Iranian revolution were not the exception but the rule—for foreign observers and Iranians alike.

Genuine social revolutions in large, powerful, strategically situated nations are rare. The likelihood that the peculiar combination of events that produced the Iranian revolution will be duplicated elsewhere is remote. Yet there are patterns in the Iranian experience that closely resemble revolutionary events in many other nations and suggest some general lessons.

First, can the events in Iran be regarded as a true revolution, compared, for example, with the American, the French or the Russian revolutions?

Within certain circles of scholars and political activists, many of whom were bitterly disappointed with the emergence of a repressive theocratic regime in Iran, there was a tendency to regard the events of 1977–1981 as a historical aberration, an unfortunate interruption of the historical process that they believed was leading Iran toward a more liberal political system providing for wider public participation, freer public expression and expanded civil rights. In this view, Khomeini's seizure of the instruments of power and his imposition of his own esoteric doctrine was, at best, a diversion of the true revolutionary (or evolutionary) process in Iran. This frustration of the political aspirations of the Iranian people, it was argued, did not deserve the glorious name of revolution.

There is no need to spend much time on this interpretation, for it says more about the political views of those who espouse it than about the revolution itself. It can be argued that Khomeini "stole" the revolution or at least distorted its original aims into something quite different and unexpected. But revolutions seldom if ever achieve in practice the ideal objectives that their supporters or partisans had hoped for. Moreover, the "legitimacy" of Khomeini's political ideas would appear to be at least as great as those of the Bolsheviks. Unlike the Bolsheviks, who seized power *after* the popular uprising had succeeded, Khomeini was popularly acclaimed as the sole leader of the revolution almost from the start, and the uprising was carried out in his name. Khomeini's ideas were no secret, and it is no use to complain after the fact that politicians and intellectuals inside and outside Iran refused to take them seriously.

Hannah Arendt describes a true revolution as one "where change occurs in the sense of a new beginning, where violence is used to constitute an altogether different form of government, to bring about the formation of a new body politic, where the liberation from oppression aims at least at the constitution of freedom . . ."[2] That is a precisely accurate description of the mass movement in Iran that resulted in the overthrow of the shah, albeit that the *aim* of "constituting freedom" in Iran was less than perfectly realized in the period following the shah's demise.

One of the most intriguing truths about all revolutions is that they occur not in conditions of abject misery but rather in societies that are experiencing a relative improvement in economic conditions. Revolutions, it appears, are born out of the perception that misery is not inevitable and that genuine improvement of man's lot is indeed possible. As Crane Brinton observed more than forty years ago in his classic work *The Anatomy of Revolution,*[3] the danger of revolution seems to arise in a society when general expectations of improved political, economic or social conditions are thwarted or interrupted.

Iran provides an almost textbook case. As a nation, Iran had experienced a long period of sustained growth and economic development. That growth had been spectacular during the decade following the shah's declaration of his White Revolution in 1963. However, by the mid-1970s, distortions had emerged in virtually every sector of the economy, due at least in part to the shah's determination to transform Iran almost overnight into a modern industrial giant, and the boom faltered badly.

Perhaps even more important was the total failure of political instruments to keep pace with economic growth. All power resided in the person of the shah, and the shah surrounded himself with a tiny group of advisers and technocrats whose tenure in office was determined by their absolute loyalty to the person of the shah and to his grandiose schemes. Although education was vigorously promoted, the new class of intellectuals, professionals and industrialists, together with the semiliterate masses who flocked from the rural areas to participate in the economic boom, was systematically excluded from the political process. Although the shah toyed with various experiments intended to create political parties, he never permitted these parties to become more than forums of praise for his programs and his personal rule, and they were regarded as little more than mouthpieces for the regime.

In every sector of the society, institutions were subordinated to the shah's rule and programs. There were many ways for ambitious Iranians to become rich, but almost no channels through which they could realistically aspire to acquire a voice in political decisions. At the same time, the greed and corruption of a privileged class at the top—most notably including the members of the royal family—assumed scandalous proportions.

By keeping the political lid firmly in place, the shah avoided messy challenges and disruptions of his programs. And as long as the general boom continued to benefit the population as a whole, the system functioned as intended. However, when the boom faltered and popular discontent began seething beneath the surface, Iranians had no outlet to express their grievances, which began to build to the point of explosion.

Lacking any political channels, people turned to the only popular institution not totally dominated by the shah's system—the mosques. And there they found a message waiting for them from Ayatollah Khomeini, who had bided his time in angry exile for more than a decade and who had occupied himself over those years developing the concept of a purely Islamic state to replace the hated Pahlavi rule. Popular discontent found both a leader and a syntax. The revolution was born.

This is not to imply that the revolution was either inevitable or easily identifiable. Organized political protest occurs in many societies—even in highly authoritarian monarchies—without turning into revolution. Moreover, even those who join together in protest seldom do so with the conscious intention of overturning a government. On the contrary, the regime usually appears impossibly strong, and the protesters typically are astonished when their initial efforts meet with success.

Michael Fischer recounts a telling incident from the early days of the revolution in Iran. When an old woman heard the crowds beginning to chant "Death to the shah!" for the first time, she fled in terror. Then, when she found that the soldiers were not going to shoot, she returned to watch the demonstration.[4] Timidity is much more common than boldness, particularly in the early stages, and self-confidence (as well as more ambitious objectives) grow only after repeated testing meets with an unanticipated degree of success. When and whether scattered discontent will crystallize into genuine revolution is essentially unpredictable.

Nevertheless, there are several lessons to be drawn from the Iranian case that may be suggestive in other instances. The first, of course, is to be particularly alert to the implications of an economic setback in any society that is experiencing an upward curve of growth and development. That is surely a sign of serious trouble, if not necessarily revolution. Second, if normal institutions for the expression of political and economic discontent are stifled or absent, observers should be sensitive to the messages being conveyed through other, perhaps unorthodox channels. When political dissent is blocked, like water rising behind a dam it will seek whatever avenues are available to it. Dissent will grow in the interstices of a political system if it must, in corners where embassies do not normally direct their attention.

Finally, a careful observer would do well to take a jaundiced view of the security apparatus of the state, for there is almost always a tendency to overestimate its effectiveness in dealing with demonstrations of deep-seated popular dissatisfaction. Certainly one should guard against casual judgments that *any* regime is so strong or so well established that it is immune from revolutionary contagion. No regime could have appeared stronger, richer or more firmly entrenched than that of the shah in the mid-1970s.

"The Best Lack All Conviction"

All of this, of course, is much easier said than done. Genuine revolutions do not occur frequently, and their symptoms are always easier to detect with the benefits of hindsight than for the observer on the spot who is inundated with conflicting information and contradictory signals. Still, there are a few symptoms that seem to be common to the pre-revolutionary condition. One is what Crane Brinton has called "the desertion of the intellectuals."[5]

If the most talented and best educated men and women that a society produces are outraged and contemptuous of the system in which they live, one may suspect that similar views are endemic within the less articulate masses of the body politic. A certain amount of bickering and criticism is inevitable among intellectuals; otherwise, as Brinton notes, they would not be intellectuals. Nevertheless, he suggests, there is a qualitative and quantitative difference between revolutionary and non-revolutionary conditions. The writers, teachers and preachers in genuinely revolutionary societies seem to share an almost universal belief that the world "needs making over."

The phenomenon is most immediately apparent in the disillusionment of the ruling class itself. Brinton recounts the comments of a czarist minister reflecting on the days before the Russian Revolution: "Even the very highest classes became *frondeurs* before the revolution; in the grand salons and clubs the policy of the government received harsh and unfriendly criticism. The relations that had been formed in the Czar's family were analyzed and talked over. Little anecdotes were passed about the head of state. . . . A sense of the danger of this sport did not awaken until the last moment."[6]

The shah's ambassador in London asked himself early in 1977, "Why is it that when people talk about torture by SAVAK or bribery in high places, I feel humiliated to such an extent that I am robbed of any will to answer back? Such iniquitous deeds have been going on for a long time and, what is more, I have known about them all along. Why then this sudden feeling of revulsion?"[7] Why indeed? By October of the same year, the ambassador was hearing rumors that the shah "now visits a crony's house three times a week in the afternoon to smoke opium."[8] Reflecting on the massacre in Jaleh Square a year later, the ambassador wondered: "Does anyone, inside Iran, still view [the shah] with affection, or sympathy? Have not his false priorities and disastrous economic policies, his military grandiosity and obsession with everything that flies and fires, his unquenchable thirst for flattery and his breathtaking insensitivity to the feelings of his own people, his vainglory and ceaseless lecturing —have these not dissipated any remaining reserves of national and international goodwill towards him?"[9]

All of this from an avowed monarchist and the shah's personal representative in a major Western capital!

Uri Lubrani, the Israeli representative in Tehran, recalled an incident after a meeting with the shah on Qish Island. Returning from the meeting, he encountered a senior Iranian official who was one of the shah's closest advisers. "He said, 'Have you actually seen His Imperial Majesty?' I said yes. He said, 'Have you *really* seen this epitome of Iranian degradation?' Well, I couldn't believe what I was hearing. It meant there was something rotten at the very core of the base on which the shah relied."[10]

In retrospect, this growing sense of cynicism and disillusionment among the very individuals who had gained the most from the shah's reign was a clear signal. It marked the spread of political dry rot throughout the system, casting doubt on the essential legitimacy of the monarchy. It helps to explain the tentativeness of some of the shah's actions, for he must have sensed at some point that even his natural constituency had grown flaccid and equivocal in its support. Moreover, this phenomenon is quite easy (and inexpensive) to monitor. Too frequently the gossip of the salons, as well as the messages of novelists, poets, playwrights, balladeers and pamphleteers, are simply ignored by political scientists and embassies.

"And Lose the Name of Action"

That leads to one further observation about experiences that most revolutions seem to have in common, specifically the ineptness and lack of skill with which the rulers confront the mounting rebellion, and their almost universal unwillingness or inability to use force effectively.[11] The underlying causes for this may be complex and quite different from one case to the next, but it is the essential condition that permits the revolution to gain strength and ultimately succeed. Revolutions can be stopped, even when relatively far advanced, by a ruler who conveys a sense of strength, determination and self-confidence.

In the case of the shah, many have argued that he was fundamentally a weak and indecisive man who had shown his true colors when he fled the country in 1953 as the "countercoup" appeared to be failing. He lived in the shadow of his father's dominant presence, and his weak and muddled response to the events of 1978, this argument goes, was predictable and entirely in character. There is no doubt truth in this assessment of the shah's personality. I was struck by his shyness and diffidence when he visited the White House in 1977, and Ambassador Sullivan recalls in his memoirs that from his first meeting with the shah, he found him "tentative" and anything but the "tough customer" that he had been led to expect.[12]

Nevertheless, this reading of the shah's character smacks of the smugness of perfect hindsight. The shah had in fact shown himself to be both courageous and decisive on a number of occasions. He had survived several major political crises and two attempts on his life. His White Revolution was a bold stroke that involved confrontations with both the large landholders and the clergy. In a fractious and politically volatile nation, he had held on to his throne for thirty-seven years. By the mid-1970s, it had been a long time since anyone could recall seeing the shah wilt under pressure. I am not satisfied that the shah's collapse in 1978 can adequately be explained by the fact that, as a boy, he had been dominated by his father. At least two other factors, in my opinion, must be given equal weight.

Iran was facing complex economic and social problems that were not anticipated in the shah's grand scheme. His juggling of cabinets, beginning in 1977, and his clumsy experimentation with a new political party were evidence that he was aware things were going wrong. But the shah had run out of answers.

He seemed to cling to the belief that if he could only get his entire program in place, things would work out. Yet the problems could not be solved by more of the same medicine that had helped create them in the first place. His own expectations about Iran were beginning to be plagued by some of the same doubts that were infecting his subjects. As one close associate of the shah put it, he had been on the throne for thirty-seven years, and he was simply exhausted. Intellectually he had run out of steam.

The other key factor, of course, was his health. Military and political figures who were close to the shah during those last years have told me that in early 1978, long before the demonstrations had gotten out of hand, the shah was a "changed man." On several occasions he was reliably reported to have suddenly broken down and cried for no apparent reason in meetings with his advisers. None of them was specifically aware of his medical problem, but they knew that something was seriously wrong. Although such stories circulated

widely in Tehran and, on at least one occasion, reportedly were shared with
U.S. officials, this information never found its way to the White House.

Religion and Revolution

In her treatise on revolution, Hannah Arendt comments: "Secularization, the
separation of religion and politics and the rise of a secular realm with a dignity
of its own, is certainly a crucial factor in the phenomenon of revolution.
Indeed, it may ultimately turn out that what we call revolution is precisely that
transitory phase which brings about the birth of a new, secular realm."[13] This
passage highlights the contradictions between Khomeini's Islamic, theocratic
revolution and the Western tradition of secularizing revolutions. In my view,
this tension between the secular and the religious was a major contributing
factor to the failure of both Iranians and Westerners to recognize the revolution in its early stages and to gauge properly its actual course and eventual
outcome.

We are all prisoners of our own cultural assumptions, more than we care
to admit. Those of us who are products of Western cultural tradition—even
if our national origins are in Africa or Asia—share certain assumptions that
are so firmly ingrained that they no longer require discussion but are regarded
almost as natural law—inevitable and irrevocable. It is now two centuries since
the first modern revolution in 1776, and over that span of time the world has
grown accustomed to the most outlandish proposals for the revolutionary
change of political, social and economic conditions. We may be difficult to
persuade, but we are no longer easily surprised.

Nevertheless, Khomeini's call for the establishment of a religious philosopher-king, the *velayat-e faqih,* and clerical management of political institutions
according to religious law was so unexpected, so alien to existing political
traditions that it was less a surprise than an embarrassment. The participation
of the church in a revolutionary movement was neither new nor particularly
disturbing, but the notion of a popular revolution leading to the establishment
of a theocratic state seemed so unlikely as to be absurd.

Vision is influenced by expectations, and perceptions—especially in politics
—are colored by the models and analogies all of us carry in our heads.
Unfortunately, there were no relevant models in Western political tradition to
explain what we were seeing in Iran during the revolution. This contradiction
between expectation and reality was so profound and so persistent that it
interfered fundamentally with the normal processes of observation and analysis on which all of us instinctively rely.

On one level, it helps to explain why the early-warning functions of all
existing intelligence systems—from SAVAK to Mossad to the CIA—failed so
utterly in the Iranian case. Certainly, U.S. intelligence capability to track the
shah's domestic opposition had been allowed to deteriorate almost to the
vanishing point. But even if it had not, it would probably have looked in the

wrong place. Only in retrospect is it obvious that a good intelligence organization should have focused its attention on the religious schools, the mosques and
the recorded sermons of an aged religious leader who had been living in exile
for fourteen years. As one State Department official remarked in some exasperation after the revolution, "Whoever took religion seriously?"[14]

Even after it became clear that the revolution was gaining momentum and
that the movement was being organized through the mosques in the name of
Khomeini, observers of all stripes assumed that the purely religious forces were
merely a means to the end of ousting the shah and that their political role
would be severely limited in the political environment following the shah's
departure. The mosque, it was believed, would serve as the transmission belt
of the revolution, but its political importance would quickly wane once its
initial objectives had been achieved.

Thus Ambassador Sullivan, in his "Thinking the Unthinkable" message of
early November 1978, could take for granted that Khomeini would return to
Iran to assume a "Ghandi-like" role in the political constellation and could
feel free to focus his attention on the seemingly more important question of
who would take over actual political power. Similarly, the U.S. scholar James
Bill could assert without qualification in December 1978 that the clerics "would
never participate directly in the formal government structure." In his twenty-
page analysis of the revolution and its possible future course, Bill found it
necessary to mention Khomeini by name only once (a reference to his exile in
1964) and never once used the term "Islamic Republic."[15] What was truly
"unthinkable," it appears, was not the shah's demise but the emergence of a
clerical-dominated Islamic republic.

The mullahs, it was argued, could not run a complex government even if
they wanted to, so they would inevitably have to turn to the secular leadership.
Khomeini did his part to keep this myth alive by appointing Bazargan, Sanjabi
and others to key posts in the provisional government, but they discovered
from the start—as they had in the months before the shah's collapse—that
their freedom to exercise real authority was contingent on their willingness to
institute a fully Islamic government in accordance with Khomeini's ideas.
Contrary to the assumptions of many Western and Iranian observers, these
men were not the cutting edge of the revolution but only its handmaidens.[16]

The same instinctive rejection of the possibility of a pro-clerical revolution
infected the shah and most upper-class Iranians. They regarded the mullahs
with open contempt as medieval reactionaries whose economic and social
concepts ran counter to the entire history of modern Iran. This attitude led
the shah and most sophisticated Iranians to underestimate badly the true
power of the religious movement and to explain events by resorting to conspiracy theories. Princess Ashraf, the shah's twin sister, expressed this attitude
perfectly when, in 1982, years after the collapse of the monarchy, she said in
a radio interview: "I am sure that it couldn't be only the mullahs. . . . It was
a concerted movement from the foreigners also. It happened the same thing
with my father. It happened the same thing with my brother. There are

foreigners who saw that Iran was becoming very important . . . and Iran in ten years' time would be another Japan. They couldn't afford another Japan in Asia."[17]

She and many others like her found it easier to believe that the revolution was the work of sinister foreign influence than to revise their opinion of the clergy. To this day they have never understood, much less acknowledged, who the real enemy was and from what source it derived its strength.

The gap between perception and reality gave birth to some marvelously muddled thinking. In early 1979, Richard Falk, a professor at Princeton and an activist on issues of peace and human rights, traveled to Iran and then to Paris, where he met with the ayatollah. Shortly thereafter he wrote a paean of praise to Khomeini and his movement. Drawing particular attention to the fact that Khomeini's entourage was "uniformly composed of moderate, progressive individuals" who shared "a notable record of concern for human rights and . . . economic development," he concluded that "Iran may yet provide us with a desperately-needed model of humane government for a third-world country."[18]

Three years later, appearing on a panel with Professor Falk, I was startled to hear him describe the Khomeini regime as "the most terroristic since Hitler." Clearly, the revolution had not worked out as expected. What had changed in the meantime was not Khomeini's concept of an Islamic republic, but Professor Falk's expectations. In the intervening three years, all of the moderate and progressive individuals around Khomeini, as well as many former revolutionaries, had protested against the principle of a theocratic state, with the result that they were successively removed from office, arrested or, in many cases, killed.

All true revolutions carry the germ of an idea that is widely regarded as illegitimate or "unthinkable" by its contemporaries. In the case of Khomeini's revolution, that central idea was the union of church and state in the form of an Islamic republic with a supreme religious guide—the *velayat-e faqih.* As a consequence, the world was surprised not once but twice by the Iranian revolution. It was surprised in the first instance by the breadth and depth of popular opposition to the shah and the success of revolutionary organization emanating from the mosques. The world was surprised once again when Khomeini was able to sustain his "fanciful" notions of an ideal theocratic state.

Nothing quite like this had occurred since the Reformation, and secular observers may be forgiven for their stubborn refusal to believe that this preoccupation with theological niceties in Tehran was anything more than a minor bout of eccentricity that would soon pass. In the meantime, those who were attempting to understand the course of events were repeatedly reduced to scratching their heads in amazement at the "irrationality" of the new regime. Khomeini seemed to have his priorities reversed. The classic functions of economic performance, social order and political stability were not ignored but were routinely subordinated in practice to abstract goals.

If those goals had been articulated in familiar terms ("Liberty, equality, fraternity," "Life, liberty and the pursuit of happiness," or "From each according to his abilities, to each according to his needs"), the gap between ideal goals and political reality would have been much easier to understand; but the importance of the intense struggles within Iran over the principle of *velayat-e faqih* was lost on most secular observers inside and outside Iran. It did not correspond to our image of the kind of question worthy of serious and prolonged political discourse.

The point is not to suggest that the Iranian revolution, because of its theological content, was somehow divinely ordained or endowed with moral superiority. On the contrary, in the Iranian case as in most revolutions, ideological purpose was grafted on a vast and inchoate swell of social protest through accidents of circumstances and personalities. All successful revolutions acquire a miraculous aura by virtue of the sheer improbability of the triumph of a mysterious popular will over a seemingly invincible structure of authority, and all revolutions impute sacred values to their central principles, however mundane or materialistic they may be.

The Iranian revolution was neither immutable nor inevitable in the form it assumed, and the fact that it proclaimed a religious rather than a secular doctrine is in itself no assurance that it will ultimately prevail. Instead, the first few years of Khomeini's rule in Iran offered a grim reminder that inhumanities performed in the name of religious extremism may equal and even exceed the abuses of materialistic regimes motivated by simple political expediency.

The point is simply this: the religious origins and doctrine of the Iranian revolution set it apart from all revolutionary movements of modern times. Observers inside and outside Iran, instinctively confident that the religious dimension was only superficial, attempted to "fit" the Iranian events into more familiar models of revolutionary experience. Not understanding what the revolution was about and profoundly skeptical of the notion of religion as the rallying point for a social revolution, almost everyone misjudged the power, the organizational capacity, the nature of the popular appeal, the motives and the purposes of the revolutionary movement.

In the absence of any relevant analogies, predictions and policies proved to be not so much wrong as irrelevant. Both the best-case and the worst-case expectations were confounded. The hopes for a liberal, democratic system and the fears of a rapid slide to radical, leftist positions were both rendered meaningless by the emergence of a clerically dominated theocratic regime that rejected democratic forms and leftist nostrums equally.

Moreover, even after the truly unthinkable had happened and Khomeini's exotic vision of the ideal state was well on its way to realization, policy judgment continued to be impaired by an unspoken but intrinsic conviction that any regime so wildly contrary to all the rules of accepted political behavior would inevitably destroy itself through its own excesses. Although never articulated, this theme ran like an undercurrent through U.S. policy during the hostage crisis, where it distorted in subtle ways assessments of the immediate physical threat to the hostages and the capacity of Khomeini's regime to absorb punishment in the form of sanctions.

Much of the deep emotion that permeated the policy-making process during the hostage crisis can, in my opinion, be traced to the underlying belief that we were dealing not only with a government that had flouted the law of nations (a disagreeable but all too common occurrence) but with a regime that was historically illegitimate, unfit, despicable. I suspect that all of us, reading the speeches and accounts coming out of Tehran, experienced a sense of physical revulsion at one time or another.

None of this can be quantified in terms of its effects on policy. It is entirely possible that with perfect understanding and the absence of deep cultural bias, the actual policy decisions would have been much the same, with the same results. Nevertheless, it is worth reminding ourselves that genuine revolutions tend to produce genuinely revolutionary results that may confound the normal processes of analysis and judgment. That insight was earned at the expense of so much individual and collective anguish during the course of the Iranian revolution that it is worth recording, even if it must be learned again the next time.

In Retrospect

Looking back at the period of the Iranian revolution and the collapse of the Pahlavi regime, with all its disastrous implications for U.S. policy in the Persian Gulf and elsewhere, there is a natural impulse to look for heroes and villains. For those so inclined, there is surely sufficient grist in the previous chapters to keep the mills of partisan advocates churning. However, that was not the purpose of the narrative.

On the contrary, an objective reading will reveal neither heroes nor villains. There were errors of perception and judgment in abundance, but they were distributed among the various actors about equally. No one in this crisis had a monopoly on wisdom. No one had it right consistently, and there were more than enough failures to go around.

It is more interesting to ask whether there were missed opportunities that might have changed the course of events significantly. Was there a key moment when a different policy or set of policies would have produced an outcome more favorable to the United States? The answer can never be known with any certainty, but it may be instructive to speculate on this question with respect to each of the principal actors in the drama.

"Now Does He Feel His Title Hang Loose About Him"

The shah, more than any other single individual, had it in his power to alter the course of the crisis. However, a real change of policy may have been more difficult for him than for any other actor. He brought with him thirty-seven years of experience and expectations. He had gambled audaciously with his country's future, placing all of his hopes on rapid economic development and military strength. Ultimately the failure of those policies and the shah's own flawed vision sparked the revolutionary ferment in Iran that brought him down. As early as 1976 he recognized that things were not going well and began a series of political maneuvers to attempt to relieve the growing economic and social pressures. However, he was also engaged in a race against time. He was ill, and he was determined to complete his plans for the "Great Civilization" in time to hand it to his son, possibly as early as 1980.

Thus, he was trapped in an iron vise. To deal effectively with the growing crisis, it was necessary to rethink his priorities and pre-empt—quickly, firmly and imaginatively—the growing tide of dissent. But that demanded a total reassessment of the strategy in which he had invested so much over nearly twenty years, at a moment when his creative energies were at a very low ebb. Moreover, he had so thoroughly insulated himself from reality behind a shield of docile advisers that it would have required a major act of will merely to penetrate the glossy surface of his own propaganda.

Despite the recurrent demonstrations of 1978, the evidence is overwhelming that the shah became aware of the full extent of popular opposition to his rule only in September, after the tragedy at Jaleh Square. By that time it may already have been too late for political solutions, and the confrontation in the streets could no longer be controlled by a limited application of force. The shah was thus faced with an impossible dilemma: either overhaul entirely the structure he had so painfully created over nearly four decades or launch a bloody, repressive campaign. He was unwilling to do either. Instead, he temporized and maneuvered on the margins, hoping for a break that never came.

This was more than a crisis of will. It was the crisis of an entire system that had run out of control. The assertion that the shah was paralyzed into inaction by the human rights policies of the Carter administration simply is not supported by the evidence or the shah's own testimony in dozens of conversations during the crisis. He was annoyed by these policies, to be sure, but his repeated refusals to launch either radical reforms or a bloodbath were based on calculations of self-interest and internal political realities, not on fear of offending Washington.

"Passages That Lead to Nothing"

That is not to say that Washington's response to the crisis was of no importance. It was. But it was more important to Washington than to Tehran. President Jimmy Carter and his foreign policy advisers were faced with the problem of preserving and defending U.S. security interests in the Persian Gulf. They were slow to recognize the extent of the danger, and the decision-making process was undisciplined and sporadic once the danger was apparent. This generally poor performance was the result of a number of factors.

First, the policy structure that the Carter administration inherited was inherently flawed. The decision by President Nixon and Henry Kissinger in 1972 to subordinate U.S. security decision making in the Persian Gulf to the person of the shah was unprecedented, excessive and ultimately inexplicable. The subsequent erosion of an independent U.S. capability to follow internal events in Iran was as unnecessary as it was unwise. This was the legacy of five years of prior policies—policies that were accepted and continued without serious challenge when the new administration took office.

The habit of relying on the shah and the consequent absence of reliable independent information were then compounded by the intrusion of competing policy issues—especially Camp David—which distracted and diverted attention from Iran. Ambassador Sullivan contributed to this false sense of security by his optimistic reports from Tehran that downplayed any sense of crisis until the last two months of the shah's reign. Then, once the crisis broke in Washington in November 1978, judgments were divided about the nature of the problem and possible courses of U.S. action.

"And So No Force, However Great . . ."

Zbigniew Brzezinski, relying heavily on the counsel of Ambassador Zahedi, consistently favored a military solution in Iran—initially a military government and then a military takeover if necessary. There were individual commanders within the Iranian military who were capable of a campaign of ruthless and bloody repression if given a green light. However, the shah deliberately avoided choosing these men to run the military government he installed in November 1978, and he resisted their pressure to order a military crackdown. Several of these men, notably including General Gholam Ali Oveissi, the former martial-law administrator for Tehran—an army officer with a reputation for absolute ruthlessness—as well as Ardeshir Zahedi, who had consistently pressed the shah to order a military crackdown, quietly left Iran in late December as part of the bargain struck between the shah and Shapour Bakhtiar. Thus, as long as the shah was still in Iran, he prevented the hard-liners from using the "iron fist."

When the shah left in January 1979, there was much talk of a military coup. However, it was mostly talk. As General Huyser discovered, the military had not undertaken even the most elementary planning for an actual takeover, and the senior generals were so unaccustomed to working together that cooperation on such a complex and dangerous plan was problematical at best. Moreover, as the crisis wore on, the loyalty of the military steadily disintegrated.

The Iranian military undoubtedly retained the capacity—at least in theory

—to take over the country until the moment of the revolutionary overthrow and even beyond. That technical capability was the subject of General Huyser's optimistic reports and the basis for Brzezinski's belief in a military solution. However, those judgments overlooked the political erosion going on just beneath the impressive surface of the Iranian military. When the moment of truth arrived, the military was revealed to be an empty shell.

It is not enough to ask whether a military takeover might have led to a different outcome. One must ask *when* such a takeover might have occurred and under what circumstances. The shah might have been persuaded to launch a campaign of military terror, but he would have done so only on the orders of the United States. He probably would have left the country temporarily to dissociate himself from the operation, and the United States would have been left with the task of making it work and with the moral responsibility for what would probably have been a crudely executed bloodbath. President Carter repeatedly rejected this option despite Brzezinski's best efforts, and I believe he was correct not only on moral but on practical policy grounds. Such an operation held the prospect of a Pyrrhic victory at best, and politically it never could have been sustained for long by a U.S. president.

The various schemes for a military coup upon the shah's departure appeared to be based more on wishful thinking than on a realistic appraisal of the Iranian military. The fragmented military command structure that the shah had developed over the years for his own self-defense vastly complicated the kind of military cooperation that would have been required to conduct an effective coup. The erosion of loyalty within the senior ranks, as well as among the enlisted personnel, had gone further than either Huyser or Brzezinski were prepared to admit. The most likely outcome of a military grab for power would have been a civil war, and it is difficult to believe that the Iranian military in its weakened condition would have been the victor in such a contest with Khomeini's mobs.

Underlying all considerations of a military takeover was the question of U.S. direct intervention. Once the United States committed itself to a military solution, there was no turning back. The shah and the generals would expect full U.S. support if things went wrong—as they probably would in such a highly charged political environment—or if it turned into a civil war. It was a no-win situation.

On a purely practical level, the United States was badly equipped to manage a campaign of military repression. The absence of any reliable intelligence infrastructure would have left the United States as dependent on the Iranian generals as it had previously been on the shah, and the generals did not inspire confidence. Even if the military succeeded in restoring control, the United States would have mortgaged any future relationship with Iran by associating itself with what almost certainly would have been extensive bloodletting and a direct confrontation with Islam. The risks of such a policy within Iran and the region were incalculable.

"The Centre Cannot Hold"

The alternative to a military solution was to attempt to build a moderate political center composed of nationalist secular elements. I have discussed at length in the preceding chapters why I did not (and do not) believe such a solution was workable. Essentially, the "moderates" were too weak to sustain such a strategy. Nevertheless, the "search for the center" is a classic U.S. response to a clash of political extremes, and it is worth pondering why such a solution was never attempted seriously in the case of Iran. The answer, I believe, lies in the actions of two men.

Secretary of State Cyrus Vance was the logical spokesman in Washington for such a policy, since many of his associates in the Department of State were its leading proponents. However, Vance was so preoccupied with the Arab-Israeli problem and so unwilling to associate himself with a decision that would have been perceived as backing away from support of the shah that the "centrist" solution was not carried vigorously into high-level policy discussions in Washington. As a result, the issue was never joined until very late in the day, when it was probably too late.

Ambassador William Sullivan was the other senior figure who could have pressed for such a policy. Sullivan was working under extraordinarily difficult circumstances in Tehran at the distant end of the policy-making chain. He was in an exposed and highly vulnerable position without direct contact with the shifting currents of policy attitudes in Washington. In this unenviable position, it would have required great courage to challenge the conventional wisdom in Washington that placed its hopes exclusively on the ability of the shah to act decisively. Nevertheless, as the point man in the crisis and as the sole senior policy official in direct contact with the shah on a regular basis, it was his responsibility to "make the call," i.e., to make the fateful judgment that the shah was irreparably wounded and that U.S. policy makers should actively begin seeking alternative solutions. This he steadfastly refused to do.

On three different occasions, Sullivan rejected suggestions from the Department of State that he take a more active stance of advising the shah and building contacts with the moderate opposition. Instead, he attempted to walk a perilous line between declaratory support for the shah in his reporting cables while conducting private negotiations with the opposition for plans that were to be implemented only after the shah decided to leave.

In the end, this policy produced the worst of both worlds. His support for the shah was perceived in Washington and Tehran as equivocal, thereby undercutting his credibility in both capitals. As a result, when the moment arrived to implement his plan for a brokered deal between the "moderates" and Khomeini, he no longer had the confidence of the president, and his last-minute proposal was rejected.

The likelihood that the "moderates" could ever have bargained effectively with Khomeini about the terms of a post-shah political arrangement was never very high. However, if U.S. support for such a plan was to have any realistic chance of success, it had to be carefully prepared in advance with the knowl-edge and support of the White House. The way the plan was developed and presented virtually guaranteed its failure.

The President's Role

President Carter was not the architect of the U.S. strategic relationship with Iran. Rather, he had inherited a peculiar array of policies that left the United States strategically dependent on the shah's regime, and his discomfort in that position was apparent. He recognized the consequences for the United States of a collapse of the shah's regime, but at the same time he did not feel the kind of personal commitment that he developed, for example, with President Anwar Sadat of Egypt. His attitude throughout the crisis was characterized more by duty than by any sense of passionate engagement.

That attitude was reinforced by the fact that he was simultaneously engaged in an extraordinary peacemaking process between Israel and Egypt that en-gaged his personal attention and the prestige of his office almost on a minute-by-minute basis. Carter was not averse to risk taking. The Camp David meeting was a personal gamble of historic proportions. But it was a gamble for peace to which he had committed himself from the very beginning of his presidency.

Jimmy Carter was instinctively a peacemaker and a reformer. In the cause of peace or social reform, he was capable of a degree of intensity and energy that seemed inexhaustible. But the issues for the United States in the Iran crisis were issues of military strategy and balance of power, and on that ground he was much less comfortable. Those individuals in his administration who lived and breathed military strategy—particularly Zbigniew Brzezinski and James Schlesinger—were therefore at a disadvantage in their efforts to persuade Carter to accept major risks in an attempt to shore up the U.S. strategic position in Iran. Schlesinger, who continued to promote the idea of a high-level emissary almost up to the moment of the shah's departure, would later recall that at the end Carter responded to his arguments with icy repudiation.

Whatever the reasons, Carter did not engage himself actively in the day-to-day policy making during the Iran crisis in the same way that he did in many other policy issues. Rather, his role was one of establishing the outer bounda-ries for U.S. policy at key moments of decision. Carter made it clear on several occasions that the role of the United States, in his view, was to assist the shah to save himself; however, he refused to assume responsibility for decisions that the shah was unprepared to make for himself, and he rejected policies that could have resulted in U.S. military intervention.

Whether or not a more active engagement by the president and a bolder U.S. commitment would have inspired the shah to act with more vigor and imagination seems to me improbable in view of the record, but that must remain a matter of speculation. The United States suffered a strategic setback of massive proportions when the Iranian revolutionaries overthrew the monarchy in Iran. It is almost certainly true that the worst consequences of the revolution could have been prevented or mitigated by an Iranian ruler who was strong, confident and politically creative. It is much less clear that the United States had it in its power to re-create the shah in his own image.

An alternative question, which is seldom asked, is whether President Carter's refusal to intervene in a potential civil war in Iran may have preserved U.S. options for a future situation involving neither the shah nor Khomeini. Only six years after the revolution, those circumstances are difficult to envisage. The catastrophe is still too near and the future too dim to make any meaningful judgment. All that can be said with any confidence is that the story is not over. It has just begun.

IX

HOSTAGES

The second great encounter between the United States and the Iranian revolution began, typically, with a telephone call in the middle of the night. Dawn arrives in Tehran seven and a half hours before the sun rises on the East Coast of the United States, so at four o'clock in the morning in Washington it is approaching noon in Tehran—ample time for something to go wrong.

I was awakened early on Sunday morning, November 4, 1979, by a telephone call from the White House Situation Room informing me that the U.S. embassy in Tehran had been overrun. We had been expecting trouble ever since the shah was admitted to the United States two weeks earlier, so I was not entirely surprised. After a few mumbled questions I got up and dressed in the dark, then drove through the empty streets of the capital listening to the bulletins coming in on the radio. Unshaven and a bit bleary-eyed, I had no reason to suspect that this pre-dawn shuttle was to become a routine part of my life for the next fourteen months.

This was not the first attack on the embassy. Nine months earlier on Valentine's Day (the Iranian revolutionaries had a perverse affinity for Sundays and U.S. holidays), the embassy had been attacked and the ambassador and staff had been taken captive. On that occasion, only days after the collapse of the Bakhtiar government, Ibrahim Yazdi and other members of Khomeini's retinue had personally intervened within twenty-four hours to set them free and to provide some measure of protection to the embassy in the form of a ragtag band of self-appointed revolutionary guards.

By November, Yazdi had become the acting foreign minister, whose responsibilities included the protection of foreign embassies and diplomats. In the weeks before the attack on the embassy, we had received assurances from Yazdi and Prime Minister Bazargan that the embassy would be protected. They were disturbed—as were many Iranians—by the sudden admission of the shah to the United States, but they were also men of integrity who took their responsibilities under international law seriously.

Driving through the deserted streets of Washington that Sunday morning, I felt no sense of complacency. But listening to the bulletins coming out of Tehran, I took some comfort in the belief that those charged with responsibility in the revolutionary regime would exert their best efforts to resolve this new crisis as quickly as possible. And so they did—for about thirty-six hours, until they were swept from power in a new swerve of the revolution.

But that was not yet evident as I joined the small group assembled that morning in the Operations Center of the State Department, listening anxiously to the telephone reports coming in from Tehran. Each telephone line was connected to a small speaker on the long table, and the voices were personally familiar to all of us as friends, colleagues, acquaintances. Elizabeth Ann Swift, who was reporting on an open line from the embassy, had been in my office only a few weeks earlier. Her voice from Tehran had the same unhurried professionalism and edge of determination that had impressed me during our earlier conversation when she was assessing the difficulties for a woman reporting on political developments in a revolutionary Islamic society.

There was an easy familiarity in the conversations being conducted from points halfway around the world that gave the scene an intimacy and immediacy not unlike members of a family discussing a mutual problem. Each of us in the room bore some measure of responsibility for the circumstances these familiar voices were now describing, and in those long morning hours, as one telephone line after another abruptly went silent, each of us had to ask ourselves the questions that would trouble many Americans in the long months ahead: Why had we let it happen? Could it have been prevented? And especially: Why had the shah been allowed to come to the United States at this delicate moment?

The Peregrinations of the Shah

A lot had happened in the last nine months. The shah had proved to be as indecisive in exile as he had been in power, and this presented a disagreeable problem for the U.S. government. Originally, the shah was supposed to fly from Iran direct to the United States. However, he decided to stop in Egypt, and his visit there continued for a week. Then he flew to Morocco as the guest of King Hassan. In the meantime Khomeini returned to Tehran, the Bakhtiar regime collapsed and, on February 14, the U.S. embassy was attacked by armed militants.

Had the shah come to the United States in January 1979 as expected, his presence would have been regarded as entirely normal. Even Khomeini had expressed no objections. But as the political situation deteriorated and the United States maneuvered to retain some measure of political contact with Iran, the shah's indecision and procrastination gradually transformed what would have been a routine event into a political issue.

Washington had had no direct contact with the shah during his visit to upper Egypt and was not consulted about his further travels to Morocco. A senior U.S. intelligence official was sent privately to establish contact with the shah and his party in Morocco, spending nearly two hours with the shah in Marrakesh on February 11. He found the shah to be virtually a broken man, traumatized by events and lacking any plans for the future. The shah reiterated that he had deliberately prevented a military bloodbath, and he continued to hope against hope that this act would keep open the possibility of a future role for the monarchy, although he insisted he had no direct contact with the military leadership in Iran. The shah gave no indication of a desire to move to the United States, and no further arrangements were made, although the invitation remained open. Three days later the first attack on the embassy occurred, and Washington began to reconsider the wisdom of permitting the shah to come to the United States.

It seems likely that the shah, during these first initial weeks, continued to hope that events would turn in his favor, as they had in 1953; and if he was to be called back to Iran, it would obviously be preferable to return from an Islamic country rather than the United States. However, after the military collapse on February 11, the shah may have concluded at last that any hope of returning in the near future was unrealistic and that he should begin thinking about a permanent residence. On February 22 the shah sent a message to Richard Parker, the U.S. ambassador in Morocco, that he had decided to move to the United States within the next week or so, and he inquired about possible arrangements for his reception.

In a meeting the following day, the Special Coordination Committee of the National Security Council met and decided to send the intelligence officer once more to talk to the shah. He was to inform the shah that the invitation remained open, but he was to let the shah know as discreetly as possible that the worsening situation in Tehran and the large numbers of pro-Khomeini Iranians in the United States created difficult problems of security. The shah should also be made aware that the U.S. government would not be able to prevent possible legal or congressional actions directed against him as a private citizen residing in the United States. In short, the message to the shah was intended to suggest that he forgo, at least for the moment, accepting the U.S. invitation.

As usual, Brzezinski chaired this meeting, and he joined the recommendation to step back from the unqualified invitation previously issued to the shah, even though he found it personally repugnant. The timing of the shah's request was impossibly bad. In addition to the attack on the embassy, the collapse of the Iranian military, and the sudden emergence of komitehs (self-appointed revolutionary "committees"[1] that sprang up spontaneously in almost every neighborhood and that were randomly arresting Americans throughout the city), there was a further problem of which almost no one—including the shah —was aware.

At the very moment when the shah let it be known that he wished, finally, to accept the January invitation, Ambassador Sullivan was engaged in the most delicate negotiations with the revolutionary authorities in Tehran to protect the lives of a group of official Americans trapped at a remote location in northern Iran and to secure their safe departure from the country. A move by the shah to the United States at that moment would have endangered directly the safety of these individuals, would have invited mass arrests of Americans in Tehran, and almost certainly would have prompted still another attack on the embassy, which was still digging out from the damage of the week before. There was no responsible choice but to postpone any visit by the shah.

Ironically, Brzezinski found himself in the awkward position of delivering personally the message agreed to by the SCC. In the middle of the night on February 26 former Iranian Ambassador Ardeshir Zahedi called Brzezinski from Switzerland, inquiring whether the shah could come to the United States in the next three or four days. Brzezinski reiterated that the invitation remained open but described some of the difficulties the shah would face by a move to the United States. He told Zahedi that someone would talk to the shah in the next few days.

The next day Brzezinski, who was intensely uncomfortable about denying asylum to a man who had been an ally of the United States for many years, raised the matter with the president, suggesting that the decision be reconsidered. President Carter reacted angrily to the suggestion, commenting that he did not want the shah in the United States playing tennis while Americans in Tehran were kidnapped or killed. That ended the discussion.

By the first week in March, both the shah and his hosts were becoming anxious. King Hassan of Morocco was politely letting the shah's entourage know that his continued presence in the country was becoming a political liability. The shah, in turn, had contacted a series of other governments without success. The Moroccans, in an effort to accelerate a process that was becoming an embarrassment to them, engaged a U.S. public relations firm to make the necessary legal and practical arrangements for the shah to move to the United States.

Summarizing these contacts on March 6, David Aaron informed President Carter that if the shah came to the United States, it was entirely possible that a "guerrilla group could retaliate against the remaining Americans, possibly taking one or more Americans hostage and refusing to release them until the shah was extradited." President Carter approved a plan to seek other countries of possible asylum for the shah.

The shah, understandably, did not wish to take no for an answer. He told the visiting representatives of the U.S. public relations firm that regardless of the admittedly serious problems it might create for the United States, he had unequivocally decided to go to the United States. Furthermore, Ardeshir Zahedi remained characteristically active. He retained a distinguished U.S. lawyer and former U.S. government official as counsel for the shah's interests in the United States and then asked him to assist in arranging for the shah's arrival. This man met with David Newsom of the State Department and after some discussion agreed with Newsom that this would be an "inauspicious" time for a visit. Instead, he agreed to assist in the widening efforts to locate an alternative site for the shah until things quieted down.

On March 14 the problem was discussed again in the White House Situation Room in advance of a mini-SCC meeting on the crisis in Yemen.[2] Vice President Walter Mondale, David Aaron, David Newsom and Frank Carlucci (deputy director of the CIA) reviewed the shah's travel plans. They agreed unanimously that the danger to Americans in Tehran would be extreme if the shah came to the United States. Four countries were identified as possible sites of temporary refuge for the shah, and efforts were initiated to sound out each of those countries on a very quiet basis.

As part of this effort, Vance and Newsom telephoned both David Rockefeller, chairman of the Chase Manhattan Bank, and former Secretary of State Henry Kissinger to seek their assistance in convincing the shah to postpone any travel to the United States for the time being. Both men were close friends of the shah, and both indignantly refused to cooperate, on the grounds that the shah had long been a friend of the United States. In their opinion, to refuse him admittance—even at the admitted risk of U.S. lives—would be a national disgrace.

Nevertheless, both Rockefeller and Kissinger were to play a central role in this evolving drama of a man without a country. The shah, recognizing finally that he could not travel to the United States for the time being, and under growing pressure from Morocco to depart, appealed directly to David Rockefeller to help him find asylum. Rockefeller and Kissinger consulted and came up with the idea of the Bahamas. On March 30 the shah flew there on an aircraft provided by King Hassan of Morocco.

By this time, communications between the shah and the U.S. government were almost impossibly strained. The shah had let it be known to anyone who would listen that he attributed the loss of his throne to the policies of the Carter administration. This theme was picked up and embellished by Henry Kissinger in a public campaign on the theme of "Who lost Iran?"[3] Moreover, by this time the shah had come to rely heavily on the advice and assistance of Robert Armao, a young U.S. public relations consultant and aide to former Vice President Nelson Rockefeller, who had died only a few weeks earlier. Armao was a perfect example of the aide who becomes *plus royaliste que le roi.* He was protective, secretive, combative and decidedly hostile to the Carter administration.

As time went on, whatever problems the shah encountered were referred first to David Rockefeller and his organization and only secondarily to Washington. Although Washington was not entirely displeased with this arrangement at the start, Armao's suspicions and lack of cooperativeness severely complicated relations and communications between Washington and the shah during the course of the hostage crisis.

The Bahamas proved an unhappy choice. The villa where the shah was housed was visible from the public beach and provided no security. Moreover, the cost of the villa and associated quarters for his retinue proved to be prohibitive, even for a man of the shah's wealth.[4] He remained there for more than two months, unhappy and exposed to the curious gaze of any tourist who could afford entrance to the exclusive Paradise Island Resort.

In the meantime David Rockefeller, Henry Kissinger and John McCloy[5] maintained a drum fire of appeals for the shah to be admitted to the United States. Kissinger called Brzezinski on April 7, and at Brzezinski's suggestion, followed up with a telephone call to President Carter. David Rockefeller saw President Carter two days later and raised the issue again. Carter was irritated by these approaches and rejected them. Kissinger responded with a speech on April 9 attacking the Carter administration for treating the shah "like a Flying Dutchman looking for port of call."

Although the president's views were shaped by the need to protect the lives of Americans in Iran, his attitudes were far less absolute than they may have appeared at the time to those arguing in favor of the shah's early admission to the United States. In early May, arrangements were quietly worked out for the shah's children to continue their education in the United States. Tehran was informed of these plans, resulting in the first official warning that there would be "serious problems" if either the shah *or his wife* were admitted to the country.

During this same period, there was an exchange of messages between the president and the shah in which the shah inquired whether his wife might visit the United States for medical treatment. In view of the Iranian warning, Secretary Vance recommended against it. President Carter disagreed and indicated that he would be prepared to permit the shahbanou (literally, shah's consort) to visit the United States for medical treatment. To the best of my knowledge, this offer was never accepted by the shahbanou, but it suggested that President Carter made a clear distinction in his own mind between a visit for medical treatment and a visit for other purposes. That distinction became critically important some five months later.

The shah shifted his residence to Mexico, but throughout the summer of 1979 the issue of his possible entrance into the United States continued to be discussed, largely as a political problem. Governmental chaos in Iran, combined with continuing reports of executions and gross violations of human rights, increasingly tended to make the shah's regime look relatively mild in comparison to Khomeini's extremism. Moreover, the debate about "Who lost Iran?" gave every indication of shaping up as a major policy debate in the forthcoming presidential election.

By the end of July, Vice President Mondale had begun to shift his position toward favoring the shah's entry. He put his views to President Carter in a memorandum on July 23. Two days later Secretary Vance sent a personal message to L. Bruce Laingen, the U.S. chargé d'affaires in Tehran. Noting that the shah could remain in Mexico at least through October, Vance asked for Laingen's assessment of the Iranian government's reaction if the shah's entry was accompanied by formal renunciation of his claim to the throne and his public agreement to forswear political activity while in the United States. Laingen replied that the shah's entry would be prejudicial to U.S. interests, but that the situation might become more manageable in the late fall if progress was made in resolving the power struggle in Iran.

At the same time, Henry Precht was asked to develop a scenario for possible admission of the shah into the country that would minimize adverse effects on U.S. interests. Precht tentatively proposed waiting until the provisional government had been replaced by an elected government, then to inform them of the U.S. intention to admit the shah as part of the process of putting old issues behind us. Precht himself had serious doubts about whether this scheme would work—doubts that were more than shared by the U.S. diplomats in Tehran. At a minimum, Precht believed that the embassy would require a more effective local guard force than the ragtag group of revolutionaries who had installed themselves in the embassy compound after the February attack, and he also proposed sending additional U.S. security guards to reinforce the embassy before undertaking such a move.

The Shah's Secret Illness

The shah had moved on June 10 from the Bahamas to Cuernavaca, a resort town southwest of Mexico City. There Robert Armao had located a large, walled villa that provided excellent natural security, permitting the shah and his family to live a more normal life. For some months the shah seemed to be settling into his new life in Mexico rather comfortably. He received a series of visits from political figures and old friends and even participated in some local social events. But there was also a dark side. Ever since his departure from Morocco, the shah's grievous illness, carefully concealed for so many years, had begun to flare up dangerously.

According to the medical history that eventually became known,[6] the shah had discovered a lump above his abdomen while on a skiing trip to Switzerland in 1974. He contacted two French doctors, Dr. Jean Bernard and Dr. Georges Flandrin, who discovered that the shah had an enlarged spleen. They diagnosed the shah's malady as lymphoma—a cancer of the lymph system that resembles leukemia. During the following five years the shah was treated with a drug known as chlorambucil, which reduced the swelling and kept the disease in check. However, by the time the shah arrived in the Bahamas, his condition had begun to deteriorate markedly. The lymph nodes in his neck had become swollen and painful, and Dr. Flandrin, who was called to the Bahamas, diagnosed a second form of cancer known as Richter's syndrome, which is usually fatal.

Under normal circumstances a patient with this condition would have been admitted to a hospital for tests and at least exploratory surgery. In this case, treatment was confined to a stronger series of anti-cancer drugs known by the acronym MOPP, which succeeded in reducing the swollen glands but also interfered with the normal production of blood-forming cells. The side effects of the treatment were so serious that the use of drugs had to be discontinued during the shah's stay in Mexico, where his health continued to deteriorate.

The shah's cancer was, without question, one of the best-kept state secrets of all time. The U.S. government did not learn that the shah had a serious illness until informed by aides to David Rockefeller at the end of September 1979, and discovered that the illness was cancer only on October 18. We were not alone. Despite theories and rumors to the contrary, French intelligence was unaware of the shah's condition, although his two doctors were French. The shah's wife, Farah, and his twin sister, Ashraf, learned of it only after he had left Iran in early 1979.

Once the fact became known, many of the shah's associates recalled events that they had been unable to explain at the time but that now, in retrospect, appeared to have been related to his medical condition. A minister in the shah's government told me of his vivid memory of one such instance that occurred approximately in September 1978. He had requested to see the shah urgently about a policy matter. Instead of being directed to the shah's office, he was brought to an anteroom outside the shah's bedroom. Eventually he was ushered into the room where the shah lay in bed, weak and pale, ostensibly suffering a bout of the flu. The minister completed his business quickly, and as he departed he met some unfamiliar men carrying equipment toward the shah's bedroom. He took them for TV technicians, and he remembered thinking it odd that the shah would be giving an interview while sick in bed. Only in retrospect, recalling that the men were speaking French, did he realize that the "technicians" must have been doctors and that their purpose was far more serious than taping an interview.

The shah no doubt realized that knowledge of his medical condition would have serious political implications, so he took extreme measures to keep it secret. However, by failing to take proper medical precautions, he may also have shortened his own life. By September 1979 the shah was suffering from a variety of complications that could no longer be concealed and that required urgent medical attention. In addition to the two cancers and the dangerous side effects of the drug treatment, gallstones were blocking his bile duct, causing him to become jaundiced. His condition had incorrectly been diagnosed as malaria by doctors in Mexico, and in the course of treatment his jaundice became worse, he had sharp stomach pains, fever, chills and nausea. His physical appearance worsened almost by the day.

Finally Robert Armao contacted Dr. Benjamin Kean of New York Hospital, a specialist in tropical diseases who had treated both Armao and Joseph

V. Reed, a senior aide to David Rockefeller. Dr. Kean visited the shah on September 29 and quickly determined that he was not suffering from malaria, but he was unable to pinpoint the true nature of the problem. The shah volunteered nothing and refused a blood test, so Kean returned to New York. Several weeks later Robert Armao called him again to say that he had learned that the shah had cancer, that he had had it for years, and that Dr. Flandrin had arrived from France. Dr. Kean returned to Cuernavaca on October 18.

In the meantime the U.S. government had learned almost nothing of the shah's condition. Joseph Reed had called David Newsom on September 28 to say that the shah had fallen ill in Mexico and might need to come to the United States for medical treatment. Newsom was aware of David Rockefeller's great interest in getting the shah into the United States, and treated the report with extreme caution. Ironically, only the night before, Secretary Vance had spoken to the Council on Foreign Relations in New York, laying out the reasons why the shah had not been permitted to enter the United States. Those reasons had not changed from February, and they had been reinforced only days earlier by Bruce Laingen, who was in Washington for consultations and who continued to advise that the entry of the shah would be extremely dangerous for Americans in Tehran. Laingen was now contacted once again by message, and he reiterated that the very tenuous U.S.-Iranian relationship could not weather the shock of the shah's arrival in the United States.

On October 17, as Dr. Kean was leaving for his second trip to Mexico, Joseph Reed again called David Newsom to inform him that the shah's condition had deteriorated further and that the diagnosis was contradictory. Newsom asked that Dr. Kean examine the shah and then consult with the State Department director of medical services, Dr. Eben H. Dustin.

On October 18, Dr. Kean met the French doctor in Cuernavaca and was given the entire medical history of the shah's illness for the first time. On the basis of the evidence available, it appeared to Dr. Kean that the shah was probably suffering from obstructive jaundice. The condition had been allowed to go untreated for more than six weeks and now required immediate surgery. In addition, it was likely that the shah had a cancerous spleen and a cancerous tumor in his neck that no longer responded to drug treatment. Further complications were added by the effects of his previous drug treatment and uncertainties about the extent of the effects of his lymphoma. At a minimum, the shah required the medical attention of a team of doctors and specialists with access to sophisticated tests and analyses of the sort that could only be provided by a large medical center. Dr. Kean strongly recommended admitting the shah to a facility in the United States.

Secretary Vance received a preliminary report of this startling news that night, and he summarized the situation for the president and his key advisers at the regularly scheduled foreign policy breakfast on Friday, October 19. After hearing of the shah's condition, Vance had concluded that the United States could not in good conscience refuse the shah access to medical treatment and he now recommended permitting the shah to enter the country.

Thus, President Carter now found all of his advisers unanimous in their view that the shah should be admitted. The president gave his approval in principle to proceed on the assumption that the shah would be admitted, subject to confirmation of Vance's preliminary information. But Carter had no illusions about the risks involved. Looking at his assembled group of advisers, he wondered aloud what advice they would give him when the Iranians took the embassy in Tehran and held the Americans hostage. Unfortunately, his sardonic comment was to prove more prophetic than he had expected.

The Shah Is Admitted

On Saturday, October 20, the State Department medical adviser submitted a formal report based on his consultations with Dr. Kean and the medical adviser to the U.S. embassy in Mexico City. He agreed with Dr. Kean that a series of highly technical tests were required that could not be carried out in any of the medical facilities in Mexico. That judgment was shared by the medical adviser to the U.S. embassy in Mexico City. Dr. Dustin concluded that the situation was medically urgent and becoming increasingly so, since each day lessened the chances of successful surgery to open the obstruction to the bile duct.

This report was forwarded to President Carter at Camp David by Warren Christopher (Vance had left for Bolivia), together with a proposal developed by Secretary Vance.[7] Vance's recommendation to the president called for an immediate approach to Prime Minister Bazargan and his provisional government in Tehran, notifying them of the shah's medical condition and the humanitarian need for him to be admitted to the United States for treatment. A judgment would then be made on the basis of the reaction in Iran. If the reaction was not strongly negative, the shah would be informed that he would be admitted into the United States.

President Carter said that the State Department should not make any request, but rather inform Iran that the shah would be coming to New York. On the following day, Sunday, October 21, the U.S. chargé, Bruce Laingen, accompanied by Henry Precht, who had recently arrived in Tehran, called on Prime Minister Bazargan and acting Foreign Minister Ibrahim Yazdi. Laingen described the circumstances and indicated that Washington had decided to admit the shah to the United States purely for humanitarian purposes. He stressed that the decision was not politically motivated and did not reflect a decision with regard to the shah's permanent residence.

Bazargan and Yazdi made it clear that this was unwelcome news. They expected that the shah's arrival in the United States would cause problems, and they were skeptical about the accuracy of the U.S. statements, but their overall reaction was subdued. They were clearly surprised to learn of the shah's malignancy. (An Iranian Foreign Ministry official remarked to a U.S. embassy official ten days later that although Iran was a "porous rumor mill," the revolutionaries had "never heard any rumors that the shah had cancer.") Bazargan and Yazdi asked for a review of the medical findings by Iranian doctors to verify the accuracy of the diagnosis. They strongly preferred that medical treatment take place outside the United States, possibly in Western Europe; moreover, if the shah had to come to the United States, they disliked the choice of New York, evidently on the grounds that the shah would have direct access to political elements hostile to the revolution. A location such as Texas would be marginally preferable.

Laingen and Precht agreed to pass on to the shah's doctors the names of two Iranian physicians identified by Yazdi to see what might be worked out.[8] Laingen requested additional protection for the embassy and for Americans in Tehran. On the following day additional police took up positions around the embassy, personally supervised by the Tehran chief of police. They remained on duty in the days that followed.

Based on Laingen and Precht's report of their discussion with Bazargan and Yazdi, the president gave the order later that day, October 21, to admit the shah. The possibility of directing the shah to a city other than New York was considered and rejected, on the grounds that treatment would have to be delayed during the process of locating facilities that were adequate both medically and in terms of security.

Joseph Reed, of David Rockefeller's staff, was contacted and informed that the shah could enter the United States on the condition that his household in Mexico be retained intact and that the shah agree not to engage in political activities while in the country. The shah was contacted personally by the president of Mexico, who assured him that he would be welcome to return to Mexico after his medical treatment, a promise independently confirmed by the Department of State. The shah was issued a tourist visa, and he arrived in New York by chartered jet the following day.

In the aftermath of the November 4 hostage taking, there was a great deal of controversy about whether the shah could in fact have been treated in Mexico rather than come to the United States. In retrospect there is little doubt that he could have been, even though all the required expertise and technical equipment were not necessarily available in a single location in Mexico. It was believed—with considerable justification—that the shah was on the verge of death, and there was no inclination to risk his life further by disputing the weight of unanimous expert opinion.

There was also considerable speculation that President Carter made the decision to admit the shah on the basis of political expediency. As suggested above, President Carter had months earlier displayed a willingness to look favorably on a request for medical treatment in the United States—even in the face of a direct warning by the authorities in Tehran. He had said bluntly that he was not prepared to place Americans in jeopardy so the shah could play tennis or his wife go shopping in the United States. However, in this case the president was convinced that the shah was dying and that he needed urgent medical attention. That was, beyond doubt, the primary reason for his decision, just as it was the sole reason for Secretary of State Vance to reverse his earlier position on the issue. No one who knows Cyrus Vance could seriously suggest that he would have exposed the personnel of his department to serious risks in the hopes that it might somehow improve the president's standing in the polls.

On the other hand, it would be naive to argue that President Carter and his advisers were oblivious to the political consequences of this decision. As indicated, many of the president's advisers had come to the conclusion that the shah should be admitted, long before his medical condition became known; and the president himself was uncomfortable refusing U.S. hospitality to a former ally. In short, there was an underlying disposition to permit the shah into the country, and the shocking news of his illness swept away any remaining inhibitions.

President Carter could scarcely have hoped that this decision would suddenly improve his political fortunes. However, he could be certain that if he refused to allow the shah access to medical treatment in the United States—possibly contributing to his death—he would be severely criticized not only by David Rockefeller and Henry Kissinger but by virtually all Americans, who would have seen his refusal as an abject rejection of humanitarian traditions. So far as I could tell, President Carter felt exactly the same way. Once the seriousness of the shah's condition became known, there was simply no question of refusing him medical attention.

More serious is the question of why the U.S. government did not take more extensive precautions to protect the safety of its people in Iran once the decision had been made to admit the shah. That question haunted all of us who shared responsibility for what happened later. The answers may help to shed light on the fundamental attitudes and assumptions that shaped U.S. policy in the months prior to the crisis, and, in some cases, long after the hostages were taken.

The Summer of 1979

In the very limited sense of providing for the physical security of the embassy itself, nothing was left undone. After the attack on the embassy in February, a full-scale security survey was conducted, resulting in major modifications. The entrances to the chancery building—certain to be the principal target of any attack—were equipped with heavy steel doors, backed by automatic alarm systems, electronic surveillance cameras and remote-controlled tear-gas devices. Windows were fitted with bulletproof glass, steel boxes filled with sand for ballistic protection, and steel grills. The embassy was stocked for self-defense, and contingency plans were developed for staged withdrawal in the event of an attack. Defenses were designed to permit the embassy to hold out unassisted for two to three hours until help could arrive. In fact, it worked exactly as planned with only one crucial exception—help never came.

Ultimately, every embassy in the world must rely on the good faith and protection of the host nation, as provided by treaty and customary international law. Physical attacks on embassies and diplomats are distressingly frequent, and nations occasionally react slowly to such attacks, particularly if they wish to make a political point. However, until the incident in Tehran, there was no modern precedent for a nation renouncing its international obligations entirely and throwing its support to the mob. That was not expected even in nations where the veneer of civilization was thin and new. For a nation such as Iran, with centuries of tradition in law and diplomacy, it was unimaginable. So much for the first assumption.

The second fundamental mistake was to place an unrealistic degree of confidence in the "moderates" who were nominally in charge of the provisional government. This was part of a pattern that had emerged immediately after the fall of the shah and that had dominated U.S. policy toward Iran throughout the summer of 1979. During that period, as Washington turned its attention to successive crises in Yemen, Afghanistan, the Arab-Israeli dispute and other areas, day-to-day policy on Iran took the form of small, incremental decisions on such issues as embassy staffing, the myriad commercial tangles that had to be unraveled, and local negotiations about embassy security. This was the natural province of the State Department, and the man in charge at the State Department was Henry Precht, the country director for Iran. Throughout the summer of 1979, as the internal politics of the new regime struggled to cope with bureaucratic chaos, tribal dissidence and subterranean political disputes over the shape of a new constitution, Henry Precht essentially ran a one-man show.

Precht had been one of the earliest to argue that once the shah was gone, moderate elements would reassert themselves and gradually establish a regime compatible with long-term U.S. interests. When Mehdi Bazargan and his moderate associates were appointed to head the provisional government in February, Precht had a personal stake in showing that he had been right, that these new forces of moderation were the true wave of the future in Iran.

Only three weeks after the collapse of Bakhtiar's ill-fated government, Precht prepared an analysis of the situation in Iran intended to serve as the basis of discussion with NATO capitals. This assessment, which purported to be the official U.S. government position, was written and sent without any coordination outside the State Department. Although the message briefly listed the serious problems facing the Bazargan regime, it devoted most of its discussion to the "elements of strength" that Henry Precht perceived. He thought that Iranians were fatigued with the turmoil of the previous year and sought a return to normal conditions under a moderate, anti-Soviet leader such as Bazargan. Iranians, he said, were basically a pragmatic people. Even during the height of the revolution, they had found solutions to pull back from the brink of anarchy. Consequently, he expected them to find face-saving compromises to their problems, particularly since he saw no apparent alternative to the Bazargan government.

This message inspired a scathing retort from Ambassador Sullivan in Tehran, who commented that the factors listed as strengths of the Bazargan government simply did not exist. Politically and economically, things in Iran were getting worse, not better, and a battle was shaping up between Khomeini, who wanted total Islamization of Iranian society, and moderates such as Bazargan, who were trying ineffectually to be all things to all Iranians. Precht was also challenged directly in a meeting at the State Department, where several of us argued with him at length that his interpretation was unrealistically optimistic and flew in the face of all the facts.

However, in that meeting and in every other encounter throughout the summer, Precht argued doggedly that Bazargan and company were steadily gaining strength. Although he did not again make the mistake of putting his views in writing as official U.S. policy, Precht never wavered in his opinion. Many of his colleagues at the State Department and elsewhere in the government vigorously disagreed, but Precht had the ear and the confidence of Assistant Secretary Harold Saunders, and it was his optimistic philosophy that shaped the many small but important decisions about manning and operating the embassy. Among those hostages who had been aware of his role in the months prior to the takeover, Henry Precht was—to put it mildly—unpopular.

Bazargan and his associates were extremely critical of the past U.S. role in Iran, and they made no attempt to conceal their displeasure with U.S. policies supporting the shah during the revolution. Nevertheless, they were interested in resolving the many problems the revolution had left in its wake, and they were prepared to deal coolly but correctly with U.S. representatives. No such contact was possible with the clerical factions around Khomeini, so almost by necessity the United States came to rely more and more on these individuals as its essential link to the new regime.

Government-to-government contacts became more frequent and more significant in the month prior to the attack on the embassy. In early October, Ibrahim Yazdi arrived in New York to attend the opening of the UN General Assembly. On October 3 he met with Secretary Vance for the first high-level policy discussion between the two countries since the departure of the shah. Yazdi arrived at the meeting in an open-neck shirt, looking rather rumpled, as befits a true revolutionary. He had just come from Havana, and he was clearly enjoying his new role.

Before launching into a lecture on the new revolutionary realities in Iran, he pointedly reminded the secretary that the last time he had been at the UN was as a protester in the street outside. Now that he was inside, he made clear, things were going to be different. After listening grimly to Yazdi's harangue, Vance outlined U.S. interest in the continued independence and territorial integrity of Iran and suggested that the two countries would do well to put the past behind them. Yazdi raised the question of the shah's suspected assets in the United States, and Vance recommended that Iran pursue its case through U.S. courts. Yazdi referred to a former SAVAK official who he said was now living in the United States. Vance was unfamiliar with the case but said he would be prepared to look into the matter with the attorney general.[9] Yazdi asked about U.S. policy with respect to the shah. Vance replied that we had told the shah that we did not believe he should come to the United States at this time. What the future might hold, he could not say. The meeting was more symbol than substance, but it was a wary first step by each side toward a speaking relationship.

The following day Yazdi and an Iranian general spent several hours meeting with U.S. political-military officials for a discussion of the very thorny issues relating to Iran's arms purchases in the United States. Most of this meeting was spent attempting to explain to the Iranians the complex tangle of financial and contractual rights and obligations they had inherited from the shah's regime. The Iranians were almost totally uninformed and intensely suspicious; however, the meeting was businesslike and served to clear away some of the more obvious misunderstandings. It was agreed that talks would continue with defense officials in Tehran, and shortly thereafter the United States announced that it was prepared to make a small quantity of military spare parts available to Iran on a selective basis.[10]

In view of the deep animosities on both sides, these first high-level contacts were about as productive (or unproductive) as might realistically have been expected. A dialogue had begun that was at least civil, and some preliminary steps had been taken to address a few of the difficult issues that the revolution had created. Although both sides were wary and skeptical, there appeared to be a genuine prospect of establishing some limited but useful dialogue.

That impression was reinforced even after the shah entered the United States. On November 1, Zbigniew Brzezinski found himself at an anniversary celebration in Algiers with Bazargan, Yazdi and Mustapha Ali Chamran, the Iranian minister of defense. A few days earlier, when Bruce Laingen learned of the forthcoming Algiers meeting, he had urged that Brzezinski or others in the U.S. delegation meet with the Iranians, in the belief that "the more contact with this group the better." He had mentioned the possibility to Bazargan, who seemed interested.

When the Iranians arrived in Algiers, they suggested a private meeting and Brzezinski agreed. Yazdi used the occasion to stress to Brzezinski that the shah's presence in the United States disturbed them. Brzezinski emphasized the strategic interests that Iran and the United States had in common, and held out the possibility of cooperation, including the possibility of continued U.S. military aid. When Brzezinski returned to Washington, he was quite positive in his evaluation of the three Iranian leaders as intelligent and sensible men who had impressed him with their seriousness of purpose and their realistic appraisal of the problems facing the new revolutionary regime. It was therefore doubly ironic that this meeting, which visibly swayed the harshest U.S. critic of the revolution, provided the excuse four days later for expelling Bazargan and Yazdi from the government.

These high-level contacts, together with some others throughout the summer, served to divert attention from the intense ideological battles being waged in Iran and to raise unrealistic expectations in Washington that in time it would be possible to establish a workable *modus vivendi* with the new regime in Tehran. Dealing with these men in the daily language of diplomacy, it was easy for Americans to forget that their very political existence hung from the slenderest of threads. The weight that we placed on them almost certainly hastened the day when the thread finally snapped.

At the same time that U.S. policy was coming to rely more and more on the moderates in Tehran, a more insidious process was under way at the bureaucratic level, essentially invisible to policy makers in Washington. During the nine months between the two attacks on the embassy in Tehran, each embassy office gradually attempted to build itself back to a relatively normal operating capacity. Daily problems had to be researched, routine reports had to be compiled, and standard bureaucratic procedures quietly reasserted themselves as they do in any governmental organization.

All embassies operating overseas are acquainted with the problem of bureaucratic "creep," the impulse to add additional personnel and resources to deal with the complex array of issues encountered in the relations between any two major nations. This process is inevitable, and it normally occurs at the working level where it is essentially invisible to the policy maker. Only the most stringent management controls can keep this process in check and prevent an embassy from becoming bureaucratically bloated.

In the case of the Tehran embassy, the governing attitude (as reflected in the views of Henry Precht on the desk in Washington) was to encourage normalization and therefore to permit the embassy to increase gradually in size and operating capacity. That process was further stimulated by pressures from groups in the United States to re-establish full consular operations as quickly as possible so Iranian Jews and Baha'is,[11] who felt threatened by the new Islamic regime, could get visas to leave the country.

In the days immediately following the attack on the embassy in February 1979, the White House had insisted on reviewing plans for restaffing the embassy. In early March a "bare bones" plan was formally approved. However, no agency likes to have the White House looking over its shoulder on matters of strictly "internal" (i.e., personnel) decisions. Over the summer, each agency gradually increased its representation in Tehran. By the time the attack occurred on November 4, the number of persons assigned to the embassy had increased significantly beyond the number originally approved. The total of about seventy persons assigned to the embassy at the time of the takeover was not necessarily excessive in terms of the number and complexity of issues demanding their attention, but it was no longer the skeletal force that had originally been approved.

More difficult to explain is the proliferation of files. Prior to February 1979, Ambassador Sullivan had properly ordered all reference files boxed and shipped back to Washington, retaining only a thin working file in each office. These working files were destroyed quickly in mid-February as order collapsed in Tehran. Unknown to anyone in the White House, when the embassy was reconstituted after the February attack, the various agencies simply shipped back many of the boxes of original files, which included the voluminous accumulation of years of memos, papers and reports. As a result, when the crisis began to mount in October, the embassy found itself with a massive quantity of extraneous paper to be protected.

Even more inexplicably, the embassy failed to take advantage of the time between the entry of the shah into the United States and the attack on the embassy to rid itself of this paper albatross around its neck. As a result, when the attack finally came, it was impossible to shred and burn all of these files in the short time available, with the result that a very large quantity of classified information fell into the hands of the student militants. Chargé d'Affaires Bruce Laingen, who performed with such dignity and courage throughout the hostage ordeal, bears a heavy responsibility for this failure to take the most elementary precautions.

The militants who took the embassy later made a great show of laboriously piecing together shredded documents, but most of the embassy files were taken intact. All of the most sensitive policy documents, for example, were held in Bruce Laingen's office. When the attack occurred, Laingen was at the Foreign Ministry and the Marine guards were unable to get into his office; consequently, the files in their entirety fell into the hands of the students. Copies of these and other documents were subsequently published in Tehran in a series of volumes (a total of at least forty by the end of 1984), including messages, letters and memos dating back as far as the early 1950s.

The most regrettable effect of the files falling into the hands of the students was that every Iranian who had had any contact with the embassy in the normal course of diplomatic reporting was potentially subject to blackmail or prosecution on the presumption that he was working for the United States. Thus, a number of Iranian patriots who had worked for the revolution were harassed and threatened in a campaign of guilt by association.

The effect was particularly devastating for Mehdi Bazargan and his Liberation Movement, since several members had been in touch with embassy officials in the course of the revolution to attempt to work out arrangements that would minimize violence. Khomeini was aware of many of these contacts and presumably sanctioned them. However, in the "spy" hysteria that followed the hostage taking, evidence of association with U.S. embassy officials was popularly accepted as proof of disloyalty, and it was used to devastating effect in the factional political wars being waged in Tehran.

Otherwise, the effects of the loss of the embassy files were more embarrassing than substantive. The students who captured the embassy were convinced that the United States had secretly managed political events in Iran for years, that it had directed the shah's campaign against the revolution, and that it was engaged in efforts to destabilize Iran and undermine Khomeini's regime through nefarious contacts with dissident tribes and disaffected political elements.

They must have been very disappointed when they looked through the documents, for, of course, they found nothing to support these paranoid notions. The students assumed that they would find a "smoking gun" to prove their charges about U.S. interference in Iran's internal politics. In fact, the most striking feature of the many volumes of material published by the students—at least for anyone familiar with the normal operation of an embassy—was the absence of anything sensational. To a practiced eye, these papers were merely the flotsam and jetsam of political reporting and internal management that might be found in the files of almost any embassy of any nation in the world. In fact, in one of the many ironies of the hostage crisis, the United States was well aware that several Iranian embassies were engaged in intelligence operations *throughout the hostage crisis* that would have made the documents in the U.S. "nest of spies" look pale by comparison.

That being said, it is nevertheless obvious that no nation would willingly permit its private political communications to fall into the hands of a hostile enemy where they could be used for blackmail and political extortion. When the embassy was overrun on November 4, those of us who had been involved in preparing contingency plans for an attack assumed that some material would be overlooked in the pressure of the moment and would fall into the hands of the attackers. However, it was not until thirteen of the hostages were released more than three weeks later that we learned that a huge archive of papers had been lost. That came as a stunning surprise.

Because of the quantity of material, we could never be sure exactly which items were in Iranian hands or how those items might be used, either as propaganda or in some political trial of the hostages. As a consequence, President Carter eventually ordered a complete review of all material relating to U.S.-Iranian relations so we would not be taken by surprise. However, the student militants seemed content to reserve their secret library for use in the internecine political warfare in Tehran. With the exception of the show trial of Liberation Front member Abbas Amir-Entezam in March 1980 (which resulted in a sentence of life imprisonment for treason and must have sent shivers down the spine of any Iranian who had ever talked to a U.S. embassy official), the purloined documents had very little practical effect on the evolution of the crisis.

The final question that must be addressed is why the embassy was not evacuated when the shah was admitted to the United States. In retrospect, it is curious that this issue was scarcely discussed at all, not only in Washington but even among those in the embassy itself who felt most directly threatened. The explanation seems to lie in a combination of three factors. First and most important, of course, was the belief that the formal assurances from the government of Iran would be honored in the event of an attack. That belief was not rooted merely in historical precedent and wishful thinking. It seemed to be given practical substantiation on November 1 when an attack on the embassy was widely anticipated.

On that date, a massive anti-American demonstration was scheduled that could easily have escalated out of control. The November 1 demonstration was considered a test case of the willingness and ability of the governmental authorities to provide for the security of the embassy. In preparation, the embassy staff was dispersed throughout the city, with only essential security forces remaining in the embassy compound, and maximum security precautions were put into effect. A series of meetings was held in Washington to review contingency plans. After one of these meetings on October 31, I reported to Brzezinski's office that the situation would be monitored on a minute-by-minute basis, and if there was any evidence that Iranian authorities were not prepared to provide adequate protection, we would have to consider evacuation.

However, the Iranian government went to great lengths to prevent an incident. Augmented police protection was provided around the embassy, and the route of march was altered at the last minute to keep the bulk of the demonstrators at some distance from the compound. Despite a massive turnout and some fiery rhetoric by the ayatollah, the demonstration was controlled in an impressive manner, with no significant physical threat to the embassy. This seemed to be convincing evidence that the Iranian government, for all its displeasure about the shah's presence in the United States, had both the will and the means to prevent a major diplomatic incident.

At the end of the day, on November 1, Bruce Laingen was able to comment that perhaps the worst had now passed. There is no doubt that the prompt and effective action by the Iranian government on that day allayed the worst fears of Americans both in Tehran and in Washington. It may also have contributed to a somewhat reduced state of alert that made the surprise attack three days later all the more effective.

The second factor that inhibited any consideration of a total evacuation was the awareness of the overwhelming importance of Iran in the politics of the region. Vital U.S. interests were at stake, and there was a deep reluctance to cut the remaining diplomatic, commercial and even personal ties that had bound the two nations together for so many years. A total withdrawal would have symbolized America's willingness simply to wash its hands of the revolutionary regime, and inevitably it would have complicated the process of maintaining the tenuous but important links that had been nursed through the difficult months after the shah's departure.

Finally, and closely related to the point above, was the dedication and professionalism of the men and women who had accepted to serve in Tehran at a difficult and dangerous time. Many of these individuals had long experience in Iran. Many of them spoke the language, and they knew and liked the Iranian people. All of them were there not because they expected it to be easy or pleasant, but because there was an important job to be done. Many of them disagreed sharply with the decision to permit the shah to come to the United States, and they were intensely aware of the animosities building in the society in which they lived. Yet they resisted the impulse to turn and run.

In retrospect, that attitude may appear to be unduly romantic, and many of the hostages would later regret that they had not spoken out more forcefully.

When these men and women were welcomed home many months later to an unprecedented outpouring of national love and respect, I would like to believe that some of that intense emotion was a tribute to all those Americans who daily serve their country in conditions of great uncertainty and personal risk and who choose to stay rather than run.

X

THE EMBASSY
IS TAKEN

S unday, November 4, was a working day at the embassy. Offices were open and manned, and the chargé d'affaires, Bruce Laingen, together with the political counselor, Victor Tomseth, and the embassy security officer, Michael Howland, had gone to the Foreign Ministry to seek additional assistance and protection from the government. In mid-morning a crowd began to assemble around the embassy, shouting anti-American slogans. Then, at about ten-thirty, just as Laingen and his colleagues were leaving the Foreign Ministry, as many as three thousand demonstrators poured over the walls and forced their way into the basement and first floor of the chancery building. Laingen was notified of the attack on his car radio and returned immediately to the Foreign Ministry to seek help. Most of the embassy staff barricaded themselves behind the steel doors of the chancery, where they would hold out for more than two hours.

Prime Minister Bazargan and Foreign Minister Yazdi were on their way into Tehran from the airport at the time of the attack, having just returned from Algiers and their meeting with Zbigniew Brzezinski. In their absence, Bruce Laingen was offered the use of Yazdi's office upstairs, and from there he set up a direct telephone connection with the State Department Operations Center in Washington. His two colleagues remained on the first floor of the Foreign Ministry, where they could watch what was happening outside the building. They also established a direct telephone line to Washington. Other direct lines were established with the approximately sixty embassy staff people trapped on the second floor of the chancery and with the U.S. Cultural Center some three miles from the compound.

These open telephone lines from four different locations provided Washington with more rapid and accurate information than was available to anyone in Tehran. The situation was not without its element of humor. At one point Michael Howland, on the first floor of the Foreign Ministry, saw a group of student guerrillas arrive at the entrance to the Foreign Ministry, apparently seeking the three missing Americans to add to their collection of hostages. Howland informed Washington immediately. Washington passed the word to Laingen and he in turn informed Yazdi, who by that time had arrived back at his office. Yazdi was dumfounded to be informed by Washington of what was happening only a few floors below him in his own ministry.

Kathryn Koob may have earned her way into some record book for what must have been the longest continuous telephone conversation in history between Tehran and Washington. From her location at the U.S. Cultural Center, she learned of the embassy takeover shortly after the initial attack. She immediately called Washington and she and her staff maintained unbroken telephone contact throughout all that day and most of the following day until she, too, was discovered and taken hostage. Many months later, as she languished in captivity, Kathryn Koob was presented by her captors, in all seriousness, with a staggering bill for her marathon telephone connection. She informed them, with equal seriousness, that she did not have that much cash, and they finally gave up. Presumably, good Islamic militants do not accept credit cards.

The Iranian Foreign Ministry was obviously taken entirely by surprise by the attack on the embassy, and they did everything in their power during those first hours to attempt to resolve the problem as quickly as possible. Although Bruce Laingen had to evacuate Yazdi's office, he remained in the Foreign Ministry, with immediate access to government officials. From the very start, Laingen (and Washington) received Yazdi's assurances that the events at the embassy were comparable to a sit-in at a U.S. university and that the situation would be resolved "within 48 hours." Although the police protection of the embassy had melted away in the face of the mob, Yazdi was confident that once he succeeded in contacting the ayatollah and his retinue in Qom (the holy city some ninety miles south of Tehran), the religious leaders would be able to convince the students that they had made their point and should withdraw.

It was therefore with a considerable measure of relief that we learned that the ayatollah's son, Ahmed, was at last on his way to the embassy. What Yazdi (and we in Washington) had not expected was that Ahmed Khomeini would clamber excitedly over the embassy wall, losing his turban in the process, and congratulate the students for their action. As that fact gradually became known, the deadly seriousness of the situation became apparent for the first time. Prime Minister Bazargan submitted his resignation in protest, and it was accepted by Khomeini. Government operations were turned over to the radicals of the Revolutionary Council, and the siege began in earnest.

Preparing the Takeover

By all accounts, the students who had organized the attack were no less surprised than Bazargan, Yazdi and those of us in Washington when the ayatollah threw his support to the students. According to subsequent articles by the students themselves, as well as interviews after the event, the students had planned the takeover as a symbolic demonstration and had expected it to last no more than three to five days.[1] It was only after they were in control of the embassy and showered with praise that they began to comprehend the full implications of what they had accomplished. The confrontation with the United States had risen to a new level. It was, as they later proclaimed, the "second revolution."

One of the major unanswered questions of this episode is the extent to which Khomeini knew of the plan in advance. The whole truth may never be known, but there is considerable evidence to suggest that Khomeini was aware of it, that he openly encouraged it, and when it succeeded, he was prepared to exploit the situation quickly and deftly for his own political purposes. The key figure in the shadowy unfolding of this event was a fiery young cleric, the Hojjat-ol-Islam Moussavi-Khoeini.

When the students first began planning their attack shortly after the shah was admitted to the United States, they met with Khoeini, who was close to the fervent Islamic circles around Khomeini. Khoeini, who later became the spiritual adviser to the students in the embassy and their primary liaison with the Islamic leadership, has remained silent about his role, but it is difficult to believe that he did not let the ayatollah's advisers know that such a plan was being developed.

In any event, in the days following the shah's admission to the United States, the ayatollah gradually escalated the level of his rhetoric. On October 28 he made a speech denouncing "westernized" Iranians (which could be understood to include Bazargan, Yazdi and other "moderates" who were opposing Khomeini's plan for a clerical-dominated government) and calling for them to be confronted "in a different manner." It was Khomeini's Islamic Republican Party that planned the giant anti-U.S. demonstrations on November 1, and on that same day his office issued an ominous statement:

It is therefore up to the dear pupils, students and theological students to expand their attacks against the United States and Israel so that they may force the U.S. to return the deposed and criminal Shah.

There is no reason to doubt that this statement was precisely what the students themselves believed it to be—an unequivocal signal authorizing them to proceed with their plan. Once the attack had proved successful, there was no evidence of surprise or hesitation on the part of the ayatollah or his advisers. On the contrary, all the signals from Qom were positive.

The exact truth of what happened must remain speculative, but on the basis of the available evidence, a very strong case can be made that the ayatollah was at least generally aware of the plans for an attack on the embassy and consciously exploited it for his own domestic political purposes. The arrival of the shah in the United States had provided the necessary trigger to set events in motion, but the fate of the shah was never the real issue. The real issue was Khomeini's constitution and the realization of his vision of an Islamic republic dominated by a religious guide—the *velayat-e faqih*—and the Shi'i clergy. The shah, the hostages and even the students in the embassy became pawns in a high-risk political strategy intended to ensure that the "second act" of the revolution would be played out according to Khomeini's script.[2]

The Politics Behind the Hostage Taking

The events in Iran from the time of Khomeini's takeover in February 1979 through the end of August 1980, when the Islamic leadership decided that the hostages were no longer an asset to the regime, should properly be understood as a constitutional crisis played out in the form of a national psychodrama. The various forces and factions that carried out the revolution had been united on only one objective—to break the overwhelming power of the monarchy. Once that goal had been achieved—more swiftly and more completely than they dared hope—the alliance quickly began to disintegrate. Three basic factions emerged, each of which had a very different view of what the revolution was really about and what the shape of a future revolutionary Iran should be.

First, of course, was the dominant vision of Khomeini himself. In a lifetime of teaching and writing, he had evolved a highly idiosyncratic concept of an ideal Islamic state. Its laws would be drawn from the *shari'a* (traditional Islamic jurisprudence) under the supervision of a supreme guide—the *velayat-e faqih,* a unique institutional invention envisaged as a sort of Islamic philosopher-king and tailored to Khomeini's personal measurements—with the support and assistance of those versed in Islamic law, i.e., the clergy.

Although Khomeini elaborated his ideas as an extension of classic Shi'i theology, the concept of direct involvement by the clergy in the operation of government represented nothing less than a revisionist interpretation of Shi'i doctrine that was regarded by many of his co-religionists as radical, if not heretical. Perhaps for that reason Khomeini initially soft-pedaled his views, concentrating on the campaign against the shah and contenting himself with delphic pronouncements that minimized the profound differences separating him from many of those who accepted his leadership. Khomeini's closest followers seemed to have little understanding of his basic political ideas; and even those who were familiar with his writings and teachings tended to regard them as too idealistic and impractical to provide a workable basis for governing a large and complex nation such as Iran.

A second body of opinion was represented among those whom I have frequently dubbed the "moderates." Although lacking any formal cohesion, and often at odds among themselves, this loose assemblage could best be identified as those who sought a return to the liberal, Western-inspired constitution of 1906, with its emphasis on democratic procedures, human rights and civil liberties. Some of these individuals, such as Mehdi Bazargan, were deeply religious and readily accepted the concept of government oversight by a committee of Islamic jurists as provided in the 1906 constitution. Others, such as National Front leader Karim Sanjabi, were essentially secular in orientation and probably envisaged a largely symbolic role for the clergy. These men were nationalists in the classic sense, and their political philosophy was derived from the experience of the early 1950s. All of them revered Mossadegh and the ultranationalist principles that he embodied. Although patriots and committed Iranian nationalists, these men tended to think in classic terms of national interest and power politics, as opposed to Khomeini's millenarianism.

A third large grouping, which encompassed many of those in the younger generation in Iran, might be classified roughly as Islamic progressives. Again, this grouping was really more of a state of mind than an actual political movement. However, a common touchstone was the philosophy and writings of Ali Shariati. Shariati was a brilliant and prolific Islamic sociologist who, at the age of forty-four, suffered an untimely death just as the revolution was gaining momentum in 1977. He was widely regarded as the ideologist of the revolution, and his portrait was often carried beside that of Khomeini in demonstrations.[3]

Shariati attempted to fuse Islam and modern progressive political doctrine into an "ideology of permanent progress and revolution" suitable to the newly emerging Third World. Although his ideas were not rigorously developed, the impulse to redefine Islam as a humane, progressive and *modern* force was more important than formal structure. He had a profound effect on the educated youth of Iran, who were experiencing anguishing tensions between their own religious and traditional roots and the pervasive and glittering materialism of the West. Shariati's great appeal was his attempt to synthesize these apparently opposite poles, retaining the best of both worlds in an indigenous, revolutionary Third World doctrine. The adoption of these ideas by young urban guerrillas of the *mojahedin-e khalq* and other opponents of the shah during the revolution gave rise to the shah's bitter denunciation of what he called "Islamic Marxists."

Needless to say, Shariati's impressionistic reinterpretation of Islam, with its strong emphasis on human freedom and its subordination of the role of the traditional clergy, which seemed to be moving in the direction of an Islamic "Reformation," was not well accepted by conservative religious opinion. But Khomeini was wise enough to realize the dangers of a public clash with such a powerful idea. In his public pronouncements during and after the revolution, Khomeini dealt with Shariati the same way he dealt with Mossadegh—he simply never mentioned either of them directly. Rather, he tacitly encouraged both camps to believe that he shared many of their own fondest beliefs and hopes for the future of Iranian politics and society.

As long as the struggle was directed against the shah, it was possible for these three groups to ignore their fundamental disagreements and to maintain a fragile façade of unity. However, when the revolutionaries assumed power, they could no longer avoid the necessity of making fundamental choices, and differences quickly began to emerge.

The Komitehs

The first of these disputes concerned the proliferation of new revolutionary bodies. As noted in chapter VIII, the blossoming of local bodies of authority seems to be a universal characteristic of revolutions. In Iran, the collapse of the existing order was paralleled by the sudden appearance of neighborhood komitehs, usually dominated by the local mullah or other religious authority and backed up by self-appointed revolutionary guards who were often nothing more than eager teen-agers with weapons.

Varying greatly in composition, scope and behavior, these groups acted quickly to assert control over specific pieces of territory and proceeded to establish a rough-and-ready system of law enforcement and revolutionary justice over the citizens within their domain. Similarly, komitehs sprang up within industrial sites, the oil fields and even the government ministries. The government had virtually no control over this patchwork of do-it-yourself power centers, and every order by the provisional government was subject to negotiation or disregard by each local komiteh. Bazargan and his cabinet ministers found it virtually impossible to perform their functions, prompting the prime minister at one point to declare that his government was a "knife without a blade."

Khomeini attempted to restrain some of the worst excesses of the komitehs, but despite repeated pleas from Bazargan, Khomeini refused to disband these local expressions of revolutionary zeal. Instead, Khomeini moved slowly and carefully to harness the komitehs and incorporate them into his own political structure. It was a brilliant political stroke, for gradually the komiteh system evolved into a loosely organized but enormously powerful channel for political action and control down to the grass roots. In some respects, this revolutionary power structure could be compared to the Bolshevik creation of a party structure parallel to but separate from the government bureaucracy.

In the Iranian case, the mosque appeared to be the unifying element that tied these fractious power centers together, and discipline (where it existed at all) was informal and tenuous. Nevertheless, the system ensured that government operations at every level would be subject to revolutionary vigilance, and real power was effectively retained in the hands of those most committed to Khomeini's personal leadership. One by one the old-line "moderates" who wanted to use their government positions to establish order and central control were defeated and disillusioned. They quietly dropped away and were replaced by others closer to Khomeini's liking.

The Islamic Constitution

The second major area of dispute was the shape and composition of the new Islamic government. The first step in this process was the national referendum on the monarchy, held on March 30–31, 1979, just seven weeks after the collapse of the Bakhtiar government. The moderates in the government attempted to offer the electorate a genuine choice, but Khomeini prevailed. The ballot offered only a stark choice between the monarchy and an undefined Islamic republic. Not surprisingly, the populace voted unanimously for an Islamic republic.

Once the referendum was completed, the emphasis shifted to the constitution. A number of National Front leaders were lawyers and legal scholars, and they had begun preparing a draft constitution even before the transfer of power occurred. At least one version of such a document was circulated in the early months of the new regime, and as might have been expected, it placed particular stress on democratic procedures and guarantees of civil liberties and human rights.

In structure and content it was very similar to the Western-inspired constitution of 1906, with the obvious exception that it made no provision for a monarchical role. Like the 1906 document, it provided for a supervisory committee of scholars versed in religious law to ensure that the laws of the nation were compatible with Islam. Otherwise it was decidedly secular. The return to the 1906 constitution was an article of faith for the leaders of the National Front and other like-minded political figures who had participated in the revolution, and they may have believed they could steal a march on Khomeini by being the first to produce a draft constitution. But they were to be disappointed.

Khomeini studiously ignored the National Front draft. Instead, his Islamic Republican Party (IRP) proceeded with plans to call a constituent assembly to draft the constitution. Contrary to Khomeini's earlier promises of a freely elected assembly, the IRP now proposed that Khomeini appoint a 75-member body. At this, the National Democratic Front of Hedayatollah Matin-Daftari, himself a grandson of Mossadegh, launched a series of protest rallies in late June. Throughout the following months, intense backstage battles were waged about the size of the constituent assembly and the credentials of those to be elected, with Khomeini's party insisting on heavy clerical representation.

The elections were held in early August under rules imposed by Khomeini's Islamic Republican Party. The National Democratic Front and eighteen other newly formed political parties protested the election as hopelessly rigged and marked by widespread electoral fraud, but their objections were dismissed. The constituent assembly, which began its deliberations in August 1979, was overwhelmingly religious in composition and pro-Khomeini in orientation. Fewer than a dozen of its 73 members were prepared to oppose the Khomeini steam-roller, and they soon found themselves muzzled by parliamentary tactics or, in some cases, physically persecuted by the komitehs and revolutionary guards for their "un-Islamic" views. One of the most outspoken opposition voices, Maragham Maraghei, eventually had to go into hiding and find his way out of the country to avoid prosecution by the revolutionary courts.

The constitution that emerged from this process was a very different docu-ment from what the "moderates" had wanted. The centerpiece of the constitu-tion was, of course, the *velayat-e faqih,* which effectively made Khomeini the ruler of Iran for as long as he lived. Moreover, all the ringing declarations of human rights and civil liberties that the "moderates" had believed they were fighting for in the revolution were watered down and made contingent on absolute submission to Islamic law and practice. Thus, freedom of the press was guaranteed "except when . . . contrary to Islamic principles," and freedom of political expression was assured, "provided [it does] not violate principles of independence, freedom, and national unity, or [is] contrary to the principles of Islam or the Islamic Republic." In short, Iranian citizens were free to speak out as long as they did not question or oppose the views of the theocratic leadership.

The practical effect of these limitations was made unmistakably clear even before the constitution was formally ratified. Numerous political parties emerged whose vigorous opposition to the rigged elections for the constituent assembly was not at all what Khomeini had in mind as proper behavior for the citizens of his Islamic Republic. Therefore, in August, he systematically set about silencing the opposition. His methods were effective and very instruc-tive.

First, he launched a major public campaign to whip up popular sentiment against the Kurds. The Kurdish leaders of northwest Iran had joined the revolution against the shah in return for assurances that they would be granted a considerable measure of local autonomy. They were quickly disabused of this notion after Khomeini came to power, and they had been in open rebellion during the summer. In August, Khomeini and the IRP made this a national issue, attacking the Kurds from every public forum. Buses with loudspeakers were sent through the streets of Tehran calling for young men to volunteer to fight against these opponents of the Islamic regime.

With public opinion distracted, Khomeini's forces moved swiftly to close down the press and opposition political parties within a period of less than two weeks. Matin-Daftari was forced into exile, the headquarters of the *mojahedin-e khalq* were attacked, and stringent new regulations were promulgated that prohibited the operation of 22 opposition newspapers and magazines. With the opposition dazed and in disarray, Khomeini proclaimed in early September that the Kurdish rebellion had been crushed, and the public campaign was terminated. (In fact, the rebellion continued for years thereafter.)

In some respects, the "phony war" against the Kurds could be regarded as a model of the political techniques that Khomeini was to use on a much larger scale in the hostage crisis in late 1979, the Iran-Iraq war in late 1980, and even in the climactic confrontation with the *mojahedin* in 1981. Although Khomeini did not necessarily seek these confrontations, he exploited the dramatic circumstances of each case to whip up public emotions, to mobilize popular support behind his own leadership when it showed signs of erosion, to weaken or crush domestic opposition to his programs, and to press single-mindedly for the adoption of controversial elements of his theocratic plans even at the risk of multiplying turmoil and sacrifice. The Kurdish campaign of August 1979 was more obviously contrived than the major conflicts that followed, but it provided a foretaste of the ruthlessness and political adroitness that would confound Khomeini's enemies repeatedly in the months and years to come.

The repressive tactics of August succeeded in stilling much of the organized public opposition to the constituent assembly; however, it did not remove the intense opposition within the government itself. From late August until the day he was removed, Mehdi Bazargan conducted a courageously outspoken campaign against what he regarded as a profound distortion of the true purposes of the revolution. He carefully avoided any hint of criticism against Khomeini himself, and Bazargan may even have believed that the IRP and the radical clergy were operating contrary to Khomeini's desires.

Bazargan called on Khomeini to return from Qom to take over operation of the government, which was constantly thwarted in its disputes with the komitehs. In a public oration at the funeral of Ayatollah Taleqani,[4] Bazargan sharply criticized the "reactionary" Shi'i clergy for having deceived the public by changing the draft constitution, and he declared that it was a mistake to reject all Western values, since some could be of benefit to Iran. Although he was rebuffed and subjected to public ridicule, Bazargan persisted in his lonely crusade. In late October, not long before his departure to Algiers and the fateful meeting with Brzezinski, Bazargan traveled to Qom and delivered a personal protest to Khomeini about the travesty of procedures in the constituent assembly and what he considered to be the ominous implications of the proposed constitution.

That was the situation Khomeini faced in the first days of November 1979. He and his party had succeeded in drafting a constitution to his liking, and the most troublesome opposition parties had been coerced into silence, at least temporarily. However, the referendum on the constitution was scheduled to occur in one month, and there was growing doubt that he could muster the kind of overwhelming support that he had enjoyed during the earlier referendum on the monarchy. The universities were scheduled to open within a few weeks, and they had already become the site of demonstrations protesting the course of the revolution. The middle class was depressed and disillusioned with the continued economic chaos and religious extremism of the new regime. The intelligentsia was shocked by the shape of the new constitution and the heavy-handed repression of civil liberties that had accompanied it. The traditionalist clergy was openly expressing doctrinal misgivings about the concept of *velay at-e faqih* and direct clerical management of government affairs. In the provinces and tribal areas, particularly in Kurdistan and the oil-producing area of Khuzestan, restiveness was hardening into outright rebellion and sabotage. And, most distressing of all, Khomeini's own prime minister was openly leading a campaign against the constitution that Khomeini intended to be the cornerstone of his new Islamic society. Khomeini badly needed a new cause to mobilize public opinion behind his leadership, to neutralize the growing opposition to his policies and to distract attention away from the radical innovations he was introducing in the name of the revolution.

Enter the Shah

There is no evidence that Khomeini immediately seized on the shah's entrance into the United States as a possible issue to revive his flagging revolutionary support. On the contrary, the initial reports of the shah's arrival in New York were mostly relegated to the back pages of Iranian newspapers and received little public attention. There were no demonstrations, and Khomeini limited his own public comments to concern that the shah might die before the revolution could retrieve his "stolen wealth." He called for demonstrations at the shah's hospital in New York and warned the United States not to give the shah permanent residence.

However, within a week of the shah's arrival, Khomeini began to refer to a "plot" associated with the shah's presence in New York; and he linked this comment to a scathing attack on his domestic opponents, characterizing them as "traitors . . . dependent on the West." "These American-loving rotten brains must be purged from the nation," he declared on October 28. It took no great political acumen to conclude that Bazargan was in very serious trouble. In the event the point was missed, Khomeini two days later denounced the entire government bureaucracy, calling for a purge of those still under the influence of the shah. The following day the Islamic Republican Party called for a mass demonstration at the U.S. embassy to protest American imperialism. As indicated previously, that demonstration on November 1 was rerouted at the last minute, resulting in no physical attack on the embassy. The rerouting of the march probably was due to the insistence of the Bazargan government, and it was Bazargan's last significant exercise of authority before departing for Algiers.

It was during this same period that those around Khomeini became aware of the students' plans to attack the embassy. On October 31, the Iranian Foreign Ministry delivered a formal note of protest to the U.S. embassy, stating that Iran "did not accept the American government's excuses for granting entry permission to the deposed shah." Privately, Foreign Ministry officials warned the embassy that "outside pressures" for a stronger reaction were increasing.

Those around Khomeini had no way of knowing if the student attack would succeed, and it was presumably important for Khomeini to be able to dissociate himself from the operation in the event of failure. Nevertheless, after November 1 the tenor of Khomeini's remarks shifted significantly. In a speech on November 2 he again referred to the shah's arrival in the United States as a plot and added: "We protest that they have taken in our enemy. . . . We shall demand that they hand him over to us." Finally, on November 3, in a statement issued in Khomeini's name to commemorate the clash between the shah's forces and students at Tehran University on November 4, 1977, which the students had chosen for the date of their attack, he openly called for action, exhorting the "students and theological students to expand with all their might their attacks against the United States and Israel, so that they may force the United States to return the deposed and criminal shah." According to one of the students who participated in the attack, the revolutionary guards had been alerted in advance and had cooperated by withdrawing their forces assigned to protect the embassy.

Once the attack had been successfully completed, the reaction from all the key individuals and institutions around Khomeini was immediate and totally consistent. On November 5, statements of support for the takeover came almost simultaneously from Khomeini, Ayatollah Beheshti (who headed the IRP and the Revolutionary Council), Ayatollah Montazeri (now the spiritual leader of Tehran), the leader of the revolutionary guards, and the theological seminary in Qom, among others. On the same day, stories suddenly began to appear charging Bazargan with an unauthorized meeting with Brzezinski in Algiers. Bazargan resigned the following day. This time his resignation was accepted, and government operations were turned over to the Revolutionary Council.

Within a brief forty-eight hours, Khomeini had silenced the last important voice opposing his program, had diverted domestic attention away from internal political disputes and had launched a major confrontation with the United States that could be expected to galvanize public opinion behind him. The risks for Iran were extremely high, but Khomeini was playing for high stakes. For him, the establishment of a theocratic society was a sacred cause worthy of great sacrifice. In the months that followed, the people of Iran paid an enormous price in terms of economic dislocation, domestic political turmoil and negative world opinion—a higher price perhaps than would have been acceptable to any other nation in the world. But in the end, Khomeini's revolution within a revolution had survived intact. In that respect, his fateful gamble won the day.

The View from Washington

This account may give the impression that the situation was clearer and simpler than it appeared at the time. The confusing crosscurrents and contradictory evidence are easier to sort out with the benefit of hindsight than they were in those first hectic days of the seizure of the embassy. Nevertheless, the fact that the embassy seizure was almost entirely a function of Iranian internal politics was fully evident at the time and was so understood by the key decision makers in Washington.

On November 5, the day after the hostages were taken, I prepared an analysis of the situation for Brzezinski that began with the assertion that internal Iranian politics were seriously complicating efforts to free the hostages —specifically, the divisions in the government between the religious authorities on the one hand, acting through the komitehs and revolutionary guards, and the secular forces of Bazargan and his associates on the other. There had been an increasing body of evidence, I noted, that Bazargan and the moderates had become aware of their inability to influence Khomeini, and information from circles close to the ayatollah suggested that he would be prepared to drop them in an instant if it suited his purposes. The taking of the embassy, I suggested, was the crunch point in this relationship that could cost them their jobs.

The presence of the shah in the United States was, I went on, a useful issue that Khomeini could exploit just as he had exploited the conflict with the Kurds in August to rally the population. Having the shah as a target took them back to the "good old days" when they could all still agree on something. As long as the shah remained in the United States, I thought, or perhaps as long as the shah lived, that would be an issue Khomeini would exploit. In my view, there was no longer any hope of working with the Tehran regime, and we should recognize that the longer Khomeini remained in power, the worse it would be for U.S. interests and no doubt for Iran itself. Khomeini would use the hostages for his own political purposes, so we should make every effort to convince him that this was a losing game by mobilizing all the resources and pressure at our command. I believed that once Khomeini had made his political point, he would release the hostages. The most serious problem in the meantime was the absence of any channel to communicate with Khomeini and those around him. I supported the proposal of sending a special emissary to present U.S. views directly to Khomeini.

Looking back now, I find no need to revise my interpretation of the immediate causes of the hostage crisis. The fatal weakness of that memorandum— which also proved to be the fatal flaw of U.S. policy over the following months —was its dual assumption that Khomeini would rather quickly "make his political point" and release the hostages, and that the United States could bring sufficient pressure to bear on Iran to accelerate his decision. No one in the U.S. government at that time had any idea that the crisis would drag on for more than a year. Perhaps that is understandable, since Khomeini himself may have had no clear sense of how long the crisis would last. More serious was the tendency to underestimate Khomeini's willingness and ability to absorb external economic and political punishment in the pursuit of his revolutionary objectives.

Although it was painfully evident that the United States had very limited means of exerting any direct influence over events inside Iran, there was a deep reluctance at every level in Washington to admit that a great power, with all the diplomatic and financial resources at its disposal, was unable to protect the interests of its citizens in such a flagrant violation of international law. The impulse to act was overpowering. As a consequence, policy attention tended to focus heavily on an inventory of action strategies while downplaying the inherent limitations on U.S. policy.

Much later, as the crisis dragged on and its implications for U.S. interests became clearer, it became popular to argue that the most rational U.S. response would have been to downplay the importance of the situation, thereby reducing its propaganda value for the extremists in Tehran. Ultimately, after a long series of initiatives had been tried and failed, that is the strategy the U.S. government adopted for lack of a better alternative; but I was aware of no significant voice inside or outside the government arguing for such a policy within the first months of the crisis. On the contrary, the outrage of the U.S. people was fully shared by Washington policy makers at all levels, and the overwhelming concern was to bring maximum pressure on Khomeini to release the hostages. That dominant theme set the tone for U.S. policy over the months to come.

The First Policy Meeting

On the morning of November 5, Brzezinski chaired a meeting of the Special Coordination Committee on the Iranian crisis that was to be the first of almost daily cabinet-level meetings over the next six months and more. The agenda was brief. The meeting opened with a discussion of the internal rivalry that was under way in Tehran and concern that the moderate elements were being undermined by the religious extremists. It was agreed that utmost caution should be exercised in any public U.S. statements to avoid making that situation worse. The SCC recognized the need to communicate directly with Khomeini and his religious circle, and it was recommended that a special emissary be sent to Iran. The two names that were mentioned were Ramsey Clark, the former U.S. attorney general, and William Miller, the staff director for the Senate Select Committee on Intelligence. Both men were well known and respected by religious and revolutionary circles in Iran.

The SCC then shifted its attention to contingency plans. A small group was designated to examine possible military steps that the United States might have to take in the event the hostages were harmed or if Iran began to disintegrate. The focus was to be on planning for a possible rescue mission, on punitive steps that could be taken in retaliation for Iranian actions, and on preserving the integrity of the oil fields in southwestern Iran. The carrier U.S.S. *Midway* was in the Indian Ocean en route to a port call in Kenya. The task force could be diverted on short notice to the Persian Gulf if military action was required to protect U.S. lives in Tehran.

That night, the Department of State managed to establish contact with

Ayatollah Beheshti, who had emerged as one of the key figures in the Islamic Republican Party and the Revolutionary Council. He was informed of U.S. willingness to send an emissary, and he received the idea positively, promising to relay the suggestion to the Revolutionary Council and to reply by midday on November 6. In anticipation of a positive response, Ramsey Clark and William Miller were called to the Department of State on the morning of the sixth and received briefings on the situation from Secretary Vance and others. A letter of instructions was prepared that outlined the first formal U.S. position with regard to the hostages. It contained several basic points:

- The key objective was to obtain the immediate release of all Americans being held in Iran; the secondary purpose was to hold discussions with the religious authorities on how to resolve the difficulties of U.S.-Iranian relations.
- Regarding the shah, the message made clear that he was seriously ill and there could be no question of his leaving while he was hospitalized. Arrangements would be sought on a confidential basis for Iran to confirm the nature of his condition by discussions with the doctors treating him. The shah was not in the United States as a permanent resident, and the length of his stay would be determined by his need for medical attention. He would not engage in political activities while in the United States, as previously announced.
- Iranian claims against the shah's assets could be pursued through legal actions in U.S. courts.
- The United States was not involved in the events in Kurdistan. On the contrary, the United States supported the independence and territorial integrity of Iran and opposed any form of external involvement in Iranian internal affairs.
- Regarding military supply issues, the message noted that progress had been made in resolving differences between Iran and the United States. It neither offered nor rejected a possible future military supply relationship.
- The message disclaimed responsibility for stories appearing in the U.S. media and suggested that Iran could best make its position known by permitting U.S. journalists to report freely on events in Iran.

In short, the message of instructions for the two emissaries was a formal statement of the U.S. position. They were not being sent to Iran as negotiators, and they carried no concessions. Their visit was seen as a symbolic gesture that would provide the Iranian leaders with an opportunity to state their views and grievances direct to the president through the good offices of two distinguished Americans who were known to be good friends of the Iranian people and who had publicly opposed the shah's rule.

At the same time that plans were being completed for the Clark-Miller mission, the possibility of a very different intervention came to light. The leadership of the Palestine Liberation Organization contacted both the White

House and the State Department through an intermediary to propose a possible PLO approach to the Iranian revolutionaries on behalf of the hostages. Yasir Arafat, the chairman of the PLO, had been warmly received in Tehran after the revolutionary takeover, and the PLO maintained an important political presence as well as some military training functions in Iran. It was evident that the PLO, by this offer, hoped to use its contacts with the new Iranian regime to build up its credit and respectability in the United States. They were quietly encouraged to proceed with their efforts.

The Third Day Begins

By the morning of November 6, it had become evident that the original hopes of a quick solution to the crisis were no longer realistic. The entire religious leadership in Iran had thrown its support to the students in the embassy, transforming the situation from a largely symbolic act of political protest into a full-scale confrontation between Iran and the United States. In the course of that day, four high-level meetings were held, three of them with President Carter, that profoundly influenced the course of U.S. policy over the following year.

At eight o'clock on the morning of November 6, President Carter convened a meeting of his principal advisers in the Oval Office. Present were National Security Adviser Brzezinski, Secretary of State Vance and Undersecretary David Newsom, Secretary of Defense Harold Brown, White House chief of staff Hamilton Jordan, press secretary Jody Powell, and myself as note taker. The president was informed that Clark and Miller were on their way to the State Department and that efforts were being made to contact Ayatollah Beheshti to get approval for the emissaries to meet with the Iranian leadership.

President Carter was very concerned about the safety of Americans who remained in Iran on a commercial basis. He felt that any U.S. counteractions to the embassy seizure could place them in jeopardy, and he directed the State Department to do everything possible to persuade all Americans to leave Iran.[5]

With regard to the hostages, Brzezinski proposed a public statement that would combine assurances of U.S. willingness to resolve the problem in accordance with civilized norms with a veiled warning that the United States would hold Iran responsible for its actions. Although the students in the embassy had no incentives to cooperate, Brzezinski and Brown felt that Khomeini and those around him were worried about the U.S. reaction.

President Carter said he was not so sure. "They have us by the balls," he said. A private threat to bomb Qom or the oil fields was possible, he acknowledged, but that would not necessarily free the hostages. Brzezinski argued that it was not necessary to spell out exactly what the U.S. reaction would be, only to make the threat credible. Vance opposed a direct threat, since that would tend to put the Iranians in a box. Instead, he recommended informing the Iranians that they would be expected to carry out the reassurances they had given on two or three different occasions that the safety and well-being of Americans in Iran would be protected.

President Carter said that for the moment there should be no public statement except to note that assurances had been given by the Iranian authorities and that we expected those assurances to be honored. The statement should note that everything possible was being done to secure the release of the hostages and that in the meantime further public comments would not be helpful or appropriate. There was to be no public mention of sending emissaries to Iran, since that might sabotage the mission.

Otherwise, the president was persuaded that the effort to build a relationship with Iran was finished. He did not believe that the presence of a few U.S. officials in Tehran would keep them from moving toward the Soviets, and the present situation demonstrated that it was not worth the effort. They could kill our people at any time. He was prepared to cut off supply of all military spares. He wanted an examination of the legal possibilities of expelling all Iranian students from the United States and of expropriating Iranian holdings in the United States. He wanted to "get our people out of Iran and break relations. Fuck 'em."

Secretary Vance expressed concern about leaks. The president said to handle the problem orally in small groups in the White House Situation Room and to keep him briefed on the results. It was essential to avoid leaks.

Newsom reported briefly on the status of the shah. The shah had indicated that he was prepared to leave the country as soon as possible, but he had several tubes in him and his doctors did not believe he could be moved safely before four to five weeks. The president commented bitterly that by that time all our people could be dead. However, he did not want to endanger the shah's life, and he asked Vance to explore the possibilities. Under no circumstances would he consider extraditing the shah.

Harold Brown noted that if they did kill the hostages, then the military options would arise. However, it was important to think through the implications. Any retaliation should be designed to hurt Iran more than it hurt the United States and its allies. The president directed that the widest possible range of retaliatory options be explored. Secretary Brown ticked off several possibilities, including the seizure of Iran's oil-loading port at Kharg Island in the Persian Gulf and the destruction of their oil-production facilities. The president said he considered that an unbelievably bad precedent, since it risked shutting down the world's oil supply from the Persian Gulf.

The Crisis Management Group

The meeting broke up at eight-thirty on that grim note, and all the participants except the president went directly to the Situation Room for a follow-up meeting of the SCC. There they were joined by Vice President Walter Mondale, Attorney General Benjamin Civiletti, Director of Central Intelligence

Stansfield Turner, Chairman of the Joint Chiefs of Staff General David Jones, Secretary of Energy Charles Duncan, and several senior military staff officers.

This meeting established the membership and procedure for what was to become the crisis management team for the hostage situation. This group, with the addition of Secretary of the Treasury William Miller, met each morning at nine in the White House for a review of the latest information on the situation and for coordination of activities throughout the government. The meetings, which often occurred seven days a week, were chaired by Brzezinski. He normally opened the meeting with a brief summary of President Carter's views or guidance to the various government departments, followed by a proposed working agenda. Each cabinet officer was free to offer additional agenda items as desired. Because of the rapidly evolving situation and in order to maintain maximum security, no agenda was circulated in advance.[6] Immediately following the meeting, I would prepare a summary of the discussion, identifying conflicting points of view and issues requiring presidential decision. Brzezinski would then review the summary and send it to the president, normally within two or three hours after the meeting was over.

President Carter read the memorandum each day, indicating his decisions, questions or observations in brief, handwritten comments in the margins. The annotated copy would then be returned to Brzezinski, and the president's comments would constitute the first item of business at the next meeting of the SCC. In this way, the president could have the benefit of the advice and opinions of his principal policy officials, without a heavy investment of his own time, while all of his advisers were kept abreast of his own thinking on a day-to-day basis.

The system was time-consuming, especially for senior officials at the Department of State and other agencies who had to give up several hours of precious time each morning to this process. However, it worked smoothly and ensured close coordination between the various agencies and departments. Since the summaries were prepared and handled exclusively within the National Security Council and the White House, the system relied heavily on good faith. There was, for example, frustration at the Department of State and elsewhere at being required to rely on verbal reports and debriefings rather than the actual notes of the meetings. However, that was an unavoidable consequence of President Carter's insistence on verbal proceedings to be held tightly within the White House.

To the best of my knowledge, the fairness and accuracy of these reports were never brought into question throughout more than one hundred such meetings covering a wide range of contentious issues; and I am aware of no instance where policy making or policy execution was adversely affected by the lack of formal documents circulating around Washington. On the contrary, the decision process was crisp, the information flow was complete and orderly, each department was responsive to presidential guidance in a disciplined and coordinated manner, and monitoring of policy action was continuous. Although it put a strain on everybody's schedule, technically the system worked in almost textbook fashion.

One innovation of these meetings was the inclusion from the beginning of cabinet members and presidential advisers from the domestic as well as the foreign policy community in Washington. The attorney general was present because of the serious policy implications and legal problems created by large numbers of Iranian students resident in the United States. The secretary of energy was called in because of the national and international problems of a cutoff of Iranian oil supplies. The secretary of the treasury had to deal with the issues of financial sanctions and the freezing of massive Iranian assets in U.S. banks.

Each of these officials brought a wealth of expertise and a special perspective to the planning of security policy that went far beyond their technical competence. In a world of increasing interdependence, it is impossible to draw a clear line between politics and economics or even between foreign policy and domestic policy. Almost any major action by the United States in the field traditionally regarded as security policy has important and often unanticipated consequences for markets and U.S. domestic policy. Yet security policy has traditionally been the exclusive province of a small group of officials who are not necessarily knowledgeable about or sensitive to these effects. Good policy would call for the inclusion of those with legal, financial or other special expertise from the outset of the policy formation process rather than expecting them to pick up the pieces of a policy decision on which they were not consulted.

During the course of the hostage crisis, a number of embarrassing pitfalls were avoided by the presence at the table of officials outside the traditional circle of "national security" advisers. Even more important, since they were fully aware of policy decisions in advance, they were in a position to anticipate problems and develop contingency plans to minimize damage before it occurred. By contrast, on those decisions where they were excluded, such as the hostage rescue mission, they were forced to improvise frantically when the news of the mission failure threatened a run on the dollar in international markets. Based on the experience of the hostage crisis, there would seem to be ample justification for any president to consider widening the circle of advisers who are involved in national security policy beyond the traditional exclusive club of State, Defense, Joint Chiefs of Staff and CIA.

The SCC meeting on the morning of November 6 included discussion of several issues with domestic economic implications. Much of the meeting was devoted to consideration of the potential effects of an Iranian cutoff of oil production on U.S. and world energy markets. At that time, the world oil market was tight, and the essential problem was to find supplies to replace the 700,000 barrels of oil that the United States imported each day from Iran.

Also, the attorney general was requested to provide a survey of Iranians living in the United States and the steps that might be available to the government in dealing with the problem of this large exile community. There was some talk of a possible mass deportation, to which Vice President Mondale responded that it would be folly for a great nation to respond to this kind of situation by "kicking out a few sad-ass students."

Finally, the group considered possible military actions. The SCC concluded that until much more preparatory work had been done, there was no way for the United States to intervene militarily to rescue the hostages without seriously risking their lives. A small group was to conduct a systematic evaluation of a possible rescue attempt and potential retaliatory actions, including a blockade of Iranian ports, bombing or seizure of Iranian military or economic targets, aid to dissident elements in Iran, or other possible actions against the regime in Tehran.

Policy Lines Are Established

During the day of November 6, the news was received from Tehran that the resignations of Prime Minister Bazargan and his cabinet had been accepted. With governmental affairs now in the hands of the mysterious but hard-line Revolutionary Council, and with the revolutionary authorities openly supporting the takeover of the embassy, the magnitude and intractability of the crisis became fully apparent. That formed the background for President Carter's formal meeting with his National Security Council at four-thirty that afternoon. Those attending were Vice President Mondale, Secretary Vance, Secretary Brown, Zbigniew Brzezinski, General Jones, and Central Intelligence Director Turner, in addition to Hamilton Jordan, Jody Powell and myself as note taker.

When President Carter entered the Cabinet Room, his face was grim and there was none of the usual banter or small talk. He had clearly spent most of the day thinking about the situation, as the news from Tehran became worse and worse, and he opened the meeting with his personal thoughts about the crisis. It was, he said, one of the most difficult problems the government had faced since he had been in the White House. American citizens had been captured, and there appeared to be no desire on the Iranian side to negotiate.

We faced the prospect, he said, of the hostages being killed one at a time, or perhaps all of them. The honor and integrity of the country demanded some form of punitive action if that should occur. First, however, it was important to do everything possible to save lives and to get people out. Second, he wished to consider what to do if a punitive action was required. President Carter said he had thought seriously about the issue and he did not incline to any action that would get the United States bogged down militarily in Iran, where extrication of U.S. forces would be difficult and any pullback would be viewed as a defeat. If we succeeded in getting our people out of Tehran, it would be his intention to break off relations with Iran.

With this, he opened the meeting to discussion. Secretary Vance reported on the status of the two emissaries, Ramsey Clark and William Miller. Ayatollah Beheshti had been contacted and had promised to raise the idea with the Revolutionary Council. A plane was standing by to fly the emissaries to a nearby country where they would wait for a decision. The plane was large enough to carry back sixty hostages if they were successful in securing their release.

Hamilton Jordan wondered if it wasn't presumptuous of us to send the emissaries off before a firm reply was received from Tehran. Vance said yes, but we wanted to have them close at hand if the answer was positive. It was extremely important that there be no public mention of this initiative until the Iranians had answered. Hamilton Jordan said that word was already circulating on Capitol Hill; it was a secret that was not well kept. The president said he did not object to having them positioned near Iran. If the answer was no, they could simply come home.

After a few minutes of discussion Brzezinski interrupted to say he had just received a note from the Situation Room saying that Richard Valeriani of NBC News had a story about the emissaries that he planned to run that evening. President Carter directed Jody Powell, Hodding Carter (the State Department spokesman) and Secretary Vance, if necessary, to talk to Valeriani and ask him to hold off. (This effort was unsuccessful. Valeriani broadcast the story on the evening news, shortly after the emissaries took off. Almost as soon as it became public, Khomeini ordered the Revolutionary Council not to meet with them. This very damaging report, which undercut the effectiveness of the mission almost before it left the ground, was one of the few instances of a major breach of security during the crisis, and it reinforced the tendency to restrict decision making to a small group operating from within the White House. The emissaries spent several days waiting in Istanbul, Turkey, and then returned to the United States.)

Admiral Turner gave a brief summary of available information on the militants who had taken over the embassy. It was believed that they had been infiltrated by the left. Their attack on the embassy had been clever and well organized. It appeared that Khomeini had given permission for the occupation of the embassy. Chances of negotiating with the militants did not appear to be good. They had publicly stated that any action aimed at freeing the hostages would result in their being killed.

With that, the discussion turned to consideration of a possible rescue mission. Secretary Brown said the option had been examined, and the Department of Defense believed that the chances of carrying it off successfully were very small.[7] General Jones briefly reviewed the problem of getting a rescue force to the embassy. Helicopters seemed to be the only possibility, but there seemed to be virtually no way at present to position the helicopters close enough to Tehran to carry out such an operation without giving the Iranians advance warning. President Carter said that the plan General Jones had outlined did not look promising. He directed that more work should be done to develop a workable plan.

President Carter then asked about punitive measures. If the hostages were killed, he said, we should be able to conduct an operation that would "blast the hell out of Iran." After some general discussion it was decided that the entire range of possible U.S. military actions should be studied in terms of their effects on Iran, the implications for broader U.S. interests in the Gulf area, the effects on America's friends and allies in the Middle East and elsewhere, and the risks of drawing the Soviets into the Persian Gulf.

At about five-forty, as this discussion was going on, Ramsey Clark and William Miller arrived at the White House, and President Carter left to meet with them in the Oval Office prior to their departure. The president said it appeared the Iranians were interested in punishing the United States and wanted to use the situation for their own domestic political benefit. He wondered if there was anyone who might have influence with Khomeini and who could make contact with him.

Ramsey Clark said he was not too optimistic that they would be received in Iran, but he was in touch with several religious and revolutionary figures to attempt to smooth the way. If Iran would not agree to see them, Clark thought it might be useful for President Carter to speak directly by telephone to Khomeini as a man of religion. Carter did not exclude the possibility but felt the language barrier would complicate direct communication. The meeting lasted about twenty minutes, after which President Carter returned to the NSC meeting, where his advisers were still assembled.

President Carter wanted to divert the carrier U.S.S. *Midway* to the vicinity of the Persian Gulf, but recalling the previous incident when a movement order to a carrier immediately appeared in the press, he asked sarcastically if the task force could move without the fact appearing on the front page of the New York *Times.* Harold Brown said the carrier was due in port in three days, and if it did not show up, it would almost certainly attract public attention. General Jones noted that the carrier would never be more than five days away from the Gulf, and we had other means of conducting a punitive strike if necessary. On balance, the risk of a damaging leak outweighed the possible benefits of having additional air power close to Iran, and it was decided to postpone any change in the sailing orders of the carrier task force for the time being.[8]

President Carter asked for an assessment of a possible embargo on Iranian assets and other economic steps that might be taken. To the extent possible, he wished to avoid the loss of life, and economic options were potentially much better than bombing. Brzezinski wondered if economic steps would be sufficient if U.S. citizens were being killed. After a long pause President Carter said no, some punitive action would be required. However, he wanted to act in a way that would avoid the heavy problems of trying to extricate ourselves militarily. He was particularly interested in an economic blockade of Iran, and he felt that we should insist that our European allies cooperate with us, even though they might resist.

Secretary of Defense Brown noted that Iran was extremely dependent on supplies of gasoline, diesel fuel and kerosene that were produced in Iranian refineries. If punitive measures were required, we might wish to consider interdicting Iranian refineries. President Carter said that was one possibility. Closing the meeting, the president said it was necessary to have the means to punish Iran without punishing the rest of the world.

The series of meetings on November 6 represented the first sustained effort at the highest levels of the government to come to grips with the policy dilemmas of the hostage crisis. By the end of that day, President Carter had outlined the essential elements of what was to be U.S. policy over the following months:

First, the United States would pursue a campaign of political, diplomatic and economic initiatives to convince the revolutionary leadership in Iran—by persuasion if possible and by pressure if necessary—that it was in their interest to release the hostages promptly and safely. Underlying this strategy was a deep, personal concern for the lives and well-being of the hostages. There was also a healthy realization of the difficulties and dilemmas created by the internal revolutionary dynamics of Iran, where an extremist leadership was intent on severing all ties with the United States and exploiting the crisis for its own political purposes.

Second, military contingency planning was to proceed on two tracks. A plan was to be developed for a rescue mission, in the event it was needed. At the same time, specific options were to be examined for a punitive military strike for retaliation in the event the hostages were harmed. The emphasis in planning was to be on secrecy, minimizing loss of life, avoiding a military situation where U.S. forces would find themselves bogged down in Iran, and ensuring that U.S. actions would be selective in their effects, i.e., to punish Iran without doing damage to U.S. friends and interests in the rest of the world.

These two strategies—the diplomatic/economic and the military—were complementary and they intersected at several critical points during the course of the crisis, most notably at the time of the rescue attempt. However, after the first few meetings the two tracks were segregated. Operational planning for military contingencies was conducted by a small group of Defense Department representatives meeting privately with Zbigniew Brzezinski in his office, outside the framework of the daily SCC meetings. Even within the SCC, the discussion of military issues was taken up only at the end of each meeting, with participation limited to senior officials of State, Defense, the JCS, the CIA and the NSC.

Other cabinet members and officials quietly resented their exclusion from these discussions, and in retrospect it is not clear that this artificial distinction was either necessary or wise. However, the existence of a "national security elite" is a firmly established tradition in Washington, and its members (who typically show no reluctance in offering advice on matters outside their special areas of expertise) have a vested interest in maintaining the aura of mystery and esoteric knowledge that pervade issues involving the political use of military power.

In any event, the distinction between national security issues and all other policy issues was carefully preserved throughout the hostage crisis.

XI

THE DIPLOMATIC OFFENSIVE

T he U.S. campaign of persuasion and pressure that was mounted in the days and weeks following the hostage seizure was probably the most extensive and sustained effort of its kind ever to be conducted in peacetime. No nation in the world had more resources at its command than the United States, and all of those resources were mobilized to bring the maximum political, economic, diplomatic, legal, financial and even religious pressure on the revolutionary regime in Tehran. The result was an onslaught of messages, pleas, statements, personal emissaries, condemnations, and resolutions of all kinds from governments, institutions and individuals around the world, descending in torrents on Iranian officials and representatives wherever they might be.

From a technical point of view, this campaign was an extraordinary achievement. Seldom if ever has world opinion been so aroused and united in opposition to the action of one nation against another. No Iranian of any political persuasion could appear in any group or any forum virtually any place in the world without being questioned and criticized about the seizure of the U.S. hostages in Tehran. Iran became an instant pariah in the world community, and the conduct of its external relations was severely impaired.

There are probably few nations in the world that would have been willing to sustain the battering of national pride and national interest to which Iran was subjected in the long months of crisis. In one sense, this campaign was a convincing demonstration of the powers of moral and political suasion that can be mustered by the world community. Unfortunately, it was also a demonstration of the inherent limitations of international public opinion to deal with a renegade nation in a state of revolutionary euphoria.

There was a tendency within the U.S. government, especially among those engaged in managing this massive exercise in international public relations, to overestimate Iran's vulnerability to external pressure. I, for one, had grave doubts about the abilities of the revolutionary leadership to cope with the pressures they were experiencing. On November 13, I commented to Brzezinski that the situation as seen from Tehran made U.S. problems seem small by comparison. Their only government had been dismissed; they lacked qualified people to take its place; there were power struggles under way in the factions around Khomeini; the various ministries were poorly staffed and demoralized; the internal war with the Kurds was not going well; demonstrations by unemployed workers were becoming almost a daily occurrence; and there were Iraqi incursions along the western border—all while they were engaged in a test of wills with a superpower. I warned that we should be alert for signs of systemic breakdown in Tehran, with the attendant risk of serious miscalculation and irrational acts of sheer frustration.

As it happened, Iran's capacity to manage near-total chaos was greater than I had expected. The exultant chants of the mobs marching before the occupied U.S. embassy helped stifle the sound of a society being pulled apart.

Many of those who had fought and sacrificed for the revolution were increasingly appalled at the ruthlessness and lawlessness of the leadership in Tehran, and they began to desert the revolution in larger and larger numbers. Politically disinherited by the shah's regime, they were doubly bitter to find themselves disinherited yet again by a regime they had fought to bring to power.[1] To their credit, many of these individuals risked their lives to argue courageously against policies they detested, but their numbers were always too few and their conversion too late to stop Khomeini's juggernaut.

The experience of the first years of the Iranian revolution was one of a steadily narrowing base of popular support and the substitution of intimidation and terror for what had been genuine popular enthusiasm. It was the triumph of one man's radical vision and its imposition on an unsuspecting and increasingly sullen population, but it was not a record that recommended itself for widespread emulation. There was no rush by other nations to seize foreign embassies, and there was reason to hope that such paroxysms of collective pathology would continue to be the exception rather than the rule in human affairs.

The President and the Ayatollah

It is one of the great ironies of history that it should have been the administration of Jimmy Carter that was called upon to deal with the exotic extremes of the ayatollah's regime in Iran. No writer of fiction could ever have conjured up a set of circumstances so ripe with contrasts and opportunities for mutual incomprehension. Each of these two national leaders embodied an aspect of his own national culture to a degree of perfection that lent itself naturally to exaggeration and caricature.

Jimmy Carter was the personification of small-town middle-American values. His religious beliefs, which were so deep as to be instinctive, were not shaped by the Old Testament vision of a wrathful God. He was quintessentially a New Testament man who prized the virtues of personal humility, charity and forgiveness. Like many Americans, he saw the world as an imperfect place but not inherently evil. He believed that adversity could be overcome by hard work, that faith without works is dead. He practiced tolerance as a positive virtue and sought peace through understanding and reconciliation, not confrontation. As an engineer, he was utterly pragmatic and a problem solver who approached each issue on its own merits.

Although he held strong beliefs on issues such as individual liberties and human rights, these views did not take the form of a highly structured system of political doctrine or dogma. There was not an ideological bone in his body. He was candid and open, almost to a fault—the very antithesis of the classic image of the wily practitioner of power politics. These attributes, together with his quick mind, appealed to a U.S. electorate emerging from the dark experiences of Vietnam and Watergate and gained him the presidency. He was later criticized when he insisted on practicing what he preached. But for anyone such as myself, who came out of the same small-town culture, the values that Jimmy Carter represented were comfortably familiar and singularly American.

The contrast with the Ayatollah Khomeini could not have been more complete. No one could claim that Khomeini's value system was representative of a broad stratum of Iranian society; on the contrary, he was as baffling and unpredictable to many of his countrymen as he was to outsiders. But it was his value system that was imposed on his nation and that in time came to represent the central reality of the revolution. Both Khomeini and Carter were deeply religious men; but those, like Ramsey Clark, who believed that this provided a common basis for dialogue failed to comprehend that their faiths had almost nothing in common.

Khomeini was the archetype of the medieval prophet emerging from the desert with a fiery vision of absolute truth. His God was a harsh and vengeful diety—full of fury, demanding the eye and tooth of retribution for human transgressions of divine law. Khomeini, in more than a decade of angry exile, had elaborated the doctrine of a utopian Islamic state and then endowed it with sacred inevitability. This philosophical system was as stark as it was comprehensive. It held the answers to all questions, and the answers were absolute and final.

In contrast to Carter, Khomeini was a total ideologue. He saw the world through the exclusive prism of his own beliefs, separating events into opposites: right or wrong, good or bad, black or white. And since he considered his ideology divinely ordained, he was the most dangerous of all ideologues. No sacrifice could be too great, no price too high, if it advanced the cause of his mission. Holy ends justify unholy means.

Khomeini's philosophy had great tolerance for pain, human suffering and political chaos, but no tolerance whatever for opposition. His opponents were satanic, and the remedy was "to cut off their arms." He was a man riven with hate—hatred for the shah, hatred for Carter and America, hatred for those who dared oppose his vision. That hatred translated itself into the frenzied curses of the mobs swirling about the besieged embassy, where it was dutifully photographed and transmitted daily into U.S. living rooms, neatly interspersed with ads for deodorants and soft drinks.

In this contest of hate, Jimmy Carter and most Americans were at a distinct disadvantage. Americans did not hate Iran, at least not until the crisis started. In fact, Americans knew little about the country, cared less, and—despite the massive television exposure and the spilling of millions of gallons of printer's ink—managed to emerge from the ordeal with their basic ignorance surprisingly intact. For Iran, the taking of the embassy was revolutionary theater of the highest order; and in the United States, where there was genuine concern for the fate of its fellow citizens, Iran found the perfect audience.

The crisis was the longest-running human interest story in the history of television, in living color from the other side of the world. Commercially it was a stunning success. Never had a news story so thoroughly captured the imagination of the U.S. public. Never had the nation sat so totally transfixed before its television sets awaiting the latest predictable chants of "Death to America" alternating with the day's interview with a brave relative of one of the hostages. It may never be known how many pairs of pantyhose and how many tubes of toothpaste were sold to this captive audience as a direct result of the hostage crisis, but the numbers were substantial. Perhaps it was the true genius of America to transform a political disaster into a commercial bonanza.

There are several possible explanations for this phenomenon. In the first place, it must be remembered, not very much happened. The hostages were taken, held for fourteen and a half months and then released. There was a good deal of political rhetoric all around, punctuated by a few moments of genuine drama and tragedy, but for the most part it was political shadowboxing, more form than substance.

More important, in my view, was the unbridgeable chasm between two impossibly different cultures, as reflected in the very different personalities of Carter and Khomeini. The eye of the television camera can record the clenched fists and glaring faces of a mob in Tehran and transmit the picture into the living room of a family in Omaha, Nebraska. But it is infinitely more difficult to make that family in Omaha understand the political and cultural context that produced those faces and fists. The problem is compounded when the alien culture is accusing you unjustly (from your point of view) and threatening the lives of those you hold dear. One may reason with a madman or attempt to subdue him physically. It is extremely uncommon to emphathize with one who is doing you harm.

The Carter administration and the U.S. public were poorly equipped to comprehend the nature of the fury and hatred they saw each evening boiling out of Tehran. That comprehension gap was of more than academic concern. It had a profound effect on the formulation and conduct of U.S. policy throughout the crisis. It helped sustain the illusion that Iran would be susceptible to traditional instruments of negotiation and political pressure. Since these were areas where U.S. capabilities were strongest, and since other alternatives, e.g., the direct use of military force, were potentially far more dangerous and unpredictable, there was a deep institutional reluctance, particularly in the Department of State, to conclude that conventional diplomacy was of little value in dealing with the revolutionaries in Tehran. As a consequence, Washington placed greater emphasis on diplomatic efforts, with a higher expectation of results, than an objective analysis of the nature and motivation of Khomeini's regime would have warranted.

The crisis was also highly personalized. To Washington policy makers, the hostages were not abstractions; in many cases they were friends. Moreover, virtually everyone in the policy circle experienced some measure of personal guilt for having permitted this predicament to occur; and that sense of culpability contributed to an exceptionally high level of emotionalism. When President Carter said, as he did on many different occasions both publicly and privately, that the fate of the hostages was on his mind at every waking moment, he was not posturing for political effect. Rather, he was expressing what was a daily reality for almost all of us who were caught up in the crisis.

I remember discussing the crisis with my family shortly after the hostages were seized and telling them that until the hostages were freed, their welfare would take priority over everything else in my life. It was almost like taking religious vows, and that sense of personal dedication remained vivid and strong until the Algerian plane carried the hostages safely out of Iranian airspace many months later.

One of the consequences of this intense personal commitment was a strong impulse to *do something*, almost as if action was a necessary end in itself. That may be another typically American characteristic, but given the mood of the time, it is fair to say that the one course of action that would have been impossibly difficult for the government would have been to do nothing at all.

Yet a coldly analytical assessment of the circumstances in Iran could have led to the conclusion that doing nothing was in fact the wisest course of action. In retrospect, it was argued that the administration, by focusing its attention so exclusively and so publicly on the hostage crisis for so long, enhanced the political importance of the issue and may even have encouraged the publicity-hungry militants by providing them the world-wide attention they craved. Certainly that view came to be accepted as the conventional wisdom among many inside and outside the government after an entire battery of policy initiatives had been tried and failed.

Particularly in hindsight, it can be argued that a realistic and prudent course of action for the administration would have been to declare that any physical harm to the hostages would result in severe punishment to Iran, but that the onus for securing the release of the hostages fell exclusively on Iran and its leaders; in the meantime the United States had other important business to attend to and did not intend to let itself be tied in knots by the illegal actions of a band of extremists.

The argument can be overdone. Given the overwhelmingly emotional response of the U.S. people and the daily diet of emotionally charged television coverage from Tehran, there were limits on the ability of any administration to move the issue lower on the national agenda. There is no convincing evidence whatsoever that such a strategy would have resulted in the hostages being released even one day earlier. On the contrary, the purpose of such a strategy would realistically have to be seen as political damage-limitation. By downplaying the importance of the crisis, Carter might have hoped to deflect international perceptions of a major U.S. foreign policy failure and to minimize domestic political reaction against himself and his administration in a situation where the United States had very limited means to affect the course of events.

The Nature of the Man

Indeed, such a strategy might have succeeded in attenuating some of the political costs that President Carter was forced to pay for his high profile efforts to mobilize national and world pressure against Iran. However, it would have been wholly unnatural for Jimmy Carter to adopt such a position and perhaps impossible for him to sustain. There has been a tendency to overlook the fact that not only was Jimmy Carter prepared to take risks, but he almost seemed to court political danger on issues that he felt were important and when he believed he was right.

Three presidents had backed away from the political quicksand of a Panama Canal Treaty, but Carter pushed it through and accepted the political consequences. The Camp David negotiations were a political high-wire act undertaken against the advice of virtually all of his political advisers. In the days immediately before Camp David, the veteran Washington correspondent Richard Rovere wrote a scathing and somewhat premature political obituary of Carter in which he commented that Carter had "made some decisions that men with a greater flair for gauging the public temper might have hesitated to make. In summoning President Sadat and Prime Minister Begin to man-to-man talks at Camp David, he is courting a failure that could be even more costly for him than for them. They risk almost nothing. . . . But Carter is involving his own and American prestige in what could be the last unarmed Middle East confrontation."[2]

At Camp David, President Carter involved himself directly in a high-profile effort to force a breakthrough in what appeared to be a hopelessly deadlocked situation. In that case he succeeded. In the hostage crisis, although the circumstances were very different, his tactics of direct personal involvement and sustained, high-level political pressure against Tehran employed the same kind of activist approach and political risk taking. In that case he failed, and he paid a very high political price. Working on the political high wire without a safety net is dangerous to your health. Even if you are right, one slip can be fatal. But I suspect that if Carter had to do it over again, he would go about it in very much the same way. It was simply the nature of the man.

Those who suggested that Carter artifically "hyped" the hostage crisis for his own political benefit got it exactly backwards. President Carter initially benefited from the hostage crisis, as presidents almost always gain public support in a national crisis, and he was quite prepared to make the most of it. However, a more cautious politician, realizing the dangers of failure, would rather quickly have attempted to disassociate himself from the consequences and would have been more inclined to adopt the kind of damage-limiting strategy that later had such appeal to pundits and academic observers. To the best of my knowledge, President Carter never seriously considered such a strategy, and that, again, was characteristic of the man.

On those occasions and issues when I had the opportunity to observe him closely, the pattern was entirely consistent. President Carter was totally absorbed by the *substance* of policy. On an important issue he would immerse himself in the facts, drawing on the best expertise he could find, and would very quickly make himself into something of an expert on the subject. He made a decision only after he was confident that he had mastered the complexities of the issue, and once he made a decision he pursued it with single-minded intensity.

However, he did not seem to display the same concern for *form* as he did for substance. He seemed unwilling to devote the same degree of care and attention to the atmospherics and public relations aspects of public presentation as he did to the decision itself. Fundamentally, he seemed to believe that if a decision was correct it would sell itself, and his disregard for the potentially dangerous political consequences of his programs at times appeared to border on recklessness. This intense concern with intellectual honesty and the willingness to let the chips fall where they might was a characteristic that I personally found refreshing and appealing. However, it made him a most unusual politician and it may even have been a fatal flaw.

Since any major presidential decision is by definition a close call, with powerful arguments on either side, the form and timing of presentation may mean the difference between success and failure. In many cases the substance of a good decision may be totally obscured by the form of its presentation, and the public will remember only the failure, not the logic underlying a complex decision.

In the hostage crisis President Carter identified himself closely with the fate of the imprisoned Americans, gambling that an intensive campaign of pressure and diplomacy would succeed in setting them free. When that high-risk strategy failed, he accepted the consequences with considerable grace, making no attempt to find a scapegoat or to deny his own responsibility. His approach may be faulted as unduly optimistic about the effectiveness of U.S. pressure on Iran or as insufficiently cautious about his own political fortunes, but it can scarcely be seen as a deliberate exercise in self-promotion.

Early Efforts

The broad outlines of U.S. policy had been set during the White House meetings in the first two days of the crisis. The two-week period that followed translated the general guidelines into action. It was a period of intense government activity on almost every front.

One of the key objectives was to encourage intermediaries with special credentials to approach Khomeini and those closest to him to persuade them to release the hostages. One of the earliest and most direct approaches originated with the Vatican. The Pope sent a special emissary to deliver a personal message to Khomeini in Qom on November 10. Unfortunately, this visit established a pattern that was to be repeated on a number of other occasions. The ayatollah received the emissary and then took advantage of the opportunity to give him a public lecture on the sufferings of the Iranian people and his own interpretation of Christian responsibility. Said Khomeini, "Had Jesus Christ lived today, he would impeach Carter. . . . You should be doing what Christ himself would do." Khomeini assured the papal envoy that the hostages were being well treated and promised him full access to see for himself. That promise, of course, was not kept, raising doubts about Khomeini's actual control over the students in the embassy.

As indicated previously, the Palestine Liberation Organization had sent a message to Washington within forty-eight hours of the embassy seizure suggesting a possible intervention on behalf of the hostages. By November 7 it was learned that a delegation of three top PLO officials had been dispatched to Iran, and Secretary Vance relayed a message encouraging the effort. Reportedly, Khomeini asked that the PLO not engage in mediation efforts, and it was agreed that the delegation would restrict itself to ensuring the physical safety of the hostages and to look into the prospects for their release.

The details of these discussions were not relayed to Washington, but there was evidence that they were contentious. The students announced they would accept no negotiations "with the PLO, Yasir Arafat or anyone else." However, there were discussions in Qom between the ayatollah and the PLO representatives, and on November 17 it was announced in Tehran that thirteen hostages, comprising women and blacks who were not suspected of espionage, would be released. They departed in two groups on the following two days and returned to the United States on Thanksgiving Day, after a medical and debriefing stop in Germany.

There was no reason to doubt that the PLO was instrumental in arranging this partial release, which the Iranians naïvely believed would split U.S. public opinion; but it was also evident that the PLO had found the going far tougher than expected. Publicly the PLO took no credit for the release and seemed chastened by the experience. My own impression, based on subsequent events, was that the PLO had significantly overestimated its influence with the Iranian leaders and had to expend far more political capital than intended, even for this limited result. They may also have been disappointed that their efforts produced no tangible political benefits on the U.S. side. In any event, the intimacy of Iranian-PLO relations seemed to subside after this episode, and the PLO never again volunteered to intercede. The real lesson of this initial approach to Khomeini—by an intermediary with impeccable revolutionary credentials—was to demonstrate the difficulty of persuading Khomeini to alter his course of action.

Interestingly, there were some individuals in Washington who had arrived independently at that same discouraging conclusion. Within a week of the embassy seizure and the resignation of the Bazargan cabinet, a group of analysts in the Bureau of Intelligence and Research (INR) of the Department of State prepared a memorandum for Secretary Vance. These analysts said there was by that time sufficient evidence to warrant the judgment that diplomatic action had almost no prospect of being successful in liberating the hostages and that no economic or other U.S. pressure on the Iranian regime, including military action, was likely to be any more successful in securing their safe release. Consequently, they concluded, the detention of the hostages could continue for some months.

At the moment when this gloomy but accurate prognosis was prepared, Secretary Vance was deeply engaged at the United Nations and elsewhere in putting together a diplomatic offensive, and the total resources of the Department of State were mobilized for that purpose. Only the day before, United Nations officials had been assured by Iranian representatives that the entire matter would be settled in two or three days. So the message was not welcome, and it was not circulated beyond a very few top officials in the Department of State.

The First U.S. Position Paper

The United Nations played a very important role in U.S. diplomatic efforts almost from the start. Secretary Vance was in close contact with Secretary General Kurt Waldheim and made a number of unpublicized trips from Washington to New York for private discussions. Abolhassan Bani-Sadr had been appointed acting foreign minister in Iran and he quickly established contact with the UN, giving rise to hopes of a workable negotiating channel.

Initially, Bani-Sadr focused on the possibility of a special meeting of the Security Council to convene a commission or some other international forum to investigate the events of the shah's rule in Iran and to provide the basis for returning the shah's assets to Iran. The United States opposed a formal debate in the Security Council on the grounds that Iran should not have access to such a platform until after the hostages were released. However, the concept of some kind of international commission became the center-piece of a negotiating package that was discussed with Iran through a variety of channels over the following five months. That idea had begun to emerge in Vance's discussions as early as November 13, and by November 17 it had evolved into a four-point proposal that was presented to Iranian representatives in New York.

The paper called for (1) the immediate release and departure of the hostages; (2) an international commission to inquire into allegations of human rights violations in Iran under the shah; (3) the availability of U.S. courts to the government of Iran to seek the return of the shah's assets; and (4) affirmation by both Iran and the United States that they would strictly observe those international conventions prohibiting interference in the internal affairs of other states and defining the rights of diplomats.

Iran replied with a counterdraft that called for (1) an international commission and U.S. recognition of the guilt of the shah; (2) return of all property and funds of the shah that might be located in the United States; (3) a U.S.-Iranian declaration of principles similar to that proposed by the United States; and (4) an evacuation of the U.S. embassy by students and permission for all U.S. citizens and government employees to leave the country.

Bani-Sadr sent two representatives to New York, where intensive negotiations with the UN and U.S. intermediaries succeeded in progressively narrowing the differences between the two drafts. By November 25, Iranian representatives tentatively accepted a draft that was not substantially different from the U.S. position, and plans were made for Bani-Sadr to come to New York to address the UN Security Council and to meet with Vance on the final details of an agreed position. It was anticipated that the Security Council would approve a resolution incorporating the points of the U.S.-Iranian agreement and would request Secretary General Waldheim either to go personally or to send a personal emissary to Iran to take custody of the hostages.

At the last minute, on November 28, Bani-Sadr was abruptly dismissed from his post and replaced by Sadegh Ghotbzadeh. Within days, Ghotbzadeh announced that he would not attend the Security Council meeting in New York and that there was "no room for negotiation at present" between the United States and Iran. Vance, describing the frustration of talks with the Iranians when it was impossible to know whether in fact they represented anyone of any real influence in Iran, commented that it was like "talking into the wind."

This initial round of negotiations provided a face-saving formula for terminating the crisis at an early stage, at a cost to Iran far less than what it eventually had to pay. Unfortunately, it also established a pattern of frustration and broken promises that was to bedevil all negotiating efforts for more than a year thereafter. Even while this effort was under way, a number of new factors had been introduced into the situation.

Oil and Dollars

One of the concerns that arose almost immediately after the seizure of the hostages was the supply of Iranian oil. The United States at that time was importing an average of 700,000 barrels per day from Iran, and experience in previous Persian Gulf crises had demonstrated that even a marginal shift of supplies could have significant effects on patterns of U.S. domestic consumption, including long lines at the gasoline pump. As a result, from the first days of the crisis, Secretary of Energy Charles Duncan began examining the potential effects of a termination of Iranian oil supplies and some measures to minimize its effects.

Within a few days it was determined that an Iranian embargo on the United States alone would be manageable by some increased conservation and by reallocation of supplies from other sources. Moreover, such a reallocation could be handled by the major oil companies without triggering the formal sharing provisions of the International Energy Agency, as long as Iran did not stop all its oil exports. Since Iran badly needed the revenues generated by oil exports, they were unlikely to impose more than a limited embargo.

Once it was clear that an Iranian embargo was not a serious threat to U.S. supplies, there were obvious advantages to pre-empting an anticipated Iranian cutoff, thereby depriving them of a propaganda victory and of any illusions they might harbor about their ability to use oil as an instrument of blackmail. Consequently, on November 12, President Carter issued a proclamation terminating all crude-oil imports from Iran to the United States, taking the Iranians by surprise. Tehran quickly announced that it was unilaterally terminating oil exports to the United States, but it was too late to have any propaganda value. The U.S. initiative had had exactly the effect intended.

A second U.S. unilateral step that proved to be a critical element in the strategy of pressure against Iran was the freezing of Iranian assets. Initial preparations for a possible freeze had begun in the Department of the Treasury almost immediately after the hostage seizure, and planning efforts were accelerated on November 9 when reports began circulating in international financial circles that Iran intended to pull its deposits out of U.S. banks. All of the preparations had been made to permit the United States to block any such effort, and on November 14, when word was received very early in the morning that Bani-Sadr had announced the intended withdrawal of Iranian assets, the decision was taken. By seven o'clock that morning Treasury began calling congressional leaders and notifying international financial officials. President Carter signed the freeze order just after eight o'clock, and it was published in the *Federal Register* by midmorning. Although the decision was made for political purposes, it had a number of legal, financial and technical consequences.

The most controversial aspect of the freeze order was its application to Iranian dollar deposits in branches of U.S. banks outside the continental United States. In effect, this provision asserted that branches of U.S. banks were subject to U.S. law rather than the laws of the nations in which they were located. This "conflict of laws" is an unsettled and highly contentious area of international law, and the freeze order was quickly challenged by Iran in the courts of Great Britain, France, Germany and other nations.

A very large proportion of Iranian assets was held in the London branch of the Bank of America, and it was feared in those first few weeks that the London courts would render a judgment prohibiting the "extraterritorial reach" of U.S. domestic law to London banks. The U.S. strategy was to use every possible legal and political device to postpone such a judgment and to let the litigation drag on as long as possible. The strategy worked.

When the assets were unfrozen as part of the hostage release settlement in January 1981, all of the overseas assets were still in place and none of the court cases had come to judgment. In fact, even years later, despite the fact that some of these cases continued on the books, none of them had been decided. Thus, although international law remains as murky as ever on this subject, the U.S. freeze was successfully sustained.

The other area of controversy and potential danger to U.S. interests was the implication of the freeze for other foreign depositors in the United States, particularly holders of large dollar deposits such as Saudi Arabia. A major effort was made by Treasury officials and others to assure those who relied on the U.S. banking system that this was a unique action resulting from a unique set of circumstances and that it was required to prevent a massive repudiation of financial obligations by Iran. The U.S. case was greatly strengthened by Bani-Sadr's imprudent and ill-advised public statements threatening that Iran would repudiate all the foreign debts acquired under the shah's regime. In fact, there was widespread feeling in Washington that Bani-Sadr's clumsy blustering did more to damage Iran's international credit position than anything the United States could have done.

In strictly financial terms, the freezing of Iranian assets may have been the most successful operation of its kind ever conducted. It severely complicated Iran's international financial position, withdrew from their use large sums of money needed to finance imports and provided a considerable measure of protection for U.S. banks that had large loans outstanding to Iran. It also provided essential leverage for negotiating a final agreement favorable to U.S. banks and businesses whose assets in Iran had been placed at risk as a result of the revolution.

However, it was not without its negative aspects. It did not succeed in pressuring Iran to release the hostages promptly, and in fact it may have slowed down the final release arrangement because of the great complexity of undoing what had been done. The freeze order undoubtedly raised fears among other foreign investors about the reliability of the United States as a haven for their deposits. Most of all, it is important to recognize that the relative success of this initiative was due to the fact that Iran had money deposited in U.S. banks far in excess of U.S. assets in Iran, a circumstance very nearly unique in the history of such cases and not likely to be repeated in the future. Thus, as argued persuasively by Deputy Secretary of the Treasury Robert Carswell, the Iranian case should not be taken as evidence that such an action will necessarily be effective or desirable in possible future cases of international conflict.[3]

Iranian Students

Another problem of an entirely different nature was the large number of Iranian students living in the United States. When the hostages were seized in Iran, the U.S. government had no accurate figures on the number of Iranian students actually in the country. These students had been coming and going freely for many years, and the Immigration and Naturalization Service made no attempt to keep track of them. It was suspected that many were "out of status," i.e., they had remained in the United States after their visas had expired or were otherwise in violation of the terms of their visas. Many of the students had made themselves extremely unpopular with the U.S. public by organizing unruly demonstrations in favor of Khomeini, and when they launched a new round of demonstrations in favor of the hostage seizure, they became the target of intense popular hostility and even violence.

This created several problems for Washington. First, it was feared that violent popular reaction to pro-Khomeini demonstrations would be played back by the media to Tehran where it might lead to reprisals against the hostages. Second, it was politically important for the government to be seen to be taking some steps to deal with this explosive issue. Third, unless the government acted quickly, there was concern that a vigilante mentality would result in indiscriminate attacks on Iranians throughout the country—many of whom were appalled by the actions of the regime in Tehran.

It was soon discovered that the government's power to deal with any of these problems was limited. President Carter wanted to institute a ban on all pro- and anti-Khomeini demonstrations, at least on federal property, on the grounds that such activity carried the risk of violence that could endanger the lives of the hostages. He soon discovered, however, that the constitutional protection of free assembly had been extended so widely and so absolutely—particularly as a result of court tests arising from the Vietnam anti-war demonstrations—that it was virtually impossible to enforce such a ban. Only after the most vigorous action by the Department of Justice, supported by personal testimony and affadavits by senior officials of the Department of State, was it possible to ban such demonstrations in the immediate vicinity of the White House and the Capitol; and it was far from certain that even those limited restrictions could withstand a concerted challenge in court. Outside those two areas, the government could do little except take every possible precaution to avoid violence.

Thus, it became common in the nation's capital to see a small band of pro-Khomeini demonstrators marching down the street surrounded by a massive phalanx of the long-suffering police of the District of Columbia, separating the demonstrators from angry and jeering spectators along the route. During the first few months of the crisis, endless hours were spent by officials at all levels of the government dealing with the problem of demonstrations. Although there were some close calls, the thoroughly professional work of law enforcement officials managed to avoid the worst. This prolonged effort was my first opportunity to become acquainted with the operation of crowd control in Washington, D.C., and I came away enormously impressed with the intelligence, dedication, sensitivity and good sense of the officers and men who have that almost impossible task.

It was also discovered that the government had very limited control over the many thousands of Iranian students. Even those who were undeniably out of status and who were known to be illegally present in the United States could not be deported summarily. Any student who wished to retain lawyers and resort to the courts could delay deportation for many months or even years. America is a nation of laws, and the protection of those laws extends to all within its boundaries, without respect to immediate passions or bureaucratic expediency. Although not without its frustrations, it was nevertheless heartening, if ironic, to observe the meticulous application of civil liberties at a time of intense national emotion, even to those mindlessly proclaiming their support of a regime acting in total defiance of the most elementary principles of human rights. It was a demonstration of civic responsibility of which Americans have every right to be proud.

After a review of the legal options available to him, President Carter limited his actions to a formal check of the status of all Iranian students. At a minimum, this would provide a more accurate inventory of the numbers, location and status of the students; it would serve as evidence to the students and to the U.S. public that the government was concerned about the problem; and, it was hoped, it would lead many of those out of status to choose voluntary departure. Although less than a perfect solution, the program generally seemed to have the desired effects.

More difficult was the problem of vigilantism. The president, the secretary of state, the attorney general and others made repeated public calls to resist the temptation of taking out national frustrations and anger on individual Iranians. Despite these efforts, almost all Iranians living in the United States at the time can attest to the anger they encountered. Most Iranians, even those who had lived for many years in the United States and who had no sympathy whatsoever with Khomeini's fanaticism, found themselves harassed in a variety of ways. A friend of mine, who considered himself a loyal American, described to me his astonishment at discovering that his local garage would no longer service his car. Some lost their jobs for no apparent reason, and there were ugly stories of attempted violence. Many Iranians pretended to be Arab or Latin American to avoid heckling and hostility. For virtually all Iranians it was a tense and very trying time.

Nevertheless, with some scattered exceptions, the U.S. public acted with discipline and restraint. Despite tensions and hostility, the size of the Iranian community in the United States almost certainly increased during and after the crisis, with many seeking political asylum. Support for Khomeini's regime gradually dwindled to a small hard core and finally eroded almost to the vanishing point, even among those who had originally supported the revolution. By the end of the crisis, the overwhelming bulk of Iranian opinion in the United States had shifted to outright opposition, and pro-Khomeini demonstrations ceased of their own accord simply for lack of support. That process was the result of Khomeini's own policies, but it was also facilitated by the responsible behavior of most Americans and of their government.

The Lucky Thirteen and the "White Paper"

By the middle of November, within two weeks of the seizure of the embassy, the basic elements of a strategy of diplomatic and economic pressure were in place, and secret negotiations were well under way through United Nations auspices in New York. At that point a series of new developments forced Washington to undertake a fundamental reappraisal of policy. It all came in a flood on November 20.

The thirteen hostages released through the intervention of the PLO were met on arrival in Germany by a team of U.S. officials headed by Undersecretary of State David Newsom. Now Washington officials got the first detailed picture of the treatment of the hostages, and it was shocking. Although these thirteen were low-level officials in the embassy who were not suspected of espionage by their captors, they had been forced to remain silent during their two weeks of captivity, and many were kept bound hand and foot for the entire period. They had been subjected to a systematic effort to break down their psychological defenses. They were repeatedly informed that they had been abandoned by their government, that no one in the United States cared about their fate. They were brainwashed with propaganda about the crimes of the shah and about America's responsibility for all the ills of Iran. Although this group had little information about the other hostages, it was apparent that those whom the students suspected of espionage would be treated more harshly, perhaps tortured.

Based on this information, the United States launched a major propaganda campaign of its own. Graphic descriptions of physical conditions in the embassy were passed on a confidential basis to many friendly governments, with the request that they approach the authorities in Tehran through whatever channels were available to them to seek more humane treatment of the hostages and to press for their prompt release. This resulted in a new world-wide barrage of statements and diplomatic demarches directed against Tehran. At the same time, Vice President Mondale made a strong statement from the White House condemning the captors for brutality and savagery, which was reinforced by background briefings for the media.

This campaign was based on the expectation that Khomeini and even the students would be sensitive to charges that they were using the same techniques as the hated SAVAK, and in fact the accusations seemed to hit a nerve in Tehran. Khomeini felt it necessary to offer public assurances of good treatment and to admonish the students to respect Islamic traditions of humane behavior. There were indications that some of the worst excesses of the students were curbed, and the way was paved for visits to some of the hostages by ambassadors and international relief agencies.

Another shock produced by the debriefings was the realization that virtually all the sensitive political files of the embassy had been captured intact by the students. This led President Carter to order, on November 20, a survey of all documents that might have been compromised in the embassy takeover and the initiation of a draft "White Paper" on U.S. relations with Iran. It was anticipated that Iran would eventually conduct a show trial of the hostages in some kind of kangaroo court or perhaps launch a propaganda attack on the United States through some international forum, such as the Human Rights Commission of the United Nations. This preliminary gathering of evidence would permit the United States to respond quickly and authoritatively to Iranian charges.

The project was undertaken by the Policy Planning Staff of the Department of State, under its director, Anthony Lake. Ultimately it resulted in a massive collection of presidential papers and official government documents plus some draft papers on various aspects of the U.S.-Iranian relationship over a period of three decades. No "White Paper" was ever produced, and as it happened, it was never needed.[4]

The issue of possible trials of the hostages was the dominating concern in Washington during the last weeks of November and early December. It was Khomeini's practice to wrap any concession or conciliatory gesture in threatening language to avoid any appearance of weakness or a softening of his position. On November 20, after the thirteen U.S. blacks and women had been released, Khomeini made a speech declaring that "if Carter does not send the shah, it is possible that the hostages may be tried, and if they are tried, Carter knows what will happen." That threat was taken very seriously in Washington. It resulted in prompt public warnings that Iran "would bear full responsibility for any ensuing consequences," explicitly drawing attention to "other remedies" available to the United States—a reference to the right of self-defense provided by the UN Charter.

The Attack on the Great Mosque

The threat of physical danger to the hostages was compounded by a bizarre combination of events elsewhere in the Arab world. On November 20 the Great Mosque in Mecca was occupied by a group of armed Islamic fanatics. This sudden attack, affecting one of the most sacred Moslem shrines on the eve of the fourteenth centennial of Islam and at the beginning of the holy month of Moharram, sent shock waves throughout the Islamic world.

Within hours, wild rumors began to circulate, including one particularly absurd story that the assault was the work of Israel with the assistance of the United States. That story was picked up by a radio station in Pakistan, where a mob formed and invaded the U.S. embassy on November 21.[5] A Marine guard and a U.S. Army warrant officer were killed, together with four Pakistanis, and the embassy was badly burned. Secretary Vance, with nearly sixty of his State Department personnel imprisoned or in hiding in Tehran, an ambassador recently killed in Afghanistan, and now the deaths and damages in Islamabad, feared that an anti-U.S. wave was sweeping the entire Islamic world. He ordered all nonessential U.S. personnel out of sensitive posts throughout the region, and some nine hundred U.S. dependents and officials were evacuated over the following weeks.

This decision, which Secretary Vance made on his own, was a reflection of the grim and fatalistic attitude that dominated Vance's thinking during this period. A moral and highly principled man, profoundly committed to the rule of reason, Secretary Vance displayed a visceral revulsion to violence and the politics of confrontation. He believed in the practice of diplomacy, the benefits of patience, and the efficacy of nonviolence. He felt a personal sense of responsibility for the people who served under him, and more than any other member of the Carter administration he measured the crisis in terms of its cost in human lives and human suffering. Vance reacted with visible pain to each of these bitter new revelations, almost as if he had been struck a blow to the body. He never wavered in his convictions, but his personal suffering was unmistakable.

His decision to withdraw as many of his people as possible from possible exposure to danger was understandable in human terms, but it was an overreaction. The decision was vigorously opposed by most Foreign Service officers in the field. For those who remained, it meant increased workloads and the added personal hardship of separation from their families. More important, the host countries viewed this partial evacuation as a vote of no confidence in their security capabilities, as a U.S. proclivity to tar all Islamic states with the same brush of irresponsibility, and as dismaying evidence of the tenuousness of the U.S. presence on which many of them relied. Although there was one further attack on a U.S. embassy (in Tripoli, Libya, on December 2), the region-wide uprising never came; and in time the evacuees quietly began returning to their posts.

A Quiet Warning to Iran

The events of November 20 and 21 had implications for almost every aspect of U.S. policy in Iran and the region as a whole. President Carter held an emergency session of the National Security Council on the afternoon of November 20; and on Friday, November 23, he assembled all of his top security advisers at Camp David for a full-scale policy review. Those attending were Vice President Mondale, Secretary Vance, Warren Christopher, Secretary Harold Brown, General Jones, Stansfield Turner, Zbigniew Brzezinski, Hamilton Jordan and Jody Powell.

The president said he had called the meeting to reassess U.S. strategy. He was concerned that Iran not be allowed to set the pace of events. His immediate concerns involved how to deter trials and physical harm to the hostages. He was also concerned about the timing of the departure of the shah from the United States, which some reports now indicated would set off a hostile and emotional reaction in Iran, especially during the mourning days of Ashura, which were to begin in a week. The available military options now included the mining of Iranian harbors and a punitive air strike on Iranian domestic petroleum facilities. He believed Iranian diplomats should be kicked out of the United States, and pressure should be brought to bear on U.S. allies to take more tangible steps than they had done so far.

Secretary Vance outlined in some detail the negotiations under way in New York. He described the four-point agreement that the Iranian representatives were close to accepting, and he noted that these representatives claimed to have the approval of Khomeini. Over protests by both Jordan and Powell that the four-point document would give the appearance of submitting to Iranian preconditions, Vance won Carter's approval to continue with the negotiations.

After some discussion, Carter also reluctantly deferred to Vance's judgment that kicking the Iranian diplomats out of the United States would interfere with the negotiations, and he agreed to postpone any action for the time being. However, he ordered continued preparations for a punitive military strike against Iran. Even if the hostages were released, Carter felt that matters had gone too far not to punish Iran for its actions. He was leaning toward the mining of harbors. Vance adamantly opposed any military action unless the hostages were physically harmed.

On the issue of possible trials, President Carter approved a message to be sent privately to Iran. The message, addressed to the highest authorities in Iran, indicated that it originated with the highest levels of the U.S. government. It recalled the U.S. preference for a peaceful solution, which was being pursued through all available channels. However, it warned that any public or governmental trial of U.S. personnel in Iran would result in the interruption of Iranian commerce. It also noted that any harm to any hostage would result in direct retaliatory action. The United States, it noted, did not intend to make this message public, but it wanted no misunderstanding of its gravity.

Secretary Vance opposed sending a direct threat, and Vice President Mondale expressed concern that the message would undermine the ongoing negotiations. President Carter overruled them, commenting that he could not "sit here as president and watch the trials." In the event of harm to the hostages, he said, the national honor comes first.

The message was relayed to Iran later that evening through a friendly government, and the United States received assurances within forty-eight hours that it had been received by high Iranian officials. No Iranian official ever acknowledged the message or referred to it in later discussions, but Iranian public and private statements immediately began backing away from the threat of trials.[6]

The group also discussed the possible departure of the shah. The shah had let it be known that he wanted to leave, and President Carter believed that on balance his departure would improve the situation by removing the ostensible cause for holding the hostages. The response of the students to the shah's departure was uncertain, and several reports had indicated that they might take reprisals against the hostages. The shah's doctors indicated that he would be well enough to travel in about one week, which would coincide with the religious emotionalism of Ashura. Consequently, President Carter ordered that preparations be made for the shah to leave—for Mexico or Egypt at his discretion—"after they stop whipping themselves."

New Pressures Rejected

Although President Carter accepted Vance's counsel of restraint at the November 23 meeting, it was evident that he was chafing at the lack of progress. After four more days had gone by without any significant change, Carter again began pressing for a more vigorous approach. On November 27, he outlined his thoughts in a note asking the SCC to comment on the following courses of action:

1. press for a strong condemnation of Iran in the UN Security Council;
2. get the shah out of the country;
3. issue a public call for a total embargo on all goods being shipped to Iran until the hostages were released;
4. seek to make the embargo universal by imposing formal sanctions against Iran under the provisions of Chapter VII of the UN Charter;
5. follow up the embargo with the mining of three Iranian ports, together with a public statement that punishment would be inflicted on Iran if the hostages were harmed;
6. prepare to destroy Iranian domestic petroleum facilities if any of the hostages were harmed; and
7. take all possible steps to restrict Iran's access to international credit and foreign commerce.

This note prompted a meeting in the White House Situation Room on November 28 of all the officials who had attended the Camp David meeting, minus the president. It was apparent to all that a fundamental turning point in U.S. strategy was fast approaching, and the meeting was one of the most contentious of the entire crisis.

Brzezinski opened the meeting by reading the president's list of proposed actions. Brzezinski commented that the United States was getting itself locked into a "litigation strategy" that tied its hands and constrained its freedom of action. He believed it would be preferable to escalate U.S. actions in a measured way rather than let the crisis subside into a situation of normalcy. Brzezinski foresaw a situation where Iran would continue to defy all U.S. diplomatic and international moves while gradually undercutting existing world-wide support for the United States by focusing on the issue of U.S. intelligence activities. Hamilton Jordan said he was surprised that the situation had not already turned sour, and he did not see how the country could go on for two or three more months this way.

Vance did not agree, but he said the question was what could be done to change the situation without making it worse. He thought the first four items raised by the president could be done without seriously threatening the hostages. The breakpoint, in his view, came with mining.

Brzezinski and Brown argued that the threat of mining could be used effectively to pressure the Europeans and others to act more forcefully. Vance said if that could be done in the context of sanctions adopted by the United Nations that would be one thing, but as a unilateral U.S. act it would be quite different. Hamilton Jordan added that UN sanctions were susceptible to veto by the Soviet Union, and if they chose to veto, it would mean the end of SALT II.

Harold Brown agreed that a decision to mine Iranian harbors would put the hostages under increased danger. He felt there was a fifty-fifty chance that some might be killed in response. The question was how long the United States could wait. In his view, the threat to the hostages increased over time, while U.S. ability to act declined. Jody Powell agreed that time worked against the United States and appeared to work for Khomeini. He favored taking some action to reverse the situation, but he recognized that military action would put the hostages in danger and probably would not result in a positive reaction from Khomeini.

Vance said it would take at least a month to exhaust available diplomatic remedies. He was extremely pessimistic that even America's closest allies would join in a blockade, noting that in 1967 the United States was unable to get a single nation to support its efforts to open the Strait of Tiran.[7] Moreover, Vance believed that a military action such as mining would set off a powerful reaction in the region. In his view, before such an action was taken the United States should pull virtually all its people out of the Moslem world.

General Jones and Admiral Turner both felt that the U.S. position in the region was eroding; however, neither believed that a military action by the United States would resolve the hostage issue or receive any significant support. That was the dilemma. Jody Powell agreed, observing that we should not attempt to press the UN for Chapter VII sanctions unless we were convinced it would be successful. A Soviet veto would be undesirable.

Brzezinski said there appeared to be a consensus on several points. A military act such as mining of harbors would increase the danger to the hostages. All diplomatic recourse should be exhausted before resorting to military action. However, if any of the hostages were killed, the United States should react forcibly. In that case, mining was not enough, although a U.S. response should be precise and not indiscriminate. We should proceed immediately with the first four steps in the president's suggested list.

Vance, apparently sensing a shift toward his own thinking, took exception to the final point. He now proposed that only the first two points of the president's list should be undertaken immediately. We should not ask other nations for an embargo until all other diplomatic recourse had been exhausted. He believed that would require three weeks to a month.

At that point Charles Kirbo, the president's close personal friend and adviser, who had joined the meeting and had sat quietly through the discussion, spoke up. Nothing he had heard thus far, he commented, offered a course of action to defend U.S. honor that would not make things worse and possibly get us mired down over the long run. He thought that as long as the hostages were unharmed, the U.S. people would stay with the administration in its efforts to free them.

Secretary Vance, picking up on Kirbo's comments, extended his position even further. Mining, he said, would produce harm to the hostages, and he would not advise it as long as they were safe, even if trials should begin. Referring to the presidential message sent to Iran several days earlier, Vance said that he did not interpret an "interruption of commerce" as necessarily meaning mining. It could also be an embargo. Brzezinski objected, arguing that without physical interruption other states would not join in an embargo. Vance insisted that a threat of mining or use of force could have exactly the opposite effect of that intended, i.e., it could turn many of our friends against us. He preferred a peaceful blockade to mining of harbors.

Harold Brown objected that a naval blockade would place the United States in the position of being forced to take the last action of sinking a ship headed for Iran, whereas mining was more passive and placed the burden on the ship that chose to enter waters known to be mined. Vance did not reply, and on that note the discussion was terminated.

This meeting also included a brief discussion of the timing of presentation of the U.S. case against Iran to the International Court of Justice (ICJ). It was agreed that the United States should proceed with the presentation of its case simultaneously with the deliberations in the UN Security Council.[8]

The Days Dwindle Down

The meeting of November 28 was a turning point for U.S. policy. Despite Brzezinski's concern that the United States was locking itself into a diplomatic strategy of inaction, he was unable to demonstrate that military action would either free the hostages or significantly strengthen the U.S. position.

On the contrary, Vance's arguments proved persuasive with most of President Carter's principal advisers, and as it turned out, with President Carter himself.

From the very beginning of the crisis Vance had doggedly pursued a strategy of relying on quiet diplomacy and of subordinating military initiatives to the diplomatic process. In the first week of the crisis, when White House counsel Lloyd Cutler proposed declaring a national emergency in order to give the president greater legal latitude to act against Iranian interests, Vance opposed it on the grounds that it would interfere with his negotiations at the UN, and his view was accepted. In mid-November, when there were suggestions of restricting the activities of Iranian diplomats in the United States, Vance opposed it on the grounds that the Iranian diplomats were personally opposed to the hostage taking, that they were working behind the scenes to change Khomeini's views and that they provided a useful channel for getting U.S. views to Tehran. Action was postponed. At Camp David, he opposed sending any direct threat to Iran on the subject of hostage trials. He was overruled by the president on that occasion, but he shifted his argument to the interpretation of the key words "interruption of Iranian commerce," arguing that the phrase did not necessarily imply mining of ports but could also mean trade sanctions adopted through the UN or in conjunction with U.S. allies. By the next meeting of the National Security Council on December 4, President Carter had accepted that position.

On only two issues was Vance completely overruled by the president. On November 20, when the Department of Defense proposed sending a second carrier task force (the U.S.S. *Kitty Hawk*) to join the U.S.S. *Midway* task force in the Arabian Sea, Vance opposed on the grounds that it would be interpreted as a U.S. military confrontation with Islam that would risk setting off a reaction in the region. President Carter disagreed and ordered the task force to proceed. Four days later, when Defense again proposed deploying some AWACS (early-warning planes) to Egypt as a contingency measure, Vance opposed the move on the grounds that it would interfere with negotiations. President Carter again disagreed, stating that such contingency preparations were essential in the event some military action became necessary. The AWACS arrived secretly in Egypt in mid-December.

With these two exceptions, Secretary Vance and the Department of State thoroughly dominated the U.S. decision-making process during the first two months of the crisis. Although President Carter and others repeatedly expressed frustration at the lack of progress, Vance argued with great persuasiveness that any dramatic action should be postponed until the PLO initiative had been completed, until Ashura was past, until the Iranian referendum was finished, until the shah was out of the country, until the Security Council had acted, until the World Court had issued its ruling, and so on. In the meantime, the U.S. people remained united behind the administration in its efforts, and there was no effective incentive to change course drastically. Time was gradually whittled away.

New Problems, New Contacts

As the second month of the crisis began, there were a number of critical new developments. Without warning or explanation, the government of Mexico suddenly experienced a change of heart and withdrew its promise to let the shah return to Cuernavaca. The Mexican announcement caught Washington totally by surprise, and the timing was almost impossibly bad.

Vance had carefully prepared a scenario in which it was hoped that the emotionalism of Ashura would pass uneventfully, that the UN Security Council would adopt a resolution permitting an active role by Secretary General Waldheim (with tacit Iranian approval), that Iran would complete its constitutional referendum, and that the shah would leave the United States. This conjunction of events seemed to offer a realistic chance to break the stalemate; however, the loss of nerve in Mexico City, and the vagaries of Iranian internal politics disrupted the plan. The Mexican bombshell came just as the Ashura marches were beginning in Tehran, just as the shah was finally sufficiently recovered from surgery to travel, and just as Iranian Acting Foreign Minister Bani-Sadr, who openly favored freeing the hostages, was summarily replaced by Sadegh Ghotbzadeh.

The collapse of this scenario was not without its intriguing aspects. On the very day that the new Iranian foreign minister assumed office, he informed Professor Richard Cottam (who had known Ghotbzadeh for years and who would serve increasingly as a contact point between the mercurial Iranian and the U.S. government) that the Revolutionary Council was frightened and anxious to find a way out of the dilemma. He sketched the outlines of a possible initiative that would permit Iran to give formal expression to its grievances against the shah, possibly in an extradition trial or some other forum, thereby paving the way for the release of the hostages.

Meanwhile, Ghotbzadeh made contact with an old acquaintance in Paris, a lawyer named François Cheron who had been active in human rights causes, and asked him to establish contact with U.S. officials. Cheron telephoned Pierre Salinger, the ABC bureau chief in Paris, who put him in touch with Warren Zimmerman, the U.S. diplomat who had conducted the discussions with Yazdi when Khomeini was still in Paris.[9] Cheron reported Ghotbzadeh's interest in arranging for non-Iranian medical personnel to visit the hostages and repeated the idea of a formal extradition trial of the shah that would permit Iran to express its grievances. It was evident that Ghotbzadeh did not intend to let any grass grow under his feet.[10]

At about the same time, another Iranian who claimed to have direct contact with individuals in the Revolutionary Council arrived in Washington from Europe with a set of proposals for resolving the crisis that involved an investigation of the shah's finances.[11] Still another Iranian with close personal ties to members of the Revolutionary Council contacted the State Department through Vice President Mondale to provide some firsthand reporting on attitudes inside revolutionary circles.

In this period there were also a number of independent initiatives by Islamic statesmen and several Islamic heads of state who were in direct contact with Tehran in an attempt to arrange visits on behalf of the hostages. One of the most significant of these was a distinguished and well-respected Moslem statesman who made unpublicized visits to Iran on several occasions to explore the possibilities of a settlement. Several embassies of Western nations in Tehran also maintained private contacts with officials close to the revolution who confirmed high-level Iranian interest in finding a way to end the crisis. Moreover, the Iranian ambassador to the UN was known to be in Tehran arguing vigorously for an early end to the crisis and preparing a proposal that he hoped to present indirectly to the United States after he returned to his post.

Unlike the early days of the crisis, when there appeared to be almost no way of communicating directly with revolutionary officials in Tehran, the problem by early December was to sort out the variety of messages and intermediaries emanating from Iran. During the month of December, Washington maintained contact with more than twenty different individuals and organizations, each of which had some degree of proven access and credibility with those in and around the Revolutionary Council. There was no doubt whatever that many of those in the Revolutionary Council were anxious to end the crisis and were engaged actively in efforts to seek a solution. That was no guarantee that the militant students and Khomeini himself could be persuaded to alter their hard-line approach, but neither was it obvious that the efforts would necessarily fail.

Prodding the Allies

This flurry of semi-covert diplomatic activity was very much on the minds of President Carter and his advisers when the National Security Council met in the afternoon of December 4. The president reiterated his concern that the status quo not be allowed to become permanent, but the principal focus of his attention was on economic sanctions and the problem of persuading U.S. allies to take more vigorous action in support of U.S. efforts. The objective, he said, was to hurt Khomeini economically, and that could only be effective if America's European allies were prepared to cooperate.

Secretary Vance was scheduled to travel to Europe that weekend for a NATO foreign ministers meeting, and it was decided to take advantage of that opportunity to seek European support for UN sanctions against Iran once the World Court had rendered judgment. Since Iran was in flagrant violation of international law, there was little doubt that the Court's verdict would go against Iran. There was also little doubt that Iran would ignore the Court's ruling. It was recognized that the process of negotiating a resolution of sanctions against Iran in the Security Council could be time-consuming and ultimately subject to Soviet veto. Therefore, Vance was to explore with the European allies the possibility of voluntary interim measures to restrict Iranian access to military credits and to European financial markets and loans. Two teams of senior officials from State and Treasury were dispatched immediately for technical discussions in Europe, to pave the way for Vance's consultations at the foreign minister level.

President Carter anticipated resistance from European leaders. He commented that if he were Chancellor Helmut Schmidt of Germany, he would try to stay out of this as long as possible. However, if he were forced to choose between Germany's broader relationship with the United States as opposed to Germany's temporary interest in Iran, he would choose to sacrifice the Iranian connection. Vance was to make it clear to the Europeans that the alternative to peaceful economic sanctions was U.S. unilateral imposition of a blockade, including the possibility of mining. The president said he was disappointed in allied cooperation to date, and if they were not prepared to join in sanctions against Iran, he wanted to know.

Secretary of the Treasury Miller reported that he had some good news on the court cases in Europe. The judge in London who was hearing Iran's case challenging the U.S. freeze of Iranian assets in Citibank had ruled that all such cases were sufficiently important to justify "full preparation." As a consequence, the judge said he did not intend to hear the cases until after Easter —a delay of some five months, during which time Iran would be unable to retrieve its assets. President Carter said that was the best news he had heard for some time. Joking, he wondered whether Treasury could have its case prepared by Easter. Lloyd Cutler responded that by Easter they could be ready to go until the following Easter if necessary.

At the end of the meeting, there was a discussion of U.S. military preparations. Secretary Brown said that, with two carrier task groups in the vicinity and AWACS scheduled to arrive soon in Egypt, he had sufficient forces to carry out a retaliatory or punitive strike against Iran if that should prove necessary. Brzezinski pointed out that since the United States was no longer able to rely on Iran as a security presence in the Persian Gulf area, this significantly increased level of U.S. presence would probably be required for the indefinite future, even after the hostage crisis ended. That raised the question of U.S. military access and support facilities.

Brzezinski had been directing an interagency review of U.S. military strategy in the region since April 1979, and the study had indicated the need for U.S. support facilities in the region, possibly at Masirah Island off the coast of Oman, at the former Soviet naval facilities at Berbera in Somalia, at the Egyptian port of Berenice (also known as Ras Banas) in the Red Sea, and possibly at the port of Mombasa in Kenya. It was not clear that access to all of these facilities would be politically possible, nor was it clear how much new construction might be required to make these sites usable. However, he felt the time had come when the United States should make an initial approach to each of the countries in question. President Carter quickly agreed and directed that a team be assembled to travel to the area in the near future.[12]

The NSC meeting of December 4 established the direction of U.S. strategy through the end of the year. Vance departed for Europe and reported back to the president on December 15 that the European allies and Japan had pledged to support U.S. efforts to get Security Council approval of international sanctions against Iran. At Vance's prodding, they also agreed that they would join with the United States in imposing sanctions even if the Soviet Union vetoed the Security Council resolution.[13] The allies also agreed to a set of voluntary interim steps that were technical in nature but helped to restrict Iran's access to credits and blocked an attempted Iranian attack on the dollar by attempting to shift oil payments to other currencies. On the whole, the European reaction was consistent with President Carter's initial assessment: at each stage they reluctantly took only what they considered to be the minimum steps necessary to prevent the United States from moving to a military solution.

The Shah and Hamilton Jordan

While Vance was traveling, a lot of time and effort in Washington was devoted to finding a new home for the shah. Plans had been made for the shah to leave New York on December 2, and the Mexican announcement on November 29 allowed only three hectic days to make alternative arrangements. After a quick survey of the possibilities, including some rather strained consultations with the shah's entourage, it was decided that the shah would go temporarily to Lackland Air Force Base in Texas while an effort was being made to find him a more permanent residence.

In Washington, Warren Christopher discreetly canvassed possible residence sites. At one point, nine different countries were under consideration; however, the list quickly narrowed to two. Egypt was the most obvious choice, since President Sadat had publicly reiterated his willingness to accept the shah, but it was feared that the shah's arrival in Egypt at a politically difficult time could weaken Sadat domestically. The other choice was Panama.

While the shah was still in the Bahamas, Panama had formally indicated its willingness to offer him asylum, but the offer had been rejected. Now Panamanian leaders quietly let it be known that the invitation was still valid, and it was decided to explore the possibility. Hamilton Jordan, the White House chief of staff, had played a key role in shepherding the controversial Panama Canal Treaty through the Congress. In the process, he had also developed a close personal relationship with General Omar Torrijos, the strong man of Panamanian politics. It was therefore entirely natural for President Carter to select Jordan as his personal representative to meet with the Panamanians.

On December 11, Jordan made a secret flight to Panama and secured a formal invitation to the shah in conversations with Torrijos. Although he did not suspect it at the time, this was the opening gambit in a bizarre negotiating process that would occupy him for the next four months and more. Because of his coincidental ties with Panama and his very close personal relationship with President Carter, Hamilton Jordan was to become a central figure in the second act of the hostage drama.

Jordan immediately flew to Lackland Air Force Base, where he joined White House counsel Lloyd Cutler to raise the matter directly with the shah. Robert Armao, the public relations man who had now become the shah's principal adviser, was strongly opposed to Panama. He raised every possible objection—the politics of Torrijos, the uncertainty of adequate medical care, the possibility of a double cross resulting in the shah's extradition. Jordan responded to each of these objections, offering assurances in the name of the president.

Although Armao continued to protest hotly, the shah eventually overruled him. The shah was sensitive to the dangers of the political situation. Although he did not believe that his departure would free the hostages, he wished at all costs to avoid charges that he had put their lives in greater danger. It was evident that he could not remain in the United States under any circumstances, and there was no real alternative to the Panamanian offer. So the following morning Jordan was joined by a reluctant and unhappy Armao to return secretly to Panama once again to examine possible living accommodations.

In the meantime Lloyd Cutler and the shah's lawyer, William Jackson, began preparing a list of guarantees that President Carter would verbally make to the shah about his stay in Panama. These assurances, which were completed on December 14 and sealed with a personal telephone call from the president to the shah, consisted of four basic points:

1. The shah's children were permitted to remain in the United States to continue their schooling, and U.S. security agencies would maintain liaison with the security personnel protecting them.
2. The shahbanou, the shah's wife, could visit the children in the United States from time to time.
3. The shah would have access to U.S. medical facilities in Panama as required. (This was particularly important, since the shah's spleen was again dangerously enlarged and his doctors strongly recommended surgery to remove it. The shah's doctors were familiar with the medical facilities in Panama and were confident that they were adequate to treat him.)
4. The United States agreed to provide the necessary transportation and assistance for a U.S. medical team to visit Panama for the operation.

On December 16 the shah left Texas for Panama City. He took up residence in the home of Gabriel Lewis, Panama's former ambassador to the United States, on the Pacific island of Contadora. Robert Armao was dissatisfied with the arrangements and obviously did not relish moving to Panama. Although he went along with the plan, he did so in bad grace, and it was evident that there would be more trouble before this sad odyssey was ended.

Plots Proliferate

The plot began to thicken within days of the shah's arrival. On December 18, President Aristides Royo of Panama told the U.S. ambassador that his government had been contacted by Iran requesting the shah's extradition. Royo said that Panama would not extradite the shah, but he was intrigued by the possibility that Panama could assist in devising a face-saving plan that might result in the hostages' release. He had two different thoughts. On the one hand, Panamanian law provided that anyone whose extradition was requested by another country would remain in custody while a judicial review was under way. He thought a declaration that the shah was under arrest, although it would not change his physical status in any way, might be helpful in Tehran. He was also considering a "coordination committee" in which representatives from Iran, Panama and the United States would meet to discuss how to end the crisis.

The United States immediately informed Royo that neither of these plans was acceptable. Ironclad assurances had been provided by Panama that the shah would not and could not be extradited under Panamanian law, and the technical "arrest" ploy was not only contrary to those assurances but a demeaning and transparent ruse. As to a meeting, the United States insisted on prior release of the hostages. Nevertheless, it was clear that Panama—which was now experiencing daily student demonstrations protesting the shah's arrival—was determined to play an active role in finding a solution to the crisis. Rumors of various schemes circulated in Panama, and these stories, combined with reports out of Tehran that a hit squad had been dispatched to assassinate Panama's new guest, could scarcely have been received by the shah with equanimity.

In the meantime, Ghotbzadeh was proceeding with his own labyrinthine schemes. With the ayatollah's blessing, he was attempting to convene an international tribunal, which he sometimes referred to as a "grand jury," to hear testimony about the shah's crimes. The Irish Nobel Peace Prize–winner Sean MacBride was invited to Iran to meet with the Revolutionary Council to consider forming such a body.

Simultaneously, Ghotbzadeh had summoned two old friends from Paris—Christian Bourguet and Héctor Villalón—to assemble extradition papers to be presented to the government of Panama. Bourguet was a French lawyer active in radical causes and a partner of François Cheron, who had earlier made contact with the U.S. embassy in Paris. Villalón was an international adventurer of Argentinian origins who operated on the shadowy margins of international business and politics. These men thrived on intrigue, as did Ghotbzadeh, and their unconventional approach was certain to strike a resonant chord in Panama. With the introduction of this new cast of characters, what had been an international drama was rapidly degenerating into political farce.

Political and Military Clouds

In late December, however, Washington had never heard of Bourguet and Villalón, and official attention was riveted on two very different concerns. The International Court had delivered its unanimous decision against Iran on December 15, which Iran rejected. Consequently, the United States was now attempting to gather support for a formal UN Security Council resolution imposing economic sanctions on Iran. Nine affirmative votes were required in the Security Council, and Ambassador Donald McHenry was finding it difficult to locate the needed support. The biggest unknown was the attitude of the USSR, which could exercise a veto. That problem was compounded by increasingly disturbing reports of Soviet troop movements on the borders of Afghanistan.

The political situation inside Iran was the most chaotic since the revolutionary takeover of power eight months earlier. The Kurds, Baluch and other tribal elements were in a state of virtual rebellion against Tehran. In Tabriz, the referendum for the new theocratic constitution had been met with demonstrations and riots of major proportions, which the revolutionary guards had put down by force. Within the ruling councils in Tehran, factionalism was rife. Khomeini was relying more and more on his clerical followers, and secular forces, including individuals such as Bani-Sadr and Ghotbzadeh, seemed increasingly powerless.

Ayatollah Beheshti was emerging as the major power in the Revolutionary Council, but the council itself seemed to have almost no control over events. The students in the embassy had emerged by now as an independent force that even Khomeini seemed unable to control. Reports were being received almost daily in Washington that in a showdown with the students, Khomeini could not be certain he would prevail. Consequently, he was avoiding any steps that might undermine his authority or bring him into conflict with the most radical elements of the revolution.

Elections for Iran's first president under the new constitution were scheduled for January, and it seemed that everyone in the country planned to run. By the end of the year, 124 different candidates had declared, forcing the Revolutionary Council to submit the list to Khomeini to be weeded out. Outside the country, exiled opponents of Khomeini were forming themselves into liberation movements, but the exiles were as divided among themselves as were the various factions in Tehran.

Rumors of plots and counterplots circulated widely. A senior cleric and close associate of Khomeini was assassinated by an unknown anti-regime terrorist organization. An attack by Iranian air force pilots against Khomeini's residence was reportedly discovered and stopped at the last minute. Beginning in early December, there were reports from Western observers in Iraq that the Iraqis were planning an invasion of Iran's oil fields, and the reports were given credence by increasingly frequent guerrilla attacks on oil installations and by the accelerated tempo of military clashes between Iraqi and Iranian forces along their common frontier.

In short, the situation was so thoroughly confused and complicated by so many uncertainties and improbabilities that it more nearly resembled the plot of some potboiler than a case of high international policy. The inherent absurdity of the circumstances was tempered only by the transcendent importance of the political and economic interests at stake and by the irreducible fact of fifty-three lives in the balance.

Inside the Embassy Walls

The U.S. public and officialdom were provided a vivid reminder of the grim daily reality in the embassy prison at Christmas time when two U.S. clergymen and an Algerian cardinal visited the compound. From the television pictures and the brief, whispered comments, it was clear that the strain was taking its psychological toll on a number of the hostages.

More disturbing was the fact that seven of the hostages were not seen by the clergymen. There had been absolutely no information on the "missing seven" almost from the day of the takeover, and it was widely feared that they had been killed or seriously injured during the two months of captivity. Despite the international outcry that greeted this new revelation, embarrassed public officials in Tehran were forced to admit their total ignorance of what was going on inside the embassy walls. Foreign Minister Ghotbzadeh confessed in a news conference that he did not know even how many hostages were being held and had been unable to find out, despite his best efforts.

Curiously, Washington's best information on the subject was provided by the students themselves. The telephone lines inside the embassy still functioned, and the Iran Task Force at the State Department had taken advantage of that fact to penetrate the embassy walls. Almost every night Foreign Service officers with Farsi-language capability placed random calls to various offices in the embassy complex and attempted to engage the students in conversation. For the most part, these conversations in the wee hours of the morning yielded nothing more than propaganda lectures, but on occasion it was possible to glean some information about the inner workings of the embassy prison. One talkative student let slip the fact that they were holding fifty prisoners, a number that exactly coincided with State Department records and seemed to confirm that all the hostages were alive and physically present in the compound. It was only one more peculiarity of the circumstances that the U.S. Department of State should have had more success eliciting information from the student captors than the foreign minister and Revolutionary Council of their own government.

Afghanistan, Russia and the UN

Two days after Christmas, the Soviet Union launched an armed invasion of Afghanistan, killing Prime Minister Hafizullah Amin and hastily bringing back from the Soviet Union his puppet replacement Babrak Karmal. The brutal Soviet intervention was the first Soviet use of its own military forces outside its own satellite empire since World War II, and the invasion dramatically transformed the entire security balance of the Persian Gulf region. The fall of the shah had removed a key pillar of U.S. security policy in the region and had stimulated planning for a more active U.S. military presence in defense of U.S. interests. That process was now accelerated. The Carter administration abandoned its efforts to seek a peaceful accommodation with the Soviet Union and moved toward a posture of enhanced military readiness and political confrontation with the USSR.[14]

The Soviet invasion also prompted a thorough review of U.S. relations with all the nations of the surrounding region. Steps were initiated to open a new dialogue with Pakistan, India, Iraq and other nations whose relations with the United States were seriously strained but who were now confronted with the new reality of a potentially expansive and militant Soviet presence on, or much closer to, their own borders.

Iran also reacted sharply to the Soviet invasion of its Islamic neighbor. Some speculated that this new threat from the Soviet Union, which shared a 1,250-mile border with Iran in the north, might persuade Khomeini and others of the folly of perpetuating the crisis with the United States. There were violent anti-Soviet demonstrations in Tehran, including a mob attack on the Soviet embassy. Ghotbzadeh seized on these new developments to denounce the Soviets and to attempt to shift popular opinion from its exclusive focus on the United States. However, there was no immediate shift in U.S. policy. On the day after the Soviet invasion, President Carter told his advisers that he wanted no let-up in the pressures against Iran.

Nevertheless, Ambassador McHenry was finding the going tough at the United Nations. Many nations had important commercial and financial relationships with Iran that they were reluctant to break. Consequently, there was powerful resistance to U.S. efforts to prohibit all normal economic transactions with Iran. On December 28, Ambassador McHenry attended a National Security Council meeting at the White House and proposed to President Carter a two-stage process intended to break the negotiating stalemate. An immediate UN resolution would direct the Secretary General of the United Nations to go to Iran to negotiate the release of the hostages. If he was unable to report progress within one week, sanctions would be imposed. The president approved this plan and directed Secretary of State Vance to go to New York to lead the U.S. efforts over the weekend of December 29–30.

Even this two-stage approach proved contentious. The Security Council did not vote the first resolution until Monday, December 31, by which time Secretary General Waldheim was already in the air en route to Tehran. The secretary general, a Viennese diplomat of the classic mode, could scarcely have imagined the reception awaiting him. On the day of his arrival the student militants succeeded in publishing on the front page of a popular newspaper a large photograph of Waldheim talking to the shah. The picture inspired popular demonstrations, and Waldheim found himself under attack every time he got in his car.

Waldheim was treated to a grotesque meeting with a large group of mutilated and deformed individuals, allegedly victims of SAVAK, who screamed and waved the stumps of missing limbs in his face. His visit to the cemetery of the martyrs of the revolution turned into a riot and had to be cut short out of concern for his life. Nothing in Waldheim's long and distinguished career as a diplomat had prepared him for the total insanity of political life in revolutionary Tehran.

Khomeini refused to meet with the secretary general, and the students at the embassy rejected his repeated requests to visit the hostages. He did hold several meetings with Ghotbzadeh and met for two hours with Ayatollah Beheshti and several members of the Revolutionary Council. At each stage the Iranians refused even to consider release of the hostages until their conditions for the release of the shah and return of his assets had been satisfied. The Iranians did suggest that the formation of some kind of international tribunal under UN auspices could be a useful step, and Waldheim agreed to report those views back to the Security Council. Visibly shaken, Waldheim left after three hectic days and returned to New York, where he said he was "glad to be back, especially alive."

Waldheim reported the results of his visit direct to President Carter and to a closed session of the UN Security Council. He was convinced that the pressure of sanctions would not be effective in getting Iran to release the hostages, but President Carter refused to withdraw the resolution. The Security Council approved it on January 13 by a margin of 10–2. However, one of the negative votes was the Soviet Union, whose veto nullified the legal force of the resolution.

The United States declared that it would proceed with sanctions despite the Soviet veto, and called for other nations to join in. Deputy Secretary of State Warren Christopher, who was in Europe for consultations on Afghanistan, reminded the Europeans of their earlier assurances that they would participate in sanctions even in the face of a Soviet veto in the Security Council. However, the Europeans, who by this time had heard from their own domestic commercial interests, unanimously refused to cooperate, citing the absence of any legal justification and arguing that severe economic sanctions would only force Iran to turn to the Soviet Union. Instead, the Europeans argued that the United States should display patience and give the political situation in Iran time to sort itself out. For the next four months, that was the perpetual refrain that Washington heard from all its allies and friends.

The U.S. strategy adopted in the first days of the crisis had been to increase pressure on Iran while exhausting all available peaceful remedies. Everything that could be done through diplomacy and international law had been done, yet the hostages remained in Tehran. What now?

A prophetic but discouraging answer to that question was offered by a senior Islamic statesman who knew Iran well and who was personally acquainted with many of the senior clerical officials, including Khomeini. "You will not get your hostages back," he told Secretary Vance in early 1980, "until Khomeini has put all the institutions of the Islamic revolution in place."

This suggested a continuation of the crisis for many months, a situation that Vance and every other high official in Washington considered intolerable. This man's words closely echoed the Bureau of Intelligence and Research (INR) assessment almost two months earlier that the hostage crisis was a function of Iranian internal politics and that there was little, if anything, the United States could do to influence the dynamics of that peculiar and unpredictable process. Like the INR report, the present judgment was duly noted at the State Department and then as quickly buried.

At about the same time, a very different conference was under way in Tehran involving a secret Panamanian delegation, Sadegh Ghotbzadeh and Ghotbzadeh's two representatives, Christian Bourguet and Héctor Villalón. Although no one knew it at the time, this curious assortment of political schemers was to dominate U.S. policy for the next four months.

XII

A LONG SHOT
THAT JUST MISSED

In late February 1980, Washington enjoyed a sudden burst of springlike weather. The nation's capital is, by its location and many of its traditions, a Southern town. Rising out of swampy land at the geographical point where North and South meet, the city has long suffered from a split personality. Like a chameleon, it has learned to adopt the political coloration of its latest inhabitants, but it never succeeds entirely in concealing the accents and rhythms of its genteel Southern origins.

The sudden shifts of political climate in the nation's capital are matched only by the city's unpredictable weather patterns. Exactly one year earlier, when the forces of Khomeini's revolution were triumphantly proclaiming victory, Washington had been buried to its neck in a massive snowfall. But on that Thursday afternoon, February 21, as I came out of the West Wing of the White House to return to my office, the brilliant sunshine and gentle breeze seemed to have transplanted us all to the president's home state of Georgia.

At the door I nearly collided with Hamilton Jordan, the controversial young chief of staff of the Carter White House, who had taken advantage of the gorgeous weather to go jogging on the south lawn. Much to his own astonishment, he had over the previous six weeks become a central figure in the seemingly endless crisis with Iran over the U.S. hostages.

In that fourth year of the Carter presidency, Hamilton Jordan had developed an unenviable reputation. As a brash newcomer to Washington, Jordan had failed to demonstrate what the permanent power brokers of the Washington establishment regarded as a proper degree of respect. They were aware—as he initially was not—that genuine influence in Washington was composed of more than personal ability and political success. It was nearly always enhanced by coalitions within a loose and informal network of powerful individuals—individuals who were already in place as each new administration arrived, and who would still be there to watch its departure, greeting its successors over drinks and lunch at one of Washington's discreet clubs.

Jordan knew none of these people when he first came to the White House, and he must have felt he owed them nothing. Ten years before, while still an undergraduate at the University of Georgia, he had signed on as a driver in Jimmy Carter's unsuccessful first campaign to become governor of Georgia. He went on to manage Carter's successful second gubernatorial campaign in 1970 and served as executive secretary in the Georgia statehouse. He arrived in Washington fresh from managing a brilliant, nationwide grass-roots campaign whose most effective themes had centered on the need for open government and the rejection of cozy power relationships. Having come so far so fast, he might have been excused the façade of youthful irreverence that offended the elders of Washington. But he was to pay dearly. When Jordan later found himself the nationwide object of devastating rumors and gossip, the establishment elite was entirely content to leave him twisting in the wind.

Washington can be ruthless and unforgiving. It can also be wrong. Ham Jordan's native shrewdness as a political analyst was unfortunately obscured by the clouds of controversy that settled about him. In dozens of meetings over a period of four years, I was struck most by the seriousness of purpose that he concealed beneath a veneer of sardonic humor. He never stood on ceremony. In a roomful of inflated egos, he wore the badge of his office lightly, almost invisibly. Unlike many of his colleagues, he was more likely to listen than to speak, but when he did speak he cut through to the heart of the issue with common sense. The crude image of Hamilton Jordan portrayed in the media was worse than caricature—it was a bad joke.

Hamilton Jordan was no Iranian expert. He had been contacted by the Panamanians for two very obvious reasons: first, he had developed relations of deep mutual friendship and trust with General Torrijos and other key Panamanian figures who had worked closely with him during the battle to ratify the Panama Canal Treaty in the U.S. Senate in April 1978; and second, he had direct and personal access to the president of the United States. Without those very special conditions—plus the coincidental fact that the shah was now resident in Panama—it is doubtful that the U.S. government would ever have become aware of the French and Argentinian lawyers who were working directly with Ghotbzadeh or have been willing to place sufficient confidence in them to pursue a complex and politically risky strategy over a period of months.

But once the contact had been established, Jordan needed help. On January 12, after being briefed by two representatives of General Torrijos at a secret rendezvous at Homestead Air Force Base in Florida, Jordan returned to Washington, and near midnight on a Saturday evening, met with Harold Saunders to discuss the bizarre story he had just been told.[1]

His decision to turn to Harold Saunders was indisputably correct. Saunders was the assistant secretary of state for Near Eastern and South Asian affairs and a seasoned veteran on U.S. Middle Eastern policy. He had served for thirteen years on the National Security Council, where he had participated in Kissinger's negotiations following the 1973 Arab-Israeli War. Later he had directed the Intelligence and Research Bureau of the Department of State. As assistant secretary of state in the Carter administration, he had played a major role in the peace talks between Egypt and Israel in 1978–1979. Saunders was the total professional—a knowledgeable, utterly indefatigable and dedicated public servant.

They were an unlikely pair—the young Georgia campaign strategist who never looked entirely comfortable in the White House uniform of pin-striped three-piece suits, and the owlish middle-aged veteran of countless bureaucratic wars. But this was no ordinary negotiation, and each of them brought special strengths that would be essential to sustain a free-flowing and thoroughly unorthodox process through months of trial and error. Jordan was able to provide flexibility and quick, authoritative responses to circumstances through his close relationship with President Carter; Saunders could be relied on to keep the negotiations on track, to ensure that every step was carefully evaluated by specialists on his staff, and never to lose sight of the central objectives despite a welter of conflicting events and contradictory information. Within days after Jordan's secret meeting in Florida, he and Saunders flew off to London for the first of a series of secret meetings with their improbable new negotiating partners.

Among the small handful of officials who were aware of these talks, there was no shortage of skepticism. From the very beginning, the melodrama of the hostage crisis had elements that would have been rejected by any grade B scriptwriter. It was international soap opera, but with real people. To those inured to a daily diet of medieval ayatollahs denouncing the "Great Satan," and other symptoms of cultural hysteria, the addition of Bourguet and Villalón was merely a minor eccentricity. It was, however, a very long shot. Why, then, was it pursued?

The simplest answer must be that when a nation (or an individual) goes berserk, one does not always have the luxury of responding in conventional or even dignified ways. By this point in the crisis, dozens if not hundreds of channels had been tested without success. Bourguet and Villalón had the confidence of the top secular leadership of Iran and were prepared to devote themselves to an effort to free the hostages. It was not the channel nor the approach the U.S. leadership would have preferred, but the alternatives were even less promising. President Carter decided to see what these unlikely intermediaries could produce.

More than a hundred hours of meetings with Bourguet and Villalón in London, Paris, Bern and Washington were conducted exclusively by Jordan and Saunders, with the invaluable assistance of a talented State Department interpreter, Stephanie Van Reigersberg (neither of the intermediaries spoke English, and neither of the two U.S. principals spoke French or Spanish), plus the occasional participation of Henry Precht, the Iranian desk officer at the Department of State.[2] Jordan and Saunders reported directly to Secretary Vance and President Carter outside the normal framework of the National Security Council structure. In organizational terms, this negotiation was the diplomatic counterpart of the small military planning group that Brzezinski chaired—also outside the NSC structure—that quietly continued its planning of a possible rescue mission or punitive military strike while the secret negotiations were under way.

Brzezinski had very little patience with this approach. He did not formally oppose it, if only because he had no realistic alternative of his own to propose at the time, but he was skeptical in the extreme about its prospects of success. In private, he was heard to mutter that he regarded the whole effort as a "disaster." The fact that it was being run almost entirely out of the State Department without his direct involvement may also have influenced his views. In any event, Brzezinski made very little effort to follow all the twists and turns of the negotiations. He received the basic position papers from Vance from time to time, and occasionally he would ask me for an evaluation. Otherwise, I was left to my own devices to try and stay informed. The best way to do that was to catch the two key participants between trips for a verbal update.

Consequently, when I almost literally ran into Hamilton Jordan outside the White House, I was particularly pleased to have a chance to bring myself up to date on the state of play. By late February, a lot had happened. Jordan mentioned that he had lately received letters of the "To Whom It May Concern" variety from Foreign Minister Sadegh Ghotbzadeh and Abolhassan Bani-Sadr, the newly elected president, providing written assurances that Christian Bourguet and Héctor Villalón were authorized to represent them in these talks.

Jordan rightly regarded it as a considerable accomplishment just to get Ghotbzadeh and Bani-Sadr to agree on anything in writing, for they were widely known to dislike and distrust each other. They had opposed each other in the presidential election of January 25. Bani-Sadr won with over 75 percent of the popular vote, while Ghotbzadeh received only an embarrassing 38,000 votes—about one fourth of one percent.

The United States had been in touch with Bani-Sadr shortly after the election to inquire discreetly whether he wished to maintain the channel of communications through Bourguet and Villalón. At that time he seemed to be unaware of their activities and was already planning to dismiss Ghotbzadeh as foreign minister. In fact, for some weeks after the election the two men refused to speak to each other, so Bourguet and Villalón found themselves in the uncomfortable position of being intermediaries not only between Iran and the United States but also between Iran's president and its foreign minister!

The Paris Meeting

It was Thursday. On the previous Sunday, Jordan had been in Paris for the only direct meeting between high-level U.S. and Iranian officials in the entire course of the hostage crisis. I had known about the meeting, but Jordan's report had been delivered direct to President Carter. I was curious about what had happened.

"Not much," Jordan said. The Iranian[3] had nothing new to offer and spent most of the time lecturing him about the evils of U.S. policy in Iran. Jordan felt that the Iranian official may have intended to use his account of the private conversation as ammunition with Khomeini, claiming that he had made an important political impact on the Americans.

That interpretation was entirely credible. One of the articles of faith among revolutionary Iranians—from the students in the embassy compound to the members of the Revolutionary Council—was that Americans would sympathize or even join with Iran in confronting the government in Washington if only they could be made to understand the depth of Iran's grievances against the U.S. government and the shah. The conviction that the American people could be won to their side—together with a pervasive sense of their own self-righteousness—accounted at least in part for the excessive duration of the hostage crisis.

Some of the leaders of the militant group inside the embassy, as well as some of the top leaders of the revolution, had spent their formative political years in U.S. universities during the height of the anti-Vietnam protests of the late 1960s and early 1970s. They never entirely abandoned the notion that the American people were only waiting for an appropriately revolutionary signal to rise in protest against their government. The fact that the kidnapping of U.S. diplomats provoked an equal and opposite reaction of righteous indignation on the part of almost all Americans was slow to be recognized. Thus, the student militants, and some key Iranian officials, hung with rapt attention on every second devoted to them on U.S. television and worked hard to make sure that they projected the proper image. One of the few visits to the hostages, at Christmas 1979, was nearly canceled because the attendant Algerian priest refused to dress according to the public relations script of that "militant Islamic" photo opportunity.

There had been one specific new proposal presented to Jordan in Paris. Not surprisingly, he chose not to mention it to me during our brief conversation. The "solution" to the crisis that his Iranian contact put forward was for the United States—or more precisely the CIA—to murder the shah.[4]

That was not the first time we had heard suggestions of the sort. Especially in the early days of the crisis, when the shah was still in the hospital in New York City, many of us received telephone calls and letters proposing, as one caller delicately put it, "pulling the plug" on the shah. I recall one telephone conversation with an individual who had a taste for the macabre. He suggested substituting a dead body for the shah and proclaiming him dead with considerable fanfare, while continuing his treatment in a secret location. All such schemes were dismissed out of hand, including that of the senior Iranian who met with Jordan in Paris.

Jordan and I talked briefly about the composition of the UN commission that had officially been announced the day before and was scheduled to depart for Tehran two days later, on Saturday, February 23. We agreed that the successful completion of the scenario that he and Hal Saunders had put together in painstaking detail over the past five weeks would depend largely on whether the five-man commission would stick closely to the agreed terms and not let itself be used or diverted by the maelstrom of political forces in Tehran.

The concept of sending a UN commission to listen to Iran's grievances against the shah had existed for some time. Bourguet and Villalón had raised it as a possibility in their first meeting with Saunders and Jordan in the home of Edward Streator, the U.S. deputy chief of mission in London, on Saturday, January 19. The two lawyers said that Ghotbzadeh had initiated extradition proceedings with Panama in order to create an illusion of progress that would satisfy hard-liners in Iran. With that as cover, he hoped that a UN commission would be permitted to visit Tehran, take note of Iran's complaints and then convince the revolutionary authorities to release the hostages.

The concept of a commission had earlier been explored by the United States, but with the proviso that the hostages would have to be released *before* the commission could travel to Iran to provide an international forum for the expression of Iran's grievances against the shah.[5] Jordan and Saunders thus regarded the possibility of a commission as a good mutual starting point for a scenario leading to the release of the hostages. However, they actively discouraged the notion of pursuing extradition of the shah, even as a political diversion.

Despite the best efforts of the U.S. team, Ghotbzadeh and the two lawyers remained convinced of the cleverness of the extradition scheme and continued to pursue it independently with the Panamanians. Thus, on January 22, only three days after the London meeting and just before the Iranian presidential elections, Ghotbzadeh announced publicly that he had been informed by President Aristides Royo of Panama that the shah was under arrest pending extradition hearings. Royo denied the story, but deliberately muddied the waters by volunteering that the shah was "under the care of the Panamanian security forces." Predictably, within a few days the shah let it be known that he wanted to move to another country. Since there were no other countries available, it was necessary to mount a new high-level campaign of reassurances to persuade the shah to remain in Panama.

The Scenario

The real scenario did not take concrete shape until the weekend after the London meeting. Bourguet and Villalón spent most of Friday and Saturday,

January 25 and 26, in Hamilton Jordan's spacious corner office in the West Wing of the White House. In a marathon session, the small group worked out a detailed schedule of interrelated and reciprocal steps to be undertaken by Iran and the United States, intended to produce the eventual release of the hostages.

Saunders had not wasted the days between these two meetings. On the basis of the first conversations, he had prepared a working paper that Secretary Vance sent to President Carter for approval in advance of the second meeting with the two intermediaries. The central thesis of the paper, which the president approved as the basis for further talks, was the reluctant admission that political circumstances in Iran simply would not permit the negotiation of a neat package in which the terms for the release of the hostages were all formally agreed in advance. On the contrary, the new proposal recognized that the release would have to come at the end of a step-by-step process in which each move helped create the political conditions for the next. In concrete terms, this meant that the United States would have to withdraw its earlier insistence that the visit of an international commission to Iran be preceded by the release of the hostages.

It was on that basis that Jordan and Saunders hammered out the terms of a scenario in an exhausting nonstop session on the twenty-sixth. The process was to begin with an Iranian request to UN Secretary General Kurt Waldheim to send a commission to Tehran to hear Iran's grievances. The Iranian request would specifically mention that the work of such a commission would help achieve an early end to the crisis. It would also stipulate that the members of the commission would have the opportunity to meet with each of the hostages. Upon receipt of this request the United States would withdraw its objections to a commission of inquiry while maintaining its opposition to any interrogation of the hostages. The commission was not to be a tribunal.

As the second step, Waldheim would then establish the membership of the commission from a list of individuals understood to be mutually acceptable to Iran and the United States. After a public announcement Iran would respond with public assurances of cooperation and an offer to arrange meetings between the commissioners and the hostages.

The commission would then visit Tehran and take testimony from the Iranians about their grievances. They would also visit the hostages. The commission would report to Iran's Revolutionary Council that the conditions of imprisonment of the hostages were inhumane and that they could not credibly report to the secretary general until those conditions had been changed. In response, the Iranian authorities would remove the hostages from the custody of the students in the embassy and transfer them to an official facility, such as a hospital.

Finally, the commission would present its report to the UN secretary general. In response, Iran would pardon the hostages and expel them from the country. The negotiating team was aware that major political announcements in revolutionary Iran tended to coincide with major religious or revolutionary holidays. February 10 was a religious holiday, while the eleventh was the first anniversary of the revolution. Consequently, the scenario called for all the steps to be completed by that time.

Early Doubts and Questions

On Monday morning, January 28, with Hal Saunders already en route to New York with Secretary Vance for a secret meeting with Secretary General Waldheim, Brzezinski asked me for an evaluation of the Jordan-Saunders conversations with Bourguet and Villalón and the proposed scenario. After reviewing the materials, I agreed with Jordan and Saunders that the basic approach of using the UN commission as the vehicle for airing Iran's complaints in return for the release of the hostages was sensible, and that the step-by-step approach, with reciprocal actions by the United States and Iran, seemed appropriately cautious. However, I had some concerns about the workability of the plan.

I thought it unlikely in the extreme that the scenario would play out the way it was intended. We were justified in taking some risks, but we should do so with our eyes open. In the first place, I noted that the political analysis that Bourguet and Villalón had offered upon their arrival in Washington had proved dead wrong. By chance, their first day in Washington coincided with the presidential election in Iran. The two lawyers gave a rather elaborate analysis of the internal political situation in Iran, concluding that the latest entrant in the race—Hasan Habibi, the spokesman for the Revolutionary Council—was understood to be Khomeini's choice for the presidency. Although they would have preferred their friend Ghotbzadeh as president, they thought that the efforts of the "master politician" (Khomeini) would ensure Habibi's success. In the course of the day, election returns from Iran reported Bani-Sadr as the overwhelming victor. This rather substantial misreading by the two visitors necessarily cast some doubt on their credentials as reliable interpreters of the admittedly chaotic political scene in Tehran.

I also commented to Brzezinski on what I considered to be a persistent quality of wishful thinking in their analysis and portrayal of developments in Iran. Bourguet and Villalón were emotionally (and financially) committed to Iran's revolution, and they wanted to see it work. To work properly, it needed to rid itself of the albatross of the hostage crisis, which was devastating to its international image, disastrous for its economy, and fatal to the ambitions of the more nationalist, nonclerical forces, e.g. Ghotbzadeh and Bani-Sadr. Thus, Bourguet and Villalón *wanted* to make a scenario work, even when logic would suggest that its prospects were slim.

In that regard, I considered the proposed time frame of the scenario—which was to be completed in less than two weeks—as totally unrealistic. I estimated that it would take a minimum of two weeks just to constitute a commission (in reality it took three), that the commission's visit to Iran would require another two weeks at a minimum (in fact, the commission remained in Iran for sixteen days), and that the scenario could not possibly be completed before March.

It was also of concern that Foreign Minister Ghotbzadeh was being set up as the goat. He was identified in the scenario as the sole negotiator or point man. Although I thought that would probably suit his *amour propre,* it would also leave him exposed as the logical target when the knives came out in Tehran. I was not at all upset at the thought of Ghotbzadeh being sacrificed for a noble cause, but I doubted that he would stand still for it. He was crafty and very much concerned about his political skin. He would not, I thought, give Bani-Sadr the perfect excuse to fire him, especially after risking the destruction of his relationship with Khomeini over the hostage issue. A double cross was, I imagined, virtually inevitable at some point.

Hence, some precautionary modifications would be desirable. Specifically, I thought that the first step of the scenario should be used as a test to clarify the nature of political authority in Iran in the post-election environment. Hal Saunders' original scenario had mentioned the desirability of establishing an American or a trusted non-American in Tehran, or if that was not feasible, in a location just outside Iran, e.g., Turkey, to pursue the negotiations on a full-time basis. Without spelling out the entire U.S. position in advance, we should, I felt, inform Tehran that we were prepared to proceed with a series of concrete and reciprocal steps. As the first step in that process, we could request that a secure form of communications be established.

If Bani-Sadr and Ghotbzadeh could agree on such an arrangement and put it into effect, I argued, we would have some tangible evidence that practical decision making was possible on the Iranian side. We would also have reduced the total reliance on what I considered to be well-meaning but possibly naïve intermediaries. If the Iranian president and foreign minister could not manage such an arrangement, then we might wish to reconsider how much political capital we were prepared to invest in them for the far more difficult matter of securing the release of the hostages.

Brzezinski did not comment on all this. He suggested only that I take up these concerns and recommendations with Hamilton Jordan, which I did the following day. Jordan listened carefully to the points I had raised with Brzezinski. He was quite realistic about the potential shortcomings of the two lawyers, although he believed that Bourguet in particular was not only well connected with Ghotbzadeh but was also a sensible and reliable interlocutor. He attributed their misreading of the election to Ghotbzadeh, for he felt they had faithfully reproduced Ghotbzadeh's views.

Jordan felt that the two lawyers had no illusions about Ghotbzadeh and his craftiness. In fact, he said, they had talked at some length about how to structure a scenario that would box in Ghotbzadeh so that a double cross would hurt him as much as us. There was no way to by-pass Ghotbzadeh at this point, but it was evident that Bani-Sadr must also be brought in. The two intermediaries were prepared to go to Bani-Sadr directly even if Ghotbzadeh objected.

Jordan was very receptive to my basic thesis that our first step should be to test the practical authority of Ghotbzadeh and Bani-Sadr by asking them to accept a reliable intermediary in place. This would help clarify the relationship between the two by forcing them to make a substantive decision. However, Jordan said, President Carter had already authorized the State Department to proceed along the lines of the scenario that Vance had proposed in his decision memorandum, and, he implied, he was not inclined to reopen the issue. Although Jordan accepted my point about the time required to carry out the scenario, he thought that things might break very quickly once the process was set in motion.

Having failed to make any headway with Jordan, I tried to reach Hal Saunders to make the same points, but couldn't. He was occupied with another subplot of the hostage crisis that was about to reach a happy conclusion.

The Canadian Caper

At almost the very moment that I was talking to Ham Jordan, six Americans who had been hiding in Tehran for nearly three months were making their way through Mehrabad Airport to safety, with the invaluable assistance of Canadian Ambassador Kenneth Taylor and his government. At the time of the hostage taking, five members of this group had left the U.S. embassy undetected through an unguarded exit. A sixth person, the agricultural attaché, had been working in a different building and was not located by the mob. The members of the group had subsequently hidden in the homes of sympathetic Canadian and other Western families until they could be provided with false identification documents. Then, on January 29, they simply went to the airport and boarded a flight for Europe. Although some members of the media were aware of the existence of this group, they were persuaded to keep the information to themselves, and the Iranians never suspected that they had some additional guests in their country until it was too late.

The story appeared on the wires that evening, just as Bourguet and Villalón returned to Washington from a quick one-day visit to Panama and were settling down in Jordan's office for a final round of discussions before taking the draft scenario back to Tehran. The visitors were understandably concerned about the reaction in Iran, fearing that the outrage of being tricked by the Great Satan would be taken out on the hostages and possibly doom the scenario even before it was presented.

Jordan, knowing that the Canadian embassy had been closed and that Canada's reputation in Iran could scarcely be made worse at that point, suggested that Bourguet call Ghotbzadeh with the explanation that the timing of this operation was part of a political maneuver intended to improve the prospects of Canadian Prime Minister Joe Clark, who was at that time engaged in a re-election battle.[6] The conspiratorial nature of the explanation had immediate appeal to Ghotbzadeh, who added his own distinctive touches to the story, claiming publicly that Clark had sent a message to Iran confirming that the release of the six Americans was a campaign stunt to improve his image with the United States. Despite a flurry of bombast and indignant charges from Iran about U.S. "illegal" behavior, this particular tempest quickly passed without serious repercussions.

The combination of the "Canadian caper" and my own hasty preparations to accompany Zbigniew Brzezinski and Warren Christopher on a trip to Pakistan left me no opportunity to raise my concerns with Saunders. Moreover, based on the reports of the meeting of the twenty-ninth, it was apparent that the idea of establishing an independent and reliable source of communications had been dropped. The die was cast. We had put all our chips on Bourguet and Villalón—for better or worse.

Good News, Bad News

One week later, when I returned with Brzezinski and Christopher from meetings in Pakistan and Saudi Arabia, I found waiting on my desk an anonymous letter from a person who claimed to be an Iranian student at a university in the Washington area, with personal contacts among the students in the U.S. embassy in Tehran. His friends in Iran had told him that three of the hostages had been killed, and he provided descriptions of two shooting deaths and a heart attack that sounded credible. There had been a number of other reports of suicides and shootings of hostages trying to escape. None of these had been confirmed, but they acted as constant reminders of the perilous conditions in the embassy compound.

Fortunately, in this case, we were fairly confident that the report was false. With Bani-Sadr's election as president, his swearing in by Ayatollah Khomeini on February 4, and his outspoken determination to put an end to the hostage crisis, there had been a notable shift on the part of the militants in the embassy. They were maneuvering daily against Bani-Sadr and Ghotbzadeh, but they seemed uncertain of their position with the ayatollah and more inclined to take an accommodating position than in the past. Many more letters from hostages were finding their way out of the embassy, and the hard-working Iran Task Force at the Department of State meticulously verified each one, keeping a running log on what was known about each of them.

On February 8 the hostages were visited by Ahmed Khomeini, the son of the ayatollah, in the company of another Iranian cleric and the Catholic archbishop Hilarion Capucci.[7] Although they did not see all the hostages, the report of this visit, together with the information in recent letters, provided convincing evidence that the story of the anonymous letter writer was false. We had fairly reliable and relatively current information on all the hostages, with the exception of Michael Metrinko. (Metrinko, we learned after the hostages were released, had refused categorically to cooperate with his captors. He spoke excellent Farsi and used it to tell them in no uncertain terms exactly what he thought of them. He spent most of the 444 days of the ordeal in solitary confinement, without ever breaking down.)[8]

Progress

On Sunday, February 10—the original date for completion of the scenario—Ham Jordan, Hal Saunders, Henry Precht and Stephanie Van Reigersberg spent the day from breakfast until after midnight closeted in the Hotel Bellevue in Bern, Switzerland. Bourguet and Villalón had requested this additional meeting to discuss minor changes in the scenario. In fact, the changes were almost insignificant, and the scenario required almost no changes. The group, which had by this time developed a strong sense of camaraderie, devoted the time to working out a day-by-day sequence of events, including the key words of reciprocal messages between Iran and the United States. The two lawyers took advantage of the occasion to extend an invitation to Jordan to meet with one of their Iranian contacts in Paris. He accepted.

During the ten days or so that the two intermediaries had spent in Tehran, all of the auguries had been good. Bani-Sadr was named head of the powerful Revolutionary Council pending the election of a new Majles and the formation of a government. Both Bani-Sadr and Ghotbzadeh acted with decisiveness and apparent self-confidence, totally dominating events in Tehran. At one point Ghotbzadeh boasted that the government would use force if necessary to seize the U.S. embassy from the student militants if they refused to accept government authority over the negotiations.

Significantly, during this entire period, Khomeini was in the hospital. By all accounts he was seriously ill with heart and prostate problems, and a hospital stay originally scheduled for two weeks had to be extended. Reporting to Brzezinski on the sudden and totally unaccustomed rash of good news, I commented: "Everything good that has happened with respect to the hostages has occurred since Khomeini's reported heart attack and hospitalization."

On the anniversary of the revolution, February 11, Khomeini issued a written message that was read by his son Ahmed. One passage in particular attracted a great deal of attention: "I have said many times and once again declare that Iran must pursue its decisive struggles until the end of all its political, military, economic and cultural dependence on America, this ruthless world-devourer. Later, provided that our alert and noble nation grants permission, *we will establish our very ordinary relations with America just as with other countries.*" (Emphasis added.)

This seemed to be vintage Khomeini—conciliation immersed in pure vitriol. Never before had he suggested that Iran could contemplate "ordinary" relations with the United States under any circumstances. Was this the influence of the more pragmatic Bani-Sadr and Ghotbzadeh who now seemed in the ascendant? Before drawing such a conclusion, one had to take note of another, less obvious passage, near the end of the message. "Dear Iranian nation," he said. "Never compromise with any power. . . . *Topple from the position of power anyone in any position who is inclined to compromise with the East and the West . . .* " If the first passage seemed to hold out the promise of eventual normalization of relations with the United States and the West, the second seemed intended as a warning specifically to the likes of Bani-Sadr not to go too far too fast.

However, Bani-Sadr appeared undaunted. On the occasion of the anniversary of the revolution, he gave an exclusive interview to Eric Rouleau, the veteran Middle East correspondent for *Le Monde.* Rouleau had befriended Bani-Sadr years before in Paris, when the idea of an Islamic revolution appeared to be one more political scheme whose life span would be measured in coffee cups in smoky Left Bank cafés. He helped the intense young Iranian find publishers for his articles on Islamic economics, and he was later rewarded by being almost the only Western journalist who had regular access to the inner workings of Iran's revolutionary politics. In this interview Bani-Sadr asserted that the release of the hostages was no longer contingent on the return of the shah and his assets to Iran.

The militants in the embassy were far from quelled. Only the week before, they had engineered the arrest of the minister of information, Nasser Minachi, on the basis of documents discovered in the embassy showing that he had engaged in conversations with U.S. Foreign Service officers during the revolution.[9] However, their response to Bani-Sadr's latest heresy was uncharacteristically subdued. They would accept a compromise solution, they announced, if Khomeini approved the plan and told them to release the hostages. At the same time Yasir Arafat, who was guest of honor at the anniversary celebration, speculated to a Western diplomat that the crisis would be over by the end of March, after the Majles election.

These positive signals were reinforced by many other sources. Over the course of the preceding months, I had become acquainted with an Iranian-American who had been active in the anti-shah movement. Like many Iranians who had made their home in the United States, this man was deeply proud of his new citizenship and considered himself a patriotic American. He was alarmed at the direction of the revolution and appalled at the hostage taking. He also feared for his life if Khomeini's agents should ever discover that he was cooperating with the United States. That fear was no idle fantasy, as would be demonstrated by the assassination of an outspoken anti-Khomeini activist, Ali Akbar Tabatabai, in Washington in late July.

This man, whom I will call Ghazi for convenience,[10] was acquainted with many of the revolutionary leaders in Tehran and was in touch with the Iranian exile community in Washington. During this period we were in contact every few days. He was afraid to talk on the telephone, so we would meet at the south gate of the White House and sit on the grass in the small park there, among the tourists and office workers on their lunch break.

Much of the information Ghazi provided was just high-level gossip about who was doing what to whom in Tehran, but there were occasional nuggets of hard information that could be compared with other reporting. It was from Ghazi that I began to develop a more rounded picture of Ghotbzadeh. According to Ghazi's various sources, Ghotbzadeh was having the time of his life. Until he joined Khomeini in Paris at the height of the revolution, he had been a student organizer hounded by the police. Never in his wildest dreams could he have imagined becoming the foreign minister of Iran. Moreover, according to his friends, Ghotbzadeh would do absolutely anything to stay there. "He likes to be a big shot," one of them remarked. "He loves the big office, the cars, the attention from journalists, and giving orders left and right." He was clever and opportunistic, but his greatest strength was that Khomeini believed in him and treated him like a son. However, Ghotbzadeh was a "dictator type" with an unquenchable thirst for power. If this is how his friends describe Ghotbzadeh, I thought to myself, he needs no enemies. Nevertheless, I considered myself fairly warned.

In mid-February, as the scenario began to be implemented, I met more frequently with Ghazi. On February 14, Ghazi said there were rumors that Khomeini had agreed that the hostages were to be released soon. The next day, he had heard that the student leaders had met with Khomeini to be informed of his views. On the morning of February 21 he told me with some excitement that although Khomeini was still too weak to do any work, the students were aware that they must give up the hostages. They had not yet agreed, he said, but it looked as if they would. "I can assure you absolutely," Ghazi told me, "that the hostages will be free before the Iranian New Year" (March 21). As usual, I immediately reported this conversation to Brzezinski and Ham Jordan. Jordan told me during our conversation that afternoon outside the White House that he had passed my note to President Carter. The president, he said, was discouraged at the way things were going, and Jordan wanted to give him some encouraging news.

President Carter had two reasons to be worried, despite the positive signals out of Tehran. First, the scenario was progressing much less smoothly than had been hoped. In fact, the very first step of the process had nearly been botched by incompetence in Tehran. According to the script, Ghotbzadeh was to send a message to Secretary General Waldheim requesting the establishment of a commission "to hear Iran's grievances and to allow an early solution to the crisis between Iran and the United States." The message was also to ask that the commission see each of the hostages. However, the message that arrived in New York on February 12, as scheduled, said the commission should investigate the "crimes committed by the shah and the funds stolen by his family," and that it could "hear the hostages" in the course of its work. To our consternation, we learned that Ghotbzadeh had departed on a grand tour of European capitals and had left the matter in the hands of assistants who were not fully briefed. After some hasty international phone calls, a "clarification" was received at the UN the following day containing the correct words.

This problem was repeated and compounded in the early morning hours of February 20. Bani-Sadr's message to the UN, which formally accepted the formation of the commission, departed radically from the "agreed" script. It described the terms of reference of the commission as "a study and investigation into the past interferences of the U.S. into the internal affairs of Iran through the regime of the deposed shah and with a view to establishing a tribunal to determine their treason, crimes and corruption. . . ."

Secretary Vance was out of the country, so Acting Secretary Warren Christopher and Harold Saunders called President Carter in the middle of the night to relay the news. They met in the Oval Office at five in the morning, and after considerable discussion the president decided to go ahead with the mission after both the White House and the UN had reiterated the terms of reference for the commission as a "fact-finding mission" to hear Iran's grievances and to "allow an early solution to the crisis." To make matters worse, Ghotbzadeh announced later that same day that the arrival of the commission (which was in Geneva) should be postponed for three days because Iran had not made the necessary "technical" arrangements to receive them. The utter chaos and vacuum of authority in Tehran had never been more apparent.

The president's second cause for concern was closer to home. The media had finally discovered that Hamilton Jordan was engaged in some kind of secret talks, and they were hot on his trail. Radio Luxembourg reported that Hamilton Jordan had met in Paris with Sadegh Ghotbzadeh at the home of Héctor Villalón during the weekend of February 19. The Iranian Foreign Ministry issued a public denial that Ghotbzadeh had met with any United States officials during his visit to Paris, but the story would not go away. There was concern that the press would uncover the details of the secret negotiations and set off a counterreaction in Tehran before the scenario could be implemented.

Things Fall Apart

These early warning signals proved prophetic. In the days that followed, things began to come apart. On February 22 an Iranian close to Ghotbzadeh told us that "something has developed underground against the release of the hostages and against Khomeini." He said there was a "real mess" inside the embassy, where there had been some fighting. He could provide no further details, but it sounded like trouble. The UN commission was due to arrive the next day.

The next day was a disaster. Khomeini, who was showing signs of recovery, issued a new message to the nation on the hostage issue. The message was unambiguous: "The Moslem and combatant students who occupied the den of espionage have by their revolutionary deed dealt a crushing body-blow against the world-devouring United States and have thereby made the nation proud. But since in the near future the representatives of the people will meet at the Islamic Consultative Assembly [the Majles, or parliament], *the issue of the hostages will be up to the representatives of the people.*" (Emphasis added.)

Khomeini's latest pronouncement was timed to coincide with the arrival of the UN commission in Tehran, and it immediately cast into doubt the ability of the envoys to perform their mission. The Majles elections had repeatedly been postponed. They were now scheduled for mid-March, with a runoff election to be held in early April. (There were several hundred seats to be filled, often with five or more candidates for each, and since a majority was required, runoffs were inevitable.) Even in the unlikely event that the elections went smoothly and that the Majles quickly organized itself and formed a government, it would still be mid-April at the earliest before the assembly could realistically be expected to address the hostage question. Moreover, given the inflammatory nature of the issue and the unpredictability of political debate among the many warring factions in Iranian politics, the outcome of a public hearing in a newly elected revolutionary forum was not promising.

The militants in the embassy had placed the issue directly in Khomeini's lap. Their rejection of any authority but Khomeini himself effectively forced the ayatollah to choose between his new president (who was identified with the nationalist, secular forces) and those who symbolized the radical Islamic politics of confrontation. It was a brilliant strategy. Although Khomeini may have recognized the validity of the arguments that Bani-Sadr and Ghotbzadeh were making—that the hostage taking had served its political purpose and was now becoming counterproductive to Iran—his acquiescence in a secret, brokered settlement could cast doubts on the "revolutionary" nature of his own leadership.

He had faced comparable choices on several occasions in the past—when the pragmatists had pressed for the dissolution of revolutionary committees that were disrupting the political and economic life of the country—and he would face the issue many times again in the future. In each case he was prepared to tolerate compromise on the part of others, but when forced to make a public choice, he always sided with the radicals. His revolutionary image—the ultimate source of his charismatic authority—was more important than public order and efficiency. In this instance, it appeared, Khomeini had weighed the political risks and had cautiously chosen to remove himself from the fray. In the process he had thrown the entire plan off track, leaving Bani-Sadr and Ghotbzadeh clinging precariously to the slenderest of branches.

The militants who controlled the embassy recognized a political victory when they saw it. They greeted this latest message with a wild celebration.

Into the Breach, Once More

Late on that Saturday afternoon, after Khomeini's bombshell, I joined Hal Saunders in his office for a review of the situation. Hal was imperturbable. He made no effort to downplay the seriousness of the situation, but neither did he dwell on it. He had looked disaster in the face in one negotiation after another over more than two decades and had concluded that despair was an emotion the negotiator could ill afford. Although his own natural optimism was legendary among his associates, he was no Pollyanna. One could not spend —as he had—a professional lifetime dealing with the issues of the Middle East without coming to appreciate the sheer intractability of some problems. Rather, he entered each new round with no illusions but with a profound conviction that even minor progress could be achieved only through dogged persistence and determination. As he told his staff on many occasions, "Our job is to take a ten percent chance of success, try to turn it into a twenty percent chance, and hope for a break."[11]

As evening turned to night, Saunders was on the phone with Henry Precht in Paris. After the Bern meeting, Precht had remained behind in Europe to provide a continuing point of contact with the two lawyers, who took turns shuttling between Paris and Tehran. That night Precht had had dinner with Villalón, who had spoken by telephone with Bourguet in Tehran. According to Bourguet, Bani-Sadr chose to interpret Khomeini's declaration that "the issue of the hostages will be up to the representatives of the people" as not relating exclusively to the future Majles. After all, Bani-Sadr argued, he was also the elected representative of the people.

According to Bourguet, Bani-Sadr, Ghotbzadeh and others remained committed to the scenario and were prepared to persevere. They took some cheer from the fact that the commission had not been prevented from entering Tehran and that it apparently would be permitted to begin its work. There was considerable discussion about the ambiguous role of Khomeini's son and even whether the statement was written by Khomeini or by some of those around him who were known to oppose a resolution of the crisis.

With respect to the scenario itself, Bani-Sadr's staff had now gone over it in some detail. They were beginning to raise substantive questions about the nature of assurances that the United States would provide to Iran on issues such as assertion of personal claims by hostages, trade sanctions, restrictions on military sales, private attachment cases, and other areas of potential dispute that could be expected to arise in the wake of any agreement to release the hostages. Saunders directed the legal staff of the State Department to begin to develop positions on each of these points.[12]

The only positive note to emerge from this was that all of those in Iran who had cooperated in devising the scenario—especially Bani-Sadr, Ghotbzadeh and the two lawyers—were prepared to continue to work toward an early settlement of the crisis, at considerable political and even physical risk. Under those circumstances, with the commission on the ground in Tehran, the United States had nothing to lose by letting events play themselves out. In Hal Saunders' formula, a 20 percent chance had just been reduced to less than a 10 percent chance, but the possibility of a break—however remote—could be sustained only if we stayed in the game.

In Khomeini's statement of February 23 he had urged Iranian "victims" of the shah's regime to testify before the commission, and this aspect of the commission's work went smoothly. Hundreds of people appeared to relate their experiences under the former regime. In accordance with its mandate, the commission met with these individuals privately, despite the interest of the Iranian authorities in making the testimony public.

The more important question was whether or not the commission would be permitted to see the hostages, as originally agreed, and whether they could succeed in securing the transfer of the hostages from the "students" to the government authorities in Tehran. Three days after the commission arrived, Ghotbzadeh went to the embassy compound to confront the students directly. He argued with them but got nowhere. By the twenty-eighth, Ghotbzadeh was reported to be depressed and very tired. He was getting very little support from Bani-Sadr and was being left to carry the political onus of dealing with the students almost entirely by himself. After a week of this, Ghotbzadeh remarked wryly to one of his associates that he did not appear to have much political future in Iran. According to one observer of the scene in Tehran, everyone could agree on one point: "There is no government."

Ominously, for the sake of the negotiations, Khomeini's health seemed to be improving by the day. In early March he was moved out of the hospital. My friend Ghazi contacted me on March 3 to confirm that the ayatollah was much stronger. According to the rumor mill, as Khomeini's health improved he seemed to regret having relinquished so much power to Bani-Sadr.

By March 5 the commission had completed most of its hearings but was apparently no closer than before to visiting the hostages. Given the stalemate in Tehran, and the apparent inability of the elected authorities to deal with the "students," the commission decided to leave.

During that same day, Ghotbzadeh apparently again visited the embassy for a showdown with the students. Reportedly the discussion was heated and the students had eventually "kicked him out—literally." Ghotbzadeh and others involved in this confrontation were beginning to fear for their lives. (Bourguet and some others in Tehran had received death threats in recent days.) Nevertheless, Ghotbzadeh persuaded the commission to postpone its departure for several more days. He thought the situation was about to break. This time, he was absolutely correct.

Early in the morning of March 6, the "Muslim Student Followers of the Imam's Line at the Den of Espionage" issued a press release. They repeated their opposition to permitting the UN commission to visit the hostages. However, they complained, "what can one do when the officials and those who are in charge in the commission have accepted that whatever the commission wants must be done? We cannot bow to and comply with a view that we do not regard as being in line with the Imam's policy. But since those in charge of government always regard our methods as a factor contributing to their weakness—always speak of a government within a government—thus, we declare to the Revolution Council, in order to allay any misunderstanding, to *take delivery of the hostages . . . from us to do with them anything they deem appropriate.*" (Emphasis added.)

The reason for this sudden *volte-face* was not clear at the time, nor has it adequately been explained since. The defensive, almost petulant tone of the announcement suggests that the "students" were sensitive to the bad press they were getting in Iran and elsewhere. The fundamental concept of the commission was to provide a "positive" act (permitting Iran to place on the record its grievances against the shah) that would permit Iran's militants to ease their position on the hostages without losing face. The underlying strategy was sound. The "students" at the embassy were put in the uncomfortable position of preventing Iran's grievances from being published by the UN. That fact, plus the drumfire of criticism that Bani-Sadr and Ghotbzadeh managed to sustain in the media, apparently had its intended effect.

However, it was probably more complicated than that. Ghotbzadeh and the two lawyers, who understood the conspiratorial nature of politics in revolutionary Tehran better than most, interpreted the announcement as a possible trap intended to draw the secular authorities into a direct and damaging confrontation with the "students." Subsequent events lend credibility to this view, for those in control of the embassy quickly arranged for hostile crowds to take up position outside the embassy to challenge anyone who tried to take custody of the hostages.

Neither Ghotbzadeh nor people in Washington, however, were inclined to look a gift horse in the mouth. Ghotbzadeh immediately went on television to announce that he had Khomeini's authorization to take custody of the hostages in the name of the Revolutionary Council.[13] He initiated plans for removing the hostages from the embassy (allegedly to be accomplished by military forces using helicopters to avoid contact with the crowds outside the embassy)[14] and moving them at least temporarily to the Foreign Ministry building, where Bruce Laingen and his colleagues reported additional cots being moved in.

Washington, in turn, began to implement contingency plans that had been carefully prepared months earlier. For the first time, State Department officials privately allowed themselves the luxury of putting on paper the phrase they had so long avoided: "*When* the hostages are released . . ." It appeared that the high-stakes gamble on Bourguet and Villalón, for all its improbabilities and lapses, was about to pay off.

Khomeini Intervenes

As usual in this drama, the cheer was short-lived. One deadline after another passed as the "students" stalled and conducted a blazing duel of press releases with Ghotbzadeh. Bourguet and Villalón asked for a new meeting with Jordan and Saunders and prepared to fly out of Tehran while the furious maneuvering was still going on. But before they could leave, Khomeini intervened once again, this time fatally.

On Monday morning, March 10, Khomeini met with the Revolutionary Council to review the situation. Bani-Sadr, who was deeply engaged in the Majles election campaign, failed to attend the meeting. After listening to the views of the clerical hard-liners, Khomeini issued a new statement. "The question raised nowadays," he said "is the United States and the American hostages and spies who are held by the Muslim and struggling students. In this connection I shall make a few points:

"1. Copies of all documents related to the U.S. Government and the traitorous shah should be made available to the [UN] commission of inquiry into the crimes committed by the U.S. Government and the shah. As for the Muslim students, if they too have any evidence, then they should provide copies to the commission.

"2. The meeting with the hostages involved in compiling the dossier on the crimes committed by the shah and the United States can take place for the purpose of their interrogation.

"3. If the commission of inquiry advances its views in Tehran about the crimes committed by the ousted shah and the interferences by the aggressive United States, then a meeting with the hostages can take place."

In short, the commission was now being asked to issue a report in Tehran *before* meeting with the hostages (except perhaps to interrogate some of them to be identified by the students). No mention was made of a transfer of the hostages to control of the government. This was contrary to all previous understandings and totally unacceptable to the United States. Within hours after this statement, the students withdrew their offer to transfer the hostages and the White House announced that the commission was suspending its activities. The commission departed the next morning.

On that bleak Monday, President Carter asked the congressional leadership to meet with him in the Cabinet Room. The meeting was extremely subdued. The president gave an unemotional, precise account of the various steps that had been undertaken in this negotiating phase. He offered neither excuses nor any particular hope. The flat tone of his voice, and his willingness to share with a roomful of political friends and enemies the details of a process which had heretofore been restricted to a tiny handful of his associates, clearly signaled his conviction that this round was over. The bitterness of his disappointment, however, did not register with me until several days later. Brezezinski mentioned in a report that according to the polls, the public considered our Iranian policy a failure. The president wrote in the margin: "The polls are accurate."

Going Through the Motions

Jordan and Saunders dutifully traveled back to Bern, where they met with Bourguet and Villalón on March 12 and 13. By this time the two intermediaries were so emotionally engaged that they had seemingly lost perspective. In this second visit ("Bern II" as the participants dubbed it) to the Hotel Belle-vue, the lawyers assured their U.S. friends that the previous week had marked a great turning point. It had, they argued, convinced the Revolution-ary Council that it must assert its authority over the students. According to their political analysis, the candidates whom Bani-Sadr was backing in the Majles election would be successful, and the foundation would be laid for a showdown with the students. They were so upbeat and confident that their mood rubbed off on their American counterparts, who constructed still an-other scenario based on the presumption of Bani-Sadr's success in the elec-tion. None of this cheer, however, managed to survive transatlantic transmission to Washington.

One concrete new development had emerged from the chaos of March 10, which was to shape the final act of this dismal episode. At the end of that Saturday, with the commission preparing to leave, Bani-Sadr sent a personal message to President Carter solemnly pledging that the hostages would be transferred to the custody of the government within fifteen days after the Majles election.

Despite its unquestioned sincerity, a promise from Bani-Sadr at that stage was scarcely cause for rejoicing. Still, the United States had very few options open to it at that point. A package of new sanctions was being prepared, but it was likely to be little more than a token gesture. More forceful, military measures were under consideration (as we shall see in the following chapter), but there was no intention to take any action against Iran in the coming few weeks. Moreover, additional time was needed to persuade the allies to join the United States in further economic pressures against Iran. Consequently, Presi-dent Carter set the end of March as his deadline for the imposition of addi-tional sanctions.

In the meantime, Washington had other matters to think about. The first was the status of the hostages. In early March, there was a new round of newspaper reports that one or more hostages were undergoing medical care after being wounded either in escape or suicide attempts. There was particular concern about Mike Metrinko. Fortunately, the presence of the commission spurred additional new visits to the hostages, and the State Department work-ing group was able to conclude with considerable assurance by mid-March that all the hostages—notably including Metrinko—were safe and reasonably healthy.

The second issue was the shah. The charade of extradition had continued despite the best efforts of the United States—and repeated assurances by Panamanians at all levels. The shah became increasingly alarmed. At the same time, his physical condition was deteriorating. His spleen was badly swollen and had to be removed. He had been promised the use of the U.S. military hospital in the Canal Zone. However, the Panamanians chose to interpret this as a slight on their medical reputation and insisted on the use of a Panamanian hospital. Then the Panamanian doctors objected to the fact that the famous surgeon Dr. Michael DeBakey had been brought from the United States to head the operating team. After several days of disputes, the operation had to be postponed.

Not surprisingly, the shah decided that he did not wish to have major surgery performed in Panama. He had a standing invitation from President Sadat of Egypt, which was now reaffirmed and, finally, accepted. As word began to circulate that the shah was considering leaving Panama, the Iranians frantically tried everything they could think of to avoid losing their prize one more time. Bourguet was in Panama with extradition papers which only an Iranian diplomat could deliver, and the nearest candidate was in New York; Hamilton Jordan was also there, to try to persuade the shah that it was safe to remain in Panama; Lloyd Cutler, counsel to the president, also arrived. But the shah had made up his mind, and he was not to be dissuaded.

Characteristically, there were several more incidents of low comedy before the curtain fell on the Panamanian venture. On March 23, the day of the shah's departure to Egypt, General Torrijos informed Bourguet that he would detain the shah in Panama if the Iranian government succeeded in taking custody of the hostages in Tehran. A new round of emergency meetings in Iran only served to demonstrate once again the powerlessness of Bani-Sadr and Ghotbzadeh in this situation.

Then, with the shah's plane in the air and Jordan on his way back to Washington, Bourguet relayed a message from Ghotbzadeh that the hostages would be transferred within one hour. He asked that the shah's plane be detained at its refueling stop at the U.S. air base in the Azores. On his own authority, Jordan called Secretary of Defense Harold Brown and requested that the shah's plane not be permitted to depart the Azores without further word. The order was given, but by the time Jordan arrived back in Washington, Bourguet again had to admit failure, and the order was rescinded. The unorthodox negotiating strategy had come perilously close to careening out of control.[15]

Imaginary Messages

In Iran, the Majles election also had not followed the script. Only a few candidates had received a clear majority, and all of those were from the clerical-dominated Islamic Republican Party, Bani-Sadr's rival. There were widespread accusations of fraud and irregularity in the voting, and a commission was formed by the Revolutionary Council to investigate. In the meantime, the runoff election was postponed. The actual formation of a capable, elected government still seemed very far away.

The fertile imagination of Héctor Villalón, however, had not run dry. On March 29 I was in my office when I received a call from the White House Situation Room. They said there was a report coming in over the Foreign Broadcast Information Service wires that I should see immediately. Minutes later I was standing in front of one of the teletype machines in the basement of the White House reading with fascination as the translation of a Tehran radio broadcast was printed out line by line.[16]

It was the text of a letter, purportedly from President Carter to the ayatollah, that had been handed to the Ministry of Foreign Affairs, which delivered it to Khomeini's office, where it was immediately released to the press. The tone of the letter was quite apologetic. At one point it stated: "I can clearly understand that occupying our embassy in Tehran could have been a natural reaction by Iranian youths." The final paragraph said: "I beg you to help me in solving the crisis between us according to just and honorable principles. I will greatly appreciate this, and our two nations will thank you for it."

I tore the copy off the machine and ran up the stairs to Hamilton Jordan's office. He was in a campaign meeting with several other people, and Eleanor Connors, his exceptionally able secretary, hesitated to interrupt. However, she had learned over the previous two months that the vagaries of events in Iran took precedence over everything else in Jordan's life, and after only token resistance she asked Ham to come to the door. I said simply, "It looks as if your friends in Tehran have been busy again," and handed him the teletype. He read down the sheet and inhaled sharply. "Those idiots!" he exclaimed, and without another word rushed down the hall to the president's private office. I did not follow, since I thought he might have some explaining to do.

Two days earlier we had had indications in Tehran that Villalón was preparing a letter, but this came as a shock. Villalón had evidently concluded that the situation was hopelessly frozen, that the United States was preparing to return to a strategy of pressure, and that some kind of direct action was required if the situation was not to deteriorate further. He had obtained some official letterhead, to provide the necessary appearance of authenticity, and then had composed a letter that assembled passages and phrases from various U.S. communications to Iran, adding his own inventions and flourishes at key points where he thought a little additional political flexibility would be helpful with the Imam. After having it typed, he delivered his masterpiece to Ghotbzadeh. Although Ghotbzadeh apparently was aware of the dubious origins of the letter, he delivered it directly to Khomeini—without even briefing Bani-Sadr.

Both Ghotbzadeh and Villalón considered themselves masters of political psychology. Perhaps they thought the ayatollah would be more prone to compromise if he were led to believe that the United States had admitted its crimes and errors. Possibly they thought that since everything else had been tried, it would do no harm to try this ploy. Whatever their reasoning, they overlooked some very simple facts. Khomeini was a vindictive man who wanted nothing so much as to humiliate the United States. He quickly recognized this as an apparent U.S. defeat and released it to the press. Several days later he addressed a new message to the nation that blandly asserted that the letter from President Carter was "another error," and that "neither excuses . . . nor confession of crimes . . . will be of any avail."

The White House immediately issued a flat denial, but it was slow to catch up with the original story. There were, of course, numerous passages throughout the forgery drawn from U.S. public and private policy statements, which gave it a ring of authenticity. Moreover, Bani-Sadr reacted indignantly to the U.S. denials, arguing with obvious sincerity that the letter was genuine—which he no doubt believed. To make matters worse, the publication of the letter came just at the moment when the United States was engaged in a campaign of pressure, trying to persuade key allies to join in imposing more stringent sanctions against Iran. The apologetic tone of the letter inevitably raised questions about U.S. resolve.

It also raised serious questions about continued reliance on the two lawyers. They had worked diligently and selflessly to try to arrange a peaceful settlement of the hostage issue, and they had nearly succeeded in spite of overwhelmingly negative odds. We owed them our gratitude. But we also owed it to ourselves to back away from the relationship as they threatened to become loose cannons on a very cluttered and dangerous deck.

Ultimatum

Unknown to the public, President Carter had sent a personal message of a very different sort to Bani-Sadr only days before the appearance of the counterfeit letter. On March 25, in the wake of several high-level sessions examining possible military options against Iran, and recalling Bani-Sadr's earlier pledge, the following message was delivered on behalf of President Carter to Bani-Sadr personally:

Over the past four months, we have followed with great interest your statements to the Iranian people and in particular your principled position on the fundamental wrong involved in the holding of the hostages. We noted your private, personal assurance on March 10 that the hostages would be transferred to the control of the Iranian government within 15 days. We hope that the transfer can be accomplished within the next few days. It is essential to give a tangible sign to the families and to the American people of the improvement of the condition of the hostages and that there is real movement toward a prompt resolution of the crisis.

In order to avoid misunderstanding, we want you to know that in the absence of such transfer by Monday (March 31) we shall be taking additional non-belligerent measures that we have withheld until now. Our quarrel is not with the Iranian people, but some will unavoidably suffer hardship if your government is not able to take the requisite steps to release the hostages. We remain ready to discuss a resolution of the crisis through any channel you choose. We must have tangible evidence, however, that Iran is prepared to move toward a resolution of the problem in order for us to explain to the American people why we are not taking additional measures.

This message was delivered to Bani-Sadr on March 27, and it provided the rationale for many of the events of the following days. It committed the United States firmly to take additional action if there had been no tangible change of circumstances by March 31. Bani-Sadr received the message with no apparent emotion. He commented only that he viewed the continued holding of the hostages as an impediment to a proper Iranian policy and that it was not necessary to encourage or threaten him. He complained that the United States had offered nothing positive to assist him, and we later heard complaints from Ghotbzadeh that the U.S. "ultimatum" offered nothing new for Iran. However, the message was taken with the utmost seriousness both in Tehran and Washington.

Late in the afternoon of Sunday, March 30, senior representatives of the principal agencies involved in the proposed new package of sanctions against Iran gathered in the Roosevelt Room of the West Wing of the White House to discuss last-minute details of the anticipated announcement. On the following day, March 31, the deadline date given to Bani-Sadr, the president convened a meeting of the National Security Council in the Cabinet Room to review the proposed imposition of sanctions.

The United States had already taken most of the steps available to it to punish Iran politically, diplomatically and economically, so the list of sanctions was not particularly long or fearsome. (A cynical journalist asked me facetiously, "When are you going to unsheath your wet noodle?") However, the decision to proceed with new sanctions marked a turning point from a policy of restraint and quiet diplomacy to a more active policy of pressure. Those present at the NSC meeting understood very well that the issue was larger than the limited package of new sanctions to be announced in the next twenty-four hours. It was the beginning of a new phase of coercion. Military actions were again under active consideration, and no one could be sure where this new policy would lead once it had begun.

President Carter had arrived at the NSC meeting for only one purpose— to discuss the nature and extent of sanctions to be imposed on Iran now that the deadline had passed. Secretary Vance, however, had a new message in hand, which he used to great effect.

Christian Bourguet had secretly visited the White House on March 25 and had spent ninety minutes with President Carter. He had been able to gauge at first hand the anger and frustration that Iran's political impotence had inspired in its most attentive observer. He had returned directly to Tehran with his own impressions to add to those of the private message that had preceded him. The combination seemed to have set Bani-Sadr and Ghotbzadeh in motion again after weeks of depression and inactivity. On the day of the deadline they sent a new message to Washington stating that Bani-Sadr had met with the student leaders and would announce the details of the hostage transfer in a speech to be made at noon on the following day.

Vance argued vigorously that it would be a mistake to announce sanctions before hearing what Bani-Sadr had to offer. Clearly, the secular leaders in Iran were making an extraordinary effort to find a way out of the crisis, and we should be prepared to give them some additional time. The president was reluctant. He had given Bani-Sadr a deadline in writing. He had let it be known publicly that he intended to impose new sanctions on Iran. To back down or equivocate at this point without any tangible movement would only give new ammunition to those who saw him as weak and indecisive. But Vance persisted. What harm could there be, he argued, in waiting an additional twenty-four hours?

President Carter looked at his secretary of state for a long moment, then asked what time it would be when Bani-Sadr made his speech. Vance replied that it would be four-thirty in the morning in Washington. After a brief pause the president said that he wanted to see Vance in his office at five o'clock the next morning. With that, the meeting adjourned.

April Fool's Day

So, at four-thirty on April 1, I found myself in my ancient Volkswagen, still half asleep, driving automatically the twenty minutes from my home in Alexandria to the White House. My radio was permanently tuned to one of the twenty-four-hour news stations in Washington, which, as it happened, featured an all-night talk show. I was not surprised that the subject of conversation was Iran. It was a national obsession. In this case, however, the talk show host seemed as sleepy as I was. He had the factions in Iran on the wrong sides, he had the latest diplomatic moves in the wrong order, and was so thoroughly confused that he kept getting calls from his insomniac listeners trying to correct him. I listened with amusement and no little sympathy for the poor fellow who had to master a new subject every night and then stay ahead of a nation of news junkies, who presumably stayed up all night studying the latest bulletins.

I arrived a bit early at the White House and joined President Carter and a few others in the darkened Oval Office before a cheerful fire. In the few minutes of small talk before a quorum was assembled, the president remarked casually that it was unbelievable what garbage got sent out over the air. I thought of the hapless talk-show host and wondered how he would have felt if he had known that the president was probably listening to his garbled interpretation of the latest news from Tehran.

April 1 was the first anniversary of the proclamation of an Islamic Republic in Iran. Both Bani-Sadr and Khomeini were scheduled to address the nation. In Khomeini's case, as had been common since his hospitalization, a message was to be read by his son Ahmed. An advance copy of Khomeini's speech was made available to Agence France-Presse, which released an exclusive report the night before. Therefore, while waiting for Bani-Sadr's speech, we were able to spend the hours contemplating the latest thoughts of the ayatollah.

Evidently the frustration of recent events was not confined to Washington, for Khomeini rose to heights of vituperation surpassing even his own past performances. He dismissed Villalón's counterfeit letter in sarcastic tones as "an attempt to deceive us with flattery," then shifted his rhetorical guns to the shah and his flight to Egypt. "Satan," he said, "is now attempting a new political project to perpetuate his domination. . . . Satan must know that to support the shah is to support his great betrayals and his pillage and that to have sent the shah, enemy of Islam and Iran, to another enemy is to deceive the Muslims of the whole world." "Today," he said, "is the birth of the hope of one day in which the world's Muslims will be able to cut the criminal hand of the looters and raise the flag of Islam. This day is the symbol of God's power."

As the group assembled in the Oval Office, President Carter referred sardonically to the Khomeini statement. "I read parts of it to Rosalynn last night," he joked, "and she went to the bathroom and threw up."

The group that morning comprised Cyrus Vance, Zbigniew Brzezinski, Warren Christopher, Harold Saunders, David Aaron, Hamilton Jordan, Jody Powell and myself as note taker. Warren Christopher said that we had just received a message from Tehran which said that although Khomeini was "very hard" in his speech, Bani-Sadr was ready to announce transfer of control of the hostages to the government. However, he set two conditions: first, the definitive release of the hostages could come only after the Majles convened, as Khomeini had decreed; second, the United States must refrain from any hostile act.

Brzezinski said we had two options. We could say the Iranian response was inadequate and proceed with the package of sanctions, or else we could acknowledge that the Iranian government had publicly accepted transfer of the hostages and hold off. He thought the latter could be justified on the grounds that Iran had responded to the U.S. message of March 25. We could ignore the conditions they set. Powell proposed announcing that we were withholding sanctions temporarily on condition that the hostage transfer was carried out. Jordan cautioned that Bani-Sadr and others in Tehran had very little room for maneuver and that we should not push them into a corner.

Meanwhile the translation of Bani-Sadr's speech was coming in over the FBIS wire. Typically, it was long, convoluted and full of awkward constructions and odd jumps of logic. I once remarked to Eric Rouleau that Bani-Sadr's speeches and interviews seemed to suffer in translation and that it was probably better to hear them in French or Farsi. "Not at all," he said, "I have known him for years, and half the time I can't figure out what he is talking about."

In this case, Bani-Sadr quoted at length from the U.S. ultimatum of March 25 and a subsequent message the State Department had sent responding to his charge that the United States had contributed nothing positive to the negotiating effort. Finally, however, he came to the central point. Speaking in the name of the Revolutionary Council, he announced, "If the United States issues an official declaration and announces that it will not, until the formation of the Majles and its decision on the hostages, make propaganda claims, speak or instigate on the issue, the Revolutionary Council will accept to take control of the hostages."

Warren Christopher, who had been writing during the initial discussion, read a draft statement that he had prepared characterizing Bani-Sadr's announcement as a positive step and acknowledging the Iranian government's statement that the hostage issue would be resolved when the Majles convened. Brzezinski said he was uneasy about taking too positive a reading of the Iranian position. He thought the president should take credit for the initiative, which his message had prompted, but we should not read too much into their statement. He was particularly concerned that the United States not lend legitimacy to the Iranian position that only the Majles was empowered to resolve the crisis.

The president said, "We are dealing with a crazy group. Bani-Sadr and others are holding on by their fingernails. If we leave out any mention of the Majles, they would come back to us for an acknowledgment of their position." Brzezinski reiterated his view that mention of the Majles weakened the statement. With some exasperation the president said, "There is no need to keep going around about this. I prefer to say something about the Majles."

Christopher proposed wording it: "The hostage issue will be resolved when the new parliament convenes." All agreed, though Brzezinski commented that we would be better off arguing the main point, i.e., the transfer of the hostages. Aaron wondered if we should say that the hostages would be transferred immediately. The president responded that he had trepidation about saying more than Bani-Sadr had stated publicly.

Jody Powell wondered if the president should make the announcement on camera. Vance thought it would be better for Jody to make the announcement. Powell said he did not like the idea of the president personally standing up and accepting conditions laid down in Tehran. The president said he regarded this as good news, at least compared to the reports of Khomeini's speech he had read last night. It gave what he had asked Bani-Sadr for in his private message, and he thought it deserved positive treatment.

The president asked everyone there to avoid making any statements except through the official press spokesmen at the White House and State Department. He anticipated that Khomeini and others on the clerical side would "say crazy things" in the next few days. He asked Vance to contact congressional leaders to request that they exercise restraint over the delicate period of the next several days. Then, near the end of the meeting, President Carter huddled briefly with Powell and Jordan to consider the political implications of the decision to forgo sanctions in response to Bani-Sadr's speech.[17]

Several minutes after the meeting broke up, Jody Powell issued the following statement from the White House press room:

> The announcement by President Bani-Sadr that the hostages will be transferred to the care and protection of the Iranian government is a positive step. Accordingly, we will defer imposing further sanctions at this time.
>
> The Iranian government has said that the hostage issue will be resolved when the new Parliament convenes. We will continue to work for the earliest possible release of all the hostages.

One hour later, at seven-twenty, the president invited journalists and TV cameras into the Oval Office, where he made the following statement:

As I am sure you realize, we have been seeking a positive development in Iran and have had in mind the transfer of the American hostages from control of the militants to the care and protection of the Iranian government.

If this action had not been taken, or is not taken, we were considering additional sanctions against Iran and had notified the Iranian government of that fact.

This morning, the President of Iran has announced that the hostages' control will be transferred to the government of Iran, which we consider to be a positive step.

In light of that action, we did not consider it appropriate now to impose additional sanctions. We will monitor the situation very closely. We would like to see this positive development continue and our foremost consideration and our constant effort will be devoted to the earliest possible release of the American hostages and their return to this country and to freedom.

During the following week in Tehran there was a frantic new round of political maneuvers—all to no avail. Bani-Sadr engineered a Revolutionary Council vote of 8–3 in favor of accepting custody of the hostages, but this was vetoed by Khomeini—ostensibly because the vote was not unanimous, but probably, as one close observer speculated, because Khomeini harbored such an all-consuming hatred for the United States that he could not bring himself to take any action that America would view as favorable.

Khomeini's second thoughts about Bani-Sadr as president also seemed to be growing more serious. The new president had staked all of his political authority on the hostage issue and had lost. Someone who saw him near the end of that grim week of successive public failures reported that he was totally despondent and wondered if he would be able to remain in power much longer.

The remark was perceptive. Although Bani-Sadr officially remained in power for another year, he had been fatally wounded by the hostage affair. In mid-1981 he was ignominiously dismissed by Khomeini and forced to flee for his life to Paris. Ghotbzadeh, similarly, clung to power for a time, then faded into obscurity. In April 1982 he was arrested in Tehran for plotting an aerial bombing attack of Khomeini's house and was eventually executed.

Neither Bani-Sadr nor Ghotbzadeh had any love for the United States. Their efforts to free the hostages were motivated entirely by the conviction that the crisis was fatally poisoning Iran's international position and eroding the accomplishments of the revolution they had believed in. But their vision of the revolution and its purposes was radically different from the vision of Khomeini, as they and many other secular-minded Iranians discovered to their chagrin. The hostage crisis was the crucible in which these domestic political tensions were heated until they either fused or separated. Bazargan's government was swept away in the first few days of the crisis, and Bani-Sadr's authority was permanently blunted during the course of the secret negotiations. A third government would have to appear before a serious negotiating process could finally begin.

In the meantime, however, Washington's patience had run out. Interest suddenly shifted from French lawyers and elaborate political schemes to the arcana of military planning. A dangerous new phase was about to begin.

XIII

THE MILITARY OPTION

T he hawks are flying," I wrote in a memorandum to David Aaron early on the morning of April 4, 1980. "I had two unsolicited suggestions for a blockade of Iran before breakfast this morning."

President Carter's controversial decision on April 1 to postpone sanctions one more time was as unpopular in the White House as in the population at large. (Despite the widespread charges of political manipulation, the decision won him no plaudits.) America had turned the other cheek once too often; Iran had gone back on its promises one too many times. There was mounting impatience and anger with a cautious policy of restraint that seemed to produce only failure and repeated humiliation.

No elaborate political polls or grass-roots surveys were required to understand this; any random conversation with almost any group of U.S. citizens would suffice. However, that was not always as easy as it sounded. The hostage crisis was perhaps the premier news event in the history of U.S. television, but many of us involved in the crisis had very limited direct exposure. The endless series of sixteen-hour working days allowed little time to sit in front of a television screen. Instead, I relied on conversations with family, friends and colleagues to get some sense of public attitudes. (There was, of course, no shortage of printed matter. At this stage of the crisis, with all the formidable information-collection facilities of the U.S. government focused on the hostage crisis, I was inundated with as much as a thousand pages of written material each day, six days a week.)

In a crisis, you never have enough information, and you take it where you find it. My own favorite strategy for expanding my range of contacts was the breakfast table. I normally arrived at my office before dawn, caught up on the voluminous overnight message traffic, prepared the agenda for the Special Coordinating Committee meeting, then stopped in the White House staff mess for a hearty breakfast before the next round of events. The staff table was a congenial meeting place, where individuals dealing with every aspect of life in the White House—from the Secret Service to consumer affairs—could meet informally and compare notes. During this period the breakfast crowd became a sort of permanent, floating seminar on Iran. I relished the good food and the easy informality of shop talk at the table. I also learned more from those sessions than most of the participants may have suspected.

The anger and exasperation that I sensed in the first week of April from my White House colleagues was repeated from several other sources, including some unexpected quarters. Bruce Laingen, Michael Howland and Victor Tomseth, it will be recalled, had been trapped in the Foreign Ministry in Tehran at the time of the embassy seizure. Despite occasional interruptions and shifting ground rules, these three managed to maintain periodic telephone contact with the Iran working group at the State Department. Unlike the other hostages, they were able to talk to their families from time to time and could share their impressions of the situation with their colleagues in Washington.

Do Something!

On the same day that I reported the hawks flying around the White House, Bruce Laingen and his two colleagues managed to place a telephone call to Washington. Although they respected the president's decision to defer sanctions and appreciated the priority that had been placed on the welfare of the hostages (notably including themselves), they thought there was a limit to the flexibility the United States could show, and they expressed doubt whether it was a good idea to let the Iranians off the hook one more time.

During this same period I was approached informally by a group of Foreign Service officers who had served in Iran. Although they were among the handful of Farsi-speaking Iranian experts in the government, they had been shunted aside from the mainstream of policy making within the Department of State.[1] They did not agree with the current policy, but their suggestions for the use of military pressure were not well received by Secretary Vance. One of them argued vigorously that a rescue operation "should be carried out at the earliest practicable moment. . . . Rescue of the hostages offers the *best* chance for getting the most hostages back safely."

Although I was unable to tell them so, their thinking mirrored that of many others in Washington, eventually including President Carter. The military option had been examined in the first few days of the crisis but had been deferred in favor of diplomacy. As the first efforts at negotiations through the United Nations failed to produce any results, interest in military planning revived. The possibility of military action had begun to appear increasingly attractive by the end of December, when the Soviet Union invaded Afghanistan.

That event abruptly altered both the diplomatic and the military track of the U.S. Iranian policy. On the diplomatic side, the USSR vetoed UN Security Council sanctions against Iran, and the United States was unable to persuade its allies to proceed with sanctions in the absence of such a resolution. On the military and strategic side, attention was diverted away from the hostage crisis. The Iranian authorities responded sharply to the Soviet invasion, and at least on this key issue, the United States and Iran suddenly found themselves pursuing almost identical efforts to mobilize opposition to the Soviet aggression. Iran, like the United States, decided to boycott the 1980 Olympic Games in protest.

The Afghan invasion transformed the entire strategic environment in the region, and it provided a compelling set of reasons for seeking a negotiated settlement with Iran instead of pressing the situation toward possible conflict. The Soviets, by their actions, appeared to have provided renewed evidence that the United States and Iran shared fundamental security interests, regardless of how much their politics might diverge. Similarly, the Soviet invasion shocked the Islamic states of the Persian Gulf into awareness of their own vulnerability and opened up new possibilities for cooperation with the United States. To have launched military action against Iran at that moment would have contributed to the political destabilization of regional governments and interrupted U.S. efforts to develop a regional security framework.

Also, of course, it was at this critical moment that a new set of possible intermediaries appeared on the scene, credibly offering the possibility of initiating a dialogue with the revolutionary forces close to Khomeini. Consequently, military plans were shelved and a new round of secret negotiations was begun that lasted until April 1980.

Quite a lot of work had been accomplished on the military side even before the Soviet invasion. In early January, I discussed the status of the rescue operation with General David C. Jones, the chairman of the Joint Chiefs of Staff, after he had returned from an inspection visit. He said the likelihood of a successful operation was greatly improved from two months earlier. One of the most hopeful signs was the gradual relaxation of security by the militants guarding the embassy. They were not professionals, and as the immediate threat of U.S. military action receded, they lowered their guard.

The possibility of military action always lay just beneath the surface of events and served as a counterpoint to the roller-coaster negotiations through Bourguet and Villalón. As the negotiations faltered, discussion in the SCC would inevitably turn to military alternatives. Thus, on January 18, after the initial shock of the Soviet aggression had begun to wear off and before the discussions with Bourguet and Villalón had begun, the SCC discussed "leaning forward" militarily through increased military deployments in the region and more belligerent public statements. Such a posture, it was felt, would accomplish two purposes: first, it would keep the Iranians off balance and uncertain of what the United States might do next; and second, it would help persuade the allies to adopt economic sanctions, which the administration considered vitally important to sustaining pressure against Iran. The allies, it was believed, would prefer the economic pain of sanctions to the much greater danger of a U.S. blockade or mining of Iranian ports.

Again, on March 11, after the breakdown of the efforts of the UN commission in Tehran, there was a heated exchange in the SCC. Secretary Vance argued against the imposition of additional new sanctions against Iran, while continuing to pursue the negotiating track. Brzezinski said that we were back to where we had been six weeks earlier. He recognized the objections to a strategy of pressure, but he thought that nothing less than the threat of a U.S. blockade would persuade U.S. allies to join in bringing pressure on Iran. He thought the Iranians would not give up the hostages unless they faced the prospect of some unpleasant consequences. The outcome of the discussion was inconclusive. However, I thought it was significant that Brzezinski assembled the small military planning group in his office that morning for its first meeting in many weeks.[2]

The same debate was repeated at the SCC a week later. The Department of State, which was responsible for preparing a list of new sanctions to be imposed against Iran, resisted breaking diplomatic relations with Iran, arguing that experience showed it was much easier to break relations than to restore them later. In the first month of the crisis President Carter had been persuaded to permit the Iranian diplomats to remain, on the grounds that they provided a potentially valuable channel of communications with Tehran, but now he had run out of patience. Commenting on the list of sanctions developed by the State Department, he wrote: "State's limited actions are worse than nothing. Be prepared to expel all Iranian diplomats."

Brzezinski argued on March 18, as he had on many occasions in the past, that the United States was being "diddled along" by the Iranians and made to look impotent. The international community was full of praise for U.S. restraint, but he detected behind those words a perception that we were weak and indecisive. He argued that an ultimatum should be delivered to Iran that promised unilateral action "highly disruptive of Iranian society" if there was no peaceful resolution of the crisis by a specific date, e.g., April 15. Some other members of the SCC proposed some intermediate steps, such as interrogating merchant ships bound for Iran, to underline U.S. seriousness. Warren Christopher argued that military pressure would not work, that Iranians openly welcomed the chance to become martyrs. Harold Brown remarked dryly, referring to Khomeini: "A man with a martyr complex seldom lives to be seventy-nine years old."

Mining

The possibility of mining Iranian harbors was discussed by the SCC on March 21. On that occasion, the Department of State was represented by Undersecretary for Political Affairs David Newsom, the senior professional diplomat in the U.S. Foreign Service. A tall, slim man of scholarly mien, Newsom seemed to be the absolute picture of the cautious diplomat. The image was completed by a quiet voice and a sense of humor so wry that it often went unobserved. The image, however, was deceiving. Beneath the donnish exterior there lurked a shrewd and able political observer who was very much his own man. Newsom's quiet understatement tended to be drowned out in a contentious policy meeting, but I learned that it paid to listen carefully. In this case, in his undramatic way, David Newsom spelled out an interesting perspective.

In response to a comment that a blockade would create a "hell" in the Islamic world, Newsom commented that if such an action were taken suddenly and without advance preparation it would indeed have an adverse effect on the moderates in Iran and could spark a new round of anti-Americanism that the hard-liners in Iran could use to their advantage. However, he suggested, if this could be relayed secretly in advance to the moderates, it might give them leverage to use in the political infighting. If handled very carefully, a case could be made that this would improve the chances of securing release of the hostages.

He thought the key issue was whether or not the United States was prepared to follow through on its threat. It was a high-risk strategy, but in the end it could go either way. This was stated in such a nonprovocative and thoughtful tone that almost no one at the meeting—including other members of the Department of State—seemed to realize that Newsom was taking exception to the central thesis that State Department representatives had been defending as an article of faith for months.

Admiral Turner agreed that such an act would arouse anger in Iran but that it would not result in the death of the hostages. It might, as Newsom had suggested, strengthen the hand of Bani-Sadr and the "moderates," but it was far from clear that this group would prevail in the resulting power struggle. We might be pressuring the weakest political element in Tehran. However, the SCC deferred further discussion of the issue, since it was expected to be dealt with in greater detail by the president and his key advisers over the weekend. An NSC meeting was scheduled at Camp David for the following day, Saturday, March 22.

Military Options

On that date, eight senior officials—Vice President Walter Mondale, Secretary of State Cyrus Vance, National Security Adviser Zbigniew Brzezinski, Secretary of Defense Harold Brown, Director of Central Intelligence Admiral

Stansfield Turner, Chairman of the Joint Chiefs of Staff General David Jones, Deputy National Security Adviser David Aaron and Press Secretary Jody Powell—met with President Carter for a complete review of U.S. strategy toward Iran. The meeting began at ten forty-five, when most of the group arrived by helicopter at the president's retreat in the Catoctin Mountains of Maryland, continued through lunch, and did not end until three-thirty that afternoon.

This meeting occurred while Hamilton Jordan and Lloyd Cutler were in Panama, negotiating with the shah about the next step in his tragic odyssey. President Carter had talked with President Sadat on the phone earlier that morning, and he opened the meeting by briefing the group on the shah's apparent intention to accept Sadat's invitation to travel to Egypt. Sadat was confident he could deal with the political repercussions in Egypt and the Islamic world, so Carter had reluctantly accepted the advice of Jordan, Vance, Saunders and others who argued that the shah's departure to Egypt was far preferable to the only other alternative—his return to the United States.

The former monarch departed by air the following day for Egypt. It was the shah's final journey. He died in Egypt four months later.

The subject of the NSC meeting at Camp David, however, concerned the possible use of military means to attempt to free the hostages. President Carter asked General Jones to begin with a detailed briefing on the prospective rescue mission. Intelligence had improved over the five months of the crisis, but it was impossible to be certain that all the hostages were in fact inside the embassy. Based on debriefing of those hostages who had been released earlier, plus reports of other observers and visitors, the locations of most of the hostages were known, but there was always the possibility that some of them might be moved from time to time. Thus, sufficient time had to be allowed to permit the rescue team to search all the buildings in the compound.

General Jones stated that if the rescue team could get to the walls of the embassy compound without warning to the students inside, and if the hostages were all inside the embassy, as it appeared that they were, then he had high confidence that all the hostages could be rescued. Brzezinski agreed that the actual break-in to the embassy and the extraction of the hostages was probably the easiest part of the operation. Getting the team to the embassy without discovery and preparing the exit route was much more complex than the confrontation with the students. Brzezinski described all the points at which detection of the operation would be possible and said that that was his greatest single concern. General Jones said that his level of confidence in the operation fell somewhere between that of the rescue team itself, which was sure that it could successfully free the hostages, and Brzezinski's more pessimistic appraisal.

The rescue effort was designed to be accomplished in a series of related steps, each of which would be reversible without escalation and with minimum casualties should something go wrong. The need to be able to terminate and withdraw at any point, together with the need for absolute secrecy, added to the complexity and difficulty of both planning and execution.

The first stage of the plan involved the prepositioning of men, matériel and support equipment at key locations in the Middle East and Indian Ocean. This movement had to be accomplished under the cover of other routinely scheduled activities to avoid signaling that an operation was being prepared. To preserve security, the bulk of this matériel had to be held back until political authorization was granted to proceed with the operation. One of the key purposes of the March 22 NSC meeting was to begin some of these preliminary steps in order to reduce the time lapse between a decision and the actual launching of the raid.

The insertion of the force into Iran was a grueling and technically difficult operation. Under cover of darkness, eight RH-53D helicopters and eight C-130 aircraft were to depart from different locations, fly at very low level beneath Iranian radar coverage across more than 500 miles of Iranian desert, and rendezvous at an airstrip that would be secretly prepared near the small town of Tabas—the site called "Desert One" in the plan. At Desert One, the helicopters were to be refueled and loaded with the men and equipment ferried in by the fixed-wing aircraft.

Following the refueling and loading, the C-130s would leave Iran. The team would conceal itself at a prepared location southeast of Tehran, and the helicopters, still under cover of darkness, would proceed to a remote site in the mountains above Tehran, where they would be camouflaged and remain in hiding throughout the following day. This delay was required in order to ensure that the assault on the embassy itself could be carried out under cover of darkness. Because of the distances involved, it was impossible to insert the necessary forces, release the hostages and depart in a single night.

For the nonspecialist, it is difficult to appreciate the demands that this critical first phase of the operation placed on men, equipment and technology. Simply flying 600 miles nonstop in a helicopter is a remarkable feat. To do so at night, without lights, in complete radio silence, and at very low altitude can only be regarded as a heroic achievement in its own right. Hence, many of those closely associated with the planning of the rescue mission believed— quite rightly as it turned out—that this was the most difficult segment of the entire operation. As Secretary of Defense Harold Brown remarked in his press conference after the mission failed, there was no other country in the world that had the resources even to attempt such an operation.

Assuming the successful insertion of the team, and its survival undetected during the following day, the actual rescue operation would have been conducted under cover of darkness on the second night. The entry of the team into Tehran would have been in local vehicles to attract minimum attention, with the helicopters making the briefest possible appearance to pick up the team and the hostages. The helicopters were then to fly to an abandoned airfield near Tehran where they would rendezvous with transport aircraft. The helicopters would be abandoned, and the Americans would be flown out of the country under heavy U.S. air cover.

General Jones described the plan to President Carter in some detail, noting that it was exceptionally complex. The chairman felt better about the viability of each of the parts of the plan, he said, than about the operation in its entirety. Making each of the parts fit together on time gave him the greatest concern.

Secretary Brown observed that in weighing the risks of this plan, it was necessary to look at the alternatives. The possibilities of a blockade and mining of Iranian ports had been examined in some detail. However, each of these also had very serious risks, including the possibility of physical retaliation against the hostages, possible widespread political repercussions in the Islamic world, pushing the Iranians into the arms of the Soviets, and the creation of severe difficulties for U.S. allies. Moreover, there was debate about whether such military acts would put pressure on the right people in Tehran. In short, the risks and costs of the rescue mission were comparable to those of other military courses of action that had been considered.

President Carter asked what steps had to be taken immediately in order to prepare the way for a rescue mission. He said he did not want to undertake a rescue operation unless there was no choice. He would prefer to wait another ninety days rather than conduct an operation that resulted in the deaths of the hostages. General Jones pointed out that the nights were becoming progressively shorter in Iran, thereby reducing the time available to insert the team and conduct the assault on the embassy. As time went on, it would be necessary to begin thinking about a three-day operation instead of the already complex two-day plan.

President Carter made it clear that he did not regard the negotiating track as finished. (Bani-Sadr's self-imposed time limit for transfer of the hostages to the government still had about a week to run at that point.) He was not prepared to make a decision on a high-risk rescue venture while there were still opportunities to work out a negotiated release. However, he authorized the taking of certain preparatory steps, including the covert flight of a small reconnaissance aircraft to the secret rendezvous site,[3] necessary to lay the groundwork for a possible future operation.

In the meantime, he asked his advisers to increase their efforts to persuade the allies to join the United States in imposing economic sanctions against Iran as a means of bringing new pressures on the Tehran regime. He hoped that the threat of new international sanctions would persuade Iran to continue its efforts toward a negotiated solution and obviate the need for military action, with all its risks and uncertainties.

As it happened, the allies were unwilling to adopt meaningful sanctions without a great deal more pressure, and the Iranians were incapable of following through on their promises. By the first week of April, all hope of a negotiated release had vanished, and attention turned almost exclusively to the search for new pressure points that the United States could use against Iran.

Three choices were left. First, the fate of the hostages could be abandoned to the vagaries of Iran's internal political processes, recognizing that this would probably mean a minimum of several more months of incarceration for the hostages while the United States confined itself to watchful waiting. Second, the United States could dramatically and unilaterally intensify the pressure against Iran by an increased show of force and ultimatums, possibly resulting in the mining of Iranian harbors or otherwise interdicting Iranian commerce. Finally, a rescue mission could be attempted which, while risky, held out the prospect of terminating the crisis without a military escalation that could push Iran toward the USSR.

Decision

On the evening of April 4, a new message was sent to Bani-Sadr reporting that pressures for action were mounting within the United States due to the repeated inability of Iran to carry out its promises. Barring some movement on the Iranian side, the message stated, the United States had little alternative to taking some decisive steps in the very near future and pressing other governments to take similar steps. The sanctions that had been deferred on April 1, the message pointedly observed, were only the first steps to "sterner measures" that would have the inevitable effect of causing hardship to many Iranians. The United States, it noted, was on the verge of important decisions, and it urged Iran's leadership to act promptly. The Iranian Foreign Ministry requested clarification of the message, but Washington responded that there would be no further clarifications.

On April 7, President Carter called a formal meeting of the National Security Council to consider the next steps in U.S. policy toward Iran. The group assembled with unusual solemnity in the Cabinet Room at nine in the morning. "The only item on the agenda today," the president announced, "is Iran." He then read aloud the most recent conversation with Bourguet in Tehran that admitted at last that the negotiating game was over. President Carter commented that the last week had shown a profound change in the situation. The militants had again offered to let the government take custody of the hostages, and this time the government had refused. We were close to the point, he said, where we must take forceful action.

We should now urge our allies to break diplomatic relations with Iran, and the United States should prepare for forceful action, including the interruption of Iranian commerce. "We have bent over backwards," he noted in a grim voice. "We have been patient and long-suffering, and we could not have been more willing to wait for responsible action by Iran." But now, he said, there were no further options available on the negotiating side. We had an obligation to the hostages. His preferred course of action at this point was to enlist the cooperation of other nations to increase significantly the pressure on Iran or, if they were unwilling to cooperate, to take forceful action on our own.

Secretary Vance noted that an announcement of new sanctions had been prepared in advance by the Department of State after discussion in the SCC. It included the following elements:

- Diplomatic relations to be broken with Iran, and all Iranian diplomatic and consular personnel to be declared persona non grata.
- All exports from the United States to Iran to be banned, with the exception of food and medicine, which were expected to be minimal.
- A formal survey of Iranian assets in the United States and U.S. claims against Iran would be undertaken by the Treasury Department. (This was a preliminary step to "vesting," or confiscation, of Iranian assets by the United States.)
- All visas held by Iranian citizens for entry into the United States to be invalidated and renewed only for reasons of compelling humanitarian concern or national interest.

There was little discussion about the list. It had been under consideration for more than a month in the SCC and was thoroughly familiar to everyone at the table. Lloyd Cutler, who had been the strongest advocate of "vesting" the Iranian assets, proposed that the announcement mention U.S. intention to use Iranian assets to pay claims at least to the hostages and their families.

Although that was a popular suggestion, it had the disadvantage of committing the United States to the confiscation of at least some of the frozen assets, thereby making it extremely difficult to return the assets to Iran at a later date. Vice President Mondale argued that the freezing of billions of dollars' worth of Iranian assets was the one thing the United States had done that really hurt Iran. "We will need to be in a position to bargain with that money for the final release of the hostages," he asserted. "If it has been attached, we lose control." After some discussion, Carter agreed with Mondale that seizure of assets was unwise, but he authorized Lloyd Cutler to draft legislation for vesting of the assets that could be available on short notice if required.

The implementation of new sanctions gave rise to one amusing and telling incident. Ali Agah, the Iranian chargé d'affaires in Washington, and his deputy were called to the State Department to be informed of the break in diplomatic relations and the required departure of all Iranian diplomats the following day. They were met at the entrance by Henry Precht, who would escort them to the office of Peter Constable, Harold Saunders' principal deputy. Waiting in Precht's office, the Iranians began talking about the hostages, and one of them commented mockingly that the hostages were really quite happy in Iran and that some of them even wanted to stay.

"Oh, bullshit!" Precht exploded. Agah announced indignantly that he would not stand for such abuse and headed for the elevator. A State Department officer had to pursue the two Iranians in a car to deliver the formal message announcing the break in diplomatic relations.

This comic sideplay was given widespread media coverage, and Precht received a torrent of congratulatory fan mail. His favorite was a handwritten note on one copy of the story that said: "One of the elements of good diplomatic language is to be concise, accurate and clear. You have shown yourself to be the master of all three." It was signed "Jimmy Carter."

On the following day, April 8, I wrote a long memorandum to Brzezinski entitled "Getting the Hostages Free," outlining what I regarded as the two basic choices remaining. The first was a campaign of escalating pressure, up to and including the mining of Iranian harbors. The alternative, which I favored, was a rescue operation that, if successful, would deprive the ayatollah of his bargaining leverage and would puncture his aura of invincibility. Both were risky, but the rescue operation offered the potential of a quick end to the crisis with minimal loss of life, while a campaign of military pressure risked unpredictable escalation.

On April 9, Brzezinski called me to his office and asked me to redraft the paper as a memorandum from himself to the president. I did so the same day, and Brzezinski forwarded it to President Carter that night with a few additions. The memorandum concluded with the following statement: "In my view, a carefully planned and boldly executed rescue operation represents the only realistic prospect that the hostages—any of them—will be freed in the foreseeable future. Our policy of restraint has won us well-deserved understanding throughout the world, but it has run out. It is time for us to act. Now."

On the morning of April 11, President Carter called another meeting of his National Security Council in the Cabinet Room. The group that assembled there at eleven-thirty was identical to the group that had met on March 22 at Camp David, with three exceptions. David Aaron, who had been at the Camp David meeting, was not included in this meeting. Hamilton Jordan, who had been in Panama negotiating with the shah on March 22, was present for this climactic meeting. Most notably absent was Secretary of State Cyrus Vance, who was represented by Deputy Secretary Warren Christopher.

The Agony of Cyrus Vance

Vance had left the previous day for a much needed long-weekend vacation in Florida. During the first three years of the Carter administration, it would have been unthinkable to take a decision on any fundamental foreign policy issue in his absence. Of all the senior foreign affairs advisers in the government, he was closest—both personally and ideologically—to President Carter. Vance alone, among the statutory members of the National Security Council, was regularly invited with his wife to spend informal weekends with the president at Camp David. His counsel was sought by the president on every foreign policy issue, and his views regularly prevailed. In the highly publicized tug of war between Vance and Zbigniew Brzezinski, the extraordinary events of Carter's fourth year in office tended to obscure in the public mind the indisputable fact that during most of the Carter presidency, it was Vance who had exerted the dominant influence on U.S. foreign policy.

The reversal of this pattern was not caused primarily by Brzezinski's tenacious infighting and policy manipulation from his vantage point in the White House. Rather, the tide definitively turned with the Soviet invasion of Afghanistan, which appeared to be a thundering repudiation of the policies that Vance (and Carter) fundamentally stood for.

On New Year's Eve 1979, Jimmy Carter told Frank Reynolds of ABC-TV that "this action of the Soviets has made a more dramatic change in my own opinion of what the Soviets' ultimate goals are than anything they've done in the previous time I've been in office."[4] The choice of words was infelicitous, and it earned him derisive criticism for his alleged naïveté about Soviet behavior. However, the import of Carter's words was unmistakable to those in the policy community. The statement was, in effect, a public admission of the failure of a policy of quiet diplomacy and patient, nonbelligerent negotiation of differences that he and Vance had adopted as the cornerstone of their policy toward the Soviet Union, and it clearly presaged a shift in those policies to a more confrontational approach. Vance understood this very well:

Afghanistan was unquestionably a severe setback to the policy I advocated. The tenuous balance between visceral anti-Sovietism and an attempt to regulate dangerous competition could no longer be maintained. The scales tipped toward those favoring confrontation, although in my opinion, the confrontation was more rhetorical than real.[5]

In retrospect, it seems clear that the Soviet leaders committed a blunder of historic proportions when they misjudged the depth of the U.S. reaction to their aggression in Afghanistan. Jimmy Carter and Cyrus Vance represented an important but often invisible dimension of U.S. attitudes toward the Soviet Union. They believed deeply in the importance of dialogue and mutual accommodation between the two superpowers on vital issues of peace and international security. They were not starry-eyed idealists about the USSR, but they were profoundly convinced that the way to peace was through careful communication and persistent discussion of issues rather than threats and bluster.

Carter, more than any recent U.S. president, was prepared to walk a second mile in pursuit of nonviolent solutions to security problems. For three years he stubbornly refused the advice of his more hawkish advisers in the hope that the USSR would respond to a historic opportunity to develop peaceful means of managing East-West competition. The Soviets, whose own historical experience provided scant basis to comprehend a policy founded on principles of mutual respect, chose to interpret U.S. behavior as a policy of weakness, thus setting in motion a new round of confrontation and arms competition. The two great powers, disturbingly, failed utterly to communicate.

The Soviet invasion was a body blow to Vance, and he seemed to age visibly under the impact. It marked the end, at least for some time, of the policies to which he had devoted his professional life. American policy was taking a dangerous new turn that he was powerless to prevent. He had run out of ideas, and he seemed to distance himself from the day-to-day policy process.

Several weeks after Carter's statement, Vance repeated to the press that he did not intend to remain in office past the November election,[6] and this self-imposed lame-duck status seemed to be reflected in the fact that Warren Christopher increasingly took his place at meetings and conducted the daily work of the State Department. "Vance is just fading out," said one of his critics in the State Department.[7] Observing Vance during this period, I thought he appeared intensely unhappy, frustrated and demoralized by a job that had lost its zest.

It was in that context that the decisive meeting of April 11 was conducted, with Secretary Vance absent and not informed of its results until he returned to Washington the following week. His views were well known, and President Carter, who arrived at the meeting with his mind all but made up, had taken them into account in advance.

The meeting was something of an anticlimax. General Jones gave an updated briefing on the mission, and the issues were rehearsed again as they had been on several previous occasions. This time, however, everyone at the table with the possible exception of Warren Christopher was convinced that the negotiating track was entirely dead and that it would be impossible—politically and morally—to sit patiently and quietly, hoping for the best, while Iran sorted out its political chaos sufficiently to release the hostages.

The real debate turned on imponderables. If a campaign of military pressure and threats was set in motion, no one could be sure where it would lead. If a rescue mission was launched, no one could be sure it would succeed. Of the two available choices, however, the risks associated with the rescue mission appeared more easily containable and less prone to uncontrollable escalation than a campaign of threats and rhetoric that led to the mining of Iranian harbors or bombing strikes against Iranian industrial targets.

Once one accepted the necessity of action, the selection of the rescue mission quickly asserted itself as a logical inevitability. President Carter had concluded by April 11 that action could no longer be deferred. From that moment, a rescue attempt was virtually assured. After a little more than one hour of discussion, the president decided that the mission should proceed without delay. The first available date was April 24.

Secretary Vance returned from Florida on April 14 and was understandably dismayed that such a momentous decision had been taken in his absence. He spoke to the president privately, and a secret meeting of the National Security Council was convened on Tuesday, April 15, to permit him to express his objections. He outlined his concerns in some detail, but he received no support from the president or any other member of the NSC. The die was cast.

The objections that Secretary Vance raised centered on the risks that a rescue mission would entail. There were four key elements:[8]

- America's allies were being persuaded to adopt more stringent sanctions in the belief that the alternative was unilateral U.S. military action. Launching a military rescue mission without prior warning or consultation would be perceived as a betrayal of their trust.
- The mission inevitably risked an armed confrontation within the city of Tehran that could result in very high loss of life among the rescue team, the hostages themselves or the Iranian population.
- The Islamic world might react to such an armed confrontation by sparking a conflagration with the West generally and the United States in particular. (As Vance expressed it, "Our national interests in the whole region would be severely injured, and we might face an Islamic-Western war.")[9]
- Even if all the hostages were removed successfully, Iran might retaliate by imprisoning a new set of American hostages, specifically the many U.S. journalists who were present in the country.

These risks were undeniable, and they were addressed directly by President Carter and others in taking the decision to proceed. It was true that the allies had been pressured by the threat of possible U.S. military action to take more effective action against Iran. However, even under that threat, the actions they were prepared to take were minimal in terms of bringing effective pressure to bear against Iran. They were unwilling to institute the sanctions voted by the United Nations but vetoed by the Soviet Union, and they were not prepared to break diplomatic relations. If a rescue mission succeeded in bringing the crisis to an end, the allies might be annoyed at the lack of consultation but they would be delighted to have the issue behind them. If it failed, their criticism was predictable but not unmanageable.

The possibility of an armed confrontation in Tehran was, of course, a real concern. That concern had led to the design of an exceedingly complex plan relying on total secrecy and surprise rather than massive military force. If the students in the embassy had advance warning of the assault, the bloodshed would be unacceptably high; so the operation was designed as a series of independent stages, capable of being terminated at any point if the mission was compromised. Militarily, it would have been infinitely simpler to come into Tehran with guns blazing, but that possibility had been rejected from the start.

It must be remembered that the student guards were in fact students, not trained military personnel. After nearly six months of guard duty, activities had settled into a comfortable and generally relaxed routine. How would these individuals react in the wee hours of a weekend night when confronted suddenly and without warning by seasoned combat troops? No one could say with certainty that the students would not react by beginning immediately to shoot the prisoners they had been guarding for months, but human nature and past experience suggest otherwise.

There was a curious parallel only a week after the rescue attempt, when a group of terrorists invaded the Iranian embassy in the center of London and held its occupants hostage. On the sixth day of the siege, in broad daylight, with the terrorists on guard and alert, and with crowds and TV cameras filling the streets below, a small group of British commandos attacked suddenly, overcoming the five terrorists with no loss of life to the hostages. Would a U.S. commando team achieve the same success striking without warning in the middle of the night in Tehran? The answer will never be known, but those planning the operation believed that the odds were in their favor if the team could be delivered undetected to the embassy walls.

The possibility of an anti-American uprising throughout the Islamic world had been at the center of Vance's concerns since the attack on the Great Mosque in Mecca and the subsequent burning of the U.S. embassy in Islamabad in November 1979. It was in response to that event that he had ordered as many official Americans as possible out of the region. Vance's assessment was regarded as excessively cautious by almost everyone else associated with U.S. Middle East policy, including many in the Department of State. The Foreign Service officers who had protested to Vance about U.S. Iranian policy believed that the Islamic states, which were being pressured by Iran, "would undoubtedly exult privately in the wake of a rescue which cut the Iranians down to size. This would prove of incalculable value in restoring our position in an area of critical importance to us." It was a risk, but the potential payoff was substantial if the mission succeeded.

Finally, there was the risk that Iran, having lost its prized possession of the hostages, would retaliate by seizing a new set of U.S. prisoners. For obvious reasons, this criticism had special appeal among journalists, particularly those in Tehran, who were furious to learn not only that they had been taken unaware by the rescue attempt but that they might have been its victims.

In the weeks prior to the mission, the administration made it illegal to conduct even the most innocuous financial transaction with anyone in Iran. Paying a hotel bill in Tehran became a criminal offense under U.S. law. Repeated warnings were issued that individuals traveling to Iran did so at their own risk and that the U.S. government could offer no protection or support in case of trouble. However, journalists correctly regarded themselves as immune from prosecution because of First Amendment protection of freedom of the press, and they were accustomed to traveling in high-risk areas.

Despite the apprehension of journalists in Tehran, it was uncertain whether the Iranian students would have launched an intensive search for other Americans to replace the hostages at the embassy. It is even less certain that the government would have acquiesced in such a roundup. The only rationale for holding the Americans at the embassy was that they were U.S. "spies" against Iran. Even that flimsy pretext would have been missing if the hostages were replaced by a random selection of Americans plucked off the streets of Tehran.

The entire context of the crisis would have been transformed. There were many in the Iranian government—even among those opposing Bani-Sadr— who were anxious to see an end to the crisis, although they were not prepared to challenge the "students" directly. It is far from certain that they would have permitted a perpetuation of the crisis once the original subjects had vanished.

Nevertheless, if the casualty level was high during the rescue, the likelihood of some nasty incidents of retribution against private Americans in Iran was considerable. It was for that reason that Brzezinski proposed on several occasions that the Delta Team bring back a number of Iranian prisoners as counter-hostages.[10]

Indisputably, the points that Vance raised in objection to the rescue mission highlighted the major risks and imponderables associated with a high-risk venture, and they were issues on which reasonable men could draw different conclusions. However, the essence of Vance's critique went beyond this catalogue of identifiable risks to the underlying premises of the decision. If the president was prepared to wait patiently for the Iranian political process to play itself out over a period of months, then there was at least a reasonable prospect that the hostages would eventually be released without any need for risky military action.

Vance was prepared to wait. As he expressed it later: "Our only realistic course was to keep up the pressure on Iran while we waited for Khomeini to determine that the revolution had accomplished its purpose, and that the hostages were of no further value. As painful as it would be, our national interests and the need to protect the lives of our fellow Americans dictated that we continue to exercise restraint."[11]

That statement reflected an honorable and very special view of the world, of the United States' role in the world, and of international politics generally. In proposing a U.S. policy of "waiting for Khomeini," Vance focused exclusively on the dangers of direct action and discounted the costs of inaction, except to acknowledge that they would be "painful." Vance's formula could as easily have been turned on its head, stressing the considerable costs of still another endless period in which U.S. policy was held hostage to the whims of Iranian political developments, with its leadership reduced to a state of professed impotence.

The image of U.S. weakness generated by months of humiliating setbacks and frustrations was not healthy for relations with allies or adversaries. In domestic politics, continued passivity not only condemned the president to self-immolation at the polls but it risked generating a popular backlash in favor of forces who opposed everything Vance and Carter represented.

No one who was acquainted with Cyrus Vance could question the depth of his commitment to peace and nonviolence. His reverence for human life shone through every decision he made. Throughout his distinguished service as secretary of state he was absolutely consistent in counseling against the employment of military instruments—even for purposes of political symbolism. He was prepared to accept temporary political defeats and humiliations rather than set in motion a chain of events that might at some point result in even limited loss of life. With all due respect, one is led to ask whether the world is ready for that degree of selflessness in international politics.

However noble the intentions, there is no such thing as a risk-free foreign policy. Inaction and excessive caution bear their own penalties, especially when interpreted by an adversary as weakness or compliance. Empty bluster and constant sword-rattling are unworthy of a responsible power, but a perceived unwillingness to act in the face of provocation may be just as deadly. Those who lent their support to the rescue mission were seeking a judicious balance between those extremes. Their choice may have been only the best of a bad lot, but the decision does them no dishonor.

The Mission Fails

Unfortunately, there was never an opportunity to test alternative theories. The rescue mission failed long before it arrived at the embassy walls. In the early evening of April 24, eight helicopters took off from the carrier U.S.S. *Nimitz* in the Arabian Sea. Some two hours into the flight, after entering Iranian territory, helicopter number 6 of the formation began receiving warning signals in the cockpit of a possible impending rotor blade failure. The pilot landed and abandoned his craft. The crew was picked up by one of the other helicopters, and the flight continued.[12]

The warning signal (known as BIM, for "blade inspection method") on the RH-53D helicopter is intended to provide advance warning of a crack in the rotor blade. The rotor blade is filled with gas under pressure. The BIM is supposed to flash if there is a loss of pressure, indicating a possible hairline crack in the blade. However, the BIM can be triggered by a number of nonthreatening circumstances. In the flight history of this aircraft, from its introduction into the fleet until the time of the rescue mission, a total of 43 warning-light episodes had occurred. Inspection revealed that in none of those cases—or in any other case in the 38,000 hours of total flight experience with the RH-53D—had a rotor crack actually been present. Even if a crack is present, it does not prevent the craft from flying for a considerable period of time. Peacetime safety regulations prescribe that an RH-53D not fly more than five hours after the appearance of a warning light. At the time this helicopter was abandoned, it was approximately three hours from Desert One.

Shortly after this event, the flight of helicopters unexpectedly encountered a cloud of suspended dust, making visual observation extremely difficult. Since the helicopters were maintaining strict radio silence and were unable to maintain contact visually, they became separated. The flight broke out of the dust cloud, only to encounter another shortly thereafter that was denser than the first. Because of the thick, swirling dust, the helicopters were forced to rely almost entirely on the inertial navigation equipment and instruments specially designed for this operation.

Approximately four hours into the flight, helicopter number 5 began to experience malfunction of essential flight instruments. The pilot reversed course, flew back for more than two hours through the dust cloud and returned safely to the carrier. Because of radio silence, the crew of helicopter number 5 was unaware that at the moment when the decision was taken to turn back, they were only 25 minutes from the end of the dust cloud and that the weather conditions at Desert One—less than one hour away—were clear.

At approximately the same moment that helicopter 5 reversed course, helicopter 2 was beginning to experience hydraulic problems. Number 2 continued on to the rendezvous site and arrived safely. However, inspection after arrival revealed that a hydraulic leak had occurred, leading to the contamination of the hydraulic system and the failure of a pump. Repair of this malfunction required not only replacement of the pump but a thorough flushing of the entire hydraulic system, a process that could not be accomplished at the desert site. The helicopter would have to be abandoned.

At this point the mission commander at Desert One was faced with a critical situation. Because of the dust clouds, the helicopters had arrived as much as 85 minutes late. Dawn was fast approaching, and he had only five workable helicopters. It had been determined in advance that a minimum of six helicopters was required in order to proceed with the second stage and to ensure the availability of sufficient lift to conduct the assault mission the following night. As a consequence Colonel Charles Beckwith, the mission commander at the site, concluded that the operation should be aborted. This decision was relayed to the White House, where President Carter concurred, and the force prepared to withdraw.

During the refueling operation preparatory to withdrawal, one helicopter, maneuvering in the swirling dust kicked up by the rotor blades, collided with the C-130 refueling aircraft, which immediately burst into flames. Eight crew members died and five others were wounded. The remaining helicopters were abandoned in the inferno of fire and exploding ammunition, and the force withdrew on board the C-130s. The rescue operation, which had been developed in elaborate detail and rehearsed over a period of months, collapsed in ignominious failure and human tragedy within its first hours.

Because of the time difference, the drama described above encompassed a full working day in Washington—from 10:30 A.M., when the helicopters took off from the carrier, until 6 P.M., when the first news arrived of the fatal collision and fire.[13] President Carter had decided to maintain a normal work schedule in order to avoid any hint that something unusual was afoot, and the small group of senior officials at the White House and the State Department did the same.

This continued the pattern that had been established over the previous weeks, when meetings were held in the Situation Room of the White House late in the evening after office staffs believed that their bosses had left for home. The most important of those meetings had occurred on Wednesday evening, April 16, for about two and a half hours. On that occasion the Delta Team leader met with the president, Vance, Brown, Brzezinski, General Jones, and other key aides for a detailed review of the entire plan. A further meeting, without the president and Vance, was held on Saturday night, April 19.

The president had lunch at noon with his key advisers who were following the mission: Vice President Mondale, Secretary of State Vance, Secretary of

298 All Fall Down

Defense Brown, Brzezinski, Hamilton Jordan and Jody Powell. At this time word arrived about the unexpected dust storms and the fact that two helicopters had gone down. (In fact, only one helicopter had gone down at this point. The confusion probably arose from the fact that the lead helicopter, upon encountering the dust cloud, reversed course and landed in the desert briefly before deciding to proceed.) Still, the reports were basically encouraging.

Shortly after 3 P.M. word was received that the eight C-130 transport and refueling aircraft had landed safely at Desert One. However, in what was perhaps an omen of things to come, three vehicles appeared on the road that bisected the landing site almost immediately after the aircraft landed. One of these was a bus with forty-three passengers and a driver. It was halted and its occupants were taken into protective custody. It was known in advance that this road had occasional traffic at night, and a plan had been developed for such a contingency. The prisoners would be flown out on the C-130s to Egypt. They would be held there until the operation was completed the following night and then released.[14]

The other two intruding vehicles gave at least momentary cause for alarm. A small fuel truck appeared, followed closely by a pickup truck. Shots were fired by the Road Watch Team, setting the fuel truck on fire. The driver jumped from the cab, ran back to the pickup, and it escaped over the desert. Brzezinski and Brown conferred on this and—judging from the behavior of the drivers—concluded that these individuals were engaged in smuggling or some other unlawful pursuit and were not likely to go to the police. They may even have believed that the U.S. team was the Iranian police, as Colonel Beckwith suggested. In any event, no alarm was raised then or later.

By 4:30 P.M. everything appeared to be on track and under control. The helicopters had been delayed by the dust storm, but the required six had arrived safely at Desert One. Refueling was expected to be completed within forty minutes. The site where the Delta Team would hide was prepared, and local transport was waiting. Optimism mounted.

At 4:45 the secretary of defense received word of the hydraulic problem on the sixth helicopter and immediately called Brzezinski at the White House. With daylight fast approaching, a decision had to be made within minutes whether to abort the mission or to continue with fewer helicopters than prescribed in the plan. Brzezinski asked Brown to get the recommendation of Colonel Beckwith at Desert One. All of the principals had met Beckwith and had absolute confidence in his courage and professionalism.

Brzezinski called the president out of a meeting in the Oval Office, and the two of them huddled in the president's small private office. President Carter spoke with Brown on the secure phone and was told that Beckwith and all other officials in the chain of command recommended aborting the mission in accordance with the plan, since the team could not be assured of the necessary lift to accomplish the assault the following night. The president listened quietly, then said, "Let's go with his recommendation." It was 4:57 P.M. The mission had failed.

President Carter assembled his advisers—Mondale, Vance, Brown, Brzezinski, Christopher, Jordan and Powell—and they sat somberly for a few moments while the reality of the failure sank in. Then, in businesslike fashion, they began thinking through the steps of notifying other nations, the Congress, the U.S. people and the Iranians. Iran was certain to find the helicopters that had to be left behind, and President Carter did not want them to believe that a military invasion was under way.

Just before 6 P.M., the president's secure-line telephone rang. It was a call from General Jones. As the president listened, his face turned white. "Are there any dead?" he asked. Then he hung up and softly told the group of the collision on the ground and the probability of several deaths. The anguish was complete.

That night I did not sleep at all. The disastrous failure at Desert One was a terrible blow to the United States at a moment when it badly needed a victory. It removed any realistic possibility of freeing the hostages for months to come, and it placed them in great physical jeopardy. It was a fatal wound to President Carter, who had shown extraordinary courage only to inherit new charges of ineptness. But to every individual who had made a commitment to this dangerous enterprise, the events at Desert One were experienced as a crushing personal defeat.

The public announcement was delayed until 1 A.M. to ensure that all members of the mission team were out of the country. I sat in the dark living room of my home, listening to the incredulous first reports on the radio starting to build to a crescendo. During the long hours of that endless night, a curious archaic phrase rose monotonously to the surface of my mind like a muffled drumbeat. What I was tasting, I said to myself again and again, was "ashes in the mouth."

Post-mortem

A military raid is, by definition, a high-risk venture that operates on the outer margins of the possible, relying on skill, daring and a goodly measure of luck. When a raid succeeds, it acquires almost magical qualities and endows its authors with the badge of genius. Hence the appeal. When it fails, it invites ridicule and the second-guessing of armchair strategists. All of those involved in the rescue operation were conscious of the risks of failure, and they accepted their bitter disappointment with remarkable dignity and a total absence of recriminations.

One week later, after discussing at length the sequence of calamities that demolished in a few brief hours the months of planning and preparation of the mission, I asked David Aaron what he thought was the ultimate cause of the failure. He thought for a moment, and then, only half joking, said, "Allah's will." The ayatollah would have been pleased.

Although the extraordinary string of bad luck which called itself the hostage crisis often seemed to defy all earthly odds, the events were man-made. That was especially true of the rescue mission, and the real lessons of that painful experience can only be gleaned by a dispassionate look back.[15]

Historically, U.S. military forces have not demonstrated a capacity to plan and conduct successful raids. The reasons for this less than impressive record are not immediately apparent, and it would be presumptuous to generalize from the particular circumstances at Desert One. Nevertheless, there are some broad observations about the rescue mission that may be worth pondering in connection with any future small-unit action of this nature.

The first, and perhaps the most important insight to emerge from a close review of the operation was the fact that human judgment was decisively influenced—even overridden—by technology. The men who conducted the operation had all volunteered, and all were aware that they risked their lives. Yet, in two critical cases, when machines failed to operate as anticipated, the mission was abandoned. In one case, a warning light in the cockpit led a helicopter crew to leave the craft in the desert. In the other, a failure of instruments led the commander of the second helicopter to turn back when he was only one hour away from the objective. In both cases the machines were technically capable of going on, though with reduced reliability. The decision to abandon the mission was a purely *human* response to technological uncertainty.

That is also a thoroughly American response. One of the first lessons learned by anyone who drives an automobile or operates complex equipment is that the erratic functioning of a machine or a flashing warning light is not to be ignored. As members of the premier technological culture, we have been trained from infancy to heed and even to subordinate ourselves to machines. They assert their precedence in the commonplace acts of our daily lives, as when an insistently ringing telephone is permitted to intrude on the most solemn conversation.

If either of the pilots had chosen to ignore the malfunction and to proceed with the mission, the nature of the decision at Desert One would have been changed. That is not to say that the rescue would have succeeded—only that the odds would have been altered slightly in favor of success. But in an operation skirting so close to the outer limits of human and technological endurance, even tiny changes in the odds are not to be discounted.

The second fundamental issue concerns the relationship between a civilian commander in chief and his professional military advisers. To what degree should a president have confidence in the professional judgment of his military advisers and to what extent should he question it? John F. Kennedy was widely criticized, especially within military circles, for insisting on civilian control over military operations in the Cuban missile crisis down to the most minute detail. Lyndon Johnson was similarly criticized for asserting presidential control down to the unit level during operations in Vietnam.

President Carter consciously attempted to avoid these extremes. He spent many hours with the military planners and members of the rescue team, educating himself about the plans in advance. Once the decision was taken to proceed with the mission, he left the details in the hands of his military specialists. Yet, the post-mortem of the operation by Admiral Holloway and his military colleagues was quite critical of the planning, coordination and training for the operation on a purely military, professional level.[16]

Two of those criticisms concerned elements of fatal importance. As early as December, research had identified the phenomenon of low-lying clouds of suspended dust as a possible hazard that might be encountered along the helicopter flight path. A table in the weather annex of the operations plan indicated, by location and month, the frequency of such occurrences. Pilots, however, were not briefed about this possibility and had no instructions about how to deal with it.[17] Technically, the massive dust clouds could have been grounds for aborting the mission. The fact that each of the helicopter crews —acting independently and without radio contact with the mission commanders—chose to proceed despite the virtually impossible flying conditions was a tribute to their courage and determination.

However, the problem could have been overcome in several ways. A low-level weather reconnaissance flight in advance of the mission would have provided warning of the seriousness of the dust problem. Such a flight would have added to the danger of detection of the mission, and it was rejected for reasons of security. With perfect hindsight, it is easy to fault that decision as another example of placing undue reliance on technology ("satellite imagery" as noted in the Holloway Report) in place of human observation. It would also have been possible to employ a fixed-wing aircraft with better navigation equipment as a pathfinder for the helicopters. That was not considered by the mission planners.

The other major criticism of the mission plan was the failure to conduct a full-scale rehearsal integrating all elements of the operation. Each segment of the operation had been rehearsed on several occasions, and some of the parts had been combined in practice. However, there was no exercise that brought together all of the participants under the demanding conditions of physical endurance and timing imposed by a very complex plan. Thus, some of the participants actually encountered each other in person for the first time on the ground in the Iranian desert. The reasons for this departure from normal military practice were secrecy, the contingent nature of the plan over a period of many months, and the very short time between approval of the mission and its launch.

Could an operation of this magnitude have been conducted several times in the United States without coming to the attention of the press and hostile intelligence? Sadly, the U.S. experience in keeping secrets—even in matters of the most sensitive military security—is exceptionally poor, and the mission planners had good reason to be wary. In contrast to many other nations, a U.S. military planner preparing an operation that relies heavily on secrecy for success begins with two strikes against him—it is the price of an open society. We pay that price gladly, but its effects must be taken into consideration in preparing for an operation such as the rescue mission.

Many Americans admire Israel's ability to conduct swift and effective military operations relying on small able forces and surprise; however, if the price for such a capability were the routine Israeli practice of censoring all news broadcasts and publications for items considered adverse to national security, the same Americans would reject it out of hand. In the case of the rescue mission, secrecy was preserved at the cost of less than adequate rehearsal. At least partially as a consequence, the disorder and confusion at Desert One were considerable and may have contributed to the collision, fire and deaths.

How does a civilian president assure himself that the advice he is receiving from his military leaders is based on the best possible professional judgment and experience? No military leader wants to be put in the position of telling the president that his forces are incapable of carrying out a mission that is important to the national interest, and every president should be aware that the "can do" spirit so characteristic of the military is a mixed blessing. It may get the most difficult and dangerous tasks done, but it may also involve an almost unconscious tendency to understate the risks once a commitment is accepted. Presumably it was his disastrous experience at the Bay of Pigs that led President Kennedy to insist on civilian control of every detail during the Cuban missile crisis.

In the case of the hostage rescue mission, there would have been great merit to an independent review of the plan by a small group of professionals in advance of the operation. An independent check by several respected military or civilian experts who had personal experience with special operations but who were not personally committed to the existing plan could have revealed weaknesses which, unfortunately, only became evident during the mission itself.

The decision to undertake the rescue mission was a choice that touched directly on U.S. national values and raised questions of profound, even philosophical, importance. How does a nation or its leadership reconcile the contradictions between the protection of innocent human lives and the preservation of national honor? To what extent should a great nation be prepared to accept short-term humiliation in the interest of long-term strategic objectives that are themselves uncertain? At what point does such humiliation itself begin to produce strategic consequences? It is questions such as these—honor vs. life —that endow great events with qualities of heroic or tragic proportions, and it is the lessons to be derived from such stark choices that draw the historian, the policy maker and the scholar back again and again.

To lead is to choose. When the political stalemate of the hostage crisis became intolerable, President Carter approved a rescue mission. He gave the military planners everything they asked for; he made every effort to inform himself about the plan but resisted meddling in the operational details; and when the mission failed he accepted full responsibility without excuses or scapegoating.

The rescue mission was a failure, but it was a failure of military execution, not of political judgment or command.

XIV

THE FIRST YEAR ENDS

O n Sunday morning, two days after the failure of the rescue mission, Brzezinski called me into his office with General William Odom, his military assistant. Bill Odom had been a personal friend of Brzezinski's for many years, and he had served over the previous six months as the principal liaison between the White House and the Defense Department for the operational planning and execution of the rescue mission.

Brzezinski wasted no time. His face was lined with the strain of the previous weeks, but the only outward change in his behavior was the characteristic narrowing of his eyes that always signaled that he was angry or under great pressure. He said that a full-scale investigation had been initiated at the Department of Defense to determine the causes of the mission failure, but he was not inclined to fret over spilt milk. Instead, he said, he had obtained the president's permission to begin immediate planning for another rescue mission.[1]

"We must go back in," he declared, and he asked Odom and me to prepare a paper outlining alternative plans for a new mission that would be less complex and less dependent on high technology than the previous operation. In retrospect, I realize that this announcement should not have startled me as much as it did.

By this time I had known and worked closely with Brzezinski for several years, and I knew as well as anyone that his dominant personality trait was a dogged refusal to submit—even to the most daunting odds. He was always on the attack. Occasionally he lost, but he never regarded defeat as anything more than a temporary setback, apparently in the conviction that, in time, his intense energy and the audacity of his strategies would wear down even the most determined opponent.

In this sense, perhaps more than any other, Brzezinski was the very antithesis of Cyrus Vance. Vance seemed to arrive in office with a fixed store of intellectual and physical energy that he expended over time in the struggles, triumphs and defeats of a nearly impossible job. One could almost see him decline, like a balloon, as his resources were exhausted. Brzezinski, on the other hand, seemed to acquire new energy from each battle, as if the very act of combat pumped new adrenaline into his veins. He was a formidable and infuriating opponent who refused to quit under any circumstances and whose response to defeat was to launch a counterattack at his adversary's most vulnerable point.

This restless energy and persistent pursuit of fresh approaches made Brzezinski a natural alter ego to Jimmy Carter's activism. Although the two men were psychologically very different and never really became personally close, they complemented each other in very special ways. Carter was dissatisfied with things as they were and was determined to use his presidency to generate change. Brzezinski sparked new ideas at a dazzling rate and refused to be constrained by the status quo in devising his strategies. Although Carter probably rejected more of Brzezinski's ideas than he accepted, he obviously valued the irreverent inventiveness that Brzezinski brought to any subject.

Brzezinski's approach to the jousting and jostling of the policy arena was characteristic of his response to any contest or challenge. He had a passion for games of all kinds, and he always played to win, whatever the stakes. Each summer Brzezinski and his wife, Muska, hosted a picnic for members and families of the NSC staff at their comfortable, rambling home in the wooded Virginia suburbs of Washington. Activities featured tennis, volleyball, soccer and other sports, with Brzezinski as a vigorous participant. For the soccer game, Brzezinski wore heavy combat boots. It did not improve his speed, but when he charged the ball on the small playing field, others soon learned to get out of the way.

His first love, however, was chess. He played at every available opportunity, whiling away long hours of air travel in the spacious presidential aircraft with endless games of chess. He deliberately sought the toughest competitor he could find, then approached each encounter as a personal test, throwing himself into it with all the energy and guile at his command. Brzezinski's favorite photograph from his White House years was a snapshot of himself sitting in deep concentration across a chess set from Israeli Prime Minister Menachem Begin during the Camp David negotiations.

Begin, like Brzezinski, was Polish-born, and the similarities between the two men were striking in many respects. Both of them reveled in the complex rough-and-tumble of high-stakes policy; both regarded themselves as masters of strategy and maneuver, though Begin had a substantial edge in practical political experience; both men were fascinated by the instruments of military force; and they shared a streak of ruthlessness and dogged persistence in the pursuit of their objectives. Both men were supremely confident of their mental and verbal skills in any confrontation, and they seemed deliberately to seek opportunities to display their talents at the expense of an adversary. Unforgiving in defeat and relentless in victory, they cultivated an aura of menace and unpredictability designed to intimidate those less bold than themselves.

At the same time, Brzezinski, no less than Begin, was a devoted family man who was anything but domineering in his personal relationships. Despite the "bad guy" image he nurtured so carefully in public, in a social situation he seemed almost shy. An intensely private man, Brzezinski was unfailingly generous and considerate of friends and colleagues. He placed heavy demands on his subordinates and was capable of acid criticism, but he consistently demonstrated respect and concern for the members of his staff. In his memoirs, he carefully identified and gave credit to each individual who worked with him.

Brzezinski shared with Begin a fundamental respect for history, a deep capacity for personal loyalty, and a streak of romanticism and an exaggerated individualism that almost seem to be Polish national characteristics. Although both of these men appreciated a good press, the lure of popularity was never as strong as the taste for victory. Menachem Begin had risen against all odds to become the undisputed leader of Israel; Zbigniew Brzezinski had vaulted to one of the most powerful positions in the world of international politics. A chess game between these two was no routine event.

Brzezinski recounts his match with Prime Minister Begin in some detail in his memoirs.[2] Setting up the board, Begin told Brzezinski that his last game of chess, thirty-eight years earlier, had been interrupted when the NKVD came to arrest him. As Brzezinski learned to his chagrin, Begin was not as rusty or out of practice as he tried to suggest, but Brzezinski always told the story with relish and with undisguised admiration for an adversary who understood the psychological value of disarming an opponent and who was not above a bit of deviousness to improve his chances.

Brzezinski, perhaps overconfident, made a critical error and lost the game to Begin. He immediately demanded a rematch, and playing with less abandon, won handily. Similarly, I should have known that Brzezinski would not be prepared to accept the failure of the rescue mission as final. He would want a second round.

In response to Brzezinski's request to develop alternative proposals for a second rescue mission, I drafted a memorandum that started from the premise that a second attempt had to succeed or it would only make the situation worse. However, the difficulties of a second effort were immensely complicated by an absence of reliable information about the location of the hostages.[3] That problem was compounded by the consternation of regional governments friendly to the United States that had been embarrassed by charges of complicity in the first operation and would therefore be unlikely to lend support to a second, as well as by the heightened security measures on the part of the captors, who would not likely be caught napping. For these reasons I regarded the prospects of a second rescue attempt as extremely dim.[4] I appreciated the need to develop contingency plans for a military rescue of the hostages *in extremis,* but the nature of the situation had changed dramatically because of the failure of the raid, and there seemed to be no reasonable chance of conducting another rescue attempt for quite a long time.

I knew this was not the answer Brzezinski was looking for. Not surprisingly, I received no response to this memo and Brzezinski never raised the issue with me again.

Waiting for the Ayatollah

Very little happened over the summer months of 1980. The failure of the rescue mission had cooled the political climate. The voices calling so insistently for the government to "do something" fell silent. Secretary Vance resigned in disagreement over the rescue mission and was replaced by Senator Edmund Muskie of Maine, who needed time to master the intricacies of his new post. The allies proceeded to enact enabling legislation to tighten economic and diplomatic sanctions against Iran, but no one expected that to produce any dramatic new effects on the Iranian economy or on the hostage situation.[5]

President Carter returned to active campaigning for the first time in many months, and there was a widespread, if tacit, recognition that nothing further could be done for the moment. The tragedy of the rescue attempt had at least created a breathing space to permit Iranian internal politics more time to grope toward a solution.

The new Iranian Majles was finally inaugurated on May 28, more than three months late, and the overwhelming dominance of the religious parties in the parliament dashed whatever hopes Bani-Sadr may have retained to assert non-clerical leadership over the revolutionary government. Close observers quickly concluded that Bani-Sadr was finished, although he continued to maneuver desperately. Similarly, Foreign Minister Ghotbzadeh, together with Bourguet and Villalón, never ceased plotting to find a way out of the political morass in Iran, but none of their activities, or those of other intermediaries, had any significant effect.

Bani-Sadr convened an international conference in early June to criticize U.S. intervention in Iran. Over the objections of his government, former Attorney General Ramsey Clark insisted on leading a delegation of ten Americans to this conference. Ironically, Clark, who had been rejected by the Iranians in November as an emissary of the president, was now welcomed in Tehran for defying the president. In the end, nothing came of it.

Economic conditions in Iran reflected the disorganization, purges, ideological battles and displacement of competent leadership that had accompanied the revolution. Oil exports were running below one million barrels per day, less than half the level required to sustain operating revenues of the government. Inflation was rampant, unemployment was running near 40 percent, investment in manufacturing had fallen to near zero, industrial production was off

50–70 percent, and the gross national product was down at least 20 percent from pre-revolutionary levels. The sanctions imposed by the United States and other nations were not the cause of these conditions, but the sanctions immensely complicated the task of Iran's new and inexperienced managers who were attempting to cope with multiple crises simultaneously.

At the same time, internal dissension was on the increase. Khomeini launched the Iranian equivalent of a cultural revolution during the summer, denouncing government use of letterhead from the former regime as "satanic" and insisting that women employees in government offices wear the *chador*. Women responded by staging demonstrations, and those in Western-style clothing were denounced on the street as prostitutes. Demonstrations were also conducted by bazaar merchants in protest against the interference by young Islamic fanatics in their business. Three fourths of the nation's doctors went on strike in early July after the execution of a doctor by a self-appointed Islamic court. The *mojahedin-e khalq,* the urban guerrilla organization that fought against the shah but opposed clerical rule, found itself under direct attack from the *hezbollahi* ("partisans of God"), who broke up demonstrations and attacked mojahedin headquarters.

Simultaneously, the border tension with Iraq was heating up, the Kurds were once again in full revolt, tribal opposition was growing throughout the country, and sabotage in the oil fields became almost a daily occurrence. Top military commanders were shuffled and reshuffled (the top ranks of the air force were purged on the grounds that they had been accomplices to the U.S. rescue attempt), and there were occasional defections of trained military personnel. The regime seemed to be on the verge of political, economic and military collapse.

Various exile groups, sensing the vulnerability of the revolutionary regime, began plotting with Iraq and calling for the military to revolt. Unsuccessful military coup attempts were reported in late June and early July, suggesting that these calls were being heeded in at least some quarters. The sense of siege and paranoia in Tehran became intense.

Tehran responded by some counterterror of its own. In Paris, a band of five men working for the Islamic Republican Party attempted to assassinate the former prime minister, Shapour Bakhtiar, the most visible representative of the anti-Khomeini exile forces. On July 22 in Washington, D.C., Ali Akbar Tabatabai, a prominent anti-Khomeini organizer, was shot to death at his home by a U.S. Black Muslim with close ties to Iran. The assassin quickly escaped out of the country, probably to Iran.

Anti-clerical politicians in Iran came under public attack. Admiral Ahmed Madani, the former head of the navy, minister of defense, and candidate for president, was hounded into resigning from his seat in the new parliament. Madani went into hiding to save his life and eventually fled to Europe. At the end of the fasting month of Ramadan, Khomeini's announcement that "we cannot tolerate those people who have been educated in Europe," sounded an ominous warning to the Paris-educated Bani-Sadr and seemed to signal open season on anyone who did not espouse Khomeini's belief in the supremacy of theocratic rule.

Throughout the long, empty months after the failure of the rescue mission, the Department of State persevered in a dogged effort to find new lines of communication into Tehran. Harold Saunders and Henry Precht again visited a series of European capitals, meeting secretly with Bourguet and Villalón and touching base with several key European leaders and private citizens about possible diplomatic initiatives. In anticipation of the installation of a new cabinet in Iran, letters were prepared from U.S. members of Congress to their Iranian counterparts and from Secretary of State Muskie to the new Iranian prime minister. Most important, the departments of State and Treasury began drafting the technical and legal documents that would be required if and when serious negotiations began.

On July 11 one of the hostages, Richard Queen, was suddenly released. Washington had heard rumors that one of the hostages was sick, but the Iranian decision came as a total surprise. It was later learned that Queen was suffering from multiple sclerosis. The Iranian doctors knew that he was seriously ill and that they could not treat him. Presumably fearing that he might die and that his death would risk U.S. military retaliation, Khomeini ordered him released immediately.

Two weeks later, on July 27, the former shah of Iran died in Cairo of complications associated with cancer. The shah's death was greeted in Iran with a laconic radio announcement that "the bloodsucker of the century has died," and with reports of scattered celebrations. Otherwise, Tehran treated the report as a one-day story that scarcely seemed to be heard above the din of dissension and contending factions.

Throughout the entire month of August, President Bani-Sadr was locked in an intense and losing battle with the Islamic Republican Party over the selection of a prime minister and a cabinet. Bani-Sadr's choices were brushed aside, and he was forced repeatedly to yield to the demands of the clerical forces that dominated politics in the Iranian capital.

On September 10, 1980, the Iranian Majles formally approved the fourteen-man cabinet of Prime Minister Mohammad-Ali Rajai. For the first time since the revolution, Iran had an elected government. Although more than four months late, the institutions that Khomeini had proclaimed necessary for settlement of the hostage crisis were finally in place.

Iran Decides to Move

On the same day that the Majles voted in Tehran, Secretary of State Muskie and Deputy Secretary Warren Christopher requested an urgent meeting with the president. They arrived at the White House just before ten o'clock in the morning and joined President Carter and Zbigniew Brzezinski in the Oval Office.

Warren Christopher informed the president that on the previous day there had been a meeting of Sadegh Tabatabai (a relative of Khomeini's by marriage and one of the ayatollah's inner circle), Ahmed Khomeini (the ayatollah's son) and Hashemi Rafsanjani (the hard-line president of the Majles) to discuss the hostage crisis. Tabatabai had subsequently contacted German Ambassador Gerhard Ritzel in Tehran and informed him that Iran was prepared to release the hostages on the following basis:

1. the unfreezing of Iranian assets and their transfer out of the United States;
2. a binding commitment of no U.S. military or political intervention in Iranian affairs; and
3. that the assets of the former shah and his family be returned to Iran or at least that the United States commit itself to that objective through court action.

After more than ten months of delays and fruitless efforts, the Iranians now said they were in a hurry. Tabatabai planned to arrive in Germany on Sunday (it was now Wednesday) and was prepared to meet with U.S. representatives to discuss the issue on the basis of the three conditions. According to Tabatabai, there were fears that the ayatollah would die at any time, and he said Iran was prepared to release the hostages within two days after agreement on the substance of the procedure. Surprisingly, Tabatabai insisted that the issue be resolved before the first anniversary of the hostage taking, i.e., November 4, 1980, the date of the U.S. presidential election.

This was the first approach to the U.S. government from anyone within Khomeini's inner circle since the beginning of the crisis. Consequently, on the U.S. side, there was genuine concern that the approach might be a false alarm. On the basis of past experience, there was reason to be skeptical that this approach in fact represented Khomeini's own thinking, particularly since the Iranian demands made no mention of an apology. Moreover, President Carter was aware that the unfreezing of the Iranian assets, many of which were subject to attachment in the U.S. courts, would not be a simple matter, and he was reluctant to initiate legal action against the shah's family or to freeze whatever assets the shah might have had in the United States.

Nevertheless, the three points of the Iranian message provided a satisfactory basis for discussion, and the president believed that the Iranians were becoming increasingly aware that the continued holding of the hostages was working to their disadvantage. He directed Warren Christopher to meet with Tabatabai in Germany, and a message was sent to the Iranians through the German embassy that evening indicating that a small delegation would be prepared to meet Tabatabai in Germany and discuss each of the three points in a "positive and constructive manner."

The next few days were a blur of activity. On Thursday morning a small group assembled in the private conference room behind Warren Christopher's office on the seventh floor of the State Department. The participants were:

Robert Carswell, deputy secretary of the Treasury; Lloyd Cutler, counsel to the president; Harold Saunders, assistant secretary of state for Near East and South Asian affairs; Roberts Owen, legal adviser of the Department of State; Arnold Raphel, special assistant to Secretary Muskie and a Foreign Service officer with experience in Iran; and myself. This "core group," under Christopher's direction, and occasionally augmented by Attorney General Benjamin Civiletti and a handful of other officials, was to serve as the nerve center of the government for the long negotiation that was about to begin.

From the outset, there were two sets of questions that had to be addressed. The first related to technical issues of finance and law. The problem of unraveling the maze of conflicting claims surrounding the frozen assets presented a unique test of the superb array of legal talent assembled at that small table, and those of us without specialized training frequently felt that we were listening in on a foreign language.[6] The second set of issues concerned judgments about Iranian intentions and an effective negotiating strategy. In those first days, the critical issue was whether or not this message from Iran was an authoritative statement of their position or whether, as had so often occurred in the past, it represented the views of a single faction that lacked the support of Khomeini.

Some of those concerns were soon laid to rest. In a speech to a group of Iranian pilgrims on September 12, Khomeini delivered an unusually long, rambling speech about Islam, international affairs and the meaning of the revolution, in the form of a general exhortation to the Iranian people. At the very end of this speech, in a passage that had obviously been spliced onto the body of the text, Khomeini abruptly turned to the question of the hostage taking and announced: "On the return of the deposed shah's wealth and the cancellation of all the U.S. claims against Iran, a guarantee of no U.S. military and political interventions in Iran and the freeing of all our investments, the hostages will be set free."

Although the text of the speech was read over the radio by an announcer rather than by Khomeini himself, the rhetoric of the speech was unmistakably that of the ayatollah, not a speech written by his "office." The points inserted in Khomeini's speech were very similar to those delivered to Washington two days earlier through the German embassy, although the speech added a fourth condition—the cancellation of all U.S. claims against Iran. There was no longer reason to doubt that this was a serious proposal, delivered with Khomeini's knowledge and acquiescence.

Act I: September–October 1980

Warren Christopher met secretly in Bonn with Iranian Minister of State Sadegh Tabatabai on September 16 and 18, in the presence of German Foreign Minister Hans-Dietrich Genscher. Tabatabai noted that the situation had progressed substantially even in the first few days of initial contact. After receiving the U.S. response on the eleventh, the four Iranian conditions had been formulated and incorporated into Khomeini's speech. These had now, he noted, become the official guidelines in Iran and would serve as the context for the decisions of the Majles. The conditions, he commented, would have been much stiffer if left to the Majles on its own.

Further, a decision had been taken that the hostages would not be placed on trial, and the composition of a parliamentary commission to develop recommendations for the Majles had been decided. Tabatabai stressed that only three or four people in Iran were aware that these talks were being conducted and it was essential that absolute secrecy be maintained. He made it clear that Foreign Minister Genscher's presence was desired by Iran as a witness and as a "guarantor" of whatever agreements might be reached.

In response, Christopher conveyed President Carter's satisfaction at the initiation of direct talks. He outlined a U.S. response to the Iranian requests that was carefully phrased to emphasize the positive elements of the U.S. position while hopefully also educating Tabatabai about some of the technical difficulties that might be expected in a negotiated settlement.

Christopher described for Tabatabai the various types and locations of Iranian assets, noting that some (e.g., the gold and letters of credit on deposit with the Federal Reserve Bank) would be available immediately upon release of the hostages, while other assets (e.g., deposits in foreign branches of U.S. banks) could be expected to be released relatively promptly. Together, these two categories comprised some $5.5 billion. It was proposed that these funds be placed in escrow with a third party (possibly the German Bundesbank) until certification was received that the hostages had been released. A third category was the assets on deposit in banks in the United States. All of these deposits had been placed under court attachment by Americans who had claims against Iran. This amount, estimated at $2-plus billion could not be freed immediately.

The Military Issue

One troublesome problem in preparing for this initial encounter was the issue of military spare parts. The September 10 message from Tabatabai had referred in passing to military equipment as a possible trade-off for the Iranian assets that would remain under attachment in the U.S. courts, so the U.S. side was well advised to expect the military issue to play a major role in the negotiations. In anticipation, I had prepared for Christopher's use an inventory of Iranian military equipment being held in the United States and an accounting of the trust fund that the shah's government had maintained with the Department of Defense.

The potential supply of large quantities of military equipment to the new revolutionary regime in Tehran was not a prospect regarded with relish by anyone in the administration. A border conflict with Iraq seemed to be brewing, and a sudden influx of U.S. arms would be interpreted as a signal of U.S.

involvement in favor of Iran. The oil-rich Arab states perched nervously across the Gulf from the unpredictable and hostile regime in Iran could be expected to greet such a development with dismay. For President Carter, who had excoriated the regime in Tehran as "terrorists" and who had associated himself with a policy dedicated to the reduction of arms transfers, the exchange of large quantities of military equipment for the hostages would be personally distasteful and embarrassing.

I prepared a list that divided the Iranian equipment and spares into three categories: (1) items that were not subject to security classification and that were not lethal in themselves; (2) items that were technologically sensitive and/or of high lethality; and (3) a "gray area" between the two extremes. The hope was that negotiations could be restricted only to the first. That hope was not entirely unrealistic, since the Iranians had lost most of their records in the course of the revolution and could not be certain what equipment had been ordered by the shah or was in the United States. Part of the negotiating strategy was to keep the Iranian side as unenlightened as possible on this issue.

When Tabatabai alluded to the question of military spare parts, Christopher acknowledged that approximately $50 million worth of military spares (the value of the "category I" items) that Iran had ordered and paid for were in storage in the United States. Christopher said that the inclusion of military equipment would complicate any agreement, but this matériel could be made available to Iran once all other aspects of the dispute were resolved. Tabatabai did not press.

On the issue of the shah's assets, Christopher informed Tabatabai that it was the considered judgment of the U.S. Treasury that the value of any assets owned by the shah in the United States was much less than the Iranians apparently believed—indeed, probably less than the interest earned on the funds frozen by the United States. Consequently, he told Tabatabai, Iran should not anticipate locating and retrieving large quantities of money or property belonging to the shah. The magnitude of the shah's personal wealth was not known to the U.S. government, but almost certainly, little of it was held in the United States in a form that could be identified or retrieved through the courts.

Other elements of the Iranian position were discussed at some length, with Christopher spelling out in each instance the degree to which the United States would be able—or unable—to respond. Valuable support was provided by Genscher, who, for example, assured the Iranian envoy that the U.S. position on the shah's wealth was reasonable and went further than would have been possible under German law.

Christopher sought clarification of the Iranian demand for cancellation of all U.S. claims against Iran. Tabatabai said this was specifically intended to prevent claims from the hostages or their relatives against Iran, claims arising from the U.S. suit against Iran in the World Court or other such possibilities. Christopher noted that this would be a difficult emotional issue, and he could make no commitment until he had had the opportunity to discuss it with President Carter.

In general, Tabatabai listened carefully to Christopher without raising serious objections. After the second meeting he informed Christopher that he intended to return to Iran on September 22 to meet with Khomeini and others. Following that meeting, a decision would be made about how to proceed. A further meeting was anticipated near the end of the month. Both Genscher and Christopher indicated satisfaction with this schedule.

Iraq Invades

Ironically, on the very day Tabatabai was scheduled to return to Iran from Germany, the conflict that had been simmering along the border between Iran and Iraq erupted into full-scale hostilities. Iraqi bombers launched surprise attacks against military targets in Iran, and Iraqi ground forces poured across the border into the oil-rich province of Khuzestan. With normal air traffic in and out of Iran suspended, Tabatabai remained in Germany, maintaining occasional telephone contact with Tehran.

Despite the war, the Majles debated the hostage issue in late September and established a seven-man commission empowered to define the precise terms of Iran's demands of the United States. However, the commission was prohibited from having any direct contact with U.S. officials or deviating from the four conditions formulated by Khomeini. Despite this restrictive mandate, produced only after a raucous public session where members came close to blows, Tabatabai (who remained in Düsseldorf into early October) continued to assure his German hosts that the scenario was proceeding on track.

This soothing message was reiterated on October 10 after Tabatabai had returned to Iran and met with the top leaders. Although there was evidence that the regime in Tehran was making an effort to work its way out of the crisis, I commented to Brzezinski that it was becoming doubtful that they could hold to their original timetable of release before November 4.

At the same time, it became evident that the Iranian leaders were becoming increasingly concerned about the war with Iraq and the lack of military resupply or availability of spare parts. The Iranians sent a separate message on October 10 via the Germans requesting an inventory from the United States of all goods that Iran had ordered from the United States during the time of the shah but that had not yet been delivered. By definition, such a listing would include military equipment, since there was relatively little other material that had been held in storage in the United States, with the exception of a large quantity of oil and gas equipment that had been trapped when the embargo was imposed. Again it appeared that the Iranian side expected to insist on a military supply relationship as a necessary component of any final settlement.

The "core group" assembled on October 11 to consider the U.S. response to this request. The objective was to construct a package of military equipment that would be attractive to Tehran while avoiding items that were very sensitive (such as electronic counter measures devices) or highly lethal (such as missiles, bombs and torpedoes). After a brief discussion the issue was narrowed to the question of whether or not to include approximately $100 million worth of spare parts for various types of aircraft in the Iranian inventory.

This equipment, which was stored in military warehouses throughout the United States, comprised almost a random selection of items that happened to be in the pipeline at the time of the revolution. Many of the items would be of little value to the Iranian air force, but others could potentially be quite important. After nearly two hours of discussion, a draft message was prepared for President Carter's approval offering a military package of about $150 million (including the aircraft spares) that would be made available upon release of the hostages.

I hurried back from the meeting to the White House, where I was scheduled to meet my sister for lunch. It was a peculiar meal. While we tried to carry on a family conversation, I was repeatedly interrupted by phone calls and even one quick trip to the White House gate to receive the sealed envelope with the draft message. Finally we had to give up, and after seeing her out, I briefed Brzezinski on the morning's discussions and then transmitted the message with maximum security to Camp David. The president approved the draft, and it was sent out that evening.

The Iranians never acknowledged its receipt. President Carter alluded publicly to the military-supply issue during the presidential candidates' debate on October 28, when he said "If the hostages are released safely . . . we would make delivery on those items which Iran owns." Tehran, however, remained silent. The initial Iraqi thrust across the border had, by that time, run out of steam and the need for military resupply may have become less critical. It was also evident that a debate was under way in Iran about the desirability of re-establishing a military relationship with the "Great Satan." Thus, Rafsanjani, president of the Majles, told French correspondent Eric Rouleau on October 23 that "Iranian opinion and the Iranian Majles are so hostile to the United States . . . that there is a possibility that we would only ask for the money we paid for the weapons to be refunded."[7]

Nevertheless, the conjunction of the Iran-Iraq war and Tehran's efforts to find a way out of the hostage crisis sparked a wave of press speculation that a swap of military equipment for the hostages was imminent. For example, a television station in Chicago reported on October 15 that five U.S. Navy cargo planes loaded with aircraft spare parts were due to arrive in Iran within forty-eight hours. Press spokesmen at the White House and State Department were required to issue almost daily denials of such reports—often filled with convincing details—that cropped up in the media from Seattle to Miami.

The Chicago TV report referred to "military reserve pilots" that it claimed had been alerted to assist in the (nonexistent) airlift to Iran. Although no significance was attached to this curious remark at the time, in 1983 it was revealed that the Reagan campaign had mobilized a network of retired officers to watch U.S. military installations, apparently believing that President Carter would launch some form of military action against Iran in the final days of the campaign. This operation may have been the source of some of the numerous media reports that many in the White House regarded at the time as a disinformation campaign.[8]

Enter the Algerians

In mid-October, Iranian Prime Minister Mohammad-Ali Rajai paid a visit to the United Nations in New York to present Iran's case against Iraq as a result of the September invasion. His reception at the UN was exceptionally cool. Rajai, who had been a provincial schoolteacher and who was generally regarded as a rather simple man with blind faith in Islam, Khomeini and the revolution, was astonished to discover that his interlocutors at the United Nations were, almost without exception, much more interested in the hostage crisis than in Iran's plight in its war with Iraq. The tightly controlled press and radio in Iran routinely suggested that most of the world sympathized with Iran's actions in the hostage taking, and this visit (Rajai's first outside Iran) may have been his first acquaintance with the considerable hostility this act had aroused throughout the world.

On October 18, Rajai met in New York with several Algerian officials who argued persuasively that termination of the hostage crisis would be in the best interests of the revolution and Iran's national security. The Algerians had been contacted by the United States in advance of this conversation, and it represented one of the earliest instances of direct Algerian involvement in a quasi-intermediary role.[9] Rajai stopped in Algiers on his return trip to Tehran, and there were indications that the Algerians took advantage of this second opportunity to discuss the hostage issue with the Iranian prime minister.

When Rajai returned to Tehran on October 22, he took an uncharacteristically conciliatory line. In answer to questions, he said he was sure the United States was prepared to respond to conditions posed by Khomeini. "The hostages are not really a problem for us," he added. "We are in the process of resolving [the crisis]. The nature of the hostage taking was important for us. We got the results long ago." Significantly, he explicitly excluded military equipment from any role in a settlement. "We do not link the release of the hostages with spare parts," he said. The Algerians had evidently made quite an impression.[10]

In the meantime, however, the Majles delayed taking up the report of the special commission on the hostage issue. First, the Iranian legislature postponed the report, then began to debate it in open session, and finally moved into closed session to continue the debate. On October 30 a key vote was prevented by a number of die-hard members who disapproved the terms offered by the commission. By their failure to appear in the Majles, they succeeded in preventing a quorum, thus thwarting the majority that favored a resolution.

The Iranian inability to come to terms with the issue was given special poignancy by the fact that the U.S. election campaign was coming to an end. In the last week before the presidential election on November 4, the media speculation about a last-minute deal that could swing the election became almost hysterical.

On Saturday morning, November 1, I received a telephone call at home from Martin Agronsky, a Washington journalist who hosted a weekly television news show. While taping the program the night before, columnist George F. Will, who made no secret of his support for Ronald Reagan, reported that he had two independent reports from sources in Europe and the United States that U.S. military aircraft loaded with spare parts were on their way to Iran. Will said that a deal had been struck with the Iranians to swap the hostages for military equipment and that the release was going to take place on Saturday.

Agronsky, who had great respect for George Will as a journalist, was in a quandary. He was scheduled to fly to Bermuda in a few hours, but if Will was correct, they would have to retape the show. I told him I also respected Will, but that in this case he was dead wrong. Much as we would like to see the hostages out, there was no swap in progress. I advised him to go to Bermuda.

On the same day, columnists Rowland Evans and Robert Novak distributed a special "bonus" column to their subscribers, citing "multiple U.S. and foreign sources," to the effect that a "deal exchanging American hostages for military equipment" had been completed two weeks earlier. They also asserted that critical parts for Phoenix air-to-air missiles had recently been moved from storage in preparation for delivery to Iran. The similarity between the Evans and Novak column and George Will's report was striking, as was the timing of this news—just three days prior to the election. Not surprisingly, when Secretary Muskie met with the press that morning, the questioning was dominated by the military-supply issue.

Iran Acts, but Too Late

The news that the Majles had finally taken action came, typically, in a telephone call just before four o'clock on Sunday morning, November 2. I dressed hastily and drove through the dark streets to the State Department, where a baker's dozen of officials were gathering in Warren Christopher's spacious office.

Christopher, who was impeccably turned out in a trim blazer and crisply creased slacks, made an interesting contrast to the groggy crew sprawled around the room, most of whom were unshaven and apparently wearing whatever was closest to hand when they were rousted from their beds. By the time I arrived, Christopher had been in touch with the president to inform him of the resolution just passed by the Majles, and he had also briefed Edwin Meese, who was with the Reagan campaign in Ohio.

President Carter was in Chicago on a campaign trip, and he immediately decided to return to Washington to confer with his foreign policy advisers. After the elections, some White House wags said Carter's fatal mistake was to get the White House press corps out of bed in the middle of the night, fly them to Washington and then make them sit all day waiting for a story, just before the election. It was certainly true that the press coverage was less than enthusiastic.

Waiting for the president, we were treated to a spectacular sunrise. The seventh floor of the State Department has one of the most glorious views in Washington. The first rays of the sun reflected off the tall apartment buildings on the crest of the Arlington ridge, transforming windows and balconies into a sparkling light display. The Capitol dome, the Washington Monument and the Lincoln Memorial were each illuminated in turn. Anyone involved in the Iranian crisis had to develop a special affection for Washington at sunrise, but on this occasion the show was enough to silence even the hardiest veteran.

I arrived at the White House as the presidential helicopter settled onto the South Lawn at precisely eight o'clock. President Carter came down the steps of the plane with scarcely a glance. Brzezinski was waiting for him at the foot of the ramp and handed him the latest Iranian text. Carter took it without a word and began reading as he walked toward the Cabinet Room, where his advisers were assembled.

By the time he sat down at the long oval table, he had read through the jumbled text. "There are several things in the list of conditions that we cannot do," he began. "The best we can do for the next few days," he said, "is to indicate our willingness to pursue negotiations" with the new executive committee appointed by the Iranians. He asked for comments about the various points raised in the resolution and how he should respond, and a long discussion ensued.

After the meeting had been going on for about an hour, Rosalynn Carter came into the room and sat quietly near the door. She looked drawn and tired. She had been campaigning almost without a break for months on end, and the strain showed. At one point President Carter left the discussion and went over to the window with his wife, where they stood talking softly and holding hands. After a few minutes they kissed and she stepped out the French door into the sunlight of the Rose Garden. Shortly thereafter the muffled sound of a helicopter could be heard lifting off the South Lawn, taking her back to her endless round of campaign appearances.

Everyone in the room was intensely aware that a national election was only two days away, and several of the president's advisers pressed him to take some immediate action in response to the Iranian resolution. Lloyd Cutler suggested that the president could announce that he was freezing the shah's assets. Carter replied that any legal steps on the U.S. side should be effective only on release of the hostages, not before. The president asked Warren Christopher, Lloyd

Cutler and Jody Powell to prepare a brief statement leaving the door open to negotiations.

Warren Christopher observed wryly that the president was faced with a "devil's choice": if he spelled out U.S. objections to the Iranian resolution, he risked slamming the door on further negotiations; if he limited himself to the positive elements of the offer, he would be criticized for playing politics. Carter said he wanted to reassure the American people that any response to Iran would be strictly in accordance with U.S. law and the principles he had outlined from the start. The Iranians already knew what was possible for us and what was not. He said he had drafted a contingency statement some days before at Camp David when it had become apparent that Iran might act at the very last minute. Christopher could draw on that in preparing a response.

At two o'clock that afternoon, Warren Christopher presented three drafts to the president. The first was a fairly lengthy statement outlining the U.S. position on the Majles conditions, for possible use in a public announcement. The second was a much briefer statement that avoided specifics. The third was a draft message to be sent to the Iranians through the German embassy.

President Carter said that he found the dual-track approach attractive, i.e., keeping his public statement brief and essentially positive while informing the Iranians privately of the limits on U.S. actions. That avoided the risk of provoking an instant rejection from Iran while keeping U.S. options open for serious private negotiations. He noted that the media were interpreting the Iranian action as a transparent attempt to interfere in U.S. domestic politics. He wanted a clear statement that the Iranians would get no better deal before the election than after and that we rejected any such interference.

Most of the president's advisers then withdrew to the vice president's office to finish drafting the statement. Although the statement was written primarily by Warren Christopher, various members of the campaign staff drifted in and out of the office during the afternoon. They were relaxed and upbeat. There was a universal feeling that this major break on the hostage issue would work to Carter's benefit. Ham Jordan said to me, "We were going to win the election anyway [i.e., without the Iranian offer], but we'll take it." The polls at that time without exception showed the election as "too close to call," but Jordan, Powell and others had been through close elections with Carter in the past and they were confident he would pull it off in the end.

Two days later, the optimism of that sunny Sunday afternoon turned hollow. Most observers would later agree that this final attempt by Iran to manipulate U.S. domestic politics served only to remind the American public of the long year of anger, frustration and policy failures. Iran, like a rock around the president's neck, helped pull him down.

XV

ENDGAME

The Iranian leaders had originally proposed to terminate the hostage crisis by November 4, 1980, for reasons known only to themselves. Some observers believed that they intended to preserve Jimmy Carter in office, in the belief that he was less dangerous than Ronald Reagan. Others suspected that Iran planned to set Carter up so they could yank the rug from under him at the last moment and destroy him. In retrospect, it is likely that both of these diametrical conspiracy theories were wrong.

Events demonstrated convincingly that the revolutionary regime in Tehran was capable of making painful and controversial decisions only under pressure of an absolute deadline. Otherwise, feuding internal factions would prevent any consensus. The U.S. elections provided a convenient target date. The Iranian leaders could reasonably argue that whatever the outcome, Iran was likely to get a better deal before the elections than after.

The Iranian revolutionaries never had more than a rudimentary understanding of the U.S. political process. They seemed genuinely surprised, for example, to learn that Reagan would not take office the day after the election. However, they were shrewd bargainers; and they would probably calculate that any president, assured of four years in office, would be less likely to compromise than a president fighting for his political life. In that judgment, they may have been correct. The package that finally resolved the issue some ten weeks later was, in several key respects, less advantageous to Iran than the offer the United States had on the table in October.

There is every reason to believe that the top Iranian command made a concerted effort to end the crisis in September and October. Although they finally managed to hammer out an agreed position in the last two days before the election, the pressures of the war with Iraq and their own internal disagreements evidently delayed them weeks beyond their own timetable. Consequently, on November 4, both Washington and Tehran were forced to stop and re-examine their basic strategies.

In the meantime, one entirely new element had been injected into the situation in the persons of the Algerian mediators. When Algerian Ambassador Redha Malek delivered to Deputy Secretary Christopher the official text of the Majles declaration on November 3, he reported that Algeria had officially been charged by Iran with its implementation. Although Washington would have preferred dealing with Iran directly, this was regarded as a positive development and was accepted without hesitation. Ambassador Malek was immediately provided with a paper detailing the formal U.S. position as it had been developed over the previous eight months. From that point, all communications with Iran were conducted through the good offices of the government of Algeria.[1]

Act II: Mediation Begins

One week later Warren Christopher and a small group of officials from State and Treasury arrived in Algiers for the first formal discussion of the U.S. response to the Majles' action. On that first night, more than three hours were spent in discussions between Christopher and Algerian Foreign Minister Mohammad Benyahia and the other members of the Algerian team, which now consisted of Ambassador Malek, Algerian Ambassador Abdelkarim Gharaib who had returned from Tehran, and Seghir Mostafai, the governor of the Algerian Central Bank. The Algerians made clear from the outset that they viewed their role strictly as that of intermediary. However, they left open the possibility that they might adopt a more direct role if that seemed to be required at some point.

During that long first night, the Algerians established a method of operation that was to become routine over the months that followed. They played the role of devil's advocate with the U.S. position paper. Politely but firmly they identified every issue they thought might be challenged by the Iranians and then pressed Christopher and his team to defend and justify the U.S. position as fully and as clearly as possible. At times the Algerians suggested possible changes in wording, which the U.S. team considered and on occasion incorporated into the text of the paper.

These exchanges accomplished a dual purpose. First, they provided an external check—by individuals sensitive to the ideological requirements of the Iranian revolutionaries—on the drafting work that had been done in Washington. In some cases, a possible clash was averted by a simple change of words that had no legal effect; in others, substantive problems were brought to light and remedied. Second, the U.S. negotiators were required to present in great detail the constitutional, legal, financial and other considerations that had gone into the preparation of the U.S. response, thereby providing the Algerians with the necessary ammunition to make a persuasive presentation in Tehran.

The U.S. side had quite a different objective in these lengthy talks. Basically, the Christopher team hoped to persuade the Algerians of the merits of the U.S. arguments and to convince them that the offer was truly at the outer limits of what the United States could deliver in practice. In short, it was hoped that the Algerians could be transformed into knowledgeable and credible advocates for the U.S. position.

By the end of the first night of meetings, some minor problems were identified, but the main thrust of the U.S. position held up well under Algerian probing. Christopher made it clear to the Algerian team that the United States, while prepared to demonstrate flexibility on form and phraseology, had almost no room for maneuver on substance. After lengthy and exhaustive probing, the members of the Algerian team seemed to understand this very well. Nevertheless, they felt strongly that the mere delivery of the U.S. position to the Iranians would be a disaster. While appreciating the constraints on U.S. actions, they believed the paper would be regarded as too general in nature and as failing to address positively certain key points in the Iranian resolution, e.g., the cancellation of all claims against Iran.

To minimize this problem, the U.S. team provided the Algerians copies of proposed presidential draft orders to be presented with the formal position paper, thus lending the paper additional weight and legal substance. These documents would be augmented by oral explanations from the three-man Algerian team, based on their detailed conversations with Christopher and his team. The Algerians believed—correctly as it turned out—that such a presentation would engage the Iranians in the substance of the U.S. position while avoiding the likelihood of an immediate rejection.

The text of the U.S. note of November 11, 1980, read as follows:

The Government of the United States has received and has carefully reviewed the resolution adopted on Nov. 2, 1980, by the Islamic Consultative Asembly of Iran.

The United States accepts in principle the resolution as the basis for ending the crisis and hereby proposes the following series of Presidential orders and declarations in response to the resolution. Each of the Presidential orders and declarations is to be made public and become effective upon safe departure from Iran of the 52 hostages.

I

The United States is prepared to deliver to the Government of Algeria a copy of a formal declaration signed by the President of the United States in which the United States states its policy, which is to refrain from interfering, either directly or indirectly, politically or militarily, in the internal affairs of Iran.

II

A. The United States is prepared to deliver to the Government of Algeria a copy of a signed Presidential order unblocking all of the capital and assets of Iran within the jurisdiction of the United States, whether located in the U.S. or other countries, in order to allow the parties to move expeditiously toward a resumption of normal financial relations as they existed before Nov. 14, 1979.

B. An accompanying Presidential order will direct the Federal Reserve Bank of New York to make available to the Government of Iran all Iranian capital, assets and properties held by the bank, amounting to approximately $2.5 billion.

C. An additional accompanying Presidential order will also remove all U.S. legal restrictions from additional sum of approximately $3 billion on deposit with the U.S. banks abroad.

D. In order to bring about the cancellation of all judicial orders and attachments relating to the capital and assets of Iran within U.S. jurisdiction, the United States is prepared to deliver to the Government of Algeria a copy of a signed Presidential declaration committing the United States to join with the Government of Iran in a claims settlement procedure which will lead to the cancellation of such orders and attachments as rapidly as possible.

III

A. The United States is prepared to deliver to the Government of Algeria a copy of a signed Presidential order revoking all economic and financial sanctions and all legal prohibitions imposed since the seizure of the hostages against exports to, imports from and transactions with Iran in order to allow trade between the two countries to be resumed on the basis of conditions prior to Nov. 14, 1979.

B. The United States is prepared to deliver to the Government of Algeria a copy of a signed Presidential declaration committing the United States to withdraw all claims pending against Iran in the International Court of Justice and to refrain from pursuing any other claims for financial damages on account of injuries or harm emanating from the seizure and detention of the U.S. Embassy and the hostages in Teheran.

C. In addition, as indicated in paragraph 2(D) above, the United States is prepared to commit itself to join with the Government of Iran in a claims settlement procedure which will lead to the cancellation and annulment of all claims asserted by U.S. nationals, including U.S. companies, and by agencies, instrumentalities and controlled entities of the U.S. Government against Iran.

IV

A. The United States is prepared to deliver to the Government of Algeria a copy of a signed Presidential order prohibiting the transfer out of the United States of any properties owned by or derived from the estate of the former Shah.

B. The same order will require the compilation, for delivery to the Government of Iran, of all information which is in the possession of U.S. nationals or in the financial records of the U.S. Government and which may serve to identify any properties of the former Shah in the United States.

C. The order will also direct the Attorney General of the United States to give notice to all appropriate U.S. courts that it is the position of the United States Government that (1) no claim of the Government of Iran to the property of the former Shah should be considered legally barred either by principles of sovereign immunity or the act of state doctrine and (2) that all decrees and judgments of the Government of Iran relating to such property may be enforced in the courts of the United States in accordance with U.S. law.

V

A. The United States believes that this response to the decision of the Iranian Majlis represents the completion of the penultimate stage in resolving the hostage issue. The final step, which the United States believes should be taken in the next several days, would be to arrange, through the good offices of the Government of Algeria, release of all hostages concurrent with the United States taking all the specific steps noted above.

B. To implement this final step, the United States will deposit with the Government of Algeria copies of the Presidential declarations and orders noted above, to be effective upon the safe departure of all the hostages from Iran. When their safe departure is confirmed by the Government of Algeria, the Government of the United States will publicly release the Presidential orders and declarations.

The three Algerian diplomats arrived in Tehran on November 12 and delivered their initial presentation to the Iranian commission the same day. During this first round of indirect discussions, there was considerable concern on the part of both the Algerian and the U.S. teams about the problem of maintaining some degree of confidentiality. On the one hand, it was feared that the Iranian side would immediately publicize the details of the U.S. position, thereby forcing a public debate and complicating the negotiating process. That did not occur. The Iranian committee under Behzad Nabavi[2] remained totally out of public view, and the substance of the Iranian-Algerian discussions during these initial exchanges remained entirely confidential.

There was also the endemic risk of press leaks on the U.S. side. This also did not occur, for several reasons. Knowledge of the U.S. position was limited to the members of the tiny "core group," who understood that a premature leak could directly affect the lives of the hostages in Tehran—many of whom were personal friends and former colleagues. The normally irresistible urge for Washington officials to whisper inside information to the press was also attenuated by the lame-duck status of the Carter administration, which removed many of the political incentives that encourage leaks. Finally, the choice of Warren Christopher as the chief U.S. negotiator must be credited as a major factor in maintaining an unusual degree of confidentiality. Christopher was a highly disciplined man who, by instinct and conviction, shunned personal publicity. If ever an official in an exposed position displayed a passion for anonymity, Christopher's performance in the hostage negotiations would have to be regarded as a classic example.

While talks were under way between the Algerians and the Iranians in Tehran, Washington received almost no substantive information about what was happening. However, during this first round, Washington heard through the diplomatic circuit in Tehran that Nabavi was dissatisfied with the U.S. response. He let it be known that he had anticipated a yes or no answer, while the U.S. paper seemed to be a new proposal in its own right. That was, of course, an accurate representation of the U.S. reply, but it provided scant grounds for optimism.

In view of the extremely tight control over information in Tehran, it is very likely that this report was part of the Iranian negotiating strategy and was intended to reach U.S. ears. In any event, it accurately presaged the contents of the formal Iranian reply delivered to the Algerians on November 21 and relayed to the Department of State on November 26.

The Second Exchange of Notes

The Iranian note characterized the U.S. response as "not to the point" and as straying from the demands spelled out by the Majles. It claimed that the Iranian government had no authority to deviate from the Majles' resolutions and therefore could not reply to "unrelated" proposals such as those included in the U.S. paper. It asked either for a positive or negative response or else a request for clarification. It then reiterated what Iran regarded as the key points left unresolved by the U.S. paper. As expected, these centered on annulment of claims, transfer of all assets without exception to Iran, and access to the assets belonging to the shah.

Brzezinski found the Iranian response "insulting" and recommended rejecting it out of hand. The Christopher group, however, chose to interpret the Iranian message as the opening gambit in a negotiating strategy, and President Carter authorized Christopher to proceed on that basis. The trick was to find a formula that appeared to respond to Iran's purported requirement for a simple "yes or no" answer while maintaining the substance of the U.S. position.

In the course of two intense days of discussions and drafting, a U.S. answer was prepared that provided brief and positive responses to each of the Iranian requests. In each case, however, the reader was referred to a separate set of "comments" or "procedural steps" that would be required to carry out the necessary steps. In this way the Iranians could have their brief positive answer —if only for public consumption—while the U.S. conditions were preserved in the "small print" at the back.

Iran also requested detailed information on the lawsuits pending in U.S. courts, a survey of all Iranian assets, and other data where their own information was presumably scanty or nonexistent. In each case the U.S. reply referred the Iranians to their own lawyers[3] or else informed them that the United States had no precise information of the sort they were seeking.

Verbally, Christopher made it clear to the Algerians that Tehran could not expect to receive any cooperation from the United States regarding location of assets as long as they were unwilling to provide a detailed accounting of the location and condition of each of the U.S. hostages. Although the U.S. written reply was stated in the neutral language of the legal profession, it was no less a rebuke of the Iranian request than their own message had been from the U.S. point of view.

Back to Algiers and Tehran

Warren Christopher carried this paper to Algiers for a new set of discussions on December 1. One of the most significant points to emerge from this second round of discussions was a proposal that all U.S. private claims against Iran be channeled into a mutually-agreed-to claims-settlement procedure. Such a mechanism would permit Iran to claim technically that attachments and court proceedings had been annulled (on the grounds that settlement action had been transferred from the courts to the claims-settlement procedure) while at the same time protecting the U.S. claimants.

The Christopher group had not proposed such a solution, thinking that the Iranians would perceive it as contrary to their own interests. In fact, relying on traditional claims of sovereign immunity, Iran's position in the U.S. courts was very strong; but if all claims were transferred to a settlement procedure —where Iran would have to accept adjudication—Iran would likely be required to pay far more in compensation in the end.

However, the Algerians believed that Iran would find such an arrangement attractive, since it would permit them to contend (as the Majles resolution required) that all claims against Iran had been terminated. Although no one on the Algerian side ever expressed it in such bald terms, they were suggesting in effect that Iran was more interested in finding an acceptable political formula than in protecting its tangible interests. Again, their judgment was on the mark.

In the meantime, President Carter was receiving some alternative advice in Washington. Admiral Stansfield Turner, the director of central intelligence, had argued from the beginning of the mediation that a detailed response to the Majles' resolution was a mistake. He believed that prolonged "haggling" with Iran risked undermining the fragile consensus that had been put together in the weeks prior to the U.S. election. He felt that a detailed, legalistic approach would inevitably fail to satisfy the Iranians, since the United States could not meet the Majles' terms in several key respects.

Although Brzezinski and Turner had more than their share of differences, on this they agreed. On December 3, Brzezinski sent a memorandum to the president relaying Turner's concerns and recommending that the Iranians be informed that no further adjustments were possible on the U.S. side. He agreed with Turner's suggestion of a clear demarche telling the Iranians that time was running out and that they must be prepared to accept some financial loss, just as the United States had suffered a great deal of human cost as a result of the hostage taking.

President Carter called Secretary Muskie on December 3 and discussed these alternative views of the negotiating process. Later that day Muskie called Christopher in Algiers and asked him to relay to the Iranians, via the Algerian mediators, the president's views that the present package was the U.S. "final offer."

On December 3 the Algerian team returned to Tehran with the clear intention of applying maximum pressure for a resolution of the stalemate by the end of the year. All participants were keenly aware that time was slipping away. If the issue was not resolved satisfactorily by the time a new president was inaugurated on January 20, 1981, no one could predict what would happen. The Algerians understood that very well, and although they were careful not to discuss the nature of their conversations with the Iranians, they presumably made this point with some vigor when they returned to Tehran for their second round of discussions.

Several days after the Algerian team arrived back in Tehran, a Third World diplomat in Tehran provided his own interpretation of the course of events. According to this observer, the Algerians believed that the United States had accepted 80 percent of what Iran wanted, and they were cautiously optimistic that a resolution of the problem could be achieved by Christmas. However, given the difficult political situation in Iran, where the least deviation from the Majles' formal conditions could have drastic political repercussions, the outcome was not entirely predictable. This diplomat believed that the Algerians would seriously consider withdrawing from the process if the Iranians rejected the most recent U.S. proposals. The Algerians did not share their personal assessments or intentions with the United States, but this independent analysis had the ring of credibility.

The Third Exchange of Notes

On December 11 the Algerian team relayed a message from the Iranian commission to Washington. In this message the Iranians agreed not to press for the information in the five lists attached to their previous note, which Christopher had flatly refused. They did ask, however, for an accounting of the total value of assets belonging to the shah and his relatives in the United States. That information, they said, was necessary for them to respond properly to the latest U.S. position. In an interesting departure, they asked for the amount of the shah's assets in the United States on November 4, 1979 (the date of the hostage taking), and the total remaining in the United States now that more than a year had gone by, implying at least tacit recognition that the shah and his family might have chosen to transfer assets away from the United States as a consequence of the hostage crisis.

A second Iranian demand in the December 11 message concerned the renunciation of all U.S. claims arising out of the seizure of the U.S. embassy in Tehran and the holding of U.S. hostages. This posed a particularly difficult problem, for it would prevent individual hostages and their families from asserting claims against Iran for its actions. In practical terms, such a renunciation would mean very little, for private claims against a foreign government virtually never succeed; but it was important psychologically and symbolically.

The administration conferred on this point with members of the hostage families, who had formed an organization known as FLAG—Family Liaison Action Group. The families agreed, with reluctance, that it would be futile to insist on claims as a matter of abstract principle at the expense of letting the crisis drag on even longer. Consequently, draft presidential orders were drawn up agreeing to withdraw and to forgo prosecution of any claims arising out of the seizure of the embassy in Tehran.

On the question of the shah's assets, there was simply no information available. Christopher informed the Algerian foreign minister that even if the United States were willing to launch an immediate investigation of the suspected holdings of the shah and his family in the United States, there was no possibility that such a survey could be completed before the change of administration. Still, Christopher recognized the deadly seriousness of this point for the Iranians. Therefore, as an attempt to square the circle, the U.S. reply to the Algerians included a draft executive order blocking all assets of the shah and his family once the hostages had been released.

The U.S. response also referred to the sum of $56.5 billion as the amount Iran's lawyers claimed as the shah's wealth in the United States. The United States (and presumably the Iranians) knew that number was totally speculative —if not entirely fictitious—and the U.S. note carefully avoided suggesting that it had any validity. However, the U.S. side recognized that, for political reasons, the Iranians could not officially accept the fact that the shah's wealth, whatever its size, had almost certainly fled from the United States and would no doubt prove as elusive for Iran as claims for personal damages would be for the hostages and their families.

The new U.S. message, incorporating responses to Iranian questions on the shah's assets and renunciation of claims, was reviewed and approved by President Carter at the regular Friday morning foreign policy breakfast with his key advisers on December 12. The message was transmitted to Algiers late the same night, giving the Algerian foreign minister the choice either of transmitting it directly to Tehran or of requesting clarification or changes. He chose to send the message to Tehran without further contact with Washington, and the Algerian team presented it to the Iranians on December 15.

Act III: The $24 Billion Misunderstanding

On December 17, Washington learned that the Algerian team had received an answer from the Iranians and had begun making preparations to return to Algiers. However, Washington did not receive the 3,000-word text of the Iranian note until December 19. The note included some recommendations for minor wording changes in the text of the U.S. response, reflecting Iranian political sensitivities; but the most startling feature of the Iranian reply was its proposal for the handling of financial assets.

First, the message demanded that $9.6 billion of Iranian assets, plus interest, together with the gold deposited in Iran's account with the Federal Reserve Bank of New York, be delivered to the Central Bank of Algeria prior to the release of the hostages. Immediately upon release, these assets were to be placed at the disposal of the Iranian government.

In addition, the U.S. government was to deposit $4 billion with the Algerian Central Bank as security for eventual repayment to Iran of Iranian funds held under attachment in the United States. The message repeated a request for the United States to accept liability for any claims against Iran for damages associated with the embassy takeover and incarceration of the hostages. It further demanded a full accounting of Iranian assets and a written U.S. commitment to return any assets that might be identified in the future but that were not included in the existing lists.

In turn, Iran agreed to bring current the outstanding payments on loans from U.S. banks and authorized the Algerian Central Bank to hold $1 billion as a guarantee against future payments of loan installments. Most significant, the Iranian response formally accepted the notion of some form of claims-settlement procedure, and it offered to set aside another fund of $1 billion to cover payment of such claims against Iran. The note agreed to replenish this account as necessary to ensure that it never dropped below a level of $500 million until the claims-settlement process was complete.

It was, however, the question of the shah's putative assets in the United States that caused the greatest difficulty. The Iranian message asked that the United States establish a thirty-day deadline for collecting information about the size and location of the shah's assets in the United States. Until that process was complete, a freeze was to be maintained on such assets, and the U.S. government was to deposit $10 billion with the Central Bank of Algeria as a guarantee of the proper "discharge of its obligations."

Taken as a whole, the Iranian message was so thoroughly outrageous in its demands that the instinctive reaction of U.S. officials was to regard it as a rejection. In the face of such a response, it was felt that further negotiation could only be futile and humiliating. The Iranian side had almost totally disregarded the detailed breakdown of frozen assets provided to them through the Algerians, and they had replaced the actual figures with numbers seemingly of their own invention. For example, their request for $9.6 billion in assets included $800 million in the Department of Defense trust fund—a figure ten times higher than the actual amount in the fund at the time. Moreover, when one considered the $10 billion requested to guarantee the shah's assets, together with the demand that the United States accept financial liability for all of Iran's litigations and claims in U.S. courts, the Iranian message appeared so far removed from the reality of what was possible for the United States—legally or morally—that it appeared to be a calculated insult.

The Algerians seemed to feel the same way. When asked about a possible future meeting, they replied blandly that they had nothing further to add to the Iranian message. Apparently, the Algerians did not wish to associate themselves with a set of demands that they knew not only was outside the realm of the practical but even strained the limits of credibility.

Within Christopher's small group, the Iranian message was immediately dubbed the "$24 billion misunderstanding." To make matters worse, on December 21 the Iranians published a summary of their message to the United States as part of a propaganda effort to justify their own position. The United States, in turn, published the texts of its own communications with Tehran to set the record straight.[4] Given the immense gap between the Iranian and U.S. positions, the apparent Algerian withdrawal, the breakdown of confidentiality, and the rapid passage of time (less than one month remained before the inauguration), it seemed that the negotiations had broken down totally and irrevocably.

Just before this message was received in Washington, I had my first conversation with Richard V. Allen, who was designated to become the national security adviser when President Reagan assumed office. As part of the normal transition process, he had temporarily moved into an office in the Old Executive Office Building next to the White House, where he was preparing himself for his new duties. He asked me only one substantive question: "Will the hostages be released before the inauguration?" I paused for a long moment, then replied, "Yes." By December 21, I began to think I would have to eat my words.

Second Thoughts

The initial response to the Algerian message was uniformly negative, but within the small group of individuals around Warren Christopher, two alternative interpretations emerged that held out the possibility of continued talks. First, it was suggested that Iran was merely engaging in traditional bazaar haggling. The $24 billion figure should, in this view, be regarded as nothing more than an opening gambit to which the United States should respond with a counter offer. This interpretation was offered, as might have been anticipated, by an individual who had served in Iran.

The second point of view, which ultimately prevailed, held that the Iranians genuinely wished to terminate the crisis but were boxed in by political circumstances. A careful reading of the December 19 message revealed a number of positive elements. It accepted the basic concept of a claims-settlement procedure and an escrow agreement with the Bank of Algeria. Iran also agreed to pay U.S. banks all overdue installments of loans made under the shah. The Iranian negotiators had shrugged off the U.S. refusal to provide additional detailed information without making it an issue. They had also accepted—in a left-handed sort of way—the principle that the shah's assets could be recovered only through the courts and that attachments on assets frozen in the United States could be undone only through court action over time.

However, it was argued, to cover themselves politically and to avoid the appearance of being taken in by the Americans, they had proposed financial guarantees. In that way they would not be seen as relying solely on the word of the Great Satan. The size of the guarantees was essentially arbitrary (although Iran would have a natural incentive to make them as high as possible), and some of the ambiguity could be attributed to the U.S. refusal to provide a detailed accounting of assets, which the Iranians had obviously sought for that purpose.

In other words, putting aside the instinctive U.S. anger at what seemed to be an insult, it was possible to see the Iranian response as a rather far-reaching effort to accommodate the U.S. position, but with some protective factors built in to ensure that they would not be cheated by an enemy they hated and distrusted. After the initial shock, it was this interpretation that came to be accepted within Christopher's "core group," and President Carter authorized the group to proceed on that basis. Nevertheless, the gap between the Iranian position (now public) and what the United States could offer was immense. Was it possible to close this gap in less than one month?

On December 21, after conferring with President Carter, Christopher sent a message to the Algerians, which relayed the U.S. reaction to the "deeply disappointing" message from the Iranians. The U.S. note provided some new draft material and requested Algerian comments. Christopher also asked the Algerians whether or not it would be worth sending still another message to Iran or whether the talks should simply be permitted to remain dormant until the Reagan administration took office.

Christopher left open the possibility of another meeting with the Algerian team if they felt such a meeting would be worthwhile. Christopher noted that judging from the lack of understanding reflected in the Iranian message, Washington had only a "slight expectation" that the original timetable could be preserved, but remained willing to explore whatever possibility might remain.

The principal new element in this late-December position paper was a draft Memorandum of Understanding that Iran and the United States would each sign with the Algerians. The MOU did not substantially change the basic U.S. position, but it attempted to reformulate it more in accordance with what Washington understood to be the essential political requirements of the Nabavi commission in Tehran. Thus, the MOU called for the transfer of as many of the Iranian assets as possible to escrow outside the United States in advance of the hostage release, with arrangements for their further transfer to Iran as soon as the release had been accomplished.

This new approach expressly rejected Iran's request for $24 billion as inconsistent with the principle of re-establishing the status quo prior to the hostage taking and as legally infeasible, but it maximized the amount of Iranian assets that could realistically be collected, short of court action. The Iranians, it was felt, might prefer to take what they could reasonably expect to get in the short run, rather than prolong the negotiations in the dubious hope of squeezing more out of the next administration.

The new U.S. proposal established a deadline of January 16, 1981, as the final date for a settlement. If this deadline was exceeded, the United States reserved the right to withdraw from whatever arrangements had been concluded to that time.

The Algerians welcomed the new U.S. proposal. They had originally been led to believe that the Iranians regarded the U.S. position of December 15 as positive and requiring only a few minor changes, so the Iranian reply had taken them by surprise. Nevertheless, on reflection the Algerians had come to the same conclusion as the members of the U.S. team, i.e., that the "$24 billion misunderstanding" was in fact a clumsy attempt by the Tehran commission to solve the political problems of implementing the agreement.

On December 23, U.S. Ambassador Ulric Haynes, Jr., was called to the Algerian Foreign Ministry and informed that Algeria was prepared to proceed with its mediation efforts on the basis of the latest U.S. position. However, before deciding whether or not to transmit the U.S. paper to Tehran, the Algerian team felt that further in-depth discussions with Christopher and his associates were needed. Consequently, the Algerians said they were prepared to leave immediately for Washington if this was acceptable to the U.S. side.

Uncertain Signals

On the following day, Christmas Eve, there was a significant change in the situation in Tehran. The United States was informed that the three U.S. diplomats who had until now been held at the Iranian Foreign Ministry (Bruce Laingen, Victor Tomseth and Michael Howland) had been taken away to join the other hostages. According to this report, all fifty-two hostages were now in "the safekeeping of the government."[5]

On Christmas Day the Algerian ambassador in Tehran and his deputy visited the hostages. The next day Washington was informed that all fifty-two hostages had been sighted. This was the first visit by outside officials to the hostages since before the rescue attempt exactly eight months earlier and the only positive confirmation in nearly fourteen months that all the hostages were physically safe. Paradoxically, however, the Algerians in Tehran reported that Bruce Laingen and his two colleagues were visited in a different site from the others, thus leaving open the question of whether a transfer of all the hostages to government control had actually occurred.

It was difficult to know how to interpret the meaning of these events. It had been a basic objective of the United States from the earliest days of the crisis to get the hostages out of the hands of the student radicals and into the official custody of the government. On the basis of the contradictory evidence available, it was unclear whether or not this had finally been accomplished. On balance, it seemed that Iran was at least moving toward the assertion of government control over the hostages, paving the way for their eventual release. That view was strongly reinforced by the Algerian team when they arrived in Washington on the night of December 29.

Act IV: Cliffhanger

Talks began the following morning and continued through a luncheon hosted by Secretary of State Muskie. By the end of the afternoon of December 30, after more than eight hours of intensive consultations, a thoroughly revised package had been put together.

This new package, which the Algerians carried back to their own country on New Year's Eve, was in the form of a "declaration" by the government of Algeria, incorporating the points of agreement between the two parties. By this device, Iran and the United States would each be making promises to Algeria, not to each other—a point of great psychological importance for the Iranians.

The new package addressed each of the four points in the original Majles resolution and described how the agreement would be implemented:

- It provided for an escrow account, with funds in the value of approximately $7.3 billion (plus interest) to be turned over to Iran when Algeria certified the safe release of all the hostages. (Some $2.2 billion in U.S. banks had been attached by the courts and could not be released immediately.)
- It established a claims-settlement procedure with binding arbitration, and incorporated the Iranian idea of a $1 billion Iranian account designated for payment of claims, to be replenished so as never to fall below a level of $500 million.
- With respect to the shah's assets, the United States reiterated its willingness to freeze existing assets, to direct the collection of information about the size and location of assets, and to facilitate Iran's access to U.S. courts.

On January 3 the Algerians met with Nabavi in Tehran to explain the latest U.S. proposal. They emphasized that time was running out if an agreement was to be reached before the change of administrations in Washington. (The deadline of January 16 was retained as the date when the United States was authorized to withdraw unilaterally from any obligations.) Nabavi acknowledged the point and indicated that an Iranian response would be forthcoming within two or three days.

In Washington, there was still great uncertainty about the location of the three diplomats in the Foreign Ministry. There was also grave concern that if agreement was not reached, the Iranians would put all the hostages on trial. Contingency plans were prepared to deal with that eventuality.

Late on January 5, Washington was notified that the three diplomats had been transferred to an unknown location with the other hostages as of January

4. In relaying this information, the Algerians counseled the Americans to remain cool and provided personal assurances from the Iranians that all fifty-two hostages were now in the hands of the government.

On January 6, Ambassador Haynes was informed that the Algerian team felt they were not far from a solution and were much more optimistic than before. It was suggested that the United States avoid mention of the January 16 deadline, apparently to avoid the impression that Iran was working under a U.S. ultimatum.

Return to Algiers

At this juncture Washington began to receive requests for clarifications or changes on many different points. These requests would be presented to the Algerian team in Tehran, relayed to Algiers, and passed to the U.S. ambassador, who sent them to Washington; then the entire process was repeated in reverse with Washington's reply. A question and answer required eight exchanges and four translations (Farsi-French, French-English, and vice versa).

In order to streamline this cumbersome procedure, Warren Christopher flew to Algiers with a small group of aides on January 7 in order to have direct contact with the Algerian side and to deal directly with questions as they were relayed from Tehran. Although the participants originally expected this process to continue only for a brief period of time (one member of the team packed only enough clothes for an overnight visit), the team was in fact required to remain in Algiers until after the hostages had been released on January 20.

As Christopher began his consultation in Algiers on January 8, it was becoming evident that the Iranians were prepared to accept most of the Algerian declaration in principle. However, the details of handling the vast quantities of money and goods involved in this transaction were emerging as very serious issues as each side got down to the fine print. The most troublesome of these issues was the prospective transfer of Iranian assets frozen in accounts of U.S. banks overseas. Some of these assets had been offset against outstanding Iranian loans, and it would be necessary for Iran to settle the loan accounts before the remaining balance could be determined. Negotiations between the Iranian Bank Markazi and the U.S. banks had been under way for almost a year, and a variety of plans had been developed to deal with the problem. However, final agreement remained elusive.

Also, the Iranians had to be persuaded that the United States was unable to terminate attachments on the $2.2 billion of Iranian deposits in U.S. banks prior to the actual release of the hostages. These funds could not be placed in escrow—and hence would not be available in cash form—at the time of the exchange. For the Iranians, this was extremely serious. They had publicly identified some $9.5 billion in frozen assets for immediate return, and to this sum they had added $14 billion more in "guarantees." They were now being asked to accept a grand total of $7.3 billion (plus interest), with an additional

$2.2 billion to follow upon completion of U.S. court action. The decision to publicize their demands in December must have seemed a great embarrassment as they struggled with the realities of a settlement in January.

The Algerians also found it exceedingly difficult to believe that the Iranians would ever agree to reduce their demands below the level of $9.5 billion. Christopher's return to Algiers and his analysis for Foreign Minister Benyahia of what the United States could and could not do had been critical in persuading the Algerians even to raise the question of the $7.3 billion with the Iranians. The Algerians agreed to present this position to the Iranians only when Christopher stated flatly that the Iranians had the choice of taking the $7.3 billion now, with the remainder to come later, or else to wait for the entire $9.5 billion until spring, after the administration had changed. Presumably, that is what Nabavi heard from the Algerians a few days later.

During this period, there was a flood of cabled messages back and forth between Algiers and Tehran. Every word of the declaration and the supporting documentation was the subject of scrutiny, queries and suggested changes. Copies of this message traffic were dutifully relayed to Washington, where they literally piled up in mounds. Those of us in Washington who were involved only indirectly in most of this trilingual swirl could only watch with respect bordering on awe as the small U.S. team in Algiers managed to deal with each new issue calmly and precisely, never losing sight of the larger picture. Just keeping the telegrams in order was virtually a full-time occupation.

By January 10 the $7.3 billion escrow proposal had been presented to the Iranians, who promised to study it. The Algerians at this stage felt that despite the flurry of minor changes and alterations, the momentum of negotiation was well established and that almost nothing stood in the way of an agreement except the amount of money to be placed in escrow. The U.S. side, submerged in the blizzard of details, was less sanguine.

Among other things, time was rapidly running out. Reports from Tehran indicated that Iran planned to respond to the latest U.S. position on about January 15. That was only one day from the original deadline—selected on the basis of practical considerations, not as a negotiating strategy—and there was growing awareness that every hour that passed subtracted one more hour of precious time to complete the complex and unprecedented arrangements necessary for a successful transfer. In Washington, at the request of Secretary of State–designate Alexander Haig, Lloyd Cutler briefed three senior members of the Reagan administration transition team about the status of negotiations. They listened very soberly and without comment to the circumstances it now appeared they would inherit in less than two weeks.

Benyahia indicated he would be willing to travel personally to Tehran if absolutely necessary, and he formally requested that Deputy Secretary Christopher remain in Algiers for the time being. Christopher agreed to remain at least one more day. Then on January 12 he again acceded to Benyahia's request. In this fashion the length of his visit was gradually extended, one day at a time. However, by early on the thirteenth, as rumors began to circulate about a formal meeting of the Majles on the hostage issue, Christopher had personally concluded that the chances of completing a settlement by January 20 were remote.

Not least of Christopher's concerns during this tense period of waiting for an Iranian reply was the status of negotiations between the Bank Markazi and the U.S. banks being conducted in New York under the supervision of Deputy Secretary of the Treasury Robert Carswell and Counsel to the President Lloyd Cutler. The Iranians balked at the demand of the U.S. banks that they maintain a guarantee fund greater than the total value of the loans themselves. They were also quite unhappy about the interest rates being offered by the U.S. banks.

Iran Blinks

This deadlock continued until January 15 when, to the astonishment of the U.S. side, the Iranians unilaterally introduced a new memorandum offering not only to bring their loans current but to pay them off entirely, thus eliminating the issue. This option had been considered from the very beginning of the bank negotiations, but it had been dropped along the way, since it had appeared to be too costly to the Iranians. Now the Iranians chose to reintroduce it to break the stalemate. Although this decision was a major breakthrough, it also meant that virtually every paper that had been prepared during the long bank negotiations had to be completely redrafted under extreme time limits.

Also on January 15, former U.S. Treasury General Counsel Robert Mundheim and Department of State Deputy Legal Adviser William Lake were dispatched to London to assist in the financial arrangements. Iran had by this time agreed that the Bank of England would be acceptable as the escrow bank, and the financial activities associated with the transfer and certification of billions of dollars of assets from a wide variety of sources were increasingly focused in "the City."

The Majles met as scheduled and voted approval on January 14. Questions presented to the Majles were intentionally restricted to approval of the claims-settlement procedure and the nationalization of the shah's assets, apparently in an attempt to avoid a prolonged political wrangle about the actual text of what was now being referred to as the "Algiers Declaration."

However, it was not until January 17 that Nabavi formally notified the Algerians that his commission was prepared to reduce its demands below the $9.5 billion level. To this concession, the Iranians added two caveats: first, they insisted that the actual level of assets, including interest, should be no less than $8.1 billion; second, they insisted on a U.S. guarantee that the remaining $2.2 billion under attachment in the United States would be freed no later than May 31, 1981.

Although the United States recognized the major concession that Iran had offered in lowering its publicly stated goal, there was still considerable doubt that $8.1 billion could in fact be produced. Part of the problem was the fluctuation in the price of gold on the world market. Iranian bullion in the Federal Reserve had lost about $150 million in value since the talks had begun. Moreover, the Iranian securities on deposit with the Federal Reserve also fluctuated in value.

After some extended computation and soul-searching, the United States agreed to accept an aggregate figure of $7.955 billion as the required "trigger" to free the hostages. The Algerians were able within a matter of hours to persuade the Iranians to accept this figure, which was then written into a series of formal documents prepared and signed in Washington on January 18.

By this time the area around the Cabinet Room in the White House had been converted into a twenty-four-hour operations center. Messengers from the Situation Room came and went with the latest dispatches, telephone conversations went on in all corners, and the large oval table in the Cabinet Room was permanently strewn with stacks of messages and drafts. January 18 was a Sunday, when the White House mess is closed, so the confusion of the scene was compounded by the litter of fast-food containers carried in from restaurants near the White House.

One of the implementing documents was to be signed by the secretary of state, who was at the State Department. So I picked up the paper to go get Muskie's signature. When I got to my car, I looked at the paper in my hand and realized too late that I had been eating pizza. There was no time for redrafting, so future historians will have to puzzle over the significance of a greasy fingerprint on the corner of the document that assigned Warren Christopher authority to sign the final documents in Algiers.

The Final Roller Coaster

The Iranians formally acceded to the agreement early in the morning of January 19, and Deputy Secretary Christopher initialed the documents in Algiers on the authority of the fingerprinted document. At that point the crisis appeared to be over. The transfer of funds began from various accounts into the Federal Reserve preparatory to transfer to the escrow account in the Bank of England. Although the transfer mechanism was complex and cumbersome, it appeared briefly for a time on January 19 that only technical compliance remained. Two Algerian aircraft had already been dispatched to Tehran for the hostages. The stage seemed to be set.

But in the Iranian crisis, nothing ever went according to schedule. Within hours, the exhilarated and exhausted team in Algiers learned that the Iranians had rejected a technical supplement to the basic escrow agreements, thus halting in its tracks the banking transfer process that had only begun. The clause that Iran found offensive (denouncing it repeatedly as an "underhanded" maneuver) was a conventional statement that transfer of specified deposit amounts to the Federal Reserve would release deposit banks from further liability. The Bank Markazi, whose records were incomplete and in some cases at variance with the U.S. banks, saw this as a trick to avoid resolving such inconsistencies later. Their point was valid, if overstated.

After nearly a full day of wrangling and Iranian accusations of bad faith, the offending supplement was removed from the basic document. It was then redrafted by Bank Markazi lawyers, agreed to by all parties, and telexed as an order to begin the financial transfer.

This telex also turned into a nightmare. The text was full of typographical errors which, in a normal banking transaction, would have had to be resolved by laborious retransmission until the text was perfect. However, by this time (early morning on January 20, Inauguration Day) there was no time left. All of the banking officials conferred by telephone to no avail, until Secretary of the Treasury William Miller finally gave verbal instructions to the U.S. banks to proceed on the basis of the order as received.

At 4:17 A.M. Washington time on January 20, the Federal Reserve transferred a total of $7.977 billion to the Bank of England. A further technical glitch at that point delayed for two more hours the transfer of this amount—within the Bank of England itself—from the account of the Federal Reserve to the escrow account of the Algerian Central Bank. The holdings of that account were then verified painstakingly, line by line, by telephone between London and Algiers, where the formal certificate was finally presented at 8:04 A.M. Two minutes later the certification was passed from Algiers to Tehran, successfully completing what was probably the largest private transfer of funds in a single transaction in history.

The figures in the final agreement that Iran had accepted were startling, even to those who had followed the negotiations closely. At the beginning of the hostage crisis, some $12 billion of Iranian assets were frozen by the United States; but because of attachments and other limitations, only about $8 billion could in fact be transferred to the escrow account before the hostage release. Once the release took place, these funds were distributed as follows:

- $3.67 billion to pay off U.S. bank loans to the shah's regime
- $1.42 billion to remain in escrow as security against payment on disputed claims between U.S. banks and Iran
- $2.88 billion to Iran

In addition, approximately $2.2 billion would be freed of attachment and the claims referred to an international tribunal. Of those funds, Iran agreed to place $1 billion in an escrow account to secure payments of claims by U.S. citizens and companies against Iran as decided by the arbitral tribunal.

In short, Iran received only slightly more than $4 billion in cash, or approximately one third of the total they had originally lost as a result of the hostage taking. In retrospect, it appeared that the longer Iran negotiated, the less it got, and those in Tehran who had opposed a settlement were not shy in drawing attention to the very considerable financial concessions the Iranian team had accepted. Certainly, if anyone had proposed such an outcome when the talks began in September 1980, it would have been rejected as unthinkable.

The U.S. negotiators could not improve on the words of former Iranian Foreign Minister Yazdi: "Generally speaking, the hostage issue has not been handled well and politically we have lost in the world."[6]

PERSONAL NOTES:
INAUGURATION DAY,
1981

A t eight o'clock in the morning of January 20, President Jimmy Carter put down the phone in the Oval Office with a satisfied smile and announced that the transfer of assets was complete. It had been verified by the Algerians, and they in turn had notified Tehran by flash message. At that point, after handshakes and congratulations all around, there was nothing further the United States could do except wait. There had been so many disappointments in the past, so many missed opportunities. Would the Iranians in fact be able to carry out their obligation to release the hostages now that the moment had finally arrived?

While the small group in the Oval Office was asking itself this question, Washington was filling with a new set of faces. The streets were full of limousines, hotel ballrooms were being readied for parties, and the city's hostesses were busily replacing lists of Georgians with new lists of Californians. The nation's capital was preparing for its quadrennial celebration of the democratic process. President-elect Reagan and his supporters were preparing to launch a lavish celebration of triumph, but President Carter and the small group of advisers working with him on the final act of the hostage crisis were scarcely aware of them.

The last three days of the hostage crisis were a unique period in U.S. history. During the last two nights of his presidency, Jimmy Carter did not go to bed. Instead he remained in the Oval Office (which had become the command post for the final stages of the negotiations), taking occasional naps on the couch.

The sheer magnitude of the transfer of assets—eight billion dollars—was unprecedented, and the complexity of the operation was daunting—fourteen banks and more than five different nations interacting simultaneously. Carter's presence had been crucial at several key moments to keep the process on track. However, his determination personally to see this crisis through to completion went far beyond his executive responsibilities. It was, in a very real sense, *his* crisis. Throughout his long last year in office, it had dominated his thoughts, like an infuriating but endlessly fascinating puzzle. He had wept, prayed, sweated and cursed over it. And now that it was about to end, he was going to be there. In person.

President Carter had originally hoped to be able to greet the hostages personally, in his official capacity, and an airplane had been standing by for a trip to Europe. Even as late as the morning of the nineteenth, when it had appeared the crisis was over, there had been an outside possibility of squeezing in a meeting with the hostages before the inaugural ceremonies.

By the morning of the twentieth, that was no longer feasible; however, the president-elect had offered to put a presidential aircraft at the former president's disposal for such a trip immediately after the inauguration. It was now scheduled to depart early in the morning of the twenty-first to Germany, where the hostages were expected to arrive after a brief stop in Algiers.

President Carter was drawing up a list of those who had worked on the crisis to accompany him to Germany. He asked me if I would like to go, and I said of course I would. He showed me his list of invitees and asked if anyone had been left off. I suggested that he add Henry Precht. Henry had not been included in the Christopher "core group," and his direct role in the policy-making process had dwindled since the breakdown of the secret negotiations through Bourguet and Villalón. However, as the Iran desk officer, he was in charge of the task force at the State Department that had continued to function twenty-four hours a day over the long months since the rescue mission failed. No one in the government, I commented to the president, had worked harder or had made more personal sacrifices. Carter immediately agreed and added his name to the list.

The president was fidgety and impatient. Finally he reached into the lower left-hand drawer of the great carved desk in the Oval Office and picked up a red secure telephone. Over the telephone, he asked if there was any action in Tehran. There was, and he sat for fifteen minutes or so following events. He then asked me to pull up a chair and take over the listening watch.

I introduced myself to the seasoned watch officer on the other end. He would pass information as it came in, and I would relay it to the president. At one point Carter left the room. The watch officer and I were making conversation, waiting for something to happen, when the soft Southern voice came on the line. "Don't let me interrupt you," Carter said, "I just picked up on the other line." He was in his private office, still listening in. Then an ominous buzzing started on the line. "Don't let this bother you. I have to shave before Reagan gets here."

By ten o'clock there was still no indication that the hostages were moving in Tehran. At that point everyone left the Oval Office to permit the furniture to be rearranged for the new president, who would arrive in a few hours. Hamilton Jordan and I went down to the Situation Room, where I re-established telephone contact with the watch officer. With the secure phone at one ear, I picked up another phone and contacted the White House operator, who kept me connected to an open line wherever the president was. He would call in periodically to ask for an update. Unfortunately, there was little to report.

As 10:30 approached, I turned on a television set to follow the inaugural events. In this slightly absurd position, sitting in a tangle of wires, with a telephone at each ear and my eyes glued to a television screen, I had reason to ponder the marvels of modern communications. I would speak to the watch officer, then to the president, and then I would watch as President Carter came out of the White House to greet the president-elect. When they left the portico and disappeared back into the White House, Carter again came back on the line for an update.

Just after the motorcade left for the Capitol, I received word that Tehran Radio had announced that the hostages would leave within thirty minutes. There was no confirmation from intelligence. Watching the president's car on television as it turned the corner of Pennsylvania Avenue toward Capitol Hill, I relayed this information to him on the car telephone. A few minutes later one of the wire services jumped the gun with an announcement that the hostages were free. It was not true, and I passed this information to him while he was in a room in the Capitol waiting for the ceremony to begin.

During the ceremony, as the new president took the oath of office, I remained in contact with a presidential aide who was prepared to relay any word to Carter on the reviewing stand through the Secret Service. This connection was never used, since the hostages remained on the ground.

Finally, as the former president was on his way by helicopter to Andrews Air Force Base to fly back to Georgia, first one plane, then a second, took off from Mehrabad Airport in Tehran with all hostages on board. That word was waiting when Jimmy Carter arrived at Andrews, and he was able to whisper to one of the hostage wives who had come to bid him farewell that she would soon be reunited with her husband.

The Algerians, who were on the scene in Tehran, later insisted that the four-hour delay on the part of the Iranians in acknowledging receipt of the escrow message—from 8:06 A.M. Washington time until 12:05 P.M., five minutes after President Carter's term ended—and the final departure of the hostages shortly after 12:30, was merely due to their typical inefficiency. However, to those in the Oval Office and to much of the world, it appeared to be one final humiliating gouge at the "Great Satan."

I wrote a brief report on the hostage departure, which I transmitted to the aircraft. Then, putting down the phones and turning off the television, I asked myself what should be done next.

I stood there for a moment as the realization dawned on me that for the first time in fourteen months, there was really nothing else that needed to be done. The job was over. I picked up my accumulated notes and papers, closed my briefcase and left.

But one more surprise awaited me. As I came out of the Situation Room into the halls of the West Wing, I was greeted by giant color photographs of President Reagan on every wall. During my hours inside, the presidency had changed, and the walls of the White House had also changed.

Truly, it was over.

NOTES

1 America and the Shah

1. Kermit Roosevelt, *Countercoup: The Struggle for the Control of Iran,* New York: McGraw-Hill, 1979. Ironically, publication was delayed for some months out of concern that the appearance of the book in the midst of a budding revolution would contribute to the collapse of the monarch whose throne Kim Roosevelt had helped preserve.
2. *Ibid.,* p. 199.
3. *Ibid.,* p. 210.
4. "Towards the Great Civilization," unpublished manuscript by the former shah of Iran, Mohammad Reza Pahlavi, pp. 5, 58. The shah wrote this book during the first half of 1978, as the revolution was gathering force. It is a panegyric on the accomplishments of his rule. By the time it was completed, events had passed it by and it was never published in the West. A copy of the manuscript came into the possession of the author in the course of the crisis. In retrospect, this document provides some useful insights into the shah's thinking during the early stages of the revolution, especially when compared to the much more austere and defensive *Answer to History,* which the shah wrote during his exile and published just before his death.
5. Mohammad Reza Pahlavi, *Answer to History,* New York: Stein and Day, 1980, p. 72.
6. *Ibid.,* p. 22.
7. Yann Richard places Khomeini's birth, in the town of Khomain, in September 1902. See his essay in Nikki R. Keddie, *Roots of Revolution,* New Haven, Conn.: Yale University Press, 1981, p. 205. Shaul Bakhash, citing Iranian biographies of Khomeini, agrees. For an extensive treatment of Khomeini's life and thought, see Shaul Bakhash, *The Reign of the Ayatollahs: Iran and the Islamic Revolution,* New York: Basic Books, 1984, pp. 19–51.
8. For a fuller discussion of the issues in the 1963 rebellion, see Keddie, pp. 154–60, and Ervand Abrahamian, *Iran Between Two Revolutions,* Princeton University Press, 1982, pp. 423–26.
9. See Richard W. Cottam, *Nationalism in Iran,* University of Pittsburgh Press, 1979 ed., pp. 307–8.
10. Pahlavi, *Answer to History,* p. 104.
11. Cited in Michael M. J. Fischer, *Iran: From Religious Dispute to Revolution,* Cambridge, Mass.: Harvard University Press, 1980, p. 1.

12. For an eyewitness (and highly critical) description of the event, see George Ball, *The Past Has Another Pattern,* New York: Norton, 1982, pp. 434–36.
13. Years later, Kissinger reaffirmed that view of the shah, noting that "In his grasp of the international trends and currents he was among the most impressive leaders that I met." *White House Years,* Boston, Mass.: Little, Brown, 1979, p. 1261.
14. This account of the meeting was given by an individual in the Nixon administration who was personally familiar with the events of the Tehran visit.
15. U.S. Senate, Committee on Foreign Relations, Subcommittee on Foreign Assistance, Staff Report, "US Military Sales to Iran," Washington, D.C.: U.S. Government Printing Office, July 1976. This report, which remains the most comprehensive and authoritative analysis of the security relationship between the United States and Iran after the Nixon-Kissinger visit of 1972, was prepared by Robert Mantel and Geoffrey Kemp. Mantel later joined the Department of State during the Carter administration, where he contributed to the development of arms transfer policy. Kemp, a specialist on security affairs at the Fletcher School of Law and Diplomacy, became the senior staff member for Middle East issues on the National Security Council staff of the Reagan administration in 1981.
16. Kissinger, *White House Years,* p. 1264.
17. Henry Kissinger, *Years of Upheaval,* Boston, Mass.: Little, Brown, 1982, p. 670.

II Early Signs and Signals

1. Parviz C. Radji, *In the Service of the Peacock Throne: The Diaries of the Shah's Last Ambassador to London,* London: Hamish Hamilton, 1983, p. 23.
2. Abrahamian, p. 480.
3. New York *Times,* May 15, 1977.
4. For an account of this conversation, see Cyrus Vance, *Hard Choices: Critical Years in America's Foreign Policy,* New York: Simon and Schuster, 1983, p. 318. Vance informed the shah in that conversation of President Carter's intent to approve the sale of airborne warning and control system (AWACS) aircraft. Very few members of the administration were aware that a decision—even in principle—had been taken by that early date. At the time of Vance's visit to Tehran, work had not yet been completed on the administration's arms transfer policy, and Vance's subordinates at the Department of State were still hard at work on a study examining the pros and cons of the AWACS decision.
5. William H. Sullivan, *Mission to Iran,* New York: Norton, 1981, pp. 19–22.
6. Final negotiation of this agreement, which was intended to serve as a model for U.S. nonproliferation policy, continued into 1978. It was eventually overtaken by the revolution and was never signed. However, the text worked out with Iran later served as the basis of an agreement signed with Egypt.
7. This phrase did not appear in the original draft of the toast as prepared by the State Department and the National Security Council staff for inclusion in the president's briefing book. The text was redrafted in the forward cabin of *Air Force One* between Warsaw and Tehran. Perhaps not surprisingly, the author has proved to be unusually diffident in taking credit for his or her work.
8. I had, in preparation for the president's trip to Tehran, sought the views of several U.S. specialists on Iran. I particularly remember a long telephone conversation with Professor James Bill at the University of Texas, who gave me an excellent description of the role of the clergy in organizing opposition to the shah, and who

offered his personal estimate that the shah would not survive on the throne for more than two years.

9. Pahlavi, *Answer to History,* p. 152.

10. Sullivan, p. 136.

11. Pahlavi, p. 155.

12. For a fuller account of this episode, see Fischer, p. 194, and Abrahamian, pp. 505–6.

13. Mohammad Reza Mahdavi-Kani, Iranian minister of the interior, April 27, 1981. Foreign Broadcast Information Service (FBIS), April 28, 1981.

14. The U.S. consul in Tabriz at the time was Michael Metrinko, one of the handful of Iran experts in the U.S. Foreign Service. He was later transferred to the embassy in Tehran, where his reporting was distinguished. He was taken hostage when the embassy was invaded in November 1979. His knowledge of Iran and his stubborn refusal to cooperate with his captors marked him for special attention, and he spent much of the 444 days of the siege in solitary confinement.

15. There was a question raised later whether this incident or other bureaucratic maneuvers by the Human Rights Bureau gave the shah an impression of divided support in Washington. The shah answered that question himself: "I was never told anything: nothing about the split within the Carter administration over Iran policy; nothing about the hopes some U.S. officials put in the viability of an 'Islamic Republic' as a bulwark against communist incursions. Instead, my ambassador in Washington, Zahedi, reported the same thing I heard day after day from Sullivan in Tehran: The U.S. is a hundred percent behind you" (*Answer to History,* p. 165). The accuracy of this comment is borne out by the shah's discussions with numerous American interlocutors during 1978. Although he raised a number of concerns and fears, he seems to have been genuinely unaware of these bureaucratic tempests in the Washington teapot until he began talking to U.S. political scientists during his long months in exile.

16. A National Intelligence Estimate (NIE) is the formal vehicle for authoritative judgments by the entire Washington intelligence community. The elaborate process of interagency coordination is often ponderous, but it has the benefit of engaging the full evaluative resources of the government on a specific issue.

17. See Michael Ledeen and William Lewis, *Debacle: The American Failure in Iran,* New York: Knopf, 1981, p. 126. Uri Lubrani had been assigned to the Tehran post since 1973. He was previously Israel's ambassador to Uganda and Ethiopia.

18. Sullivan later noted that "the Israelis enjoyed an information network that was second to none" in Tehran as a result of the "large colony of eighty thousand Jews in Iran who penetrated into almost every aspect of Iranian life" (*Mission to Iran,* p. 62). In a 1984 interview with the author, Sullivan recalled general conversations in which Lubrani expressed his concern about the course of events but no explicit warning or official communication.

19. In my experience Israeli officials, like their counterparts from other nations, were not prepared to predict the shah's downfall or to attach specific time estimates to events despite their superior intelligence on Iran. In fact, although the Lubrani report created a momentary sensation when it was received in Jerusalem, the Israeli government itself did not significantly alter its policies in Iran. Lubrani was routinely rotated to a new assignment in the summer of 1978. When the shah's regime collapsed in February 1979, Israeli diplomats were trapped in Tehran and had to request emergency evacuation on U.S. aircraft after their mission was occupied by the PLO. The episode is described in Sullivan, pp. 270–71.

III   The Revolution Begins

1. Ambassador Radji at the Iranian embassy in London heard reports on July 23 of "an attempted assassination of the shah on the Caspian," which were denied in Tehran the same day. When he arrived in Tehran for a visit on August 1, he was told by a friend that the shah looked "unhealthily thin on television" and that he had been seen by a heart specialist. The doctor, however, was said to have found "no abnormalities." When the ambassador met the shah on August 8, he found him "looking well if a little thinner." See Radji, *In the Service . . . ,* pp. 202–12.
2. Fischer, p. 196.
3. The Moslem religious calendar is based on the lunar month, resulting in a shorter year than the Western calendar. Consequently, dates in the Islamic calendar advance from year to year relative to Western date-keeping.
4. As mentioned earlier, this was a refrain that ran through the shah's thinking throughout the entire revolutionary period and received attention in his memoirs. He mentioned his fears to numerous visitors and journalists, and he repeatedly dropped pointed hints to U.S. officials. Viewed from Washington, the very idea of the CIA conspiring with the religious forces against the shah was absurd. In the first place, U.S. intelligence in Iran was focused almost exclusively on the USSR, and to operate effectively it needed the cooperation of the shah and his government. Moreover, it had been many years since the CIA had had the kind of contacts within the opposition that would have permitted it to influence the course of events. At the time that the shah was expressing his concerns, U.S. intelligence was only beginning to recognize the seriousness of the political threat to the shah.
5. For a detailed account and an analysis of the conflicting reports, see John D. Stempel, *Inside the Iranian Revolution,* Bloomington: Indiana University Press, 1981, pp. 115–17.
6. *Answer to History,* p. 161.
7. Sir Anthony Parsons, *The Pride and the Fall,* London: Jonathan Cape, 1984, pp. 71, 73–74.
8. These included visits by Undersecretary of State Newsom; Deputy Supreme Allied Commander in Europe, General Robert Huyser; Commandant of the Marine Corps, General Louis H. Wilson; and Deputy Secretary of Defense Charles Duncan; as well as the president's telephone call in September, a strong presidential statement of support in his news conference of October 10, and a warm message on the shah's birthday, October 26.
9. Sanjabi was a former dean of the law faculty at Tehran University and had served as minister of education in Mossadegh's cabinet. He became foreign minister briefly in the provisional government in 1979 under Prime Minister Bazargan, another long-time prominent member of the National Front.

IV   Communications Fail

1. Curiously, in his memoirs Ambassador Sullivan quotes with approval the shah's complaint that "Whenever I met Sullivan and asked him to confirm these official statements, he promised he would. But a day or two later he would return, gravely shake his head and say he had received 'no instructions' and therefore could not comment." (*Answer to History,* p. 161; *Mission to Iran,* pp. 191–92). A review of

Ambassador Sullivan's very extensive reporting on his meetings with the shah reveals not a single mention of such an exchange.

2. Cyrus Vance, *Hard Choices: Critical Years in America's Foreign Policy*, New York: Simon and Schuster, 1983, pp. 327–30.

3. A very different reaction to the conversation was reported by the shah in his memoirs. The shah recalled this conversation more than a year later, as follows: "President Carter's National Security Advisor, Zbigniew Brzezinski, at least had his priorities straight. He called me in early November to urge that I establish law and order first, and only then continue our democratization program." (*Answer to History*, p. 165.)

4. *Answer to History*, pp. 164–5.

5. *Ibid.*, p. 165.

6. Sullivan, pp. 171–72, 191 ff. See also note 1 above.

7. As Sullivan put it later, the policy position adopted in response to his November 2 telegram "seemed to finesse an assessment that the embassy had earlier sent to Washington . . ." (*Mission to Iran*, p. 171).

8. *Ibid.*, pp. 173 ff. Ambassador Sullivan's account places this episode several days earlier and incorrectly reports that the major riots in Tehran occurred on November 4, rather than on the fifth. The message report of his meeting with the prime minister places it on November 5.

9. For example, on the same day that Hoveyda was arrested (November 8), Houshang Ansari, a former minister of finance and economic affairs, director of the National Iranian Oil Company, and a trusted insider who served as an intermediary between the shah and Henry Kissinger, hastily boarded a plane for the United States, where he remained in exile.

10. The Policy Review Committee (PRC) was the usual venue for cabinet-level consideration of policy issues. It was normally chaired by the cabinet member whose department had primary responsibility, usually the secretary of state or the secretary of defense. The Special Coordination Committee (SCC) was charged with crisis management, arms control and certain functional responsibilities such as intelligence matters. Its membership was essentially the same as the PRC, but it was always chaired by National Security Adviser Zbigniew Brzezinski. In practice, the jurisdictional lines between the PRC and the SCC tended to blur, and backstage bureaucratic battles about who would chair a specific meeting on a specific topic were not uncommon. That was not the case, however, for the November 6 PRC meeting, which had been requested by the Department of State.

v Thinking the Unthinkable

1. Mehdi Bazargan went to Paris on October 20 to propose a limited accommodation with the army to prevent massive bloodshed. Khomeini flatly refused. (See Bakhash, *The Reign of the Ayatollahs*, p. 50.)

2. Mohammad Heikal, *Iran: The Untold Story*, New York: Pantheon, 1982, pp. 145–46.

3. See Hamid Algar, *Islam and Revolution: Writings and Declarations of Imam Khomeini*, Berkeley, Calif.: Mizan Press, 1981. For a discussion of Khomeini's writings, see Bakhash, pp. 38 ff.

4. Ambassador Sullivan later related his understanding that it caused "consternation" in Washington (*Mission to Iran*, p. 203). Secretary Vance repeated this

claim in his memoirs (*Hard Choices,* p. 329). I detected no such reaction. Possibly the effects of this message were confused with those of the telegram of November 2, which did create a strong reaction in the White House and elsewhere.

5. It was later drawn to my attention that a lengthy analysis of the internal situation was drafted by George Lambrakis of the embassy political section and sent on June 1, 1978. However, because of its length, this report was sent as an airgram and was apparently never circulated to the White House, nor was it included in the reporting I reviewed on November 17. Thus, although it offered greater insight into the situation than the cable reporting, its form of distribution prevented this report from having any significant effect on policy thinking in Washington.

6. U.S. House of Representatives, Subcommittee on Evaluation, Permanent Select Committee on Intelligence, Staff Report, "Iran: Evaluation of U.S. Intelligence Performance Prior to November 1978," Washington, D.C.: U.S. Government Printing Office, January 1979.

7. After meeting with Khomeini in Paris, Sanjabi returned to Iran. He was arrested on November 11, when he attempted to hold a press conference and was being held in genteel detention.

8. Press conference, November 19, 1978. See the New York *Times,* November 20, 1978.

9. The Brzezinski-Zahedi connection resulted in an angry confrontation between Vance and Brzezinski in mid-December, when Vance accused Brzezinski in front of the president of maintaining a separate channel of communications to Iran. Brzezinski denied the charge. Vance reports this episode in his memoirs (*Hard Choices,* p. 328). Brzezinski does not mention it.

VI The End of a Bad Year

1. For a sensitive and illuminating discussion of the "Karbala Paradigm" and its significance in the religion and politics of Shi'i Islam, see Fischer, pp. 13 ff.

2. The *New Republic,* December 2, 1978, pp. 15–18.

3. As noted earlier, a version of this idea had been carried to Paris in late October by Mehdi Bazargan and other "moderates" as a possible compromise solution to avoid violence during Moharram. That approach had been vetoed by Khomeini.

4. Brzezinski, on the other hand, was hoist on his own petard. Having personally brought in George Ball to inject some new thinking into the policy debate, and having given him *carte blanche* to operate independently with the blessing of the White House, he now found himself for the first time in the crisis confronted with a vigorous and articulate opponent with sufficient stature to carry his views directly to the president.

5. James Bill, "Iran and the Crisis of '78," *Foreign Affairs,* Winter 1978/79, pp. 323–42.

6. A detailed description of the meeting is contained in Ball's memoirs, pp. 460–61.

7. Gholam Hossein Sadiqi, himself a septuagenarian, had been a cabinet minister under Mossadegh in the early 1950s and was a prominent member of the National Front. Together with Dr. Ali Amini, he had been working quietly for some weeks to assemble a new government.

8. Shapour Bakhtiar was a French-educated nationalist who was sixty-two years old at the time. He had played a prominent role in breathing new life into the National Front in the late 1970s when the shah lifted some restrictions and opposition

activities became possible again. He had consistently opposed the alignment of the National Front with Khomeini and the clerics, and this had created rifts between him and Karim Sanjabi, the National Front leader who had met with Khomeini in Paris in October. When Bakhtiar later agreed to form a government under the shah, it precipitated a break between him and the National Front.

9. In early December, following a meeting in the White House, Brzezinski had asked to meet privately with Precht in Brzezinski's office. The meeting lasted only about fifteen minutes, and neither of them talked about it later. It seemed to have no effect, however, on the low opinion each had for the other.

10. Zbigniew Brzezinski, *Power and Principle: Memoirs of the National Security Adviser, 1977–1981,* New York: Farrar, Straus and Giroux, 1983, p. 375.

11. Vance, *Hard Choices,* p. 333.

12. This was a direct contradiction of the shah's own claims earlier that the military was pressuring him for a crackdown. It is also contrary to what the generals themselves said at the time and later.

VII   Last Gasps

1. Sullivan, *Mission to Iran,* p. 223.

2. *Ibid.,* p. 224.

3. *Ibid.,* p. 222.

4. Sullivan, in his memoirs, recalls that his angry message was written in the early morning of January 5, while the president was still in Guadeloupe (p. 224). President Carter reports that the message was sent on January 10, after he had returned to Washington and the plan had been reviewed by his advisers (Jimmy Carter, *Keeping Faith: Memoirs of a President,* New York: Bantam Books, 1982, p. 446). Brzezinski's account agrees with President Carter's (*Power and Principle,* p. 381). Secretary Vance's memoirs mention neither the message nor the response it provoked from the president. However, his account suggests that January 10 was probably the date of the message (*Hard Choices,* p. 337).

5. Brzezinski used this memorandum to raise with President Carter his view that the United States might soon have to "throw its weight behind one of the sides to protect our interests," i.e., support a military takeover. President Carter, who had already indicated that he did not support a coup by the military, became irritated and jotted in the margin: "Zbig—After we make joint decisions, deploring them for the record doesn't help me" (Brezezinski, pp. 381–82 and pp. 563–64).

6. Sullivan, p. 230.

7. A distinguished expert on Iran has informed me that this may have been a mistranslation from Farsi, or it may not have been understood by Khomeini in the Western sense of the word. Specifically, there is a question whether Khomeini, at this early stage, expected to assume the dominant position in the new Islamic Republic that he eventually acquired. It is also surprising that he would have showed his hand so boldly at this point, when his aides were making extraordinary efforts to reassure the West of Khomeini's benign intentions. Nevertheless, there can be no doubt that this statement had a chilling effect (at least on me) and that it in fact proved prescient as events turned out.

8. For a description of this incident, see Carter, pp. 449–50.

9. Ambassador Sullivan initially requested additional Marine reinforcements, and a small unit of fifty Marines and six helicopters was alerted and began moving toward

Iran. However, after Sullivan talked to Bazargan's headquarters and received assurances that the revolutionary forces would assure protection of embassies and foreigners, he asked that this small force "move forward" but not enter Iran.

10. A colorful description of this episode as perceived from Tehran is provided in Sullivan, pp. 252–54.

VIII   The Politics of Revolution

1. Hannah Arendt, *On Revolution,* New York: Viking, 1963, p. 36.
2. *Ibid.,* p. 28.
3. Crane Brinton, *The Anatomy of Revolution,* New York: Norton, 1938.
4. Fischer, p. 214.
5. Brinton, pp. 52 ff.
6. *Ibid.,* p. 66.
7. Radji, *In the Service . . . ,* p. 52.
8. *Ibid.,* p. 118.
9. *Ibid.,* p. 228.
10. Statement made during an interview on a BBC radio program, "The Fall of the Shah," broadcast March 16 and 23, 1982.
11. This is, of course, a tautology. The fact that the revolution succeeded means, by definition, that the ruler was not successful in maintaining himself in power. The point, however, is that many more rebellions fail than succeed in overthrowing political systems. The competence and will of the ruler is a critical factor in determining the outcome.
12. Sullivan, *Mission to Iran,* pp. 44–57.
13. Arendt, p. 18.
14. The *New York Times Magazine,* May 26, 1981, p. 63.
15. *Foreign Affairs,* Winter 1978/79, pp. 323–42.
16. In fairness, it should be acknowledged that Khomeini probably assumed that these men basically agreed with him and would willingly cooperate in establishing the kind of government he believed in. His later speeches indicate that he was surprised, disappointed and finally angered by what he perceived as lack of cooperation on the part of these men.
17. BBC radio program, cited above.
18. "Trusting Khomeini," New York *Times,* February 16, 1979.

IX   Hostages

1. The name was derived from the *comités du salut publique* that sprang up in similar fashion during the French revolution. In the Russian revolution, the comparable phenomenon was the emergence of local governing councils known as "soviets."
2. Almost simultaneously with the collapse of the Bakhtiar regime, irregular forces supported by the Marxist government of South Yemen launched what appeared to be a concerted invasion of North Yemen. Saudi Arabia was alarmed at the prospect of expanding Marxist influence on its southern border and asked the United States for urgent assistance. During February and March 1979, this was the subject of numerous crisis meetings that resulted in the deployment of a carrier task

force to the region, formal warnings to the USSR to restrain their client, accelera-
tion of U.S. arms deliveries to North Yemen, and the first deployment of AWACS
air defense aircraft to Saudi Arabia. This event, combined with the kidnap and
assassination of the U.S. ambassador to Afghanistan on February 14—the same day
as the Iranian attack on the U.S. embassy in Tehran—generated an atmosphere of
unrelieved crisis throughout February and March that resulted, among other
things, in a full-scale reappraisal of U.S. military strategy in Southwest Asia and
the initial planning for the U.S. Rapid Deployment Joint Task Force (later the
Central Command).

3. Commenting on the causes of the Iranian revolution in the London *Economist* of
February 10, 1979, Kissinger observed in sententious tones that were almost a
self-parody: "If we attempt to take the curse off our geopolitical necessities by
placating our human-rights advocates in the middle of the crisis, we make a
catastrophe inevitable. . . ."

4. The personal wealth of the shah became a matter of myth and exaggeration. The
revolutionaries in Iran, who tried the shah *in absentia* and launched an international effort to retrieve what they considered to be assets stolen from their country,
assumed that the shah disposed of many billions of dollars. The shah acknowledged
being a millionaire, but he scoffed at suggestions that he had anything like a billion
dollars. (See, for example, the shah's interview with Barbara Walters reported in
Pierre Salinger, *America Held Hostage: The Secret Negotiations,* New York: Dou-
bleday, 1981, pp. 67–68.) This issue would assume great importance during the
negotiations for the release of the hostages.

5. John McCloy, of the New York law firm of Milbank, Tweed, Hadley and McCloy,
and a senior statesman of U.S. foreign policy, had been the U.S. military governor
and high commissioner for Germany after WWII. In addition to many other
honors and positions, he had served as chairman of the board of the Chase Manhattan Bank in the 1950s.

6. The details of the shah's medical history were carefully researched and reported
by Dr. Lawrence K. Altman, medical correspondent of the New York *Times,* in
a special edition of the *New York Times Magazine* on the hostage crisis, May 26,
1981, pp. 48–52. His account was fully consistent with (and considerably more
comprehensive than) the information made available to the U.S. government. I
have relied on his reportage for many of the medical details in the account that
follows. I am also grateful for the assistance of Dr. Morton Coleman of New York
Hospital.

7. Significant excerpts from this memorandum are provided in Carter, pp. 455–56,
and Vance, pp. 371–72.

8. Various attempts were made to bring the Iranian doctors together with the shah's
U.S. physicians to make them aware of the shah's medical condition. Both the
White House and the shah's family flatly rejected proposals that the two Iranian
doctors be permitted to examine the shah personally. A doctors' meeting was
tentatively worked out for October 31, but when the New York *Post* leaked word
of the meeting, it was canceled by the shah's retainers.

9. Yazdi later claimed that Vance had promised to locate and return the individual.
I was present at the meeting, and no such promise was made. Vance could scarcely
have done so in any event, since the United States had no extradition treaty with
Iran.

10. By August 1979, after the U.S. Congress approved the purchase of some of the ships that the shah had ordered and the transfer of those funds to the trust fund maintained by the Department of Defense, the trust fund became solvent. For the first time since the beginning of the crisis, there were sufficient funds available to cover the anticipated expense of terminating the many contracts that had been inherited from the shah's days. At that time the U.S. government began to release some of the equipment and spare parts that Iran had paid for but that had been frozen in U.S. warehouses from the beginning of the year. Some $3.2 million worth of equipment was released during September and October. Following the talks in New York in early October, when Yazdi expressed great interest in the question of military spares, it was further agreed to permit Iran to make selected new purchases of spare parts. The negotiations on this additional package of spares were still in progress when the hostages were taken. At that point, all arms deliveries were halted. No further deliveries of any kind were made after November 4, 1979.

11. Baha'ism is an offshoot of Shi'i Islam that originated in Iran in the nineteenth century and has subsequently attracted followers around the world. The orthodox Shi'i regard it as dangerously heretical. Although Khomeini, while in Paris, offered explicit guarantees to Christians and Jews in his proposed Islamic Republic (which were subsequently written into the constitution and, for the most part, respected), he excluded the Baha'is. This group was later persecuted mercilessly under the Islamic Republic.

x   The Embassy Is Taken

1. The most authoritative account of which I am aware was the series of articles in the Iranian publication *Mojahed* (issue Nos. 101–6, some undated) in December 1980 by one of the students who became disillusioned with the political in-fighting associated with the hostage taking. Those articles, together with some original interviews and investigative reporting, formed the basis of several reports in the U.S. media. For example, see Bill Baker, "Iran Militants Planned to Hold U.S. Embassy Only Days, Student Claims," *Christian Science Monitor,* December 31, 1980; and John Kifner, "How a Sit-in Turned into a Siege," the *New York Times Magazine,* May 26, 1981.

2. Some of the students later concluded that they had been manipulated by the Islamic Republican Party (IRP) for its own political purposes, i.e., to ensure the success of the referendum on the constitution and to defeat the political moderates. They claimed that many of the documents in the embassy that would have incriminated IRP leaders such as Beheshti, who had met with U.S. officials in the course of the revolution, were removed or stolen to prevent them from being used for political attacks on the IRP. As one of the students later wrote, after quoting extensively from a cable reporting a conversation that Laingen and Precht had with Beheshti, "It is truly shameful that people who toppled the Bazargan government because it met with Brzezinski would consider [the embassy] documents to be infamous. Our people are not aware that Mr. Beheshti met with officials of the American embassy [and] asked the help of the Americans" (*Mojahed,* No. 102, December 2, 1980).

3. Shariati died in London in June 1977 after having been permitted to leave Iran following a long confinement in the shah's prisons. Many in the revolution sus-

pected foul play by SAVAK; but Shariati was in poor health after his incarceration, and his death may have been due to natural causes. For an excellent discussion of Shariati's life and his intellectual influence on the revolution, see the essay by Yann Richard on "Contemporary Shi'i Thought" in Keddie, *Roots of Revolution,* pp. 215–25. I rely heavily on this source for the remarks that follow. The entire chapter on "Modern Iranian Political Thought" by Keddie and Richard, pp. 183–230, is an invaluable survey for anyone who wishes to understand the political and philosophical undercurrents that shaped the Iranian revolution.

4. Ayatollah Mahmud Taleqani was the leading religious figure in Tehran. He was a key personality during the revolution and was credited as the principal organizer of the mass popular demonstrations that contributed to the overthrow of the shah. He had close ties to the *mojahedin* and was considered one of the most progressive of the senior religious figures. He had supported Mossadegh in the 1950s and was a close friend and associate of Bazargan. He also enjoyed great popularity; he won more votes than any other candidate for the constituent assembly. Because of his great popularity, his demonstrated leadership capacity and his more tolerant views, many considered him a potential rival to Khomeini. In April 1979, shortly after the revolutionary takeover, two of Taleqani's children were arrested for their opposition to the dictatorial methods of the fundamentalist clergy. Taleqani went into hiding for several weeks, then emerged to reiterate his support of Khomeini, whereupon his children were released. He died, reportedly of a heart attack, on September 9, 1979, and Khomeini immediately replaced him as the spiritual leader of Tehran with Ayatollah Montazeri, a man of mediocre abilities but a pliable supporter of Khomeini. (See Keddie, pp. 210–13.)

5. The largest single group of Americans remaining in Iran after the summer of 1979 were the employees of the Fluor Corporation, who were building a new refinery in Isfahan. The company had a performance contract with Iran and feared that it would be liable to penalties if the U.S. experts were withdrawn from the project.

6. It was my practice to arrive early in the morning, review the latest information, and prepare a proposed agenda that I delivered to Brzezinski's office about thirty minutes prior to the meeting. I routinely conferred with my counterparts in other departments by telephone to seek their inputs and to facilitate their own preparations.

7. General Jones had had lunch with Israeli Chief of Staff General Raphael Eytan, who happened to be in Washington, and they had discussed the possibility of a rescue mission. General Eytan, after reviewing the location of the embassy in an urban environment far from an airport, had concluded that such a mission would be much more difficult than the Entebbe raid.

8. Both Secretary Brown and General Jones were embarrassed by their inability to give absolute assurances that a movement order to the carrier could be kept confidential. This lack of confidence in the security of normal military reporting channels was a major contributing factor to the obsession with security and the reliance on unorthodox channels that later hampered the planning and coordination of the rescue mission.

XI The Diplomatic Offensive

1. Years later, Khomeini was to refer obliquely to this flight of talent as an explanation for the direct involvement of the clergy in government affairs at every level.

The secular followers of the revolution, he said, "did not want to follow the road which we wished to follow" and had to be replaced by the clergy. (See Khomeini's speech on June 21, 1982, translated in the Foreign Broadcast Information Service dated June 22.)

2. *The New Yorker,* August 28, 1978, pp. 77–78.

3. Robert Carswell, "Economic Sanctions and the Iran Experience," *Foreign Affairs,* Winter 1981/82, p. 247–65. For a detailed discussion of the decision making, implemention and broader implications of the financial sanctions that the United States imposed on Iran, see the chapters on economic and financial sanctions by Robert Carswell and Richard J. Davis and on the bank negotiations by John E. Hoffman, Jr., in Warren Christopher, *et al., American Hostages in Iran: The Conduct of a Crisis,* New Haven: Yale University Press, 1985.

4. The central fact that emerged from this mammoth research project was the constant, if less than totally successful efforts of one U.S. administration after another to persuade the shah to moderate his taste for expensive weaponry and to focus his primary attention on the economic and social problems of his nation. That theme, which ran through the policy papers of every president from Franklin Roosevelt through Lyndon Johnson, was reversed only in 1972 when President Nixon and Henry Kissinger visited Iran and gave the shah a blank check for weapons purchase with none of the incentives for accompanying economic and social development that their predecessors had attempted to sustain. The other fact that emerged from the documents was the shah's single-minded pursuit of his own vision of Iranian independence, strength and national greatness and his remarkable ability to adjust his policies as required to win the cooperation and support of five successive U.S. presidents until he finally got exactly what he wanted from President Nixon. A fair reading of the record would demonstrate that the shah was far more adept in manipulating U.S. policy over a period of more than thirty years than was the U.S. government in manipulating him.

5. Saudi officials had been expecting trouble from Iranian Shi'i pilgrims in Mecca, and there was speculation immediately following the attack that it was conducted by Shi'i fanatics. That proved to be false. Perhaps in response to those early suspicions, Khomeini made a statement on November 21 in which he said that "it is not farfetched to assume that this act has been perpetrated by the criminal American imperialism so that it can infiltrate the solid ranks of Muslims by such intrigues." Although this statement added fuel to the flames, its timing came after the attack in Pakistan was already under way and probably was not the specific cause of the mob action in Islamabad.

6. Army Colonel Charles W. Scott, who was a hostage, later wrote that he began to realize that the torture that he had endured during the first weeks of his captivity was suddenly beginning to end during the period around Thanksgiving Day (November 22, 1979). He felt, he said, that "the militants have been told by their government that they may continue to hold us and harass us, but that they had better not kill or permanently injure any of us. There are still some advantages to being a citizen of the most powerful nation in the world–even as a hostage . . ." See Scott's *Pieces of the Game: The Human Drama of Americans Held Hostage in Iran,* Atlanta, Ga.: Peachtree Publishers, 1984, pp. 191, 203.

7. In May 1967, Egyptian President Gamal Abdel Nasser announced the closure of the Strait of Tiran, on which Israel relied for all its shipping to and from the southern port of Eilat. President Johnson, in an effort to reopen the strait, at-

tempted to form a multinational fleet to sail through the strait. However, the idea attracted very little support from U.S. allies, and it was overtaken by the outbreak of the Arab-Israeli war on June 5, 1967.

8. Originally there had been some concern that raising the issue in the ICJ would provide a convenient excuse for Iran to divert anticipated criticism in the Security Council by claiming the issue was under judicial review. However, as the Security Council debate was progressively delayed, it was decided to proceed. The case was presented to the court on November 29. In the end, Iran boycotted both the Security Council and the World Court. The Court acted with unprecedented speed, and on December 15 unanimously ordered the immediate release, without exception, of all U.S. nationals being held in Iran and the restoration of U.S. property to the custody of the United States. The order was rejected in Tehran.

9. A colorful account of this episode is related in Salinger, *America Held Hostage,* pp. 57–59.

10. In this instance, as in almost every other case of an intermediary whose credentials seemed reliable, the United States relayed a message back to Tehran reiterating the U.S. position that had been worked out in mid-November. This had the benefit of exercising the channel, provided the basis for a response from Tehran and ensured that the U.S. position was consistently presented as often as possible to as many officials as possible in Tehran. One additional fillip was added to the message relayed through Cheron. It proposed that Charles Kirbo act as a personal intermediary for high-level discussions on the hostage issue. Ghotbzadeh did not pick up on the suggestion and it was not pursued.

11. This individual worked through a U.S. lawyer who had good contacts in the Department of State. Harold Saunders, the assistant secretary of state for Near Eastern affairs, had several secret meetings with him, and I also met him on one occasion. However, as time went on, it became apparent that his contacts with the leadership in Tehran were less reliable than he liked to suggest and that his own financial interests may have been his paramount concern.

12. A team representing the State Department, Defense Department and NSC departed for the area later in the month. Access arrangements were negotiated with each of the four countries during the spring and summer of 1980.

13. They later backed away from this commitment on the grounds that they had no legal authority to impose sanctions in the absence of UN authorization. However, when Vance returned from Europe he believed he had a clear understanding.

14. For an examination of the effects of the Afghanistan invasion on U.S. security policy in the region, see Gary Sick, "The Evolution of U.S. Strategy toward the Indian Ocean and Persian Gulf Regions," in Alvin Z. Rubinstein, ed., *The Great Game: Rivalry in the Persian Gulf and South Asia,* New York: Praeger, 1983, pp. 49–80.

XII   A Long Shot That Just Missed

1. For a detailed personal account of this and other episodes in the "secret negotiations" with Tehran, see Hamilton Jordan, *Crisis: The Last Year of the Carter Presidency,* New York: Putnam, 1982.

2. Lively firsthand accounts of all the meetings are provided in Jordan's memoir.

3. One of the conditions of the meeting was that this individual be granted permanent anonymity.

4. See Jordan, p. 165, and Carter, p. 488.

5. A five-point statement of the U.S. position was delivered to Secretary General Waldheim on New Years Eve, 1979. On January 12, that statement was expanded considerably to take account of reports that some of the more nationalist members of the Revolutionary Council were anxious to persuade Khomeini to end the crisis in the wake of the Soviet invasion of Afghanistan.

6. See Jordan, pp. 142–44.

7. Archbishop Capucci of Jerusalem had once been jailed in Israel for alleged gun-running to Palestinians. Ironically, in one of the twists that seemed to pop up repeatedly in the hostage crisis, Capucci's lawyer on that occasion was Christian Bourguet. Capucci's clerical and political background gave him special status and credibility in revolutionary Iran.

8. See, for example, Robert D. McFadden, *No Hiding Place,* New York: Times Books, 1981, pp. 130–31.

9. In fact, many of the leaders of the revolutionary movement had met with embassy officials during that period, as the United States attempted to expand its contacts among opposition groups. Since only the "students" had access to the embassy files, they were in a position to blackmail their political opponents. The Minachi arrest was a clear warning to others who might oppose them.

10. Out of consideration for his safety, I never used this man's name even in my reporting memos inside the White House. His identity was–and will remain–known only to the two of us.

11. See the chapter by Harold Saunders in Warren Christopher, *et al.,* p. 84.

12. The work that was initiated at this point proved invaluable later in the year when substantive negotiations began.

13. This was a serious tactical blunder. Apparently Ghotbzadeh had told Khomeini of his intentions to take custody of the hostages. The old man had listened silently, which Ghotbzadeh took as approval. When he was later challenged on this point, he had to admit that he had only "indirect" approval. Khomeini's office, in the meantime, issued a statement that "the Imam . . . prefers to remain silent on this . . ." Despite this contretemps, however, the official offer to transfer custody of the hostages seemed to remain valid.

14. See Salinger, *America Held Hostage,* pp. 178–85.

15. The details of these hectic few days are recounted in detail in Jordan, pp. 195–227. For a slightly different account as seen by Bourguet and the shah's entourage, see Salinger, pp. 187–216.

16. The Foreign Broadcast Information Service (FBIS) is a service of the U.S. government. This remarkable organization monitors ordinary commercial radio broadcasts throughout the world and provides almost instantaneous translations of important items, which are made available on a subscription basis to news organizations, research institutions and interested citizens, as well as the government. These reports provide an extraordinary wealth of timely information on political and economic developments around the world. The speed and accuracy with which complex texts were translated and transmitted never ceased to amaze me. Often, FBIS was the only source of information about what was going on in Tehran. The men and women of FBIS are among that large band of unsung heroes who do vitally important work but seldom receive any credit.

17. Many journalists contended that this decision was deliberately timed to coincide with the Wisconsin primary on April 1 and that it represented a cynical manipula-

tion of the hostage crisis for political purposes. That view came to be accepted as part of the conventional wisdom of the campaign. I disagree with that judgment, as do all of the participants in the decision process. I have provided a very complete summary of the events leading up to the April 1 announcement in order to provide a more balanced perspective on the rationale and timing of the decision.

XIII   The Military Option

1. John D. Stempel, who had served as deputy chief of the political section in the U.S. embassy in Tehran during the revolution, later described this situation in his book in the following words: "By April all efforts to deal directly with the Iranians through channels both normal and abnormal had fallen through. . . . A plausible argument can be made for the fact that the State Department would leave no stone unturned in seeking the hostages' immediate release. The emotional commitment of the President and Secretary of State Vance to that position, however, severely minimized the influence of Farsi-speaking State Department officials who had served in Iran and were knowledgeable about Shi'ite politics in discussions about whether pressing to negotiate a settlement might be impossible or inappropriate" (pp. 296–97).
2. The core members of this planning group were Brzezinski, Secretary of Defense Harold Brown, Director of Central Intelligence Admiral Stansfield Turner, Chairman of the Joint Chiefs of Staff General David Jones, General John Pustay (deputy to General Jones), and General William Odom (Brzezinski's military assistant).
3. Brzezinski had proposed such a flight as early as March 1, and when his recommendation was rejected, he returned to the president with the same proposal a week later after securing Vance's concurrence. (See Brzezinski's *Power and Principle,* pp. 489–90.) The background of the reconnaissance flight and the report on April 2 of its positive findings are described in Carter, pp. 501 and 504.
4. New York *Times,* January 1, 1980.
5. Vance, *Hard Choices,* p. 394.
6. New York *Times,* February 15, 1980.
7. *Ibid.*
8. See Vance, p. 410.
9. *Ibid.*
10. Brzezinski, p. 494.
11. Vance, p. 408.
12. Because the helicopters were maintaining radio silence, the White House was unaware that the crew of helicopter 6 had been picked up. The uncertainty about the fate of this crew was a concern throughout the day.
13. The following description of events as seen from the White House benefits greatly from four firsthand accounts: Carter, pp. 514–18; Brzezinski, pp. 496–500; Jordan, 265–81; and Vance, pp. 411–12.
14. The selection of the Desert One site, straddling a public road, was a point of criticism later. An extensive search had been conducted for months to find a better site within a prescribed distance from Tehran that would be adequate to accommodate the eight C-130s and eight helicopters, but none could be found. Originally the plan had called for seizing a little-used airfield near Tehran, but that idea was dropped in January in favor of a more remote location. It was finally decided to

use the Desert One site only on April 7, after an exhaustive survey had failed to reveal any better alternative.

15. The essential facts about the operation are readily available in the comprehensive "Rescue Mission Report," prepared by former Chief of Naval Operations Admiral James L. Holloway III, and five senior military officers, active and retired, representing all four services. Shortly after the mission failure, this distinguished panel was asked to conduct a professional, independent assessment of all aspects of the operation as a basis for recommending changes and improvements for any future special operations. Most of their report was made public in August 1980. It received only a brief flurry of attention, but anyone who is interested in the operation will be rewarded by a careful reading.

16. *Ibid.*

17. The flight path was across virtually uninhabited territory, for obvious reasons. The "Rescue Mission Report" of Admiral Holloway notes on p. 40: "Satellite imagery was extremely useful but incapable of revealing the presence of low-level clouds or other restrictions to visibility hidden beneath an overcast and was of limited value at night." Ironically, there were two automatic weather stations along the flight path that might have provided useful information; however, they had broken down and had not been repaired, probably due to the internal confusion in revolutionary Iran.

XIV The First Year Ends

1. I was unaware at this time that President Carter and Brzezinski had paid a secret visit earlier that day to the members of the team that had participated in the rescue attempt. During that visit Colonel Beckwith asked to be permitted to go back and the president had indicated assent. (See Carter, p. 519.)

2. Brzezinski, p. 259.

3. At that time, only days after the failure of the mission, there were wildly conflicting claims and reports. The student captors announced that the hostages had been dispersed to remote locations. There was a school of thought within Washington that tended to discount these reports as a bluff, on the grounds that the students would never relinquish central control. In fact, many of the hostages were dispersed to locations in other Iranian cities, in some cases to abandoned U.S. consulates.

4. President Carter, in his memoirs, indicates that he did not seriously contemplate launching a second rescue attempt, which he believed would be "suicidal" (p. 519). Others, however, took his words of encouragement to Colonel Beckwith literally and initiated a major effort to develop the capacity for a second mission.

5. At the final moment, the British government reneged on the EEC decision to cancel all contracts with Iran signed after November 4, 1979. Instead, the British agreed only to ban any new contracts from May 22, 1980. This weakened even the psychological effect of the new sanctions and dramatized divisions among America's allies.

6. This account will make no attempt to analyze the legal and financial issues except in the most general fashion. For those readers who wish to pursue this aspect of the negotiating process, see Warren Christoper, *et al., American Hostages in Iran.*

7. *Le Monde,* October 24, 1980, p. 44.

8. The White House view is discussed in Jody Powell, *The Other Side of the Story,* New York: Morrow 1984, pp. 252 ff.

9. Algeria had played a special role during the crisis in several respects. Algeria had been chosen by Iran to represent its interests in Washington when relations were broken in April 1980. The Algerian embassy, under the direction of Ambassador Redha Malek, had performed this contentious role with great skill. The U.S. ambassador in Algiers, Ulric Haynes, Jr., had established an excellent working relationship with Algerian officials, and he had been instrumental in arranging for the archbishop of Algiers to visit the hostages during the previous Christmas holidays. The Algerian ambassador in Tehran, Abdelkarim Gharaib, was acknowledged to be one of the best informed observers of the political scene in Tehran and one of the few ambassadors who had access to key revolutionary figures. He had been among the first group of ambassadors to visit the hostages, and he had continued to follow the issue closely but discreetly. In September, Algeria had delivered a letter from the hostage families to the authorities in Tehran, and throughout September and October the Algerians dropped hints that they might be interested in an intermediary role under certain circumstances. The Algerian foreign minister had explicitly raised this possibility with Undersecretary of State for Political Affairs David Newsom during a meeting at the United Nations in early October.

10. In the midst of this delicate process, a message was received from Prime Minister Begin indicating that Israel had been contacted by the Iranians seeking military equipment and spare parts. He said that one plane load of matériel had already been dispatched and he sought U.S. approval to continue to provide spares for Iran's U.S.-built aircraft. At a time when every effort was being exerted by the United States on its allies to ensure the integrity of the embargo, this request was received with astonishment bordering on disbelief. Begin was informed that any leakage in the embargo would be regarded as unhelpful to U.S. efforts to bring pressure on Iran to end the hostage crisis, and he was asked to desist. He said he would.

xv   Endgame

1. Throughout the crisis, there was the problem of distinguishing genuine messages and interlocutors from those who were self-appointed "messengers of good will," entrepreneurs seeking to turn the crisis into fame or fortune for themselves, or representatives of a political faction among the many in Tehran. This problem became particularly acute in late 1980, when Iranian President Bani-Sadr was engaged in a grim battle with the clerics. The head of the Iranian Central Bank, Ali Nobari, who was engaged in behind-the-scenes negotiations with the U.S. banks on the handling of the frozen assets, was a political ally of Bani-Sadr's. Not only was he often unaware of what the parliamentary commission (appointed by the Majles) was saying to the United States through the Algerians, but he had some incentive to sabotage its efforts. At least one group attempted to initiate a swap of military spare parts for the hostages through an individual close to one of the U.S. presidential candidates. Shortly after the Algerians were designated as intermediaries, Washington informed all of these individuals that any future discussions on the hostage issue would have to be conducted through the parliamentary commission and the Algerians.

2. Nabavi was known as a radical who headed the extremist Islamic guerrilla group known as "the *mojahedin-e enqelab-e eslami* (the mojahedin of the Islamic Revolu-

tion, not to be confused with the *mojahedin-e khalq*), a movement formed by the merger of five small Islamic guerrilla groups and . . . given to attacking the rallies of political opponents" (Bakhash, p. 67). Earlier, he was reported to have been a committed Marxist. In the hostage negotiations and later, Nabavi became the point man for the Islamic regime in a series of politically difficult, even dangerous issues. However, despite his association with a series of explosively controversial problems, he seemed immune from the kind of personal political attacks that had destroyed so many others. He remained an elusive but important presence in the revolutionary regime.

3. The Iranians retained counsel in the United States. Initially, this was seen as potentially troublesome, especially if the two U.S. lawyers should offer legal advice significantly at odds with what their government was saying to the Algerians. So Warren Christopher called the lawyers in to the State Department and reviewed with them some of the key legal points in the U.S. position. Although the two men did not agree to every fine point of law, they did recognize that the U.S. position was indeed near the outer limits of what could legally be done by any administration.

4. See the New York *Times,* December 29, 1980, p. 10.

5. This was, at best, a half-truth. Although the hostages were all moved during this period to more comfortable quarters and began to receive more humane treatment, they remained under the immediate control of the same captors until their departure. It is possible that the government had overall control of the building and policy, but that was not evident to the prisoners except in the quality of treatment they began to receive. (See, for example, Scott, pp. 373 ff.)

6. Ibrahim Yazdi, foreign minister of Iran at the time of the hostage taking, in Tehran, November 6, 1980.

INDEX

Aaron, David, 36, 67, 96, 100, 105, 107, 115, 128, 138, 149, 178, 179, 299
Afghanistan, 36, 247, 282, 291
air force, homafar rebellion in, 147, 154–55
Algeria, medication in hostage negotiations, 315, 320–21, 323, 324–25, 326, 327, 329, 330, 331, 332–34, 335–36, 359
Americans in Iran
    admission of shah and, 178
    evacuation of, 78, 100–101, 106–7, 117, 128–29, 149
    hidden by Canadian embassy, 259–60
Amini, Ali, 9–10, 47, 93–94, 110
Arafat, Yasir, 209, 262
Arendt, Hannah, 157, 159, 164
Armao, Robert, 179, 180, 181, 182, 183, 243
arms sales
    and arms package request, 43–44
    AWACs controversy in, 26–27
    to Barzargan government, 189
    Carter directives on, 25–26, 27, 44, 45
    contract restructuring agreement in, 148–49
    cutback by shah, 56
    Defense advisory role in, 14, 15–17, 24
    entire systems purchase stipulation in, 43–44
    F-4 aircraft wiring question in, 44–46
    in hostage negotiations, 311–12, 313–14, 315, 316
    interagency study of, 17–18
    Iranian five-year plan for, 49
    Nixon-Kissinger arrangement on, 13–15, 18–19, 20
    see also crowd control
AWACs controversy, 26–27
Azhari, Ghomam Reza, 75, 79, 82, 119, 122, 124

Bakhtiar, Shapour, 111, 118, 126, 154, 307, 348–49
    Khomeini and, 145, 147–48, 150–51, 158
    and military, 139, 141, 142–43, 146
    and shah, 125, 130–31, 139
    U.S. support for, 153
Ball, George, 105, 348
    characterized, 103–4
    Council of Notables plan of, 107–8, 109
    on evacuation of Americans, 107
    impact on Iran policy, 116–17

knowledge of Iran, 103–4
    Washington mission of, 102–3, 104, 114–16
Bani-Sadr, Abolhassan, 55, 228, 239, 261, 263–64, 270, 271, 306, 308
    and Bourguet-Villalon negotiations, 253, 258–59, 266
    Carter ultimatum to, 273–75, 288
    elected president, 253, 257, 260
    in hostage negotiations, 225–26
    on hostage release, 262
    on hostage transfer, 270, 276–79
Bazargan, Mehdi, 84, 141, 147, 148, 154, 191, 195, 199, 204
    on admission of shah, 184–85
    government, 187–88
    meeting with Brzezinski, 189
    opposition to constituent assembly, 203
    resignation of, 196, 205
    and Sullivan plan, 134–36
Begin, Menachem, 51, 304–5, 359
Beheshti, Mohammad, 132, 140, 148, 205, 208, 214, 245, 248
Benyahia, Mohammad, 320, 334
Bill, James, 112, 165, 344–45
Blitgen, Glenn, 16
Blumenthal, Michael, 88, 89, 96–97, 102, 115
Bourguet, Christian, 244, 274, 308
    intermediary in hostage negotiations, 251–59, 260, 266, 268, 269–70, 271
Bowie, Robert, 99, 105
Brezhnev, Leonid I., 95, 96
Brinton, Crane, 159, 161–62
Brown, Harold, 67, 68, 115, 116, 125, 143, 210, 215, 236, 237, 283, 286, 287, 298
Brzezinski, Zbigniew, 24, 36, 46, 60, 67–68, 70, 77, 90, 97, 110, 116, 119, 120, 143
    and admission of shah, 177, 178
    Bazargan-Yazdi meeting with, 189
    on Bourguet-Villalón negotiations, 253, 257, 258
    characterized, 303–5
    on contacts with Khomeini, 133
    in crisis management team, 211, 216
    dispute with Vance, 95, 348
    and George Ball, 102–3, 115–16, 348
    in hostage negotiations, 324–25
    and military option, 126, 141, 142, 152, 156, 170–71, 349

on military sanctions, 236–37, 241, 283
opposition to Council of Notables, 109
private emissary of, 87–88
and rescue mission, 285, 290, 298, 303, 305–6
telephone call to shah, 72–73, 74
Zahedi and, 50, 61, 66–67, 71–72, 99
Byrd, Robert C., 88, 99–100

Canada, Americans in Iran hidden by, 259–60
Carswell, Robert, 310, 335
Carter, Jimmy, 88, 116, 132, 142
on admission of shah, 178, 180, 184, 185–86
arms sale policy of, 25–27, 44, 45
attitude to shah, 22–23, 30
characterized, 33, 109, 219, 304
on contact with Khomeini, 133
counterfeit letter to Khomeini, 272–73
decisionmaking by, 26, 223
distrust of Sullivan, 137, 138, 151–52
doubts shah's survival, 110, 131
in hostage crisis management system, 211
and hostage negotiations, 269, 308–9, 314, 317, 318, 324, 326, 339–40
and hostage release, 340–41
human rights concerns of, 66
on intelligence failure, 88
and military-economic sanctions, 209–10, 213, 214–15, 227, 234, 235–36, 238, 241, 248, 270, 283, 288, 289
on military presence, 215, 238
political risk taking by, 222–24
postpones sanctions, 275–79, 280, 281
and rescue mission, 285, 287, 292, 297, 299, 300–301, 302
role in Iran policymaking, 173–74
on security leaks, 153–54, 215
support for Bakhtiar, 153
support for shah, 51–52, 53, 62, 110, 117, 126
Tehran visit of, 29–31
telephone call to shah, 51–52, 53
ultimatum to Bani-Sadr, 273–75
White House reception for shah, 28–29
Carter, Rosalynn, 28–29, 317
Central Intelligence Agency (CIA), 6–7, 92–93, 346
Cheron, François, 239, 244
Christopher, Warren, 67, 68, 70, 115, 116, 152, 155, 156, 184, 242, 248, 276, 277, 283, 292
in hostage negotiations, 308–9, 310–13, 316–17, 318, 320–21, 323, 324–25, 326, 329, 330, 333, 334–35, 336
Clark, Ramsey, 308
emissary in hostage crisis, 207–8, 209, 213–14, 215
clerics (mullahs)
attitude of shah to, 11, 165–66
failure of intelligence on, 165–68
in riots of 1963, 10
see also Iranian Revolution; Khomeini, Ruhollah
Constellation, U.S.S., 78, 125
security leak on movement of, 127–28

constitution
Islamic, 201–4
of 1906, 63, 117–18, 19–20, 158, 201
Cottam, Richard, 54, 55, 57, 239
Council of Notables, 107–8, 109, 111, 116, 118
crowd control, 35–36, 49, 59–60, 78
Cutler, Lloyd, 238, 241, 243, 271, 289, 310, 317–18, 334, 335

Defense Department
and arms sales policy, 14, 15–17
in contract restructuring agreement, 148–49
Derian, Patricia, 35, 36
Duncan, Charles, 58, 59, 77–78, 115, 131, 211, 227

economic sanctions, 215–16, 235–37, 287
freezing of Iranian assets, 227–29, 241, 289
international, 240–41, 242, 245, 247–48
oil import termination, 227
Eisenhower, Dwight D., 6, 8, 14
Eliot, Theodore L., Jr., 133
embassy in Tehran
failure to evacuate, 192–94
files of, 190–92, 232
increase in size, 190
physical security of, 155, 181, 185, 186–87, 193
reporting on dissidence, 32, 36, 37, 91–93
takeover of, 195–98, 204–5
Valentine's Day attack on, 175
voice communications with, 78, 246
see also Sullivan, William H.
European sanctions, against Iran, 240–41, 242, 248, 287

Falk, Richard, 166
F-4 aircraft sale, 44–46
Flandrin, Georges, 181–83
Ford, Gerald, 17, 23
foreign policy establishment, decision-making in, 38–41

Gast, Philip C., 154, 155
Genscher, Hans-Dietrich, 310, 311, 312
Gharabaghi, Abbas, 140, 146, 150, 152, 156
Ghotbzadeh, Sadegh, 55, 226, 239, 244, 246, 247, 248, 261
and Bourguet-Villalón negotiations, 253, 258–59, 260, 266, 271, 272
characterized, 263
and embassy militants, 267
Great Britain
boycott of Iranian oil (1951), 6
occupation of Iran (1941), 5
see also Parsons, Anthony
Great Mosque in Mecca, attack on, 232–33

Habibi, Hasan, 257
Hallock, Richard, 15–17
Haynes, Ulric, Jr., 331, 333, 359
hostage crisis
break in diplomatic relations, 289
Clark-Miller mission, 207–8, 209, 213–14, 215
cultural differences and, 218–21

downplaying of, as policy option, 221–22
economic sanctions in, *see* economic
    sanctions
and embassy militants, 245, 246, 254, 262,
    263, 265, 267–68, 352
and embassy takeover, 195–98, 204–5
exploitation by Khomeini, 206
first reports of, 175–76
influence of Vance in, 238
management team in, 211–13
military options in, 209, 210, 213, 214–15,
    234, 235–37, 283, 287
mobilization of world opinion in, 217–18,
    231–32
Palestine Liberation Organization (PLO)
    mediation in, 208–9, 224–25
papal emissary in, 224
policy limitations in, 206–7
presidential election and, 318, 319–20
prognosis for, 225, 249
proposed murder of shah in, 254–55
rescue mission in, *see* rescue mission
United Nations commission on Iranian
    grievances in, 226, 248, 255, 256–57,
    263–64, 266–69
U.S. military presence in, 215, 238, 241
hostage negotiations
Algerian mediation in, 315, 320–21, 323,
    324–25, 326, 327, 329, 330, 331, 332–34,
    335–36
with Bani-Sadr, 225–26
Bourguet-Villalón, 251–59, 260, 261, 266,
    268, 269–73
claims settlement in, 311–12, 325–27, 332,
    337
confidentiality of, 323–24
final agreement process in, 332–38
frozen Iranian assets in, 311, 328, 330,
    333–34, 335–37
independent initiatives in, 239–40
Iranian response in, 324–25, 327–30
Khomeini and, 264–65, 268–69, 310
loan payments to U.S. banks in, 328, 335
Majles resolution in, 313, 315, 316, 317–18
military supply issue in, 310–11, 313–14, 315,
    316
shah's assets in, 225, 226, 312, 326, 327,
    328, 332
Tabatabai approach in, 309–10, 311–13
U.S. position in, 321–23, 330–31
hostages
dedication of, 193–94
false reports on, 260
in Foreign Ministry, 195–96, 281, 331, 332
number of, 246
partial release of, 224–25, 231
personal commitment to, 221
release of, 340–41
renunciation of claims on Iran by, 326–27
threat of trials, 234–35, 238
transfer to government custody, 270,
    276–79, 288, 331–32, 333, 356, 360
treatment of, 231–32, 354, 360
visits to, 232, 240, 246, 260–61, 267, 270,
    331
Hoveyda, Amir Abbas, 50, 76–77

Howland, Michael, 195, 196, 281, 331
Husayn, Imam, 89, 105
Huyser, Robert
    as communications channel, 137, 138, 139,
        145
    and military, 131, 132, 136, 139, 140
    on military collapse, 156
    report to Carter, 151–53, 155

intelligence
    embassy reporting, 32, 41, 65–66
    failure, 38, 41–42, 90–91, 164–68
    Lubrani report, 37, 345
    private emissary in, 87–88
    unofficial sources of, 66–67
Iran
    Bakhtiar government, *see* Bakhtiar,
        Shapour
    Bazargan government, 187–88
    British oil boycott of 1951, 6
    conflict with Iraq, 245–46, 307, 313
    freezing of assets, 227–29, 243
    Majles elections in, 265, 270, 271, 306
    military in, *see* military
    military government in, 75–76, 79–80, 93,
        105
    oil production in, 78, 141
    oil strikes in, 58, 78
    political repression in, 23, 24, 160
    resistance to Western values in, 10, 11
    wartime occupation of, 5
    see also hostage crisis; hostage
        negotiations; Pahlavi, Mohammad Reza;
        United States–Iran policy
Iranian Revolution
    cyclical demonstrations in, 34–35
    factions in, 198–200
    foreign policy decisionmaking in, 169–70
    goals of, 157–58
    influence of left on, 105–6
    intelligence failure in, 32, 37, 41–42, 164–
        68
    Islamic constitution of, 201–4
    Islamic progressives in, 199
    Jaleh Square Massacre, 50–51
    Khomeini opposition in, 54–55, 57, 63, 82,
        101, 147–48, 150–51, 158, 199–200
    komiteh system in, 200
    moderates in, 55, 62–63, 73, 82, 85–86, 94,
        111, 134–37, 138, 171–73, 198–99
    Moharram processions in, 105, 110–11
    referendum on monarchy, 201
    religious nature of, 164–67
    Rex Cinema fire, 47, 56
    roots of, 159–62
    shootings in Qom, 34
    Sullivan scenario for, 81–84, 86–87
    Tabriz riots, 35
    Tehran riots, 74–75
    as true revolution, 158–59
Iranians in United States
    anti-shah demonstrations by, 28, 31
    and deportation issue, 211–12, 230
    diplomats, 238, 289
    pro-Khomeini demonstrations by, 229–30
    vigilantism against, 230–31

Iraq, 57, 245–46, 307, 313
Islamic Republican Party, 201–2, 204, 208,
    307, 308, 352
Israel, 29, 35, 37, 41, 345

Jaleh Square massacre, 50–51
Jam, Fereidoun, 130–31
Jones, David, 67, 211, 214, 215, 236
    in rescue mission, 282, 285, 287, 292, 299
Jordon, Hamilton, 88, 114, 214, 234, 236, 318,
    341
    in Bourguet-Villalón negotiations, 251–56,
    258–60, 261, 264, 269–70, 271, 272
    characterized, 250–51
    and shah's Panamanian asylum, 242–43

Kean, Benjamin, 182–83, 184
Kennedy, John F., 8, 9, 14, 47, 52, 300, 302
Khoeini, Moussavi, 197
Khomeini, Ahmed, 196, 260, 261, 275, 309
Khomeini, Ruhollah, 34, 56, 101, 145
    benign image of, 85, 112–13, 138–39, 165
    and constituent assembly, 201–2, 203–4
    cultural revolution of, 307–8
    and embassy takeover, 197–98, 204–5
    flight to Paris, 57–58
    on hostage release, 264–65, 268–69, 310
    illness of, 261, 267
    imprisonment and exile of, 10–11
    and Islamic Progressives, 199–200
    and komitehs, 200
    Kurdish campaign of, 202–3
    and military, 84–85
    moderate opposition and, 63, 85–86
    on normalization of relations, 261–62
    receives counterfeit Carter letter, 272–73
    reception of emissaries, 224
    return to Iran, 148, 150
    revolutionary goals of, 158, 159
    in riots of 1963, 10, 52
    and Soviet Union, 96
    U.S. contacts with, 54–55, 133, 137, 140,
    141–44, 146, 147
    value system of, 219–20
Kirbo, Charles, 237, 355
Kissinger, Henry, 50, 153, 170
    and admission of shah, 179, 180
    in arms sale arrangement, 13, 14–15, 17, 19,
    20
komiteh system, 200
Koob, Kathryn, 196
Kurds, opposition to Khomeini, 202–3, 307

Laingen, L. Bruce, 189, 193
    on admission of shah, 181, 183, 184
    and embassy files, 191
    hostage in Foreign Ministry, 195, 196, 281,
    331
Lake, Anthony, 128, 232
Lubrani, Uri, 37, 41, 162, 345

McCloy, John, 180, 351
Madani, Ahmed, 307
Majles
    elections to, 265, 270, 271, 306
    in hostage agreement, 313, 315, 316, 317–18,
    335

Matin-Daftari, Hedayatollah, 201, 202
Metrinko, Michael, 260–61, 270, 345
military
    and Bakhtiar government, 139, 141, 150
    collapse of, 155–56
    homafar rebellion in, 147, 154–55
    Huyser mission to, 131, 132, 136, 139, 140,
    145
    and Khomeini, 84–85, 140
    lack of coordination in, 141
    pro-shah demonstrations by, 118–19
    reliability of, 56–57, 83–84, 89, 122, 140,
    145, 146, 151, 152
    threat of coup, 142–43, 152–53, 170–71
Miller, William, 211, 241, 337
    emissary in hostage crisis, 207–8, 209,
    213–14, 215
mining of harbors, 234, 236, 237, 284, 287
Mondale, Walter, 179, 180–81, 210, 213, 231,
    234, 289
Montazeri, Husayn-Ali, 101, 205
Mossadegh, Mohammad, 6
mullahs, see clerics; Khomeini, Ruhollah
Muskie, Edmund, 306, 308, 326, 332

Nabavi, Behzad, 323, 324, 332, 335, 359–60
Nassiri, Nematollah, 76–77
National Front, 138, 201
    in coalition plan, 62–63, 73, 94, 111
National Intelligence Estimate (NIE), 37, 92,
    345
Newsom, David, 45, 123–24, 156, 179, 183,
    210, 231, 284
Nixon, Richard M., 7–8, 13–15, 18–19, 170
nuclear power plants, sale of, 25, 29

oil imports, termination of, 212, 227
oil production, decline in, 78, 141
oil strikes, 58, 78
Oveissi, Gholam Ali, 99, 170

Pahlavi, Mohammad Reza Shah, 4, 5
    admission to U.S., 127, 132, 139, 140–41,
    177–86
    on Afghanistan coup, 36, 44
    arrest of associates, 76–77
    assets of, 188, 208, 225, 226, 312, 326, 327,
    328, 332
    assurances of U.S. support for, 51–52, 53,
    59, 62, 67–68, 72–74, 110
    attitude to Carter administration, 22–23,
    25, 31
    attitude to clerics, 11, 165–66
    and Bakhtiar government, 125, 130–31, 139
    belief in return to Iran, 177
    Carter telephone call to, 51–52, 53
    and Carter visit in Tehran, 29–30, 31
    and celebration at Persepolis, 12
    characterized, 28–29, 163
    coalition plan of, 62–63, 73, 75, 94, 111
    conspiracy theory approach of, 32, 33, 36,
    48, 346
    death of, 308
    departure from Iran, 142, 146–47
    departure from U.S., 235, 239, 243
    disillusionment of ruling class with, 162
    in Egypt, 285

extradition requests for, 244, 255, 270–71
image as modernizing ruler, 48–49
indecisiveness of, 36–37, 42
influence on U.S. policy, 19–21, 48–49, 354
internal opposition to, 30–34, 36, 41–42,
    43, 164–68, see also Iranian Revolution
and Khomeini, 56, 58
medical condition of, 13, 163–64, 181–83,
    210, 351
medical treatment of, 181–86, 270–71
in Mexico, 181–84, 185, 239
and Middle East peace, 29, 35
military expansion program of, 8–9, 56, see
    also arms sales
and military government, 75–76, 170
military option of, 58, 59, 63–64, 111, 122,
    124–27, 153, 170
and Mossadegh, 6–7, 8
and Nixon, 7–8, 13, 14
in Panama, 242–43, 244, 255, 270–71
policy characterized, 168–69
and political reform, 9–10, 23–24, 47–48,
    50
psychological state of, 52–54, 61, 88, 96,
    100, 109, 163, 177
and return to constitution of 1906, 117–18,
    120
and riots of 1963, 10–11
travels in exile, 176–77, 179–80, 181
Washington visit of, 28–29, 31
White Revolution of, 10, 11, 12, 23, 52,
    159–60, 163
Pahlavi, Reza, 23, 60–61, 62
Pahlavi, Reza Shah, 9
Palestine Liberation Organization (PLO),
    mediation in hostage crisis, 208–9,
    224–25
Panama
    asylum of shah in, 242–43, 270–71
    and extradition request, 244, 255, 270,
        271
    role in hostage negotiations, 251
Parsons, Anthony, 53, 58, 67, 75, 145
Persepolis, celebration at, 12
Policy Review Committee (PRC), 45, 77–78,
    89, 347
Powell, Jody, 213, 214, 234, 236, 277, 318
Precht, Henry, 91, 104, 105, 106, 111, 138, 289,
    308, 338
    on admission of shah, 181, 184
    on Bazargan government, 187–88
    in Bourguet-Villalón negotiations, 253, 261,
        266
    characterized, 69
    critical of support for shah, 121–22
    in policy dispute, 69–70

Qom, religious demonstrations at, 34

Rafsanjani, Hashemi, 309, 314
Rajai, Mohammad-Ali, 308, 315
Reed, Joseph V., 182, 185
Regency Council, 101, 118, 126, 127, 131–32
rescue mission, 128, 214, 216, 281, 282
    criticism of, 299–302
    failure of, 296–99
    opposition of Vance, 292–95, 306

planning of, 285–87
    and second attempt, 303, 305–6
revolutions
    desertion of intellectuals in, 161
    disillusion of ruling class in, 161–62
    in growth conditions, 159–60
    secularizing, 164
    true, 157, 158–59
Rex Cinema fire, 47, 56
Rockefeller, David, 179, 180
Rockefeller, Nelson, 33, 68
Roosevelt, Kermit, 6–7
Rouleau, Eric, 262, 276, 314
Royo, Aristides, 244, 255

Sadat, Anwar, 51, 52, 147, 285
Sadiqi, Gholam Hossein, 111, 117, 118, 119–20,
    122, 124
Sanjabi, Karim, 63, 94, 111, 112, 199, 346
Saunders, Harold, 54, 70, 78, 104, 107, 108,
    109, 128, 188, 310
    in Bourguet-Villalón negotiations, 251–52,
        256, 261, 265–66, 269–70, 308
SAVAK, 23, 28, 34, 35, 36, 46, 47, 66, 162
Schaefer, Tom, 156
Schlesinger, James, 15–16, 17, 24, 113–14, 115,
    116, 173
shah, see Pahlavi, Mohammad Reza Shah
Shariati, Ali, 199, 352–53
Shariatmadari, Ayatollah, 34, 47
Sharif-Emami, Ja'far, 47–48, 63, 75
Soviet Union
    invasion of Afghanistan, 247, 282, 291
    and Iranian Revolution, 93, 95–96, 106
    occupation of Iran (1941), 5
Special Coordination Committee (SCC), 347
State Department
    inspector generals report on Iran, 20–21,
        27, 32
    Iran policy paper, 58–60
    leaks, 123, 153–54
    Newsom's working group in, 123–24
    opposition to AWACs sale in, 26
    personnel evacuations from Islamic states,
        233
    veto of opposition contact, 55
    -White House policy dispute, 68–72
    see also embassy in Tehran
Stempel, John, 150
Sullivan, William H., 31, 32, 36–37, 51, 62,
    72, 75, 88, 93, 110, 117, 121–22, 124–25,
    126–27, 131, 139, 156, 163, 178, 188, 190
    on arms package request, 46
    contingency analysis of, 81–84, 86–87
    on Council of Notables plan, 109, 111
    on crowd control assistance, 59–60
    deference to shah, 48–49
    differences with Huyser, 145, 151–52
    on direct intervention, 108–9, 118, 119
    indicates shah's abdication, 3–4, 63–64
    and Khomeini opposition, 132–34
    on military government option, 58, 59,
        63–64
    and moderate opposition, 134–38, 172–73
    optimistic reports by, 41, 46, 53, 65–66, 170
    on overture to Khomeini, 56, 60
    policy characterized, 172–73

policy guidance for, 25, 67–68, 74, 96, 150, 151, 346
on U.S. military presence, 78
and Zahedi, 72, 98–99

Tabatabai, Sadegh, in hostage negotiations, 309, 311–13
Tabriz riots, 35
Taleqani, Ayatollah, 203, 353
tear gas, sale of, 35–36, 49, 78
Tehran
    anti-shah demonstrations in, 30
    Carter visit to, 29–31
    Jaleh Square massacre in, 50–51
    November riots in, 74–75, 347
    see also embassy in Tehran
Tomseth, Victor, 195, 281, 331
Torrijos, Omar, 242, 251, 271
Toufanian, Hassan, 16, 56
Tudeh Party, 93, 143, 152
Turner, Stansfield, 67, 68, 77, 115, 152, 211, 214, 236, 284
    in hostage negotiations, 325
    and intelligence failure, 90–91

United Nations
    commission on Iranian grievances, 226, 248, 255, 256–57, 263–64, 266–69
    in hostage negotiations, 225–26
    Rajai visit to, 315
    sanctions against Iran, 240, 245, 247–48, 282
United States-Iran policy
    on admission of shah, 127, 132, 139, 140–41, 177–86
    on arms sales, see arms sales
    on Bakhtiar government, 153, 187–89
    and Ball mission, 102–4, 114–16
    bureaucratic decisionmaking in, 38–41
    communication failure in, 31–34
    competing policy issues, 60, 65, 170
    contact with opposition, 32, 54–55, 77, 86, 133, 137, 140, 141–44, 146, 147, 172–73
    Council of Notables plan in, 107–8, 109
    direct intervention option, 98, 108, 118, 119, 171
    under Eisenhower and Kennedy, 7–8, 9–10, 14, 47

Huyser military mission and, 131–32, 137, 139, 140, 141
influence of shah on, 19–21, 37–38, 48–49, 354
intelligence in, see intelligence
Iranian security role in, 13–14, 18, 20
on "iron fist" measures, 124–27, 170–71
military presence in, 78, 125, 127–28, 215, 238, 241
and Mossadegh ouster, 6–7
Regency Council plan on, 126, 127, 131–32
on return to constitution of 1906, 119–20
security leaks and, 123, 127–28, 153–54, 215
support for shah, 25, 51–52, 53, 59, 62, 67–68, 70–71, 72–74, 96
White House vs State Department on, 68–72, 120–22
see also hostage crisis; hostage negotiations

Vance, Cyrus, 25, 26, 35, 45, 68, 77, 78, 123, 125, 132, 138, 143, 224, 233, 304
    on admission of shah, 183, 186
    dispute with Brzezinski, 95, 348
    and European sanctions, 240–41, 242
    hostage crisis strategy, 209–10, 234, 236, 237, 238, 283, 295
    in hostage negotiations, 225–26, 234
    influence on Carter, 238, 290–91
    meeting with Yazdi, 188–89
    objections to rescue mission, 292–95, 306
    policy characterized, 172
    rejects "iron fist" option, 126, 128
    and Soviet policy, 291–92
    support for shah, 70–71, 73, 96
Villalón, Hector, 244, 251–59, 260, 264, 266, 268, 269–70, 271–73, 308
Von Marbod, Eric, 17, 24, 148–49

Waldheim, Kurt, 225, 226, 239, 247–48, 256

Yazdi, Ibrahim, 54–55, 111–12, 175–76, 184–85, 189, 195, 196, 338
    -Zimmerman meeting, 140, 141–44, 146, 147

Zahedi, Ardeshir, 49–50, 53–54, 60–61, 66–67, 72, 77, 94, 98–99, 170, 178, 179
Zimmerman, Warren, 140, 141–44, 146, 147, 239

About the Author

GARY SICK, the principal White House aide for Iran during the Iranian revolution and the hostage crisis, served on the National Security Council staff under presidents Ford, Carter and Reagan. He is a captain (ret.) in the U.S. Navy, with service in the Persian Gulf, North Africa and the Mediterranean. Mr. Sick, a Ph.D. in political science from Columbia University and a member of Phi Beta Kappa, is at present with the Ford Foundation, where he is responsible for programs relating to U.S. foreign policy. He is adjunct professor of Middle East politics at Columbia University.

Please remember that this is a library book,
and that it belongs only temporarily to each
person who uses it. Be considerate. Do
not write in this, or any, library book.

DATE DUE

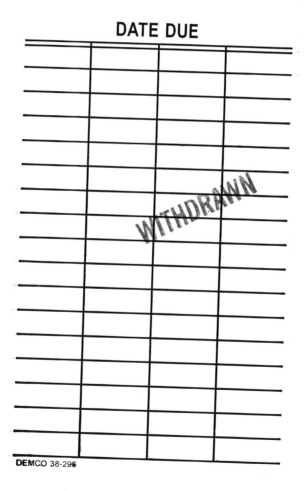

DEMCO 38-296